GROWING UP

GROWING UP

Transition to Adult Life for Students with Disabilities

DANIEL E. STEERE
East Stroudsburg University

ERNEST ROSE
Loyola Marymount University

DOMENICO CAVAIUOLO
East Stroudsburg University

Boston ■ New York ■ San Francisco
Mexico City ■ Montreal ■ Toronto ■ London ■ Madrid ■ Munich ■ Paris
Hong Kong ■ Singapore ■ Tokyo ■ Cape Town ■ Sydney

Executive Editor: *Virginia Lanigan*
Series Editorial Assistant: *Matthew Buchholz*
Marketing Manager: *Kris Ellis-Levy*
Composition and Prepress Buyer: *Linda Cox*
Manufacturing Manager: *Megan Cochran*
Cover Coordinator: *Elena Sidorova*
Editorial-Production Coordinator: *Mary Beth Finch*
Editorial-Production Service: *Modern Graphics, Inc.*
Electronic Composition: *Modern Graphics, Inc.*

For related titles and support materials, visit our online catalog at www.ablongman.com

Between the time Website information is gathered and then published, it is not unusual for some sites to have closed. Also, the transcription of URLs can result in unintended typographical errors. The publisher would appreciate notification where these errors occur so that they may be corrected in subsequent editions.

Disclaimer: The individuals portrayed in the various vignettes in each chapter are fictional and while they may bear some resemblance to persons in the general population, any specific similarities are purely coincidental.

Library of Congress Cataloging-in-Publication Data

Steere, Daniel E.
   Growing up : transition to adult life for students with disabilities / Daniel E. Steere, Ernest Rose, Domenico Cavaiuolo.
     p. cm.
   Includes bibliographical references and index.
   ISBN 0-205-44205-6
   1. Students with disabilities—Education—United States. 2. Students with disabilities—Counseling of—United States. 3. Life skills—Study and teaching—United States. 4. School-to-work transition—United States. I. Rose, Ernest David. II. Cavaiuolo, Domenico. III. Title.
LC4031.S833 2007
371.904—dc22

2005057240

Printed in the United States of America.

3 4 5 6 7 8 9 10   V0CR   15 14 13

CONTENTS

CHAPTER 5

Interaction Across Agencies   112

CHAPTER 8
Moving Out of the Family Home to Community Living 204

Nick called home first thing Thanksgiving morning. He, like so many other young adults, could not be home with us for the holiday. Celebrating Thanksgiving in his own home this year, he wanted to share in the joy of the holiday and his plans for his own celebration. This simple act of a son calling his parents on Thanksgiving perhaps was not unusual for many parents. But for us, it was no small miracle. When Nick was three, he was diagnosed with autism and moderate intellectual disabilities. As he was growing up and we faced the reality of his disabilities, we could hardly imagine that someday he would have a home of his own, live in city away from us, and have his own circle of support. Most days we seemed focused on the present, just getting through the day was challenge enough. And now, at 35, Nick has become part of the fabric of his community. He works part-time with supports and has assistance to live in his own home. Well beyond our dreams, Nick has his own piece of the American dream.

Nick's life in the community and the fulfillment of our hopes and aspirations as his parents did not happen by chance. In fact, as I think back to a time when Nick was in school, no one talked about transition. There was little attention beyond the immediate individualized education plan. His teachers were skilled, well-intentioned, and dedicated to his success; however, the future seemed so far away that we found many reasons not to focus on his life after school.

Then something wonderful happened. Many educators and rehabilitation counselors started to look at the issues of transition. Most of their work came about due to frustration with the skills young adults with disabilities lacked to be successful members of society. Quietly, but with vigor, the transition movement began to grow. Professionals began to work with families, like ours, to articulate new programs and services to help people with disabilities cross the bridge from school and family life to the realities of community living.

Nick's life today in his community is thanks to the vision, careful planning, and advocacy of numerous special education teachers, rehabilitation counselors, social workers, and human service professionals who over the years planned for his successful transition to the community. Not only did these professionals implement good practice, but also they understood that transition is hard work and requires diligence, tenacity, and a great deal of advocacy. They understood, more than most, how important it was to listen to Nick and his desires and to take into account our concerns as his parents, as well as those of his brother and sister.

Like all young adults, Nick's transition to greater independence has been neither smooth nor predictable. He has had to learn to express his own desires and learn new skills to be independent. Like all of us as we mature, Nick has had to face changing realities and make adjustments in his life. Some adjustments were rather easy, others more difficult. He has been successful in his transition because those who help him understand that transition is not an event that can be neatly planned, but rather a life process that is continually unfolding.

Nick's story is hardly unique. The thousands of young adults with disabilities who leave high schools each year desire to be a part of their communities. They want to live, work, and recreate with others. They want their own share of the American dream. Unfortunately for so many of these young adults, transition programs have been rather disjointed and lack the systematic planning and professional assistance that they need to be successful.

Now comes this new book by Dan Steere, Ernie Rose, and Domenico Cavaiuolo which sheds new light on the transition process and our collective professional responsibilities to help people with disabilities to become valued, fully functioning members of our society. I only wish this book was available when Nick was a teenager. We would have been better prepared to help his educational team prepare for his future. Had this text been used in the preparation programs of all the professionals who interacted with Nick, perhaps his transition would have been more deliberate and perhaps he would know even greater success today.

Steere, Rose, and Cavaiuolo use their vast experience with teenagers and adults with disabilities to present the critical issues surrounding comprehensive transition in an effective and easy-to-comprehend manner. They share their wealth of experience to bring new insights into the transition process and practices that will prepare professionals for the realities of comprehensive transition planning.

The book is filled with information and suggestions that contemporary professionals need to be successful in helping teenagers and young adults learn to be successful in their communities. As I read the text I was particularly impressed with

- *The rich summary of research and best practices on transition*—The research is presented in a way that not only synthesizes the best thought in the field but also integrates research findings from other aspects of disability.
- *The many pragmatic suggestions for professionals*—Of importance to any professional, the text moves beyond mere description of the challenges and provides practical suggestions for professionals. While this is not a *how-to book*, after reading this book one is equipped with the skills necessary to implement successful transition programs.
- *The emphasis on self determination*—Steere, Rose, and Cavaiuolo know the simple truth. People with disabilities, like all of us, need to live their own lives structured around their desires. While we as family members and professionals may have our own ideas about what is best for the person with the disability, the reality is that it is the individual's life, not ours. Throughout the text we are reminded to practice our most important skill—listening to the person we want to help.
- *The importance of family members in the transition process*—As Nick's dad I cannot overemphasize the importance of families in the transition process and activities. As is so powerfully presented, family members, including parents, brothers, sisters, grandparents, aunts, and uncles can and should be involved. Steere, Rose, and Cavaiuolo understand that families need to be empowered to assist and that

their help can be invaluable to professionals in building successful transition programs.

■ *The value of using friends and community members in the transition planning and activities*—If it were not for Nick's friends and other community members, I doubt that he would be successful in his home or at work. There is power in building circles of support for people with disabilities that go beyond professionals. As is pointed out, we always have been so pleasantly surprised that friends and community members want to be asked and enjoy the help that they provide. So often we are told that helping with Nick's living, employment, and recreation plans has enriched their lives.

■ *The historical notes*—Throughout the book Steere, Rose, and Cavaiuolo highlight a number of the champions whose work not only has advanced transition planning, but also our profession. These notes remind us of the importance of the work of so many who have dedicated their work to ensure the success of people with disabilities.

So now I hope that you are ready to move into this book as a way to enhance your professional skills. As you do, remember that transitioning is really about a focus on the future. Good transition programs are more than simply helping a person with a disability to have a positive future. Good transition programs also are about the future of our society. As we come to know, befriend, and learn from people with disabilities in our communities, we all will be enriched.

Thomas H. Powell
Nick's father
President
Mount Saint Mary's University
Emmitsburg, Maryland

PREFACE

In growing up, all people make the transition from school to adult life, but for young people with disabilities, this period of transition presents greater challenges. Because of these additional challenges, the process of planning and preparing for the future needs to be that much more effective. This book is designed to prepare you to help young people with disabilities make a successful transition to a happy and fulfilled adult life.

This book reflects our belief that people with disabilities should have the opportunity to be included in everyday life in their local communities. Too often, young people with disabilities have left special education services only to enter segregated adult service programs from which they rarely exit. The decisions to "place" individuals with disabilities in these programs often are made primarily on the basis of the severity of their disabilities, with little regard to their personal choices for the future. Likewise, individuals with mild to moderate disabilities may benefit from postsecondary training programs or a college education. If they are denied access to such programs, they often become underemployed and lose untold thousands of dollars in income and the opportunity for an advanced career. Instead, we believe that young people should have the opportunity to work for pay in the community, continue their education as appropriate, and begin a career. They also should have the option to live in a home or apartment of their choosing, to be actively engaged in their communities, and to have a network of friends. In short, young people with disabilities should have the option to pursue the same type of lifestyles that most of us do.

This book is written as an introduction to the topic of transition from school to adult life. We have written it for special education teachers in training (both graduate and undergraduate); for those studying in related fields such as rehabilitation counseling, school counseling, or secondary education; and for young people with disabilities and their families. In writing this book, we recognize that some of our readers may be involved actively and directly with the transition planning process, while others may not. Regardless of your specific role or connection to this topic, we feel that your work with people with disabilities can have substantial impact on their subsequent success. Even those who work with young children can contribute to their future success by teaching skills and patterns of behavior that will serve them well later in their educational career.

Laws that affect the transition planning process have changed in recent years, and they are likely to do so again. It is certainly important for us to know what these laws require and to implement services accordingly. However, our position is that, in order to truly help young people have a reasonable chance for attaining a fulfilled adult life in the community, we must go beyond mere compliance with the law, and instead, use our energy and creativity to provide what *each student needs*. In fact, we would advocate for the practices described in this book even if there were no laws mandating transition services, because they are the right approach for us to truly help young people.

Certainly, efforts to go beyond mere compliance with the law take more time, effort, and creative collaboration, but the stakes are high. When young people with disabilities make a successful transition to adult life (e.g., to a paying job, to a course of study at a community college or university, to a home or apartment, or to active participation in the life of the community), our communities and society as a whole benefit. These students become productive employees (or employers), taxpayers, homeowners, or contributing community members. Those who do not make a successful transition become overly dependent on others without the opportunity to contribute back to their local communities.

Your work, then, in providing effective transition services will have direct impact on the lives of specific young people with disabilities, on their families, and on your local communities. It is our sincere hope that this book will help you begin to develop the skills and strategies that you will need to assist individuals with disabilities in growing up and making the transition to adult life.

ACKNOWLEDGMENTS

The concept and inspiration for this book came from the many students and colleagues with whom we have worked over several years, and our friends with disabilities who have taught us so much. Among those colleagues are Thomas H. Powell, President of Mount St. Mary's University in Maryland, Ernest Pancsofar at Central Connecticut State University, John Butterworth at the Institute for Community Inclusion in Boston, Susan Gregory at Montana State University-Billings, Paul Wehman at Virginia Commonwealth University, Michael Hardman at the University of Utah; William Bursuck at the University of North Carolina-Greensboro; Barbara Wilcox at Indiana University-Indianapolis (now retired); Ed Polloway at Lynchburg College; and Tim Vogel at the Rural Institute on Disabilities, University of Montana. We sincerely appreciate the feedback from our many students and colleagues at East Stroudsburg University, Loyola Marymount University, Binghamton University, and Montana State University-Billings. We also have learned from many dedicated professionals in schools and adult service agencies in several states, including Pennsylvania, New York, California, New Jersey, Connecticut, and Montana. We extend our particular thanks to the many students and families who have taught us so much. We are especially grateful for the research assistance of Serena Bhavnani Castelda and Crystal Reed. We benefited from the insightful and helpful reviews of Debbie Case, Southwestern Oklahoma State University; Kimberly Fatata-Hall, North Central University; Margret Hutchins, Illinois State University: Kagendo Mutua, University of Alabama; Yvonne Kelley Niemann, University of Louisville; Susan Severson, Southwestern Oklahoma State University; and Darlene Unger, Kent State University. Our sincere thanks to Virginia Lanigan at Allyn & Bacon who believed in this project from the start and has supported us at every step in the writing and production process. Our thanks also to Virginia's associate, Scott Blaszak, for his support throughout the development of the project.

Of course, no project of this magnitude can be accomplished without the support and cooperation of our spouses and children, so special thanks to Kathy, Zach, and Brendan Steere; Linda Rose; and Domenico's wife Barbara Kling, children Mimmo, Kathryn, and Carlo Cavaiuolo, and parents, Vittorio and Maria Cavaiuolo, who inspired courage and commitment.

OVERVIEW OF TRANSITION TO ADULT LIFE FOR STUDENTS WITH DISABILITIES

If you are reading this book then you are probably a student majoring in special education, rehabilitation counseling, or in some field that concerns itself with the lives of individuals with disabilities during and after they leave school. You are studying to become part of a profession, and when you become employed in that profession you will be a wage earner, a tax payer, and a participant in your local economy because you have money to spend. You will pay rent or mortgage payments, buy food and clothes, spend money on transportation, perhaps purchase an automobile, and spend some portion of your income on entertainment. Wherever you live, you will integrate yourself into that community because it will be the natural thing to do. But for individuals with disabilities, this integration process, this *transition* from school to adult life, will not be automatic. It will take planning, teaching and learning, long periods of practice, family, friends and community support, and a little luck to manage what will likely be so much easier for you. If you happen to have a disability, then you are well aware of the challenges the transition to adult life poses.

The purpose of this book is to prepare you to prepare students with disabilities to make the transition from school to adult life. We will attempt to do that through a discussion of research on best practices, the telling of stories, features on individuals who have pioneered the design and implementation of transition practices that work, and exercises to facilitate your own learning. We will introduce you to two individuals who have disabilities that are very different in nature. Throughout the text, we will use examples from their lives to enliven the discussion and make it real. We want you to feel personally involved. Let's begin by meeting Sue Anne and Mike.

Sue Anne

Throughout her life, Sue Anne has been a quiet girl and young woman. But she has had dreams. It was embarrassing to her that she was among the last of her friends to learn to read. Even then, she read at a slower rate than almost everyone else and would often have to re-read each page to follow the story or comprehend the meaning of the text. The same was true in mathematics. Numbers on the textbook pages and even the ones she wrote down seemed to swim on the page and not line up as they should. As the operations became more complex, Sue Anne had more and more difficulty learning the material. One of her first dreams was to be as "smart" as everyone else in her class. She worked hard, but it was frustrating when the hard work did not pay off. Fortunately, her parents were very supportive and most of her teachers were too.

It was her second grade teacher who realized Sue Anne was falling well behind her classmates in reading and math. The teacher had tried a number of approaches with Sue Anne, but they had been only marginally successful. She talked with Sue Anne's parents and suggested that Sue Anne be referred for testing to find out why she was not learning at the rate she should. Sue Anne's parents agreed. They were aware that Sue Anne was showing signs of frustration and she was beginning to lose interest in reading stories and having stories read to her.

The school district psychologist and the school's special education teacher arranged to give several assessments to Sue Anne over a two-day period. The assessments were to determine Sue Anne's ability to learn, in general, and to learn specific skills, especially in reading and math. At the end of the two days they concluded that Sue Anne had a learning disability. According to her assessment profile, Sue Anne had a strong potential for learning, but she was clearly underachieving in reading and math, which was affecting her performance in other subjects. Without a more personalized model of instruction to meet her learning needs, Sue Anne would continue to fall farther behind her classmates.

Sue Anne received academic support for her learning disability throughout her elementary grades. During the fall of eighth grade, her last year of middle school, the Special Services Planning Team (SSPT) requested that Sue Anne and her parents meet with them to consider the courses Sue Anne would take when she started high school the next year. The Guidance Counselor from the high school attended the meeting as well. Sue Anne and her parents made it clear she wanted to attend college. Her sister was now a junior at a private college and her brother would graduate from the high school this year and probably attend the state university. Sue Anne did not want to be left behind. The SSPT told Sue Anne and her parents that, as part of her IEP, it was now important to plan services through high school with the goal of preparing her for life after high school. The team asked the Guidance Counselor to lay out a typical four-year high school program that would qualify a student to attend college. Then, they looked for courses that would present significant challenges. Advanced courses in math and science would definitely challenge Sue Anne so, the SSPT discussed ways to support Sue Anne in those courses. Other courses in English and history would mean a good deal of reading and writing. For those courses, the SSPT recommended accommodations without special instruction, for example, extended time on exams. The Guidance Counselor recommended that Sue Anne join a support group of other students with learning disabilities to talk about their special challenges and to share strategies for overcoming those challenges. He spoke of the importance for Sue Anne to develop skills of self-determination to keep pursuing her dream of attending college throughout her four years of high school. Although college still seemed to be a long way off, Sue Anne and her parents were pleased to have a map of the road ahead.

When Sue Anne reached her junior year in high school, her Guidance Counselor and the SSPT invited Sue Anne and her parents to a meeting to plan how she would prepare to apply to colleges and to discuss which colleges would be good choices for her based upon her interests and the support services available to students with learning disabilities. Also at issue was the application process, including standardized tests (e.g., SAT or ACT), an essay, and the extracurricular activities that had been part of Sue Anne's life. The biggest challenge was the standardized test. Sue Anne would need to apply to take it with extended time, so the test provider would need the appropriate documentation from the high school to verify the need for this accommodation. The team also discussed the option of Sue Anne attending the local community college for a year or two and then transferring to a four-year college. Based upon the knowledge of supports she would need to succeed in college, Sue Anne and her parents planned to visit a few campuses in the spring.

Mike

There are families that would consider Mike a daunting challenge. Born with developmental disabilities like cerebral palsy and mental retardation, it was clear from day one he would need strong support from his family and eventually from his teachers, therapists, counselors, and specialists to live in the community as an adult. Even before attending school, Mike worked with a speech therapist, physical therapist, and occupational therapist. His parents attended special classes with Mike to learn how to work with him at home and in the community. They were dedicated to creating choices for Mike that would one day serve him well as an adult. They would also have to balance their parenting of Mike with that of his older sister and give her the opportunity to live the life she hoped for as well.

Clearly, Mike would need special education services at the earliest opportunity. His parents determined those services would be focused on the future so that Mike would be as independent as possible when he reached his adult years. Like Sue Anne, Mike likely has dreams, but due to the severity of his disabilities, it is his parents who largely give voice to those dreams.

Mike is now a typical sixteen-year-old young man, and continues to have many complex challenges. He attends the East Area High School, where he participates in a Life Skills Classroom. There is one teacher and one paraprofessional for Mike and four other students, all of whom have severe and multiple disabilities. Mike is seen by the district's speech therapist one time a week for approximately two and a half hours, and the occupational therapist, once a week for three hours. He has difficulty with ambulation (walking) and therefore he uses a variety of methods to get around. He generally walks with physical support around school buildings and home but he also uses a wheelchair and a walker with wheels (one that supports his upper extremities so as to allow him to stand more erect while walking). This latter form of mobility is generally used at school. He is included in some portions of the school day, such as lunch and assemblies. He also participates in community outings such as grocery shopping and eating at restaurants. This is generally done two times a month using menu cards to order food at a restaurant, with one-on-one support from a person who is not always the same individual. While grocery shopping, a match-to-sample approach is used to shop (that is, matching labels to grocery items in order to make the correct selections). When grocery shopping he will push the cart, put items in the cart, place the items on the check-out counter, and carry the bags out to the bus.

The family has indicated some factors that they considered to be positive and negative about Mike's current educational setting. In general, the family feels that some positives are that Mike's current teacher has provided him with some good experiences. They are generally happy with her as his teacher this year. They also feel he has improved in areas such as his bathroom skills, his walking, and in some tasks that he was previously unable to do. On the negative side, the family feels that Mike has had a limited inclusive experience, has not participated in swimming and gym, and has not had music therapy from the school district as they requested.

Mike is on medication for sleep deprivation, which he takes at bedtime. The family has been the most important contributors to his development over the years. Both parents are employed, and Mike's sister attends college away from home. His home is fully accessible, allowing him mobility to every room in the house. Mike has private areas that he accesses when he chooses. His home environment encourages his independence and learning about himself and his interests.

Mike has many relationships in his neighborhood and through community recreational group activities. He has many relatives—aunts, uncles, and cousins—with whom he interacts and who support him. One aunt is designated as the legal guardian in case of a family emergency. Mike is a very active person within his community, and he frequents the mall, local park, McDonald's, community fairs, and goes on walks with his family. Mike is also involved with his church, and other activities such as therapeutic horseback riding, and a softball league for individuals with disabilities.

Some professionals think of Mike as a challenging person with whom to work. Yet, the real challenge is that they don't know enough about him to work effectively with him. That is, it has been difficult to identify Mike's motivation and interests as they relate to vocational options and other activities. One factor that has made this issue difficult is Mike's limited work-related experiences that are reflective of potential jobs that he might obtain in a community setting. As for other activities that involve some vocational component, at the therapeutic horseback riding program Mike is required to clean out the stalls and sweep a portion of the barn area when completing his ride. This activity seems to be somewhat enjoyable as well as being very challenging for him. Although he enjoys the cleaning activity, he still requires a great deal of prompting and physical assistance to complete the tasks.

In terms of physical abilities to manage a work-related activity, Mike has limited mobility and cannot stand for long periods of time, and therefore he needs an environment that will allow him the flexibility to sit or stand, depending on his preference. He also seems to need some variety in the activities and tasks he does because it seems that his on-task time is around twenty to twenty-five minutes. It is unclear whether the amount of engaged time is a true level of frustration (the point at which he loses interest or gets bored with the task) or if it is a learned behavior since his school lessons or activities seem to last about twenty to twenty-five minutes before changing activities. Mike has some difficulty with picking up or grasping objects or small pieces of work material. He will place his hand on the object, roll it in the palm of his hand until it reaches his fingers, then grasp it by curling his fingers around it. This technique is time consuming when attempting to pick up small objects but generally successful. Mike seems to be left-hand dominant, but also uses both hands with equal skill.

Despite the many challenges Mike's severe disabilities pose, both his family and the school personnel are committed to helping him plan and achieve a successful and fulfilled adult life. Clearly, much more will need to be discovered about Mike's capabilities and interests and how to build on these for his future. Although his family is unsure about what the future holds for Mike, they know that they want him to be a part of his community through work or volunteer activities, and they want him to be able to find a home outside his family's home. Mostly, they want Mike to live a happy and fulfilled adult life.

Obviously, Sue Anne and Mike have very different abilities and need very different levels of support in their school and community environments. Nevertheless, they both need the opportunity to share academic and social experiences with their friends and peers in inclusive settings at school and in the community.

THE EXTENDED CLASSROOM

We believe the educational needs of children and youth with disabilities would be insufficiently met if those needs were addressed only in a traditional school classroom (Rose, Rainforth, & Steere, 2002; Steere, Rose, & Fishbaugh, 1999). The school, home, and community are essential domains in an integrated curricula and have been proven to be fertile environments for teaching and learning (Brown, Branston, Hamre-Nietupski, Pumpian, Certo, & Gruenewald, 1979; Cross & Villa, 1992; Steere, 1997; Wilcox & Bellamy, 1987). The responsibilities of the teacher are more expansive in an extended classroom model in that he or she works as a service coordinator organizing the activities of parents and other family members, friends, school administrators, related-services personnel, public agency providers, and employers. By extending the classroom into the community, students like Sue Anne and Mike are able to develop and sustain a larger and more stable network of friends and advocates than with school peers alone (Rose et al., 2002; Steere et al., 1999).

THE IMPORTANCE OF ADVOCACY AND
SELF-DETERMINATION

For students with disabilities to gain the most benefit from their education, support systems, and learning experiences, a method of planning that includes family, friends, and advocates should be enacted during the school years. An important feature of this planning process is the preparation to assume as much self-advocacy or self-determination as possible (Martin, Mithaug, Cox, Peterson, Van Dyke, & Cash, 2003; Wehmeyer, 1996; Wehmeyer & Schwartz, 1997). The amendments to the Rehabilitation Act in 1992 and 1998 specified policy related to self-determination (West, Kregel, & Revell, 1994). The amendments required Individualized Plans for Employment (IPE) be written by the client and the vocational rehabilitation counselor with consideration to the individual's employment goals and job choices (West et al., 1994). Thus, the salience of individuals learning to contribute to their own advocacy from the school years through the adult years is by now a well-recognized practice (Steere et al., 1999; Wehmeyer & Schwartz, 1997).

TRANSITION AND THE EXTENDED CLASSROOM

Annual transition planning for students with disabilities begins with the first IEP to be in effect when the child reaches the age of sixteen as required by the Individuals with Disabilities Education Improvement Act of 2004 (IDEA 2004) (H.R. 1350). This is acknowledged as good policy for students with mild to moderate disabilities, Sue Anne for example, but students like Mike with severe and multiple disabilities need more time in planning and implementing transitions from home to school, school level to school level (e.g., middle school to high school), school to community, and school to employment (Steere et al., 1999). The spaces individuals and communities construct for living, learning, and working usually work for those of us who do not have disabilities and for those who have mild to moderate disabilities, but they often create significant barriers for persons with severe and multiple disabilities. As a society, we must be observant of children and youth with such disabilities and how they interact in the various environments of their lives. A change in environmental space and personal interaction means a transition for students with severe and multiple disabilities. Thus, it becomes especially important that transition planning include micro-level activities (e.g., moving from a van into the school building) as well as macro-level activities (e.g., using the metropolitan transportation system to get to work) (Rose et al., 2002).

You now have some beginning background on transition, which will be expanded in Chapter 1 with both regulatory and conceptual definitions. You have also met our two students, Sue Anne and Mike. As you move through the following chapters, you will experience their transitions and interactions with the various professionals who work with them. We hope, one day, you will be one of those professionals.

REFERENCES

Brown, L., Branston, M., Hamre-Nietupski, S., Pumpian, I., Certo, N., & Gruenewald, L. (1979). A strategy for developing chronological age-appropriate and functional curricular content for severely handicapped adolescents and young adults. *Journal of Special Education, 13*, 81–90.

Cross, G., & Villa, R. (1992). The Winooski school system: An evolutionary perspective of a school restructuring for diversity. In R. Villa, J. Thousand, W. Stainback, & S. Stainback (Eds.), *Restructuring for caring and effective education: An administrative guide to creating heterogeneous schools* (pp. 219–237). Baltimore, MD: Paul H. Brookes.

Individuals with Disabilities Education Improvement Act of 2004, H.R. 1350-162.

Martin, J., Mithaug, D., Cox, P., Peterson, L., Van Dyke, J., & Cash, M. (2003). Increasing self-determination: Teaching students to plan, work, evaluate, and adjust. *Exceptional Children, 69,* 431–446.

Rose, E., Rainforth, B., & Steere, D. (2002). Guiding principles for the education of children and youth with severe and multiple disabilities. In F. Obiakor, C. Utley, & A. Rotatori (Eds.), *Advances in special education: Psychology of effective education for learners with exceptionalities.* Stamford, CT: JAI Press, Inc.

Steere, D. (1997). *Increasing variety in adult life: A general-case approach.* (Innovations, #10). Washington, DC: American Association on Mental Retardation.

Steere, D. E., Rose, E., & Fishbaugh, M. S. E. (1999). Integration in the secondary school for students with severe disabilities. In M. Coutinho & A. C. Repp (Eds.), *Inclusion: The integration of students with disabilities.* Belmont, CA: Wadsworth Publishing Company.

West, M., Kregel, J., & Revell, W. (1993–1994, Winter). A new era of self-determination, *Impact, 6.*

Wehmeyer, M. (1996). Self-determination as an educational outcome: Why is it important to children, youth, and adults with disabilities? In D. Sands & M. Wehmeyer (Eds.), *Self-determination across the lifespan: Independence and choice for people with disabilities* (pp. 17–36). Baltimore, MD: Paul H. Brookes.

Wehmeyer, M., & Schwartz, M. (1997). Self-determination and positive adult outcomes: A follow-up study of youth with mental retardation and learning disabilities. *Exceptional Children, 63,* 245–255.

Wilcox, B., & Bellamy, G. T. (Eds.). (1987). *A comprehensive guide to the Activities Catalog: An alternative curriculum for youth and adults with severe disabilities.* Baltimore, MD: Paul H. Brookes.

■ ■ ■ ■ ■

CHAPTER 1

TRANSITION TO ADULT LIFE FOR STUDENTS WITH DISABILITIES

Foundations, Definitions, and Legislation

CHAPTER OBJECTIVES

Upon completion of this chapter, you will be able to

1. define transition using key phrases from the Individuals with Disabilities Education Improvement Act (2004) (IDEA 2004) definition and from the position statement of the Division on Career Development and Transition (DCDT).

2. describe how transition from school to adulthood relates to other transition points throughout the lifespan of individuals with disabilities.

3. describe important categories of transition outcomes that help define a desired future life for a young person with disabilities.

4. possess background knowledge on the nature and importance of the transition process.

This knowledge will serve as a foundation for all subsequent chapters.

KEY TOPICS TO LOOK FOR IN THIS CHAPTER . . .

- Language of the law: The Individuals with Disabilities Education Improvement Act (2004) contains key language that guides our efforts to help young people make a successful transition to adult life. Notice particularly how the law focuses on empowering students to participate actively in their own transition planning process.

- Visions of success: As you will read in this chapter, transition planning is a longitudinal process designed to help young people clarify and then work toward a positive vision of their adult life.

Transition from school to adult life centers on a systematic planning process, which we will describe in subsequent chapters, but it also can be described as a time of intense change in the lives of young people and their families. The stakes for helping young people make a successful transition are high because the impact of our efforts during this time period will affect the remainder of their adult lives. In this chapter, we will define transition and its essential elements. In doing so, we provide a framework for the remainder of the book.

WHAT IS THE PURPOSE OF PUBLIC EDUCATION?

In considering what the future holds for Sue Anne and Mike, the two young people introduced in the Prologue, we need to first ask ourselves about the broader purpose of the educational process. What do we as citizens want from the public education system? Possible responses to this question include the following:

> To prepare all children to be citizens who contribute to society
>
> To help all children learn valued knowledge and skills
>
> To prepare all children to participate in the workforce and contribute to state and national economies
>
> To invest in our communities and our country
>
> To allow all people to have a chance at a better life

Clearly, there are many potential responses to this question, depending on one's orientation. For purposes of our discussion, we would like to focus on the achievement of a *positive adult lifestyle* as an important result of the educational system. In other words, if we do our jobs well in the special education system, then graduates of our services will have an improved quality of life as adults. They will have satisfying jobs and careers, comfortable homes, meaningful involvement in their local communities, and satisfying relationships with friends and family. They will achieve the same things that most people want from their adult lives. The fact that students like Sue Anne and Mike have disabilities in no way changes their desires for happiness and fulfillment in adulthood. How well have we done as a profession in helping people with disabilities achieve these outcomes? We will address this question in the next section.

HOW WELL HAVE WE ACHIEVED THESE OUTCOMES?

In general, the outcomes of students with disabilities who exit American schools have been poor (Houtenville, 2000; La Plante, Kennedy, Kaye, & Wenger, 1996). When discussing outcomes of students with disabilities leaving school, employment is often a primary focus. Although the idea of being gainfully employed is and should be a primary consideration as a positive outcome for students leaving the special education system, it has been recognized that outcomes for individuals with disabilities receiving services in school be broad by considering the full range of students' interests and preferences. As we will discuss in subsequent chapters, the Individuals with Disabilities Education Improvement Act (2004) (IDEA 2004) focuses on several outcome areas, including postsecondary education, community participation, community living, and recreation and leisure. However, results of ongoing studies that track the status of students leaving the special education system have documented poorer results for students with disabilities than nondisabled students. These poorer outcomes include:

- higher unemployment rates
- underemployment (working in a job that demands less than one's ability and pays less than one's earning power)
- poor rates of participation in postsecondary education, and poorer graduation rates
- less extensive social support networks

The reasons for these poor outcomes may range from the challenges that schools have faced in preparing students for adult life to the struggles of poorly funded adult service programs that could aid the process of transition. We will address the ineffectiveness of schools separately, but for now, we should note here that when funding affects adult service programs, it tends to have a ripple effect on the transition of students with disabilities. Developmental disability departments in some states have provided only minimal growth in funding to adult services in the past several years. This has contributed to the difficulties that adult service agencies have had in making commitments to graduates from special education programs. That is, since many individuals with disabilities will require some ongoing support system, which usually comes from adult services programs, these programs have been reluctant and unable to provide a "seamless transition" program for students (Sax, Noyes, & Fisher, 2001). This issue has created a problem in many states where individuals with disabilities do not have a job or a program to go to upon leaving school, and are therefore placed on their state's "waiting list" for services. States throughout the country are experiencing extensive waiting list problems, and these waiting lists include people who left school when it was hoped they would receive services from adult human services (Pennsylvania Waiting List Campaign, 2002).

The transition amendments were added to IDEA in 1990 in large part due to the poor outcomes achieved by schools on behalf of students with disabilities. The overall unemployment rate for people with disabilities continues to range from 50 to 75 percent (Louis Harris & Associates, 2000). It should be noted that the success of students with the various types of disabilities has also varied significantly. For example, the success of individuals with specific learning disabilities is far better than that of individuals with multiple disabilities. The percentage of individuals with specific learning disabilities employed competitively is around 63 percent, whereas for students with multiple disabilities it is about 15 percent. La Plante, Kennedy, Kaye, and Wenger (1996) reported that an estimated 75 percent of adults labeled as having a severe disability were unemployed and 92 percent of adults labeled with a profound disability were unemployed. They also reported that students with disabilities have a higher dropout rate, are in lower paying jobs (those that do work), and have higher arrest records than do their graduating counterparts. It should be noted that more recent data from the National Longitudinal Transition Study 2 have shown some encouraging trends in the outcomes for students with disabilities who have exited school, including increased rates of school completion and of engagement in postsecondary education (Wagner, Newman, Cameto, & Levine, 2005). Despite these gains, students with disabilities are still far less likely to complete school, to go to college or other postsecondary education, or to be employed. This represents a major challenge to many schools who are preparing individuals with disabilities to enter the adult world upon leaving school. Several researchers have raised the importance of creating a seamless transition from school to adult life as a potential solution to this problem (Certo, Pumpian, Fisher, Storey, & Smalley, 1997; Fisher & Sax, 1999).

DEFINITIONS OF TRANSITION

Legislative Definitions

Since initial passage of the Education for All Handicapped Children Act (EAHCA) of 1975 (PL 94-142), the concept of transition has undergone considerable expansion (Neubert, 2000; Wehman, 2001). The EAHCA implied that children and adolescents with disabilities would have the same access to programs as students without disabilities, including whatever vocational education programs were available. However, there was no explicit language related to transition or transition services. By the end of the Act's first decade, parents and researchers were becoming quite aware of the lack of options for former special education students and the problems this created (Hasazi, Gordon, & Roe, 1985; Mithaug, Horiuchi, & Fanning, 1985; Wagner, 1989).

The Education of the Handicapped Act Amendments of 1983 and 1986 provided discretionary funding for schools to work model programs, but did not require transition services for children and adolescents with disabilities. However, in 1990, the Act was reauthorized as the Individuals with Disabilities Education Act (PL 101-476) and included language requiring identification of needed transition services in the Individual Education Plan (IEP) by age 16 or younger if deemed necessary. The 1990 definition stated:

    a. As used in this part, transition services means a coordinated set of activities for a student with a disability that—

      1. Is designed within an outcome-oriented process, that promotes movement from school to postschool activities, including postsecondary education, vocational training, integrated employment (including supported employment), continuing and adult education, adult services, independent living, or community participation. (Section 300.29) The definition also included student participation in the planning process.

      2. Is based on the individual student's needs, taking into account the student's preferences and interests; and

      3. Includes—

        (i) Instruction;

        (ii) Related services;

(iii) Community experiences;

(iv) The development of employment and other postschool adult living objectives; and

(v) If appropriate, acquisition of daily living skills and functional vocational evaluation. (Section 300.29)

From the original EAHCA (PL 94-142) to IDEA (PL 101-476), the legislation moved from a presumption that access to traditional vocational education programs would be sufficient to an acknowledgment that specific activities and specific individuals must be identified to ensure appropriate transition planning and services for students regardless of the range or severity of disability. This was further extended in the Individuals with Disabilities Education Act Amendments of 1997 (PL 105-17). These amendments changed the required service age from 16 to 14, from high school to middle school, to allow for additional planning and education for full community integration and for those students with a desire to attend postsecondary educational institutions. However, the reauthorization of the Act, the Individuals with Disabilities Improvement Act of 2004 (H.R. 1350), has changed the service age language to "beginning not later than the first IEP to be in effect when the child is 16, and updated annually thereafter" (Section 614, VIII). This language gives planning teams an upper age range starting date, but provides latitude on beginning transition planning and services at a younger age if needed.

As the official definition of transition services in IDEA 2004 now stands, some terms are important to consider (see Table 1.1). First is that of a "coordinated set of activities." This means that transition services include a number of people with responsibilities for planning and providing services, including teachers, specialized service providers from the school district, in many cases adult service providers from outside the school district, the child, and the child's parents. It is this group of individuals who are charged with determining the transition activities that are a part of the child's IEP and who are required to update the activities on an annual basis, as needed.

Another important term is "results-oriented process." This term reflects the movement toward greater accountability expected of schools that receive federal and

TABLE 1.1   Key Phrases in the IDEA 2004 Definition of Transition

"coordinated set of activities": implies collaboration among schools and diverse agencies and other support systems

"results-oriented process": implies that transition should result in an improved adult life for the child in areas such as working, postsecondary education, community living, recreation and leisure, and community participation, which is caused by greater academic and functional achievement

"taking into account the child's strengths, preferences, and interests": implies that the student should be an active participant in planning and that his or her achievement and choices should guide the planning process

state funding. That is, transition services provided by a school are expected to make a positive difference in the academic and functional achievement of children with disabilities. The individual's prospects for successful employment or postsecondary education or both, participation in community activities, and living an independent life outside the family home (with or without supports) should be significantly improved by the transition planning and service process.

Finally, "taking into account the child's strengths, preferences, and interests" is a term that affirms an individual's right to have significant input over her or his life choices. This means that, like a school district, any outside agency (public or private) that is participating in the transition planning and service delivery of a child must invite the child and representatives of other agencies who will interact with the host agency in providing or paying for the transition services under consideration.

A Definition from the Field

Although the official definition of transition brought forward in 1990 and amended in 1997 and again in 2004 made transition planning and delivery part of the IEP, the language and scope were too narrow for many professionals. Halpern (1994) wrote a position statement on behalf of the Division on Career Development and Transition (DCDT), of the Council for Exceptional Children (CEC). Halpern called his definition of transition, "a framework for guiding future work in this area" (p. 117).

> Transition refers to a change in status from behaving primarily as a student to assuming emergent adult roles in the community. These roles include employment, participating in post-secondary education, maintaining a home, becoming appropriately involved in the community, and experiencing satisfactory personal and social relationships. The process of enhancing transition involves the participation and coordination of school programs, adult agency services, and natural supports within the community. The foundations for transition should be laid during the elementary and middle school years, guided by the broad concept of career development. Transition planning should begin no later than age 14, and students should be encouraged, to the full extent of their capabilities, to assume a maximum amount of responsibility for such planning (p. 117).

Halpern (1994) explained the definition in two parts, one related to transition planning and the other related to the delivery of transition services (see Table 1.2). In the planning stage, he first stresses that students should develop an emerging sense of empowerment which will enhance self-determination in the transition planning process. Thus, DCDT was emphasizing student interests and preferences and their primary importance in developing the transition plan. Second, student self-evaluation is emphasized. In all of special education, there has been a history of standardized assessments for eligibility and program services. DCDT advocates that student self-exploration should be a pivotal part of the evaluation process and that students, whenever possible, should direct the goals of their transition plans. The third aspect emphasizes that students' postschool transition goals must be consistent with the results of their self-evaluations. For example, if the goal is employment, professionals should work with students to ensure it is competitive employment (with supports if necessary)

TABLE 1.2   Key Points in the Position Statement of the Division on Career Development and Transition of the Council for Exceptional Children

TRANSITION PLANNING

- Students should develop self-determination
- Student self-evaluation is emphasized
- Post-school outcomes or goals should be consistent with the self-evaluations
- Students should select educational experiences to fit the desired transition outcomes

DELIVERY OF TRANSITION SERVICES

- Services and programs should be based on students' interests, preferences, and skills, with an orientation toward the future
- Inclusion in general school programs is emphasized
- Community-based programs are emphasized as learning environments
- Linkages should be promoted as needed
- Community organizations should be involved

Source: A. S. Halpern (1994). The transition of youth with disabilities to adult life: A position statement of the Division on Career Development and Transition, The Council for Exceptional Children. *Career Development for Exceptional Individuals, 17*, 115–124.

with commensurate benefits to promote financial security as much as possible. Finally, students should be encouraged to select appropriate educational experiences in school and in the community that fit their transition goals. The emphasis here is to promote classroom and school inclusion and to use the community as a fully integrated educational experience, which will better prepare students for success upon leaving high school (Rose, Rainforth, & Steere, 2002; Steere, Rose, & Fishbaugh, 1999).

In part two, Halpern (1994) describes the delivery of transition services as following the foundation set by planning, which follows the four criteria discussed above. He stresses that DCDT does not advocate a specific approach to delivery, but it does recommend that approaches selected should conform to the four planning criteria. Halpern identifies five issues that should help to guide the delivery of transition services. Issue one stresses that services and programs be based on a student's interests, preferences, and skills with an orientation toward the future. Issue two re-emphasizes inclusion in general school programs. Issue three stresses the importance of community-based programs as learning environments, including transportation systems, whenever appropriate. Issue four promotes the linkage of adult service agencies as needed, especially as postschool providers. And issue five emphasizes the need to involve community organizations (e.g., service clubs, community recreation centers, etc.) in addition to service agencies (e.g., Department of Rehabilitation Services, Department of Mental Health Services, etc.). Thus, the Halpern/DCDT (1994) definition of transition invites innovation and creativity while emphasizing that the individual is the most important director of the transition plan and delivery of services. It is this definition that helps provide the framework for this book.

■ ■ ■ ■ ■

SIDEBAR 1.1
SPOTLIGHT ON HISTORY: MADELEINE WILL

During the mid 1980s, Madeleine Will, a parent of a young man with disabilities, contributed to the development of transition services through her "Bridges from School to Working Life" model. Will was Assistant Secretary of the Office of Special Education and Rehabilitation Services (OSERS), part of the federal Department of Education. Concerned about poor results from follow-up studies of students who had received special education services, she developed a model of transition from school to working life that involved three types of services or "bridges." The three bridges that she described were:

- No special services: This "bridge" would be appropriate for students with disabilities who would not require any formal or specialized adult services in order to be successful in entering the job market.
- Time-limited services: This "bridge" includes services from the federal and state Vocational Rehabilitation (VR) system, which assists people with disabilities to obtain employment. The VR system is a time-limited system that cannot provide employment supports for extended periods of time. This bridge would be appropriate for students who do need specialized adult vocational services to obtain employment but who will not need support from such services throughout the duration of their employment. The VR system is discussed in greater detail in Chapter 5.
- Ongoing services: This "bridge" includes supported employment, which is a service approach designed for people with the most severe disabilities, who will always need some level of support in order to maintain community employment. Supported employment is described in detail in Chapter 9.

Although it focused narrowly on the transition from school to employment, the Bridges model was important in describing the need for coordinated transition services that could meet the needs of students with diverse disabilities (Flexer, 2005; Will, 1983).

The work of Madeleine Will in the 1980s contributed substantially to the development of our understanding of the purpose and scope of transition planning. A brief profile of Will and her "Bridges" model is shown in Sidebar 1.1.

REMEMBER WHEN?: THE HUMAN SIDE OF TRANSITION

So far, we have discussed what transition is and why it is so important. We have also introduced key definitions from the Individuals with Disabilities Education Improvement Act (2004) (IDEA 2004) and from the Division on Career Development and Transition (DCDT). In subsequent chapters, we will go into detail about the actual transition planning process and the roles of the people who are involved with it. Before we proceed, however, we would like to remind you that all of us have experienced transition and that all young people, not just those with disabilities, will go through the transition process. In fact, this is one of the reasons this topic is of such interest, because we can all relate to the challenges that young people are facing.

Consider This!   Think back to your transition experiences. What was life like when you were between the ages of fourteen and eighteen years old? (You can include the years up to age twenty-one as well for purposes of this discussion.) Think back to . . .

Your first car or other vehicle
Your first date
Your first home away from home
Your first career choices
Your first feelings of emotional independence
Your first realization of at least some financial independence
Your first feelings of self-esteem and self-definition as a capable adult

Thinking back on these aspects of transition can be humbling, but it is an instructive exercise. First, we can remember how confusing this time can be and how many mistakes we might have made. We also remember the importance of first steps, like learning to drive or going to the store alone for the first time, first sexual experiences, first career awareness, and the first experience of moving away from home. These experiences are all part of the transition process. For students with disabilities, these same challenges exist but are compounded by the unique challenges posed by their particular disabling condition. The important point is that, regardless of the presence of a disability, the young person in transition is first and foremost a young person.

A BROADER PERSPECTIVE ON TRANSITION

The topic of transition from school to adult life typically focuses on students from ages sixteen through their exit from special education at either eighteen or twenty-one. These are the ages to which IDEA 2004's transition mandates apply, as we will discuss in subsequent chapters on the transition planning process. However, transition from school to adult life is one of many times of transition in a person's life. For example, children make a transition from home to preschool or daycare settings. Later, they make a transition to kindergarten for their first school experience. These transitions lead to transitions from grade to grade and from one teacher to the next. Maturation brings additional transitions in terms of physical changes, skill development, and changes in self-image. The profile of Sue Anne, presented earlier, highlights the longitudinal nature of these life transitions.

Edna Szymanski, a former rehabilitation counselor and now Dean of the College of Education at the University of Maryland, made this point well in an article published in the journal *Exceptional Children* (1994). Her "life-span and life-space" orientation to transition highlighted the importance of experiences in early childhood on later transition success. For example, the fulfillment of responsibilities such as chores within the home provide a foundation for later adult roles. These early experiences regarding career awareness, adult roles and responsibilities, and the development of work ethic are cumulative and are an essential basis for later planning efforts. Szymanski also pointed out that career development is considered to be a longitudinal process and is typically not complete by age twenty-one. In short, her point was that we cannot wait until age sixteen, or even fourteen, to begin to think about transition to adult life, because many foundational skills, habits, and attitudes need to be developed earlier, and we cannot stop our transition efforts at age twenty-one. These recommendations have important implications for our collaboration with other professionals, the role of the family in transition, and the importance of educators at the elementary and intermediate levels.

Consider This! What skills, knowledge, habits, and attitudes do children learn during the early childhood to elementary years that relate to later success in adulthood? In responding to this question, consider skills, knowledge, habits, and attitudes that relate to:

> Career awareness and work
> Home living
> Adult roles and responsibilities
> Successful social interaction
> Recreation and leisure
> Self-image and self-esteem

OTHER ASPECTS OF TRANSITION

Shift from Entitlement to Eligibility

As students with disabilities and their families prepare to graduate and/or leave school, one factor that challenges them is the shift from an entitlement program (the special education system) to an eligibility required adult service system. The challenge is that, unlike the special education system in which identified students are entitled to services, the adult service programs generally require applicants to meet eligibility criteria for gaining access to services. Furthermore, acceptance to services (that is, meeting eligibility criteria) does not guarantee immediate services, and waiting lists are common. This factor seems to be one that families of students with disabilities are the least prepared for during transition. It also seems to be one of the least understood factors by special education teachers and school administrators. That is, there is an assumption that once a student leaves the special education system the student will automatically be "picked up" by the adult service system. Once a student leaves a special education program, schools do not generally track their students' outcomes and placement. The concept of creating a "seamless transition" has been hypothesized as a significant needed change to the service delivery system that could impact the outcomes of students with disabilities (Sax et al., 2001). This seamless transition requires postschool systems to collaborate and participate in a student's plan to ensure a positive outcome (Sax et al., 2001).

The shift from entitlement to eligibility requirement is difficult for families and students with disabilities. Families generally struggle for years to learn and understand how to negotiate a complex special education system. Yet, when this entitlement system ends they have to learn and understand a new and equally complex eligibility adult service system, which can vary somewhat from state to state. In an eligibility-driven system there are no guarantees of funding for needed services or programs. It is a system in which one has to continuously prove one's need, despite the oftentimes obvious disability or need for the service. Families find this process frustrating and time consuming, leading in some cases to their giving up, only to have the person sit at home regressing from any progress he or she may have made while in school.

Domains of Adult Living

As previously mentioned, competitive employment is only one aspect of a successful adult life. Other aspects include living on one's own in the community or as independently as possible, participating in recreation and leisure activities, and participating as a member of one's local community. There are two very critical considerations that should be taken into consideration in designing a transition program: first, to create many opportunities for students to practice their skills in community-based settings, and second, to address the various life domains as a foundation for learning. But not all students will need the same type of program. Students will generally need to address the life domains in different ways. For example, students with learning disabilities may not need to experience the life domains as extensively as students with significant disabilities. What is important and needed is that ALL students have access to a school curriculum that helps to prepare them for the different aspects of adult living.

VISIONS OF SUCCESS

Planning effective transitions to satisfying and successful adult living requires families and professionals to assist students to envision the goal of a positive future and then to work toward that goal. This requires that students be aware of their options, have experienced work and other adult activities while in school, and have support in taking the risks associated with setting desired goals and then pursuing those goals. As this book details, there are many different facets to transition planning, but they all hinge on clarifying a vision of success. Consider the visions of success of the two young people who were introduced in the Prologue.

Sue Anne

By the fall semester of her senior year, Sue Anne had decided to apply to four colleges, including the local community college. She had qualified to take the SAT with extended time and had earned an acceptable score. She had worked hard on her essay and her guidance counselor, selected teachers, and the supervisor at the daycare center where she volunteered had all written strong references for her. Off went her applications and then, like most of her classmates, Sue Anne began the wait. Her choice of colleges was based upon her desire to become an early childhood teacher. She loved her volunteer work at a daycare center and at her church's preschool program. She had a knack for working with young children and was in constant demand as a babysitter.

After what seemed like years, the letters came back. Sue Anne was accepted at two of the three four-year colleges to which she had applied and the community college. Sue Anne and her parents talked about the two colleges where she had been accepted. One was a state college, the other a private college. Both had been welcoming and both provided good services for students with disabilities. Sue Anne could get what she needed, but she would need to use the self-determination skills she had been working on all through high school. She would also have to practice a lot of self-discipline because her parents would not be there to monitor the choices she, as a student, would have to make, such as, study or go to a movie with friends. Sue Anne talked for hours with her sister, who was a graduate of a private college, and her brother, a senior at the state university. In the end, she chose the private college for its smaller student body and more personal touch. This college had created a service office for students with disabilities well before the development of such offices on most campuses and they had a national reputation for their excellent services. In addition, they had a quality early childhood program and a preschool on campus where students in the program could intern. The members of the special services planning team (SSPT) were delighted for Sue Anne. They had worked with her and her parents to design a transition plan that would achieve this result. The plan had worked.

Now consider the impact of the achievement of Sue Anne's vision of success on her adult life. Several years have passed since she was a young high school student first planning her future. Now she is a beginning teacher. Sue Anne looked around the classroom. Everything was ready. The walls had brightly colored posters, there were learning centers, it was well organized, yet inviting. Soon parents would be pulling up in the parking lot and walking their young children into the school. Fifteen of the parents would be bringing their children to Sue Anne's classroom. She felt confident. Her college program had been demanding, but she graduated with a B average and had earned her position based upon her interview and the references from her professors and the director of the campus preschool. Although a transition plan was not required at her college, Sue Anne worked with counselors in the Office for Students with Disabilities and they had recommended she work with the counselors in the Campus Career Development Center to learn résumé writing and to practice interviewing for teaching positions. When a position came open at a preschool near her hometown, Sue Anne was qualified and well prepared to interview for the job. So here she was.

TABLE 1.3   Mike's Vision of Success, Developed with the Assistance of His Circle of Support

FUTURE HOPES

Live in a group home close to home
Fulfill community-based functions, such as work, volunteering, and recreational activities
Be happy and content
To have a good quality of life

DREAMS

To walk independently
To develop communication abilities
To have friends
To be happy and content

FEARS

Living at home full-time
No funding available
No program available
In segregated adult day care program
Total responsibility for care falls to his sister
His parents having to sacrifice their careers
His mom having to stay home and losing income

The quiet little girl with big dreams who struggled to learn reading and math would now be preparing young children to learn those essential skills. Her abilities were all that mattered now.

Mike

Because of the severity of his disabilities, Mike has difficulty expressing a vision of future success. In order to support him, his family and others who care about him formed a Circle of Support to develop a Personal Futures Plan for him (Mount & Zwernik, 1988). This informal planning approach taps into the creativity, energy, and commitment of those who care about the focus person with a disability. As described earlier, Mike has an extensive support system of family, friends, and community members, and these people are his strongest asset. The section of his personal futures plan developed by his Circle of Support and focusing on his desired future is shown in Table 1.3.

In general, Mike's vision for the future can be summarized as achieving a level of happiness and being content with his life. This involves being self-sufficient enough to live in a community residence with people of his choice, and to be involved in community activities that are relevant to his interests and that contribute to the community. This may involve a paid job or a volunteer position. Finally, his Circle of Support envisions Mike having friends who will spend time with him doing things that are mutually satisfying. A major point in his vision of success is to avoid being placed in a segregated day activity center. The Circle of Support will need to further clarify his vision of success over the next several years, but they are well on their way to describing what a positive and fulfilling future can look like for Mike.

CHAPTER SUMMARY

This chapter has introduced you to the topic of transition and its importance in the study of special education. We have also introduced the idea that our success in the field of special education is perhaps best measured by the achievement of successful adult outcomes for people with disabilities. Transition was defined using the Individuals with Disabilities Education Improvement Act (2004) (IDEA 2004) and the position statement of the Division of Career Development and Transition (DCDT) of the Council for Exceptional Children (CEC). We also described transition within a broader context of the life span, and we focused on particular domains of adult living, including work and career development, community participation, living in one's own home, and recreation and leisure. We ended our discussion by highlighting the importance of helping young people develop a vision of success for their adult lives to guide the transition planning process.

APPLICATION ACTIVITIES

The application activities listed below are essential for your continued learning and skill development in transition. Each of the activities will require your time and energy but will help you develop your professional skills in this area.

For Practice and Enhanced Understanding:

Interview two young persons between the ages of fourteen and eighteen. One of the individuals should have a disability. Design questions around the domains of adult living that were introduced in this chapter, for example, work and career development, community participation, living in one's own home, and recreation and leisure. What do these individuals tell you about their thinking at this stage of life? How well prepared for the next steps are they? What steps should they be taking now to be prepared for the future? What are the most striking differences (if any) between the two young people?

Observe three or four children between the ages of six and nine. What signs do you see that indicate a beginning awareness or development of later adult roles and responsibilities? What are they learning or experiencing at school and home that will contribute toward their eventual success in adulthood?

Review your own career development pattern to date. What steps have you taken? Did you change direction and, if so, why? When did you make a commitment to a particular career or direction of effort? Who helped or influenced you, and how?

For Your Portfolio:

If you are currently teaching or plan to teach at the secondary level, list at least six students with whom you have interacted and who are sixteen years of age or older. These students are at the defined transition age and should be participating in transition planning, as it is described in subsequent chapters. For now, identify a job and a living arrangement you think is achievable for each student. As we will note later in this book, we feel strongly that transition planning can and should begin when students are fourteen, so this suggested activity can also be completed with students of that age.

If you are teaching or plan to teach at the intermediate or elementary school level, list the subjects you teach or will teach and how each content area relates to a child's future activities in adulthoood (e.g., work, independent living, recreation, and leisure).

If you are a parent or family member, develop a description of what you want for your son's or daughter's future. Note: We will provide you with additional formats for doing this in later chapters. For now, simply list your thoughts about your child and the future.

REFERENCES

Certo, N. J., Pumpian, I., Fisher, D., Storey, K., & Smalley, K. (1997). Focusing on the point of transition. *Education and Treatment of Children, 20,* 68–84.

Education for All Handicapped Children Act of 1975, Public Law 94-142, 20 U.S.C. 1410.

Education for the Handicapped Act Amendments of 1983, Public Law 98-199, 97 STAT., 1357–1377.

Fisher, D., & Sax, C. (1999). Noticing differences between secondary and postsecondary education: Extending Agran, Snow, and Swaner's discussion. *Journal of the Association for Persons with Severe Handicaps, 24,* 303–305.

Flexer, R. (2005). History and transition legislation. In R. Flexer, T. Simmons, P. Luft, & R. Baer (Eds.), *Transition planning for secondary students with disabilities,* 2nd ed. (pp. 20–52). Upper Saddle River, NJ: Merrill Prentice Hall.

Halpern, A. S. (1994). The transition of youth with disabilities to adult life: A position statement of the Division on Career Development and Transition, The Council for Exceptional Children. *Career Development for Exceptional Individuals, 17,* 115–124.

Hasazi, S., Gordon, L., & Roe, C. (1985). Factors associated with the employment status of handicapped youth exiting from high school for 1979–1983. *Exceptional Children, 51,* 455–469.

Houtenville, A. (2002). *Estimates of employment rates for persons with disabilities in the U.S.* Ithaca, NY: RRCT for Economic Research on Employment Policy for Persons with Disabilities, Cornell University.

Individuals with Disabilities Education Act of 1990 (IDEA), Public Law 101-476, 20 U.S.C. 1401.

Individuals with Disabilities Education Act Amendments of 1997, Public Law 105-17, 20 U.S.C. 1400.

Individuals with Disabilities Education Improvement Act of 2004 (IDEA 2004), Public Law 108-446, 20 U.S.C. 1400 *et seq.*

LaPlante, M. P., Kennedy, J., Kaye, S. H., & Wenger, B. (1996). Disability statistics abstract, No. 11. Washington, DC: U.S. Department of Education, National Institute on Disability and Rehabilitation Research.

Louis Harris & Associates (2000). The N.O.D./Harris survey program on participants and attitudes: Survey of Americans with disabilities. New York: Author.

Mithaug, D., Horiuchi, C., & Fanning, P. (1985). A report on the Colorado statewide follow-up survey of special education students. *Exceptional Children, 51*, 397–404.

Mount, B., & Zwernik, K. (1988). It's never too early, it's never too late: An overview of personal futures planning. St. Paul, MN: Governor's Planning Council on Developmental Disabilities.

Neubert, D. (2000). Transition education and services guidelines. In P. L. Sitlington, G. M. Clark, & O. P. Kolstoe, *Transition education and services for adolescents with disabilities* (pp. 39–69). Needham Heights, MA: Allyn & Bacon.

Pennsylvania Waiting List Campaign (2002). A guide for transition to adult services: What you need to ensure that a waiting list is not in your future.

Rose, E., Rainforth, B., & Steere, D. (2002). Guiding principles for the education of children and youth with severe and multiple disabilities. In F. Obiakor, C. Utley, & A. Rotatori (Eds.), *Advances in special education: Psychology of effective education for learners with exceptionalities.* Stamford, CT: JAI Press, Inc.

Sax, C., Noyes, D., & Fisher, F. (2001). High school inclusion + seamless transition = desired outcomes. *TASH Connections, 27*, 17–20.

Steere, D. E., Rose, E., & Fishbaugh, M. S. E. (1999). Integration in the secondary school for students with severe disabilities. In M. Coutinho & A. C. Repp (Eds.), *Inclusion: The integration of students with disabilities.* Belmont, CA: Wadsworth Publishing Company.

Szymanski, E. M. (1994). Transition: Life span and life space considerations for empowerment. *Exceptional Children, 60*, 402–410.

Wagner, M. (1989). Youth with disabilities during transition: An overview of descriptive findings from the national longitudinal transition study. *Project Director's Fourth Annual Meeting*, Champaign, IL: The Secondary Transition Effectiveness Institute.

Wagner, M., Newman, L., Cameto, R., & Levine, P. (2005). *Changes over time in early postschool outcomes of youth with disabilities: A report of findings from the National Longitudinal Transition Study (NLTS) and the National Longitudinal Transition Study-2 (NLTS2), executive summary.* Retrieved from website of the National Longitudinal Transition Study 2 (www.nlts2.org/reports/str6_execsum.html).

Wehman, P. (2001). *Life beyond the classroom* (3rd ed.). Baltimore: Paul H. Brookes Publishing Company.

Will, M. (1983). *OSERS programming for the transition of youth with disabilities: Bridges from school to working life.* Washington, DC: U.S. Department of Education, Office of Special Education and Rehabilitative Services. (ERIC Document Reproduction Service No. ED 256 132).

CHAPTER 2

STUDENT PERSPECTIVES AND INVOLVEMENT IN TRANSITION

CHAPTER OBJECTIVES

Upon completion of this chapter, you will be able to

1. define self-determination and describe specific student actions and behaviors that are reflective of increasing self-determination. You will also be able to take steps to increase the self-determination of students whom you teach.

2. take specific steps to better prepare students for their active and meaningful involvement in the development of their own transition IEPs.

3. have the ability to assist students with disabilities in taking an active role in their own transition planning.

KEY TOPICS TO LOOK FOR IN THIS CHAPTER . . .

- Self-determination: It is critical that we help young people take an active role in the transition planning process. In this chapter, we discuss a range of ways to increase students' self-determination.

- Person-centered planning: Person-centered planning is an alternative approach to planning that helps give people with disabilities and their families greater control over the planning process. Look for how person-centered planning works and how it contributes to the success of transition planning.

Perhaps most affected by the success or failure of transition planning are the young people with disabilities who are the focus of the planning process. Regardless of the nature of their disabilities, these students are young people who are growing and changing from adolescents to young adults. This is a time of life that presents many challenges to most young people, including peer pressure, uncertainty about the future, and lack of awareness of one's own abilities and strengths. Students with disabilities face these same challenges but also face additional problems that result from their disabilities.

As introduced in Chapter 1, the Individuals with Disabilities Education Improvement Act (2004) (IDEA 2004) specifically states that transition services are "... based on the individual student's needs, taking into account the student's strengths, preferences and interests ..." (Section 602(34)(B), PL 108-446). This means that students must be active and central participants in all aspects of transition planning. Without active student involvement, we cannot do an effective job with the transition planning process. Therefore, the challenge that we face is how to help students with disabilities to have the knowledge, skills, and attitudes necessary for them to assume their rightful role in planning for the future. This chapter will describe student perspectives on planning for the future and then discuss ways for professionals and families to support students in their active participation in planning.

CONCERNS AND INTERESTS OF TYPICAL ADOLESCENTS

Before discussing the challenges that students with disabilities face in participating in transition planning, it will be useful to focus on some of the perspectives, concerns, and interests that are typical in teenagers (Wehman, 2001). Although we cannot assume that all adolescents share these concerns and interests, for many young people these issues are of major importance to them. Table 2.1 lists some of the areas of concerns of typical teenagers.

First, for young people at the high school level, peer group membership becomes an important concern. Teenagers usually try to figure out where they fit in socially and whom they can trust as friends. This often is expressed through group membership and identification. Peer pressure increases during the high school years as the opinions and feedback of one's peer group increase in importance.

Second, adolescents are often concerned about their appearance and their self-esteem. Adolescence is clearly a time of physical maturation and change, and it is fairly typical for students to be self-conscious about how they appear to others of their own age. Many may dress or groom themselves to look more adult, more attractive to

---

TABLE 2.1 Areas of Concern of Typical Teenagers

- Peer group membership and acceptance
- Appearance and attractiveness
- Self-image and self-esteem
- Mobility and transportation
- Recreation and leisure interests
- Independence from family, and greater privacy
- School work and homework
- Extracurricular activities sponsored by the school or community agencies

Source: Adapted from Wehman, 2001.

others, or simply to look more in style. For many young people, this is the age at which first serious dating takes place and first sexual experiences may occur.

Many young people at the high school level have a focus on day-to-day activities within and outside of school. Class work and homework take up a large proportion of their day, and extracurricular activities may also require fairly large time commitments. Leisure interests outside of school, including sports, music, videogames, and television, may also be preferred ways to spend time. Finally, many students begin their first work experiences during the high school years. These daily demands and activities tend to keep students focused on the "here and now" and not on the more distant future.

Increasing independence in mobility assumes greater importance during the high school years. Many teenagers need to rely on their parents for rides. However, because of the increasing importance of peers in the lives of adolescents, reliance on this form of transportation may not be preferred. Instead, independent mobility through riding bikes or walking may be desired. Once they reach the legal age, students also begin to pursue the attainment of their driving permits and licenses to allow even greater mobility.

With their focus on these issues and concerns—peer group membership and pressure, appearance and self-esteem, mobility, and involvement in daily activities in and out of school—many young people of high school age do not actively think about the future beyond their high school years. For many, it is difficult to even conceive of or envision living a different lifestyle than the one to which they are accustomed. For them, the future may appear unclear and somewhat foreboding, and they may choose not to think about it.

Nicole is in tenth grade at her local public high school. She does not have a disability. Nicole's favorite subject in school is English, and she considers herself to be a pretty good writer. Her least favorite subjects are math and science, and she struggles to maintain a low B average in these areas. Nicole has three very good friends, also girls, whom she hangs out with at school and with whom she does things after school and sometimes on the weekend, such as going shopping or out to lunch. Nicole is on the field hockey team, and she enjoys the challenge of competition. Practice and games take a lot of her time, however, so she has to be careful to schedule homework time as well. Homework is difficult for her and takes quite a bit of time each night, particularly math. She sometimes forgets major assignments until right before they are due; she is trying to work on this because her parents have become angry about her lack of planning in the past. Nicole likes the way she looks overall, but she is sometimes shy and insecure with people that she doesn't know well. She is much more comfortable with her close friends. She has not dated and does not have a boyfriend. Nicole is looking forward to getting her license when she turns sixteen. Nicole assumes that she will go to college, because her parents have always told her that she would and have pushed her to do well in school. Other than that, she really hasn't thought much about the future.

Consider This!   We suggested in Chapter 1 that you interview two young people who are between the ages of fourteen and eighteen. What did these young people tell you? To what degree are they thinking about the future?

Now compare the responses from your interview with your own awareness at the same age. What helped you to start taking a more active role in planning for your future? When did you really start to think about your life after high school?

RESEARCH ON STUDENTS' INVOLVEMENT IN TRANSITION PLANNING

In this section, we will discuss research that has been conducted relating to the self-determination of students with disabilities and to their ability to understand and participate actively in their own transition planning process. The results of the studies that we present here provide a context for the recommendations that we offer in the remainder of this chapter for increasing student involvement in transition planning.

Several studies attempted to document the extent of student participation in transition planning and their degree of self-determination. Martin, Greene, and Borland (2004) conducted a web-based survey for school administrators regarding their perceptions of student preparation and involvement in IEP meetings. One hundred thirty-two principals, sixty-three special education directors, and twenty special education teachers who were serving as building-level administrators participated in the study. Results indicated that administrators believed that students participated to a greater degree than was actually observed in a related study. In addition, the respondents generally did not expect students to direct their own meetings, and they felt that, although students were always invited to their meetings, they only attended sometimes. The authors speculate that these findings indicate that a culture in which active student participation is expected has not been fully established. Mason, Field, and Sawilowsky (2004) also conducted a web-based survey of teachers, administrators, and related services professionals through CEC (Council for Exceptional Children) online. Although the respondents generally valued student involvement in IEP meetings, only 34 percent were satisfied with the level of student involvement in such planning and only 8 percent were satisfied with the approach taken in their district for teaching self-determination skills to students. Grigal, Neubert, Moon, and Graham (2003) conducted surveys of parents and general education and special education teachers of students with both low and high incidence disabilities about their views on student self-determination. Results of the study indicated that parents strongly supported student participation in IEP meetings and in instruction on self-determination skills. Teachers slightly agreed that they were familiar with self-determination skills and that students had the opportunity to learn and apply these skills. Both parents and teachers reported a lack of opportunities for students to learn self-determination skills. An important implication of this study is that the development of behaviors and skills associated with greater self-determination require strong parental support. Martin, Marshall, and Sale (2004) conducted a three-year study of middle, junior high, and high school IEP meetings. Perceptions of 1,638 meeting participants from 393 IEP meetings were recorded in this study. Results indicated that student participation in IEP meetings was valuable to other members of the IEP teams. Families reported that they understood better the reason for the meeting, were more comfortable saying what they thought, and understood more of what was said by others. Administrators tended to talk more about student strengths, needs, and interests, and general educators felt more comfortable saying what they thought and felt better about the meeting. Ironically, students reported the lowest scores for knowing the reasons for IEP meetings and knowing what to do during these meetings. They reported lower scores related to being comfortable and confident about speaking up, saying what they thought, and making decisions. An important implication of this study is that students need training on the IEP development process and on the content and form of IEPs. An additional implication of this study is that all members of the IEP team need to do more to learn student interests and preferences prior to IEP meetings in order to better include them in a meaningful way in the planning process. Cooney (2002) interviewed nine young adults in their final year of high school, their parents, and professionals regarding their experiences during transition and transition planning. Students who were interviewed had clear aspirations for the future but few opportunities to fulfill them. An additional finding was that professionals tended to plan for student transition by matching students to existing programmatic options, rather than planning for attainment of personal aspirations.

Several researchers have attempted to train students with disabilities to participate more fully in the IEP process and/or to increase their skills and abilities associated with greater self-determination. Wehmeyer and Lawrence (1995) conducted field testing of the self-determination curriculum material *Whose future is it anyway?* with fifty-three high school students with a range of disabilities, and found that the use of the curriculum resulted in increases in students' beliefs that they could participate in their own planning meetings and in their expectations for achieving successful adult outcomes. Whitney-Thomas, Shaw, Honey, and Butterworth (1998) conducted a qualitative study of student participation in Whole Life Planning (a form of person-centered planning; Butterworth, Hagner, Heikkinen, Faris, DeMello, & McDonough, 1993) with ten students between eighteen and twenty-one years old. The authors found that students' participation appeared to increase when their conversational styles were identified and matched to the meeting size and structure. Specifically, student involvement increased when the meeting facilitator spoke directly to or directed questions toward the focus students and when language that was used included wording that was understood by the students. These findings indicate that the behavior and skill of facilitators of person centered planning meetings are key ingredients to active student participation in such meetings. (Note: person centered planning will be discussed in greater detail later in this chapter.) Mason, McGahee-Kovac, Johnson, and Stillerman (2002) used their curriculum material (*Student-led IEP's: A Guide for Student Involvement*) to train forty-three students with higher incidence disabilities to participate in IEP meetings. Students were provided preparation on what they wanted, the law, and components of IEPs. Results showed that having students lead their own meetings helped them to develop social and self-advocacy skills, and students reported increases in self-confidence, self-advocacy, and valuing their involvement in setting their own goals. General and special education teachers also reported positive perceptions of students' knowledge of the law and of their preferences and of their abilities to participate in IEP meetings. The study also suggests that having students lead their own meetings may increase parent involvement and communication between students and parents. Allen, Smith, Test, Flowers, and Wood (2001) studied the effects of teaching a modified version of the *Self-Directed IEP* to four students with moderate levels of mental retardation. The Self-Directed IEP is one of three curriculum strands in the *Choice Maker Self-Determination Curriculum* (Martin & Marshall, 1995). Student skills (leading the meeting, reporting interests, reporting skills, and reporting options) were observed during mock and actual IEP meetings, and increases were noted in all four skill areas. Thus, a functional relationship between the training and student participation in their own IEP meetings was reported. The authors recommended that student participation in their own IEP meetings begin prior to age fourteen so that students have more experience with the process prior to the initiation of transition planning. Test, Mason, Hughes, Konrad, Neale, and Wood (2004) conducted a literature review of interventions designed to increase student involvement in IEP meetings. Sixteen studies were analyzed, and results indicated that students with widely varying disabilities can be taught to participate in IEP meetings and that both published curriculum materials and person-centered planning can be effective strategies for increasing student skills related to meeting participation. Karvonen, Test, Wood, Browder, and Algozzine (2004) conducted a qualitative study of six programs from across the United States that place strong emphasis on developing self-determination skills with students of transition age. Common promising practices included (a) using curricula to teach self-determination skills; (b) teaching and coaching students to increase their participation during meetings; (c) non-instructional practices to promote decision making (e.g., making sure students make informed choices, weigh benefits and consequences of decisions, and accept responsibility for their decisions); (d) the leadership of an "impetus person," i.e., someone with the philosophy and motivation to see self-determination practices implemented; (e) teacher roles of mentor, instructor, case manager, and counselor; and (f) parents' roles of coach, role model, and advocate. One implication that the authors drew from their work was the fact that students may initially resist learning or talking about their own disabilities, decision making, and taking responsibility. Additionally, the authors stated that the programs they studied illustrated the need for a broad commitment to training in self-determination and that there is a need to promote self-determination skills among people with more severe disabilities. In another study, Martin, Mithaug, Cox, Peterson, Van Dycke, and Cash (2003) taught eight students with severe emotional/behavioral problems to use self-determination contracts to regulate the correspondence among their plans, their work, their self-evaluations, and their academic adjustments. The use of the contracts was successful in increasing students' abilities to achieve greater correspondence among these elements. Konrad and Test (2004) studied the effect of IEP writing instruction using an IEP template on the abilities of seven middle school students with mild disabilities and reported increases in all the participants as a result of the instruction. Lehmann, Bassett, Sands, Spencer, and Gliner (1999) reported on a three-and-a-half year systems change project to increase student self-determination in three schools. The participating schools established teams to address self-determination, developed curricula and infused them into existing coursework, increased student participation in IEP meetings, formed advisory councils, and increased student involvement in service learning. A major implication of this study is that school-level systems' change to increase self-determination takes planned and concerted effort and time. Zhang (2001) investigated the impact of the use of the Next S.T.E.P. (student transition and educational planning) curriculum (Halpern, Herr, Wolf, Doren, Johnson, & Lawson, 1997) on the development of self-determination abilities of high school students with learning disabilities. The Next S.T.E.P. curriculum includes nineteen lessons on (a) self-evaluation of skills needed for transition; (b) choosing goals and activities in areas of personal life, education and training, jobs, and living on one's own; (c) taking charge of one's personal transition planning meeting; and (d) following through on choices and keeping track of progress. Using an untreated control group design, the author found that the students in the treatment group made greater gains in self-determination, as measured using the Arc's Self-Determination Scale (Wehmeyer & Kelchner, 1995).

Finally, some authors have studied the career development process and the impact of increased self-determination on attainment of successful adult outcomes for students with disabilities. Lindstrom and Benz (2002) conducted a case study of six young women with learning disabilities and found that there were three distinct phases of career development: unsettled, exploratory, and focused. The implications of this study were that (a) students need a variety of experiences to make informed choices; (b) students should have the opportunity for vocational training for skill development and advancement; (c) students need trusted adult role models; and (d) goal setting, self-advocacy, and self-determination skills contribute to career development and the attainment of positive adult outcomes. Webster (2004) conducted a qualitative study of twenty-two students with disabilities who had made a successful transition to college. Five themes emerged from the students' responses: (a) college students with disabilities are insightful and reflective regarding their own transition and postsecondary needs; (b) students with disabilities are college students first and foremost; (c) students want and need access to disability-related knowledge; (d) students want opportunities to develop skills to become self-determined adults; and (e) students need opportunities to explore boundaries of their independence. Rojewski (2002) reviewed research regarding career assessment of students with mild disabilities and concluded that assessment should begin at age fourteen and should be updated regularly and adjusted as students cycle through stages of career awareness, exploration, and establishment. Wehmeyer and Palmer (2003) studied students with mental retardation and students with learning disabilities who were one to three years out of special education services. Scores were obtained during their final year of high school using the Arc's Self-Determination Scale. Those individuals with higher self-determination scores tended to do better in several postschool outcome areas, including employment, access to health and other benefits, financial independence, and independent living. Using the database of students in the Oregon Youth Transition Project, Benz, Lindstrom, and Yovanoff (2000) found that career-related work experiences and the completion of student-identified transition goals were highly associated with improved graduation and employment outcomes in adulthood.

Together, the studies reviewed in this section suggest that, although there are many benefits to active student participation in their own transition planning, such active participation has not occurred sufficiently. This research also suggests that students benefit from specific training and information about how and why to participate in transition planning and that such training programs lead to greater self-determination.

SELF-DETERMINATION: TAKING CHARGE OF YOUR OWN LIFE

As we discussed earlier, IDEA 2004 has established that transition planning needs to be based on students' needs, strengths, preferences, and interests. However, if students are uninformed, are not comfortable participating, or have simply not thought about their futures, then it is very difficult to meet this aspect of the IDEA mandate. Therefore, we must be concerned about helping young people take as active a role in their own transition planning process as possible.

Self-determination is a term that has been used increasingly to refer to the ability to take greater control over one's own life and decision making. Field, Martin, Miller, Ward, and Wehmeyer (1998) defined self-determination as "... a combination of skills, knowledge, and beliefs that enable a person to engage in goal-directed, self-regulated, autonomous behavior ..." (p. 115). This definition highlights the fact that self-determination is a combination of *knowledge*, *skills*, and *attitudes* or *beliefs*. It is critical to the success of transition that we help students to develop their knowledge about the options and demands of adult life, to develop skills that they will need in adulthood, and to develop positive attitudes about their own potential (Wehmeyer & Palmer, 2003). Table 2.2 lists important information (knowledge), skills or abilities, and attitudes or beliefs that students need to develop during the transition planning years.

As shown in Table 2.2, students in transition need to develop skills and knowledge in several areas in order to increase their self-determination. They also need to develop confidence and a belief in themselves. Clearly, not all students will achieve these attributes to an equal degree. However, we can be sure that if we do not attempt to help students develop greater self-determination, they will be at a greater risk throughout and beyond the transition from school to adulthood.

It is also important to notice that the skills, knowledge, and attitudes associated with greater self-determination develop longitudinally and begin well before the age of sixteen, at which time transition must be addressed formally. As we discussed in Chapter 1, many foundational skills for successful transition begin during the elementary and middle school years, and this is especially true with self-determination abilities. Consider students who learn early on that they have the ability to solve problems if they try hard, or who learn what they are good at versus areas where they are not so strong. Students at the elementary and middle school years can become increasingly aware of their own interests and their knowledge related to these interests. Self-determination must therefore begin to develop prior to the time formal transition planning is initiated.

Sue Anne and Mike

Think back on the two students who were introduced in the Prologue and in Chapter 1. Sue Anne had longitudinal support in developing self-determination skills. She had a clear vision of success for herself—college and a job in early childhood education—and she followed a specific plan of action to help her achieve this desired future. She also developed the necessary academic skills to allow her entry into

TABLE 2.2 Self-determination: Important Knowledge, Skills, and Attitudes

KNOWLEDGE: STUDENTS IN TRANSITION NEED TO LEARN ABOUT ...

- Themselves: their abilities, skills, interests, and areas of need
- Future options: for college, careers, living arrangements, sources of transportation
- Skills needed: for success in career, college, and community living
- Sources of support: family, friends, agencies that assist people with disabilities
- Their rights: in education, employment, and community access

SKILLS: STUDENTS IN TRANSITION NEED TO DEVELOP SKILLS RELATED TO ...

- Self-advocacy: speaking up on their own behalf, stating their needs and preferences
- Living skills: skills needed in order to live in the adult world, in areas such as financial management, daily living skills, etc.
- Self-management: skills related to setting goals for oneself, monitoring progress toward those goals, and taking action to achieve the goals
- Academic and other skills: skills directly related to their desired postschool outcomes in employment, postsecondary education, and community living
- Problem-solving and decision-making skills: determining reasonable courses of action when presented with challenges

ATTITUDES OR BELIEFS: STUDENTS IN TRANSITION NEED TO DEVELOP ATTITUDES THAT REFLECT ...

- Confidence: a belief in one's own abilities, determination to make things happen for one-self
- Self-efficacy: a belief that one's actions will have an impact and will positively affect one's own future
- Internal locus of control: a belief that the power to effect change comes from within oneself

college. She learned relevant information (for example, about colleges and the services that they provide) from family and professionals, such as her teachers and guidance counselor. Finally, she developed the confidence and determination to make her dream a reality, and these helped her handle challenges and setbacks during her high school years.

Mike, on the other hand, is struggling somewhat. He lacks information about working due to his lack of experience in actual community jobs. This makes it difficult for him and his support network to determine what he might like or what he does well. His family envisions Mike having a job and living in his own apartment some day, but they lack information about how to achieve these goals. Mike is learning some skills that he will need in order to have greater control over his life, such as shopping and accessing community environments. He is also fortunate to have a strong network of immediate and extended family members and community members who are available to help him during the transition process.

A comparison of Sue Anne and Mike in relation to self-determination may suggest that Mike's difficulties are a function of the severity of his disability and that people with more severe disabilities cannot develop the knowledge, skills, and attitudes related to strong self-determination. This is not the case. Although communication and learning difficulties certainly pose challenges, there is much that we can do to help students with severe disabilities develop self-determination to a greater degree. For example, we can:

- expose these students to more experiences to give them a base of information from which to make decisions;
- enhance and expand their communication abilities;
- afford them more experiences in making choices and decisions;
- acknowledge their choices and decisions so that they can increase their belief in their own ability;
- help develop comprehensive profiles of students so that their strengths, abilities, gifts, and capacities are clarified (Note: the development of comprehensive profiles through person-centered planning will be discussed later in this chapter.);
- communicate high expectations to them to enhance their determination in pursuing future goals

The development of the knowledge, skills, and attitudes associated with greater self-determination is clearly a central issue in helping students with disabilities take charge of their lives. Sidebars 2.1, 2.2, and 2.3 provide Spotlights on History related to the development of our knowledge of self-determination. The Spotlight on History in Sidebar 2.1 describes the work of Michael Wehmeyer, who has provided essential leadership in helping young people with disabilities develop greater

---

SIDEBAR 2.1

SPOTLIGHT ON HISTORY: MICHAEL WEHMEYER

Michael Weymeyer is Associate Director of the Beach Center on Disabilities and Associate Professor at the University of Kansas. Dr. Wehmeyer is an internationally recognized expert on self-determination for students with disabilities. Prior to joining the staff at the Beach Center, Dr. Wehmeyer worked at the ARC-US, where he pioneered the development of materials for teaching self-determination skills to individuals with mental retardation. His interests also include increasing the access to the general education curriculum for students with severe developmental disabilities, and technology use. He is the author of over 150 journal articles and book chapters, and he is the editor or co-author of 15 books on self-determination and access to the general education curriculum.

(*Source*: www.beachcenter.org.)

██ ██ ██ ██ ██ ▬▬▬▬▬▬▬▬▬▬▬▬▬▬▬▬▬▬▬▬

SIDEBAR 2.2

SPOTLIGHT ON HISTORY: ROLAND JOHNSON

Today we're gonna talk about: how to be in control; who's in control. I want to know—raising hands—who are in control.

Are you in control?

Are staff in control?

Well, I understand that you need to be in control, and some of them are not in control because staff tells you what to do; advisors tell you what to do and staff tells you what to do. I don't believe that you are in control over your life . . .

Control means being in self-control . . . who's in charge over you.

Are you in charge?

Is staff in charge?

But who's in charge?

Well. Some people tell me that sometimes staff is in control, that you don't be in control over your life. And doing things in your workshops or day programs and in where you live—staff in control.

I want to know who is telling you what to do. If you're telling yourself what to do or are you letting staff tell you what to do.

I can't hear you!

You're supposed to be in charge, right?

I can't hear you!

From Roland Johnson's presentation at the Third International People First Conference, Toronto, June 1993 (Johnson & Williams, 1994, p. 98).

Roland Johnson (1945–1994) was an influential self-advocate who served as President of the Board of Directors for Speaking for Ourselves, a self-advocacy group in Pennsylvania, from 1986 to 1990. Like many people with mental retardation of his era, Johnson was institutionalized at an early age. He was placed at Pennhurst State School, outside of Philadelphia, from 1958 to 1971. While at Pennhurst, he was sexually assaulted repeatedly and, like other residents of the institution, he was made to perform numerous work tasks for no compensation. For thirteen years, he lived a life of dependency, little control, and fear.

Despite this experience, Johnson emerged as a leader within the self-advocacy movement in Pennsylvania and, more broadly, in the United States. In addition to his leadership role with Speaking for Ourselves, Johnson went on to give numerous presentations at self-advocacy conferences across the United States and Canada. He was a keynote presenter at the 1991 President's Committee on Mental Retardation 25th anniversary in Washington, DC, and he presented an award to President George H. W. Bush in connection with the Americans with Disabilities Act in 1993, an event that was also broadcast on "Nightline."

During his lifetime, Roland Johnson overcame his nightmarish experiences of institutionalization and emerged as a powerful self-advocate who taught countless others about the basic ingredients of self-determination.

(*Source:* Johnson & Williams, 1994.)

■ ■ ■ ■ ■ ▬▬▬▬▬▬▬▬▬▬▬▬▬▬▬▬▬▬▬▬▬▬▬▬▬▬▬▬▬▬▬▬▬▬▬▬▬▬

SIDEBAR 2.3
SPOTLIGHT ON HISTORY: BERNARD CARABELLO

Bernard Carabello is another national leader in the development of self-determination. He has been quoted as saying "Self-advocacy should not even exist. But, society makes it exist." Once institutionalized, Carabello emerged as a true leader and fighter for the rights of all people who have been disenfranchised by society.

Mr. Carabello was born with cerebral palsy. He was misdiagnosed with mental retardation and committed to Willowbrook State School on Staten Island. He remained there for eighteen years. In 1972, he acted as inside informant for Geraldo Rivera's exposé on the abuse at the state facility. This led to his freedom and ultimately to the closing of the facility. Mr. Carabello was a featured speaker along with Governor Mario Cuomo at the official closing of Willowbrook.

Mr. Carabello focuses on the need to educate the public and has appeared on various television programs. He has had speaking engagements all across the United States. He was the 1991 New York Recipient of the Victory Award, Washington, DC. Mr. Carabello is the Founder and Director of The Self-Advocacy Association of New York State and the Founder of Bernard J. Carabello & Company. He has served as Director of Self-Advocacy of the ARC-US and also Director of Self-Advocacy Protection and Advocacy System for New York City. Mr. Carabello has served on the board of directors for the One to One Foundation, been a member of Consumer Advisory Board for the Staten Island Developmental Center, and served as a public educator for the One to One Foundation.

self-determination. Sidebars 2.2 and 2.3 describe Roland Johnson and Bernard Carabello, whose achievements exemplified the ingredients of self-determination.

INVOLVING STUDENTS IN TRANSITION PLANNING

Thus far, we have discussed the importance of student involvement in planning their own transition to adulthood. We have also discussed the skills, knowledge, and attitudes or beliefs that young people need to develop to have greater control over the course of the planning process and their adult lifestyle that emerges from it. In this section, we will discuss important and creative strategies for increasing and enhancing the involvement of students in the transition planning process. Later in this book, Chapter 4 will describe the transition planning process as it takes place through the development of an IEP and its relevant sections that specifically address transition to adult life. Although the transition planning process will be described in more detail at that time, this chapter focuses on the student's role in transition.

Before describing ways to involve students in their own transition planning, it is important to understand that IDEA 2004 is clear that students must be invited to their IEP meetings for transition planning. In addition, the school must document its attempts to invite the student to participate. Therefore, student participation should not be construed as a possible occurrence but as a necessity. The law is clear in its expectation: students should be involved. Also, as described in greater detail in Chapter 4, students are recipients of certain rights and responsibilities as they approach exiting from school. IDEA 2004 now requires that students who are no longer entitled to special education services due to graduation or exceeding age requirements shall be provided with (a) a summary of academic achievement and functional performance and (b) recommendations to assist them in meeting postsecondary goals (Johnson, 2005). This requirement will help students who are participating in their final transition IEP meetings. Also, the law states that students and their families must be informed of the rights that will transfer to the student upon reaching the age of majority. Together, these various requirements provide a mandate and structure for student involvement in the transition planning process.

As a framework for our discussion of student involvement in the transition planning process, we will describe strategies for better involving the student (a) before an actual planning (IEP) meeting; (b) during the planning meeting; and (c) following the planning meeting.

Before the Planning Meeting

There are a number of steps that educators and families should take before an IEP meeting takes place that can increase and enhance the involvement of the young person in the planning process.

An important first step is for teachers, guidance counselors, or family members to interview students about their current lives and their future aspirations. There are numerous formats for accomplishing this task. A simple face-to-face interview can be conducted, or this could be formatted as a writing assignment or oral presentation assignment for students. Creative teachers can format written materials to match the age and abilities of individual learners. Regardless of the format, the information that is gathered should not simply be filed, rather it should become a basis for discussion with students and their families. Such interviews should include questions about students' current interests and daily activities, followed by questions about their plans or interests for the future. Sample interview questions are shown in Table 2.3, and a sample section of a written format for gathering this information is shown in Figure 2.1.

A second step to be taken prior to an IEP meeting is to have the student gather information to help in the planning process. For example, students could investigate potential careers in which they might have an interest. This could be accomplished by using databases on career information, such as the Occupational Outlook Handbook or the ONet. These databases provide professionals, families, and students with a wealth of information about the job market, types of occupations, training requirements, and general salary ranges for virtually all possible occupations in the United States. They have been widely used by job development professionals and rehabilitation counselors, but they are also available for students and their families to use. Students could also investigate potential careers through visits to the One Stop Center nearest to them. (Note: One Stop Centers, developed under the Workforce Investment Act of 1998, are community resource centers where job seekers can obtain in-

TABLE 2.3   Sample Interview Questions

PROFILE AND FAMILY LIFE

- Tell me about yourself (age, where you live, etc.).
- Tell me about your family.
- Do your parents work?
- What kind of work does your father/mother do?
- Do you have brothers or sisters who work?
- What kind of work do they do?
- Have you always lived here, or did you move here?
- Tell me about the neighborhood that you live in.

INTERESTS AND HOBBIES

- What do you like to do in your free time?
- What are your hobbies and interests?
- What do you like to do on weekends?
- Tell me about some enjoyable vacations that you have had.

SCHOOL

- What are your favorite subjects in school?
- What are your least favorite subjects?
- Who are your friends in school?
- What do you like best about school? What do you like least?
- Are you involved in any extracurricular activities?

FINANCES

- Do you have a bank account?
- Do you earn an allowance?
- Do you know how to write a check?
- Do you know how to use a credit card/debit card?
- Do you know about costs such as electric service, phone service, and gas?

MOBILITY

- How do you get around your community?
- Where do you like to go?
- Do you have a driver's license or are you planning on getting one?

EMPLOYMENT

- Have you ever had a job?
- If you were going to get a summer job, what kind of job would you look for?
- What skills do you feel that you could build a career on?
- What are your interests in terms of employment?

(continued)

TABLE 2.3   Continued

POSTSECONDARY EDUCATION

- Are you planning on going to college?
- If so, have you considered a major?
- Did anyone else in your family go to college?
- Have you ever visited a college campus?

COMMUNITY LIVING

- Do you know how to cook?
- Do you do any chores at home? If so, what chores?
- Do you know how much it costs to rent an apartment?
- Do you like living with others?
- Do you like privacy?
- Do you know what to do if there is an emergency in your home?

FUTURE ASPIRATIONS

- What do you see yourself doing in five years?
- What careers do you plan on exploring, and why?
- What steps do you feel you need to take now to help prepare you for your future career?
- Who could help you take the steps you described in the previous question, and how might they help you?

formation about employment options.) Professionals at One Stop Centers can guide students through the aforementioned career databases or other resources related to employment. Students who intend to pursue postsecondary education can gather information about two- and four-year colleges or universities, the majors that they offer, and services to support students with and without disabilities. Much of this information may be gathered via the Internet.

A particularly valuable step is to have students visit employment sites or postsecondary institutions in order to learn firsthand about life in these environments. Students can shadow currently employed workers in a particular profession and record their questions and reactions to what they have observed. They can visit and interview at local colleges or community colleges. These activities are most valuable when they are conducted in a structured and cumulative manner, with followup from family members, teachers, or guidance counselors who discuss with young people what they have seen and what reactions they have to these observations.

An additional strategy is to have the student interview others about the demands of adult life. For example, the student could interview family members or friends who are employed about what they like, find challenging, or find rewarding about their employment. The same strategy can be used to help students find out information about other aspects of adult living, such as financial responsibility, living on one's own, or using community resources. This type of interview can be conducted in person or can be completed in writing. For example, one educator assisted a student with phys-

FIGURE 2.1 Sample Section of a Survey for Obtaining Information from Students

GETTING TO KNOW YOURSELF

Name: _____

Grade: _____

Year: _____

Directions: Listed below are a number of questions to help you get to know yourself better and to get you to think about your future goals. Although you may not have an answer to every question, try your best to give an answer.

1. What do you like to do in your free time?

2. What do you think you are good at outside of school?

3. What are your favorite subjects in school, and why?

4. What are your least favorite subjects, and why?

5. What do your friends like best about you?

6. How do you contribute to helping your family at home?

7. Have you ever worked?

8. If you were to get a job this summer, what would you like to do?

9. Have you considered going to college?

10. If so, what majors have you considered? Why?

11. Where do you want to live when you get older?

12. What type of work can you see yourself doing?

13. How much money do you think you will need to live comfortably?

14. What are you looking forward to in your future?

15. What are you nervous about or concerned about in your future?

ical disabilities in designing and distributing a questionnaire to the student's extended family and friends. In filling out the questionnaire, recipients answered questions about their perceptions of the student's strengths, abilities, and potential. The resulting completed surveys were summarized on a large chart that the student was able to present at his IEP meeting. This helped prepare the student for his IEP meeting and gave him an active role in the planning process. It also started the meeting off by focusing on his strengths and positive attributes, and not on his disabilities and deficits.

Finally, it may be very helpful for students to role-play in advance what they will say during the upcoming IEP meeting. As suggested in the research described earlier in this chapter, providing such practice will help students decrease their uncertainty and anxiety about the upcoming meeting.

During the Planning Meeting

IEP meetings can be intimidating events for young people to participate in. We may start with an assumption that most students from fourteen to twenty-one years of age would probably wish to avoid a planning meeting that focuses on their future and in which their teachers and parents participate. Yet, the intent of IDEA is clear: the assumption is that students are active participants in designing their own plan for their transition to adult living. The challenge, therefore, is how to make it more conducive for student involvement in the planning process.

One important step to take is to give the student an active role in the planning process (Mason et al., 2002). Students can invite people, prepare name tags or refreshments, or help write agendas for their meetings (Field et al., 1998). Students can also have a role in leading an IEP meeting, by making introductions or stating what will be discussed (Field et al., 1998). Clearly, this will vary according to the needs and abilities of individual students. The key issue is that students have a clear way of participating in the meeting. As one typical sixteen-year-old stated, "You would need to let them have voice, or a say in their own meeting." This includes having other participants address comments *to* the student, not *about* the student.

A major factor in helping students have an active role in their planning meetings is for them to know what to expect and how such meetings will progress. Having a clear agenda can help with this. This can be presented to the student ahead of time in either a written or picture format. Also, the student should know who each participant is, why he or she is at the meeting, and the contributions that each participant can make to the student's successful transition to adult life.

Finally, it is helpful for an action plan to be developed to clarify steps to be taken following the planning meeting. This should include a list of what steps should be taken, who will assume responsibility for completion of each step, and timelines. A sample action planning form and a sample completed section are shown in Figures 2.2 and 2.3.

After the Planning Meeting

It is essential that follow-up communication take place after an IEP meeting during which the transition to adult life is discussed. This follow-up communication should be tied to the action planning steps described above. Whenever possible, the student should have a central role in such communication. For example, the student can report back on steps that have been taken to help clarify desired future outcomes. Of course, students may require support in reporting on progress toward completion of action steps, but they should participate to the fullest extent possible. A sample format

FIGURE 2.2   **Sample Action Planning Form**

ACTION PLANNING FORM

Student Name: _____

Date of Meeting: _____

The following steps need to be taken to help _____ decide what to do in the future. These steps will help this student figure out what to do for work, where to live, and whether or not to go on for further training or education.

Focus Area (employment, postsecondary education, residential, recreation/leisure, community participation): _____

Steps To Be Taken	**Responsible Person**	**Timelines**

Focus Area (employment, postsecondary education, residential, recreation/leisure, community participation): _____

Steps To Be Taken	**Responsible Person**	**Timelines**

---

for reporting progress on action steps that have been taken is shown in Figure 2.4. A completed example is shown in Figure 2.5.

Consider This!   Each of the steps described above help make students aware of the need to start thinking about their futures. We should start with the assumption that students have not thought much about their future lives or choose not to. It is not reasonable to ask students who have not thought about the future to participate meaningfully in the planning process. Instead, we must provide them with multiple opportunities to begin to consider their future lives. This is a longitudinal, gradual process. As we stated in Chapter 1, this is one important reason why the foundations of effective transition begin prior to age fourteen. It is never too early to start the conversation!

FIGURE 2.3   Sample Section of an Action Planning Form for a Student with Learning Disabilities

---

ACTION PLANNING FORM

Student Name: *Lianne Neilson*

Age/Grade: *15 years old, 9th grade*

Date of Meeting: *September 16, 2005*

The following steps need to be taken to help *Lianne* decide what to do in the future. These steps will help this student figure out what to do for work, where to live, and whether or not to go on for further training or education.

Focus Area (employment, postsecondary education, residential, recreation/leisure, community participation): *Postsecondary Education*

Steps To Be Taken	Responsible Person	Timelines
■ *Gather information about community colleges within the local area, including entrance requirements, application processes, and major areas of study*	*Lianne, her parents and school guidance counselor*	*by 12/1/05*

Focus Area (employment, postsecondary education, residential, recreation/leisure, community participation): *Employment and residential*

Steps To Be Taken	Responsible Person	Timelines
■ *Lianne needs to start completing chores at home on a daily basis*	*Lianne, her parents*	*by 9/15/05*

CREATIVE APPROACHES TO INVOLVING STUDENTS AND THEIR FAMILIES

In this section, we describe approaches that have been developed to better involve students and their families in transition planning. First we describe curriculum materials and programs that have been developed to increase students' self-determination and enhance their participation in educational planning. We then describe person-centered planning strategies that make people with disabilities the center of their life planning process.

FIGURE 2.4   Sample Reporting Format

ACTION PLAN PROGRESS REPORT

Student: _____

Date of Report: _____

Action Steps Taken:

■

■

■

■

Next Steps Needed:

■

■

■

■

Curriculum Materials and Programs for Enhancing Student Involvement

A number of innovative curriculum materials and programs have emerged over the past decade or more that focus on teaching self-determination skills and skills for student involvement in transition planning (Baer, 2005; Sale & Martin, 2004). Several of these curriculum materials focus on the broader process of career awareness and development, while others focus on the development of increased self-determination. These materials are described briefly below. Readers are urged to review each of these products or materials for more information and to determine which best meet the needs of specific students in transition.

Several curriculum materials have been developed to involve students in the career exploration process; a selected range of these are described here. Brolin's

FIGURE 2.5 Sample Reporting Format for a Student with Learning Disabilities

---

ACTION PLAN PROGRESS REPORT

Student: *Lianne Neilson*

Date of Report: *12/15/05*

Report completed by Lianne, with assistance from her parents

Action Steps Taken:

- *I sent for catalogs and brochures from the county community college.*
- *With the help of my guidance counselor, I have reviewed the catalogs and have identified some courses of study that I might want to pursue. These are: elementary education, environmental studies, journalism.*
- *I have started doing chores at home every day. I set the table and alternate with my sister in doing the dishes. I am paid an allowance, half of which has to be deposited into my bank account.*

Next Steps That Need To Be Taken:

- *I need to find out more specific information about each of these majors in which I might have an interest. I need to look up information about them on the community college website.*
- *My guidance counselor says that I should also investigate four year colleges within the area. My parents say that is a good idea also, even if I start at community college and then transfer. With my parents' and guidance counselor's help, I will contact the University to obtain a course catalog.*

Life-Centered Career Education (LCCE) model (Brolin, 1997) describes twenty-two major competencies for the development of life skills in the domain areas of daily living skills, personal–social skills, and occupational guidance and preparation. Competencies are further broken down into subcompetencies, which progress from less or more advanced skills. *What Color Is My Parachute?* (Bolles, 1995) provides an overview of the career development process and guides the reader through activities to clarify their interests and steps to pursue those interests. *The Self-Directed Search* (Holland, 1995), based on Holland's theory of career decision making according to personality types, provides an assessment of students' personality types and then directs them to potential career options that best match their identified personality types.

Self-determination curricula include *ChoiceMaker* (Martin, Marshall, Maxson, & Jerman, 1996), *Whose future is it anyway?* (Wehmeyer & Kelchner, 1995), *Next S.T.E.P.* (Halpern, Herr, Wolf, Doren, Johnson, & Lawson, 1997), *Become Your Own Expert!* (Carpenter, 1995), and *Steps to Self-determination* (Field & Hoffman, 1995). These materials, which are particularly useful for students with milder disabilities, focus on developing students' abilities to self-advocate, make decisions, develop goals, demonstrate leadership, and participate actively in their own transition IEP meetings (Baer, 2005). Readers should refer to Baer (2005) and Sale and Martin (2004) for more complete descriptions of these different curriculum materials.

Sue Anne's Participation in Transition Planning

As described in the Prologue, Sue Anne had been actively involved in planning, with the support from her family, since her last year of middle school. From that time on, the planning team worked with Sue Anne and her family to plan out a course of study throughout high school that would lead to college entrance. The high school guidance counselor, Mrs. Reid-Meyer, emphasized the need for Sue Anne to develop self-determination skills, not only for success in high school but for her college career. During Sue Anne's freshman year, Mrs. Reid-Meyer recommended that Sue Anne learn more about how to become more actively involved in the planning process. In order to do so, she introduced Sue Anne to the *ChoiceMaker Self-Determination Transition Curriculum* (Martin & Marshall, 1996). She explained to Sue Anne how this curriculum package teaches students about seven aspects of self-determination: self-awareness, self-advocacy, self-efficacy, decision making, independent performance, self-evaluation, and adjustment through leadership and management of the IEP process. In particular, Mrs. Reid-Meyer introduced Sue Anne to the Self-Directed IEP, a component of the curriculum package that teaches students the skills that they need to clarify and discuss their own interests and to then take an active leadership role during IEP meetings. Although Sue Anne felt that she had good support from her school and her family, she did admit to Mrs. Reid-Meyer that the actual IEP meetings could be somewhat confusing and intimidating, so she agreed to work on this part of the ChoiceMaker curriculum.

First, Sue Anne watched a brief introductory video called the *Self-Directed IEP in Action* to become acquainted with the focus of the process. Next, Mrs. Reid-Meyer taught Sue Anne about the eleven steps of the Self-Directed IEP process (Martin, Huber, Marshall, Maxson, & Jerman, 1996):

1. Begin the meeting by stating the purpose.
2. Introduce everyone.
3. Review past goals and performance.
4. Ask for others' feedback.
5. State your school and transition goals.
6. Ask questions if you do not understand.
7. Deal with differences in opinion.
8. State what support you will need.
9. Summarize your goals.
10. Close the meeting by thanking everyone.
11. Work on IEP goals all year.

Sue Anne watched a longer video that showed these eleven steps in action, and then Mrs. Reid-Meyer gave have her a workbook that Sue Anne would use to plan how to implement each of the eleven steps with her own IEP meeting. Mrs. Reid-Meyer suggested that Sue Anne take the video and workbook home to show her parents.

Over the next several weeks leading up to her next IEP meeting at the end of her freshman year, Sue Anne worked her way through the workbook and discussed how she would follow the eleven steps at the upcoming meeting. Both her parents and Mrs. Reid-Meyer provided her with encouragement and support as she planned and practiced. When the day for the IEP meeting came, Sue Anne was nervous but excited about taking an active role in the planning meeting. When people were coming into the conference room for the IEP meeting, Sue Anne followed Mrs. Reid-Meyer's suggestion that she sit at the head of the table. As she had practiced so many times, she started off by saying "Welcome to my IEP meeting, and thank you all for coming to help me plan for my future." After that, she was far less nervous as the meeting progressed. She led the group in making introductions, which helped her because she now had a much better idea of who each person was and why they were there. After the team discussed Sue Anne's progress over the past year, the discussion turned to her long-range aspirations after high school. Again, as she had rehearsed, Sue Anne described how she wanted to go to college and wanted to study elementary education so that she could become a teacher. No one told her that her aspiration was unrealistic; instead, the team members were all supportive. The remainder of the meeting was devoted to discussing the courses that Sue Anne would need to take next year and the skills that she would need to continue to work on. At the end of the meeting, Sue Anne could not help but smile broadly as she thanked everyone for their help and support. She knew that from now on she would be an equal and active team member of the IEP team and that, ultimately, this was her plan.

Person Centered Planning

In the 1980s, alternative planning approaches emerged to make it easier for people with disabilities and their families to take a more active role in service planning. These strategies were developed because of shortcomings in typical service planning meetings, particularly for students with severe disabilities. Specifically, service planning meetings were often perceived by people with disabilities and their families as confusing, intimidating, and not conducive to active participation. Also, the perception was often that deficits and disabilities were overemphasized while strengths and abilities were overlooked. The alternative planning processes that have been developed are collectively referred to as *person centered planning*. This term is used to emphasize the individual's central role in the planning process; thus, planning occurs *with* the individual, not *about* the individual (Butterworth, Steere, & Whitney-Thomas, 1997; Steere, Gregory, Heiny, & Butterworth, 1995).

Table 2.4 describes several specific planning approaches that are considered to be forms of person centered planning. Although each of these planning approaches involves a somewhat different series of steps or elements, they share several common features:

- A support team or circle of support that consists of family, friends, and concerned community members is formed to support the individual with a disabil-

TABLE 2.4 **Forms of Person Centered Planning**

NAME OF PROCESS	DEVELOPERS	USES
Personal Futures Planning	Mount & Zwernik, 1988	Planning transitions from state institutions to community life; planning improved lifestyles in community life
Lifestyle Planning	O'Brien, 1987	Planning transitions from state institutions to community life; planning improved lifestyles in community life
Essential Lifestyles Planning	Smull & Harrison, 1992	Planning services for individuals with challenging behaviors in community environments
MAPS	Forest & Pearpoint, 1992	Planning inclusive educational services for students with disabilities
Career Planning	Powell et al., 1991	Planning career development and job development within supported employment programs
Outcomes-Based Planning	Steere et al., 1990	Planning transitions from school to adulthood for students with disabilities
Whole Life Planning	Butterworth et al., 1993	Planning services for individuals with disabilities in inclusive community environments; planning transition from school to adulthood

ity in the planning process. This support team is a "personal cabinet" that helps the individual make decisions about day-to-day life and about the future. It is essential that the circle of support consist of people that the individual chooses and trusts.

- The support team contributes to the development of a comprehensive personal profile of the focus person (the individual with a disability). This profile emphasizes strengths, abilities, capacities, and gifts that the individual possesses. In addition, choices and wishes that the individual makes are clarified. It is essential that this profile be comprehensive and exhaustive. In fact, the development of the profile typically requires at least two hours or more.
- Graphics are used extensively to record comments and ideas from participants in the meeting. These are recorded on large pieces of chart paper for all to see.

The use of graphics and colors helps to encourage participation by individuals with disabilities who may have limited reading abilities. They also encourage participation by other support team members who see that their comments are valued and recorded.

- The individual with a disability is a central member of the planning process. The individual participates in each planning meeting to the best of his or her ability. Comments are addressed to the individual. Efforts are made to ensure that the individual is an active participant.

- Planning typically takes place in a comfortable and familiar environment for the focus person. For example, meetings may take place within the focus person's home, or within a community location such as a meeting room in a library.

- A facilitator typically runs each person centered planning meeting. This individual should be someone who is trusted by the members of the circle of support (planning team) and who can help to create a relaxed and productive planning atmosphere. The facilitator is akin to a "master of ceremonies" and makes sure that all members of the group participate. The facilitator typically records comments that are made, as described above.

- Once a profile is developed, the support team turns its attention to envisioning a positive or desired future for the focus individual. At this time, participants are encouraged to state what they feel the individual might want for the future. This discussion must take place without negative comments about what appears to be unfeasible. Instead, the support team is encouraged to think out loud about what would be a positive vision of the individual's future life.

- With the profile of the individual and the vision of success in mind, the team lists challenges and barriers that currently exist to help the individual achieve the desired future. Action steps to help the individual overcome these challenges are then prioritized, and individual members take responsibility for implementing specific action steps.

- The support team reconvenes as often as necessary to update progress in implementing the action steps clarified above. Action steps are revised as progress is made. Planning becomes an ongoing, recurrent process.

Person centered planning has been used to address a number of specific issues in providing services to people with disabilities. Specifically, person centered planning has been used to assist people in moving from state institutions to community life (Mount & Zwernik, 1988), to facilitate inclusion of children with disabilities in typical classrooms (Forest & Pearpoint, 1992), in planning positive behavioral support for people with challenging behavior (Lucyshyn, Olson, & Horner, 1995; Smull & Harrison, 1992), in planning appropriate housing supports (Racino, Walker, O'Connor, & Taylor, 1992), and in planning for job development in supported employment (Powell, Pancsofar, Steere, Butterworth, Itzkowitz, & Rainforth, 1991). For each of these specific challenges, person centered planning was chosen to help the individual and his or her family have a more central, productive, and meaningful role in the planning process.

Person centered planning has also been used to support transition planning from school to adult life for students with disabilities (Hagner, Helm, & Butterworth,

TABLE 2.5 Ways in Which Person Centered Planning Addresses Challenges to Student and Family Involvement in Transition Planning

CHALLENGES TO STUDENTS AND FAMILIES	RELEVANT FEATURES OF PERSON CENTERED PLANNING
▪ Student lacks comfort in participating	▪ Planning occurs in a familiar and comfortable environment ▪ Planning involves familiar and trusted people
▪ Student lacks knowledge of options	▪ Support team is a source of ideas and resources about potential options ▪ Ongoing action planning allows for active investigation and discussion of options
▪ General lack of clarity in desired future outcomes	▪ Planning is designed to clarify and describe desired future lifestyle
▪ Student lacks self-awareness of strengths, abilities, and limitations	▪ Comprehensive, positive profile is developed as a basis for future action planning
▪ General lack of knowledge to take steps toward clarifying and attaining desired future outcomes	▪ Ongoing action planning by all team members takes place on an ongoing, regular basis ▪ Action planning is designed to identify and then take steps to overcome specific challenges

1996; Everson, 1995; Miner & Bates, 1997; Steere, Wood, Pancsofar, & Butterworth, 1990; Wehman, 2001). The utility of person centered planning in helping to plan the transition of a young person from school to adult life is clear when the attributes of person centered planning are considered. Table 2.5 lists challenges in involving students in transition planning and the associated features of person centered planning that help address these challenges.

Mike's Person Centered Plan

Mike, introduced in the Prologue, is unclear about his future. Concerned about this, Mike's parents decided to form a circle of support to assist Mike with decision making. They learned about this strategy while attending a session at a state-wide conference on transition planning, and they have since read more material about person centered planning. In addition to Mike and his parents, the people invited to participate in Mike's circle were:

▪ his sister
▪ his aunts, uncles, and cousins
▪ his minister from church

- his teacher from school
- his therapeutic horseback riding instructor

Each of these individuals is pleased to be invited to be part of this special group.

The first meeting takes place in Mike's home, in the living room, after school. Mike's parents help him to prepare simple snacks to have during the meeting. His aunt, Sharon, who was designated as guardian in case of emergency has agreed to try to facilitate the first meeting. She has an outgoing personality and is not nervous about getting up in front of the group. She is also very close to Mike and is willing to do whatever it takes to help him have a successful adult life.

On the day of the first meeting when people are arriving, Mike does not understand what is happening, but he is excited about these people coming to his home. Each person agrees to wear a nametag with their first name written on it. People gather informally in the living room, eating snacks and having coffee and other drinks. Blank chart paper is ready on a standing easel, and markers and tape are ready. After about fifteen minutes of informal socializing, Sharon calls everyone together to begin the meeting. She describes the purpose of the meeting: to help Mike plan his future beyond high school. Mike smiles and rocks: he does not understand everything that is being said, but he knows that it is about him, and he likes the attention. Sharon begins with a series of questions to build a positive profile, and people contribute their responses:

- What does Mike like?
- What does he not like?
- What is he good at?
- What support or help does he typically need?
- What choices does he typically make?
- What are his special gifts, capacities, and contributions?
- How does Mike learn best?
- What are some of the important events, both positive and negative, that have occurred in Mike's past?
- Who is Mike? (Team members offer descriptors of Mike.)

As more information is recorded on the chart paper, each completed piece is hung on the wall. Mike helps with this process. As the profile discussion progresses, the number of chart papers increases until the living room walls are covered with descriptions of Mike.

The group takes a brief break, and then returns for the second part of the meeting. Although this is a lot to accomplish in one afternoon, Mike's parents feel it is best to keep the momentum going. The next part of the meeting is devoted to brainstorming and envisioning a positive future for Mike. This is not an easy process, and no one is really certain what to say. Mike's father says that he wants to see his son have the opportunity to work in the community for pay, on at least a part time basis, but he is not sure in what type of work. As the discussion proceeds, it becomes evident that people do have ideas about Mike's future. They envision him . . .

- working in a part time job, possibly in an environment like the horse riding stable;
- volunteering for the other parts of his day so that he has a full daily schedule;
- living in an apartment or small group home, but with people whom he likes and gets along with;
- having time to come home and visit his parents for some weekends and holidays;
- having some friends who like to be with him and are not paid to do so;
- overall, to just be happy and safe.

Next, barriers are identified. It becomes clear that the major problem at this point is the lack of information about options. Specifically, they list these challenges:

- we don't know what kind of jobs Mike might be suited to, or like;
- we don't know if there are agencies to assist Mike with finding and keeping a job;
- we don't know the options for group homes or supported apartments;
- Mike does not have an active group of friends to do things with.

Finally, some initial action steps are identified, and people agree to take responsibility for completing them.

- Mike's teacher agrees to research and contact adult vocational agencies in the area that might be able to provide job training or support. She already is aware of a few, including the Vocational Rehabilitation office, but she agrees to contact them for more information and then bring the information back to the next meeting.
- Mike's minister agrees to try to involve Mike in some additional recreation activities through the church in the hopes that these could lead to potential friendships.
- Mike's parents agree to start teaching Mike some more skills that he will need if he is to move into a group home or apartment. Specifically, they will focus on teaching simple cooking and cleaning skills within their home. They will start Mike on an allowance system, whereby he will earn money for completing chores at home.
- Mike's relatives who are in attendance agree to brainstorm possible job opportunities of which they may be aware. They agree to think about who they know who might help, particularly in finding part time work experience.
- Mike's teacher and parents agree to reconvene the IEP meeting as soon as possible to add specific goals and objectives related to increasing Mike's work experiences in the community. This is not specifically listed on his IEP, and it is now clear that it should be.

The group agrees to reconvene within one month to discuss what has happened during the intervening time. They also agree to contact an adult service agency that employs job placement specialists and job coaches. These professionals will be integral to Mike's future success in employment.

As Mike's teacher is leaving the meeting, she is thinking about how unusual the meeting was. She was nervous at the outset, but now she realizes that this informal group will be an enormous asset to Mike. It is also helping her clarify how to best help him in her role as his teacher.

CHAPTER SUMMARY

This chapter has focused on the central role of students with disabilities in their own transition planning processes. IDEA 2004 is clear in its mandate that planning be based on students' needs, preferences, and interests, and it is clear that students should be active participants in the planning process. This has been difficult for a variety of reasons, including lack of information or awareness of options, discomfort in participating in an adult-oriented meeting, and a lack of a meaningful role in the process. We need to be aware that an underlying need of all students in transition is the need to develop greater self-determination, that is, the knowledge, skills, and attitudes that are necessary to take greater control over their lives. There are numerous activities that creative and committed educators and others can do to increase and enhance student participation prior to, during, and following transition IEP meetings. In addition, for some students, person centered planning strategies are extremely helpful in providing a clearer direction for planning and helping them to take the necessary action steps toward a clear vision of success.

APPLICATION ACTIVITIES

The application activities listed below are essential for your continued learning and skill development in transition planning. Each of the activities will require your time and energy, but will help you develop your professional skills in this area.

For Practice and Enhanced Understanding:

Develop a simple survey that focuses on student abilities, interests, and needs. This can take many forms and you should adapt it to the characteristics of students of different ages and abilities. For students with more severe disabilities, consider the use of drawings and other visuals.

Select and read an article or booklet or view a video that describes person centered planning. If possible, attend a person centered planning meeting. What aspects of person centered planning could you incorporate into your work with students with disabilities? For example, could you work with students' families to develop more comprehensive positive profiles?

Describe each of your students in terms of their degree of self-determination. For each student, ask yourself:

- What skills, knowledge, and attitudes does the student now have that can contribute toward taking greater control over his or her life?

- What skills, knowledge, and attitudes does the student need to develop more fully?

For Your Portfolio:

If you are currently teaching or plan on teaching at the secondary level, list ways to better prepare your students for increased participation in their transition IEP meetings. This may include role play, discussions, or providing them with additional information.

If you are teaching or plan to teach at the elementary or intermediate level, consider ways to increase your students' awareness and knowledge of their own strengths, abilities, and needs. Also, whenever possible, point out how certain professions require certain types of skills or knowledge.

Create a set of materials to help students describe themselves, their current interests, hobbies, and so forth. Distribute and use these materials at the beginning and end of each school year, and give copies of the results to the students and encourage them to share these results with their families.

If you are a parent or family member, develop a detailed profile or description of your son or daughter. Look back at the questions discussed under the section on person centered planning and try to answer them in writing. If possible, include your son or daughter in this discussion.

RESOURCES AND WEBSITES

The following resources and websites will allow you to extend your knowledge about how to work most effectively with families of students in transition. Consider including these resources in your professional portfolio.

Sopris West for ChoiceMaker Materials

www.sopriswest.com

Beach Center on Disabilities

Information for families of people with disabilities. Includes national listing of Parent to Parent and other organizations in all states in the United States.
www.beachcenter.org

AAMR

Information and advocacy regarding individuals with intellectual disabilities. Includes links to local chapters.
www.aamr.org

ARC of the United States

Information and advocacy regarding people with intellectual and developmental disabilities. Includes links to local chapters.
www.thearc.org

Council for Exceptional Children

Information about educational services for students with all exceptionalities. Includes links to local chapters. Also includes divisions that focus on students with specific exceptionalities and on specific issues, including the Division on Career Development and Transition (DCDT).
www.cec.sped.org

Learning Disabilities Association of America

Information and advocacy regarding citizens with learning disabilities.
www.ldanatl.org

National Alliance for the Mentally Ill

Information and advocacy about citizens with mental illnesses.
www.nami.org

TASH

Information and advocacy for people with disabilities, particularly severe and multiple disabilities. Includes links to local chapters.
www.tash.org

Self-Advocacy Organizations

Investigate your state's self-advocacy organizations for people with intellectual and other disabilities. People First is an example of such an organization. See the Beach Center site for a national map that includes these organizations.

Self-Directed Search

www.self-directed-search.com
Copyright © 2001 Psychological Assessment Resources, Inc.

New Freedom Initiative's Online Resource

Federal interagency website to give access to information and resources for people with disabilities.
www.disabilityinfo.gov

REFERENCES

Allen, S., Smith, A., Test, D., Flowers, C., & Wood, W. (2001). The effects of *self-directed IEP* on student participation in IEP meetings. *Career Development for Exceptional Individuals, 24,* 107–120.

Baer, R. (2005). Transition planning. In R. Flexer, T. Simmons, P. Luft, & R. Baer (Eds.), *Transition planning for secondary students with disabilities* (2nd ed.) (pp. 305–335). Upper Saddle River, NJ: Pearson Merrill Prentice Hall.

Benz, M., Lindstrom, L., & Yovanoff, P. (2000). Improving graduation and employment outcomes of students with disabilities: Predictive factors and student perspectives. *Exceptional Children, 66,* 509–529.

Bolles, R. (1995). *What color is my parachute? A practical manual for job hunters and career changers.* Berkeley, CA: Ten Speed Press.

Brolin, D. (1997). *Life-centered career education: A competency-based approach.* Reston, VA: The Council for Exceptional Children.

Butterworth, J., Hagner, D., Heikkinen, B., Faris, S., DeMello, S., & McDonough, K. (1993). *Whole life planning: A guide for organizers and facilitators.* Boston: Children's Hospital, Institute for Community Inclusion.

Butterworth, J., Steere, D., & Whitney-Thomas, J. (1997). Person-centered planning. In R. Shalock (Ed.), *Quality of life: Applications with persons with mental retardation, Volume II* (pp. 5–23). Washington, DC: AAMR.

Carpenter, W. (1995). *Become your own expert! Self-advocacy curriculum for individuals with learning disabilities.* Minneapolis: Minnesota Educational Services.

Cooney, B. (2002). Exploring perspectives on transition of youth with disabilities: Voices of young adults, parents, and professionals. *Mental Retardation, 40,* 425–435.

Everson, J. (1995). *Supporting young adults who are deaf-blind in their communities: A transition planning guide for service providers, families, and friends.* Baltimore: Paul H. Brookes.

Field, S., & Hoffman, A. (1995). *Steps to self-determination.* Austin, TX: Pro-Ed.

Field, S., Martin, J., Miller, R., Ward, M., & Wehmeyer, M. (1998). Self-determination for persons with disabilities: A position statement of the Division on Career Development and Transition. *Career Development for Exceptional Individuals, 21,* 113–128.

Forest, M., & Pearpoint, J. (1992). Putting all kids on the MAP. *Educational Leadership, 50,* 26–31.

Grigal, M., Neubert, D., Moon, M. S., & Graham, S. (2003). Self-determination for students with disabilities: Views of parents and teachers. *Exceptional Children, 70,* 97–112.

Hagner, D., Helm, D., Butterworth, J. (1996). "This is your meeting": A qualitative study of person-centered planning. *Mental Retardation, 34,* 159–171.

Halpern, A., Herr, C., Wolf, N., Doren, B., Johnson, M., & Lawson, J. (1997). *The Next S.T.E.P.: Student transition and educational planning.* Austin, TX: Pro-Ed.

Holland, J. (1985). *The self-directed search professional manual.* Odessa, FL: Psychological Assessment Resources.

Johnson, D. (2005). Key provisions on transition: A comparison of IDEA 1997 and IDEA 2004. *Career Development for Exceptional Individuals, 28,* 60–63.

Johnson, R., & Williams, K. (1994). *Lost in a desert world: The autobiography of Roland Johnson.* Plymouth Meeting, PA: Speaking for Ourselves.

Karvonen, M., Test, D., Wood, W., Browder, D., & Algozzine, B. (2004). Putting self-determination into practice. *Exceptional Children, 71,* 23–41.

Konrad, M., & Test, D. (2004). Teaching middle school students with disabilities to use an IEP template. *Career Development of Exceptional Individuals, 27,* 101–124.

Lehmann, J., Bassett, D., Sands, D., Spencer, K., & Gliner, J. (1999). Research translated into practice for increasing student involvement in transition related activities. *Career Development for Exceptional Individuals, 22,* 3–19.

Lindstrom, L., & Benz, M. (2002). Phases of career development: Case studies of young women with learning disabilities. *Exceptional Children, 69,* 67–83.

Lucyshyn, J., Olson, D., & Horner, R. (1995). Building an ecology of support: A case study of one young woman with severe problem behaviors living in the community. *Journal of the Association for Persons with Severe Handicaps, 20,* 16–30.

Martin, J., Greene, B., & Borland, B. (2004). Secondary students' involvement in their IEP meetings: Administrators' perceptions. *Career Development for Exceptional Individuals, 27,* 177–188.

Martin, J., & Marshall, L. (1995). ChoiceMaker: A comprehensive self-determination transition program. *Intervention in School and Clinic, 30,* 147–156.

Martin, J., Marshall, L., Maxson, L., & Jerman, P. (1996). *Self-directed IEP.* Longmont, CO: Sopris West, Inc.

Martin, J., Marshall, L., & Sale, P. (2004). A 3-year study of middle, junior high, and high school IEP meetings. *Exceptional Children, 70,* 285–297.

Martin, J., Mithaug, D., Cox, P., Peterson, L., Van Dycke, J., & Cash, M. (2003). Increasing self-determination: Teaching students to plan, work, evaluate, and adjust. *Exceptional Children, 69,* 431–447.

Mason, C., Field, S., & Sawilowsky, S. (2004). Implementation of self-determination activities and student participation in IEPs. *Exceptional Children, 70,* 441–451.

Mason, C., McGahee-Kovac, M., Johnson, L., & Stillerman, S. (2002). Implementing student-led IEPs: Student participation and student and teacher reactions. *Career Development for Exceptional Individuals, 25,* 171–192.

Miner, C., & Bates, P. (1997). The effect of person-centered planning activities on the IEP/transition planning process. *Education and Training in Mental Retardation and Developmental Disabilities, 32,* 105–112.

Mount, B., & Zwernik, K. (1988). *It's never too early, it's never too late: A booklet about personal futures planning.* Mears Park Center, MN: Metropolitan Council.

O'Brien, J. (1987). A guide to lifestyle planning: Using the Activities Catalog to integrate services and natural support systems. In B. Wilcox and G. T. Bellamy (Eds.), *The Activities Catalog: An alternative curriculum design for youth and adults with severe disabilities* (pp. 104–110). Baltimore: Paul H. Brookes.

Powell, T., Pancsofar, E., Steere, D., Butterworth, J., Itzkowitz, J., & Rainforth, B. (1991). *Supported employment: Development integrated employment opportunities for people with disabilities.* White Plains, NY: Longman.

Racino, J., Walker, P., O'Connor, S., & Taylor, S. (1992). *Housing, support, and the community.* Baltimore: Paul H. Brookes.

Rojewski, J. (2002). Career assessment for adolescents with mild disabilities: Critical concerns for transition planning. *Career Development of Exceptional Individuals, 25,* 73–95.

Sale, P., & Martin, J. (2004). Self-determination. In P. Wehman & J. Kregel (Eds.), *Functional curriculum for elementary, middle, & secondary age students with special needs* (2nd ed.) (pp. 67–93). Austin, TX: Pro-Ed.

Smull, M., & Harrison, S. (1992). *Supporting people with severe reputations in the community.* Alexandria, VA: National Association of State Mental Retardation Program Directors.

Steere, D., Gregory, S., Heiny, R., & Butterworth, J. (1995). Lifestyle planning: Considerations for use with people with disabilities. *Rehabilitation Counseling Bulletin, 38,* 207–223.

Steere, D., Wood, R., Pancsofar, E., & Butterworth, J. (1990). Outcomes-based school-to-work transition planning for students with severe disabilities. *Career Development for Exceptional Individuals, 13,* 57–69.

Test, D., Mason, C., Hughes, C., Konrad, M., Neale, M., & Wood, W. (2004). Student involvement in individualized education program meetings. *Exceptional Children, 70,* 391–412.

Webster, D. (2004). Giving voice to students with disabilities who have successfully transitioned to college. *Career Development for Exceptional Individuals, 27,* 151–175.

Wehman, P. (2001). *Life beyond the classroom: Transition strategies for young people with disabilities* (3rd edition). Baltimore: Paul H. Brookes.

Wehmeyer, M., & Kelchner, K. (1995). *The Arc's self-determination scale (adolescent version).* Arlington, TX: The Arc National Headquarters.

Wehmeyer, M., & Kelchner, K. (1995). *Whose future is it anyway?* Arlington, TX: ARC.

Wehmeyer, M., & Lawrence, M. (1995). Whose future is it anyway? Promoting student involvement in transition planning. *Career Development of Exceptional Individuals, 18,* 69–83.

Wehmeyer, M., & Palmer, S. (2003). Adult outcomes for students with cognitive disabilities three years after high school: The impact of self-determination. *Education and Training in Developmental Disabilities, 38,* 131–144.

Whitney-Thomas, J., Shaw, D., Honey, K., & Butterworth, J. (1998). Building a future: A study of student participation in person-centered planning. *Journal of the Association for Persons with Severe Handicaps, 23,* 119–133.

Zhang, D. (2001). The effect of Next S.T.E.P. instruction on the self-determination skills of high school students with learning disabilities. *Career Development for Exceptional Individuals, 24,* 121–132.

■ ■ ■ ■ ■

CHAPTER 3

FAMILIES' PERSPECTIVES AND INVOLVEMENT IN TRANSITION

CHAPTER OBJECTIVES

Upon completion of this chapter, you will be able to

1. describe specific challenges that transition may create for families of students with disabilities.
2. take specific steps to better prepare family members for and include them in the transition planning process.
3. assist family members of students with disabilities in taking an active role in their sons' and daughters' transition planning.

KEY TOPICS TO LOOK FOR IN THIS CHAPTER . . .

- Empowering families: In this chapter, look for the range of ways that schools and adult service agencies can collaborate to empower families to be active and informed participants in the transition planning process by providing them with accurate and timely information.
- Overcoming challenges experienced by families: As we will discuss in this chapter, the transition of young people to adult life affects their families as well and can present numerous challenges to everyday family life. Look for creative ways to overcome these challenges and your potential role in assisting families.

Very often, when something happens to one member of the family, the entire family may be affected. This is typically the case when a student with a disability makes the transition from the special education system to adulthood and to the adult service system (Blacher, 2001). The changes that happen in a family as a result of the transition of a young person with a disability may be positive or negative for the family. Also, different family members may be affected in different ways by such transitions. The role of educators and other professionals who are responsible for working with students in transition is to help the family gain access to needed support and information so that the overall impact of the transition is a positive one.

   As we will learn in this chapter, family members of students with disabilities are typically under-informed about the adult service system and ill-prepared for the changes that transition brings about. This makes this time of life a potentially difficult and stressful one for a family. Most notably, transition is a time of change from reliance on the special education system, which is an entitlement system under IDEA, to the adult service system, which is typically based on the need to meet eligibility criteria. In addition, lengthy waiting lists are common for many services, even if eligibility criteria are met, which results in gaps in services for young people who are leaving the school system.

Despite these challenges, we must acknowledge that, for a majority of young people who are in transition, their families will be the primary and most enduring source of guidance and support throughout their lifetimes. Special educators and others in the schools are very important to transition success, but their active involvement typically stops when students exit the special education system. Adult service personnel are likewise very important, but, again, their immediate influence is typically limited in scope and is often time limited. Families, however, are usually the most enduring source of support.

In this chapter, we will describe the potential impact of transition from school to adulthood on families of individuals with disabilities. We will also discuss what families need from educators and other professionals to meet the challenges of transition. We will also discuss ways in which educators and other professionals can better prepare families for transition and include them more fully in the planning process.

TIMES OF CHANGE IN THE LIVES OF FAMILIES

All families experience times of change and adjustment. Some of these changes are positive and joyful and some are sad and difficult. Because families of students with disabilities face many of these same changes, we will take a brief look at these events in the lives of typical families.

First, the birth of a child is a time of great joy, but also change in the life of a family. This event brings about changes in family members' roles and responsibilities, and interaction patterns may have to be adjusted. Older siblings may have to assume new responsibilities, and the family's finances may be strained. In short, the entire family is affected by this experience.

In typical families, other times of change include a child's entry into school, the child's reaching adolescence, changes from grade to grade, and finally the child's graduation from high school. For some students, entry into or graduation from college signifies an additional change for the family. Each of these changes may bring stress to a family, but they are also potentially times of celebration of the achievements of family members. In fact, formal celebrations and ceremonies accompany many of these changes, for example, confirmation or Bar Mitzvah/Bas Mitzvah, graduation or commencement ceremonies, etc.

Juan is a senior—finally he has made it to the end of his high school career! It is the spring, last quarter, and he knows that the end is in sight. He has been accepted to the State University, where he will study business administration. He is very pleased, and he knows that his family, particularly his parents, are extremely proud of his achievements. He is nervous about living on campus in a dorm, and the university is three hours from his home, but he is trying not to worry about this too much at this point—he just wants to enjoy the end of the school year and the summer. His entire family is coming for the graduation ceremonies, and he has already reserved a cap and gown. He will be taking a trip out west with his family before heading to college, and he is also excited about that. Juan knows that things are changing, and there are so many good things happening, but his life won't be the same.

Consider This!   If you are currently teaching, consider the ceremonies and celebrations that take place in the families of the students you teach. If you have children of your own, think back on the changes that have taken place in your own family, as well as changes that will be happening in the future. Even those changes that are positive can bring stress to a family. How has your family been affected by these changes or transitions?

THE FAMILY AS A SYSTEM

Turnbull, Turnbull, Erwin, and Soodak (2006) have studied families of individuals with disabilities extensively, with a focus on how professionals can support and work most effectively with families. Their work has included the description and use of a "family systems model" that describes how families function and how events in life affect the family system. Their basic family systems model is shown in Figure 3.1.

Turnbull, Turnbull, Erwin, and Soodak's Family Systems Model conceptualizes a family as a system with several components or "subsystems" that are interconnected. The *family configuration or characteristics* subsystem consists of the members of the family, their culture, their education level, socioeconomic status, neighborhood, etc. A key point here is that the concept of the "typical" family has changed dramatically over the past several years, and many different configurations of families now exist. The *interactions subsystem* consists of the relationships within a family, for example, the mother-to-father interaction patterns, parent-to-child interaction patterns, sibling-to-sibling interaction pattern, and so forth. These interaction patterns can vary substantially across families. The *functions subsystem* consists of activities that must be done on behalf of the family by members of the family. For example, someone must make money for the family (economic function); someone must maintain the home; someone must care for children within the family, etc. The final element of the Family Systems Model consists of *life cycle transitions*. These are events that can affect all other elements or subsystems within the family system. Take, for example, the birth of a child. This happy event certainly changes the configuration of the family. Interaction patterns will change of necessity, with new interactions (parent to child) now requiring a substantial amount of time, while parent-to-parent interaction may change in nature or duration. New functions will need to be completed for the family (child care and nurturance, for example) while other functions may be affected (e.g., the potential loss of one parent's income for a period of time). This example highlights the fact that even a celebrated or joyous event has impact on the entire family system.

Although this description of Turnbull, Turnbull, Erwin, and Soodak's model (2006) is cursory (readers should refer to their excellent work), it helps us to under-

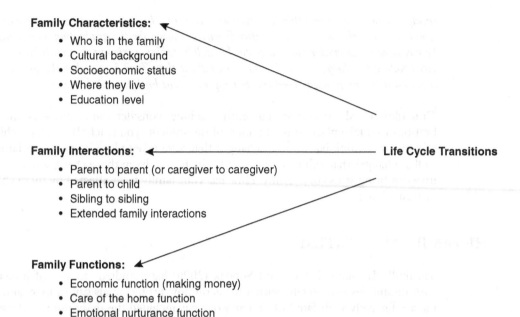

Family Characteristics:

- Who is in the family
- Cultural background
- Socioeconomic status
- Where they live
- Education level

Family Interactions: **Life Cycle Transitions**

- Parent to parent (or caregiver to caregiver)
- Parent to child
- Sibling to sibling
- Extended family interactions

Family Functions:

- Economic function (making money)
- Care of the home function
- Emotional nurturance function

FIGURE 3.1   Turnbull, Turnbull, Erwin, and Soodak (2006) Family Systems Model

Source: Adapted from Turnbull, Turnbull, Erwin, and Soodak, 2006.

stand that major life events, including the transition of a young person from school to adult life, can affect the entire family.

Consider This!   Review the following description of a student and her family. As you read this description, consider how the two possible courses of events could affect the family system.

> *Lisa is twenty years old and is in her last year of special education. She has a diagnosis of severe mental retardation and autism. Lisa receives services in a self-contained classroom for students with autism, located within the local public high school. Her teacher is committed to teaching her functional skills. To achieve this, he has arranged for her work in a community-based training site within a local business two days per week, during the mornings. He also is having her practice work skills within the school (delivering mail within the building). Lisa's curriculum also involves shopping, and other community activities, and some functional academic skills, such as using money, telling time, and reading a simple list of tasks to be completed. Although she is making good progress, she will probably always require some form of ongoing support to work, live, and recreate in her local community.*
>
> *Lisa lives with her mother, who is divorced. Lisa's mother, Amanda, works full time during the day, Monday through Friday. Amada is in a serious relationship, and her "boyfriend" spends a substantial amount of time with the family. Lisa's younger sister, Amy, who is in seventh grade, also lives at home.*

Consider two possible transition scenarios for Lisa and her family. What potential impact might each of these courses of events have on Lisa's family?

Scenario #1: Lisa is accepted for supported employment services by a local rehabilitation agency. The agency will help find a job for her and then will provide job coaching services. Her schedule will mirror her current school schedule (in other words, approximately the same hours of the day, Monday through Friday).

Scenario #2: No services are arranged for Lisa, and she will have to spend her days at home. Someone will need to monitor and supervise her.

The Family Systems Model is one of many contributions of Ann and Rud Turnbull to our understanding of the importance of families in the lives of people with disabilities and how professionals can best collaborate and support families. (See Sidebar 3.1.)

■ ■ ■ ■ ■ ▬▬

SIDEBAR 3.1
SPOTLIGHT ON HISTORY: ANN AND RUD TURNBULL

SPOTLIGHT ON HISTORY

> In communicating with families, you can come to know yourself, know them, honor their cultural diversity, affirm their strengths, promote their choices, envision great expectations, communicate positively, and warrant trust and respect. Your communication is a means by which you can create an empowering context. More than that, your communication is a way you can affect the family's motivation and knowledge/skills. When you communicate effectively, you may affect the family's motivation, enabling them to believe in themselves or acquire a greater sense of control. Likewise, you may augment their knowledge and skills by providing them with useful information or augmenting their problem-solving, coping, or communication skills. (Turnbull & Turnbull, 1997, p. 156)

Ann and Rud Turnbull have been national leaders in shaping how our profession collaborates with families of people with disabilities. First, they are parents, and one of their children is a son with cognitive and mental health disabilities. Their experiences as parents of a child with multiple challenges provides them with an empathetic perspective on the many challenges that families of people with disabilities face and how professionals can truly be of help. Secondly, they are researchers, teachers, and consultants whose work has been prolific and of enormous impact. As co-founders and co-directors of the Beach Center on Disability at the University of Kansas, Ann and Rud have continued to conduct cutting-edge research in the disability field. Their work has had such impact that they have been recognized by a consortium of seven professional and family organizations in the field of mental retardation/intellectual disability as two of the thirty-six people who, in the last one hundred years, have "changed the course of history" in the field of mental retardation. They also have been recognized by their peers as two of the most influential special educators of the past one hundred years (Beach Center at the University of Kansas, www.beachcenter.org). They are perhaps our most visible and dynamic advocates for the families of people with disabilities.

RESEARCH ON FAMILIES IN TRANSITION

As the example above illustrates, transition from school to adulthood can be a time of potentially increased stress within a family of a student with a disability. Other times of increased stress may include the discovery of the child's disability, the child's entry into school, transitions to different classrooms and teachers, and the onset of adolescence (Featherstone, 1981; Wehmeyer, Morningstar, & Husted, 1999). For older parents, their own aging process and concern about the well-being, care, and safety of their child with disabilities after they become infirm or die is an additional time of worry and concern. The transition from school to adulthood is, therefore, one transition time among many across the lifespan of a young person with disabilities.

Several studies have suggested that transition from school to adulthood may be a particularly difficult time in the lives of families that have children with disabilities. Ferguson, Ferguson, and Jones (1988) interviewed families about their perceptions of the transition process, and families' responses indicated that they experienced three aspects of transition: a bureaucratic transition (from school to other agencies), a transition in family life, and a transition in the child's status to adult. Each of these contributed to family stress. (Note, however, that this study predates the federal mandate for transition planning that occurred with IDEA's passage in 1990.) Thorin and Irvin (1992) found that there were multiple stressors for families of students with disabilities, particularly regarding their concerns about residential options for their children. Gallivan-Felon (1994) also found that parents lacked knowledge about transition planning options. Hanley-Maxwell, Whitney-Thomas, & Pogoloff (1995) reported that one parent referred to transition as the "second shock," the first being the discovery of their child's disability. Their study suggested that families of students with disabilities do have visions of success for their children but that numerous barriers exist, including waiting lists, lack of social networks for their children, the strain of their child's versus their own needs, and the sheer difficulty of making decisions about the future. Whitney-Thomas and Hanley-Maxwell (1996) compared responses of families of students with and without disabilities and found that families of those with disabilities were significantly less comfortable with the transition process and had less optimistic visions of their children's future success. Lehmann and Roberto (1996) compared interviews with parents of young people with disabilities and those of young people without disabilities who were in vocational education. Interestingly, the parents of children with disabilities described their children more positively, although they also discussed limitations of the adult service system (e.g., waiting lists and lack of transportation) to support their children. Thorin, Yovanoff, and Irvin (1996) described six dilemmas that families of young adults with developmental disabilities face. These dilemmas highlighted the need for continued intensive family involvement in the life of their children during a time during which, for typical families, family involvement often decreases as young people gain greater independence. Kraemer and Blacher (2001) found that families that they interviewed were very involved in transition planning, yet had pessimistic views about their children's future work environments, primarily due to the lack of options in the adult service system. A notable finding in this study was the discrepancy between what parents wanted for their children in an ideal service system and what they expected would actually occur. This discrepancy between what families hope for versus the challenges of limited programmatic options was also discussed in a study by Cooney (2002). Cooney's study also found that parents' goals for their children focused on the opportunity to use talents and abilities, to contribute to the community, and to be safe from harm. Chambers, Hughes, and Carter (2004) interviewed parents and siblings of students with significant disabilities and found that both parents and siblings felt that they lacked knowledge of postschool options for their family members with disabilities. Finally, Timmons, Whitney-Thomas, McIntyre, Butterworth, and Allen (2004) conducted focus groups and in-depth interviews with parents of young adults with disabilities and found that the respondents perceived the adult service delivery system as inconsistent, complex, and unresponsive. These parents also reported that the challenges of day-to-day living and general uncertainty about the future made it difficult to plan for transition to adulthood. These authors also found that families' location of residence (urban versus rural) presented additional challenges, particularly regarding transportation and the lack of programmatic options in more rural environments.

Together, these studies portray families that experience stresses that may be similar to those of families of students without disabilities but that are greater in intensity. For example, most families worry about how their children will do in college or in their first jobs, but families of young people with disabilities may experience this worry to a greater degree. Also, families of children with disabilities experience unique stresses that may not be shared by other families, such as dealing with the complexities of the adult service system. Table 3.1 provides a summary of common challenges that are faced by families in transition.

Let's consider how transition might affect the families of Sue Anne and Mike.

Transition and the Families of Sue Anne and Mike

Sue Anne is about to make a transition to college. Because of the support and efforts of her family, guidance counselor, and teachers, her dream is about to come true as she

TABLE 3.1 Challenges Faced by Families in Transition

- Lack of thought given to their child's future
- Assumption that the school system would continue to provide for their child
- Fear of the future
- Lack of knowledge of adult service agencies
- Conflicting aspirations of the parents and child
- Assumption that professionals know best and should lead the planning process
- Lack of information about what the transition planning process entails
- Expectations that are not challenging enough for the student (too low)
- Expectations that may not be attainable (excessively high)
- Lack of time and energy to devote to planning
- A focus on day-to-day concerns and not on the long-term future

embarks on the beginning of training as an educator. This is a happy and exciting time in her family. It is also a time of change. The family structure will be affected by Sue Anne's departure from home to the college dorm, and her parents, although extremely happy for her, are going to miss her terribly. Her absence will change the interactions in the family, and her parents will have more time with one another. The costs of college will be an additional burden in terms of meeting the economic needs of the family. Sue Anne's parents are understandably concerned about how she will fare in college. Specifically, they wonder if she will get the support that she needs for success in her classes and if she will speak up and advocate for herself for the accommodations that she needs. They have always been there to support her throughout high school, but now she will be more on her own.

As stated in Chapter 1, Mike's family is extremely uncertain about his future. The change from special education to adult life is still several years in the future, as Mike will continue to receive services until he is twenty-one. However, they are already concerned about what options will be available for him during the day, Monday through Friday. Both of Mike's parents have day jobs so it has worked out well as long as Mike has been in special education. A change in Mike's schedule in his adulthood would necessitate changes in his family's schedule, as someone would need to be home to supervise him. This is already a problem when Mike is ill and stays home from school because, unlike a typical sixteen-year-old, he cannot be left without supervision, except for very short periods of time. As mentioned in the last chapter, his family has organized a circle of support to help plan for Mike's future, and they are envisioning Mike working part time and volunteering or being involved in the community for the rest of his day. This all will need to be arranged, if it is possible, when he reaches age twenty-one. Mike's parents are also concerned about transportation. The school bus has always transported him to school, but how would he get to a part time job or other activities? And, although they do not discuss it openly, Mike's mother and father have nagging worries about what the future will hold if they cannot get a group home or supported living placement for Mike.

CULTURAL DIFFERENCES AND FAMILIES

As described above, one aspect of the family characteristics subsystem in the family system model is a family's culture (Turnbull, Turnbull, Erwin, & Soodak, 2006). Turnbull, Turnbull, Erwin, and Soodak (2006) refer to culture as group identification due to race, ethnicity, religion, geographic location, income status, gender, sexual orientation, disability status, and/or occupation. Any of these factors can influence a family member's perception of what constitutes success, the role of extended family in assisting younger members of the family, their comfort level with interacting with education or human service professionals, or even the importance of future planning. Because cultural differences can have such a substantial impact on decision making, educators and other professionals must take the time to try to understand each family's perceptions of the transition process and its impact on the family unit (Luft, 2005). Specifically, educators must not fall into the trap of *attribution*, that is, the erroneous interpretation of a behavior that may reflect cultural difference (Rubin, Chung, & Huang, 1998). For example, a family's choosing not to participate in an IEP meeting may be construed as a lack of interest in their child's educational program, when in fact it may reflect the parents' own discomfort with schools as a setting for family planning. Similarly, silence in response to a comment may be misinterpreted as stony disagreement, when in fact the parent or family member may simply be considering what was said. Professionals must be vigilant to avoid developing negative attitudes toward families such as "They don't care," "They are overprotective," "They are unrealistic," or "They are uncooperative." Table 3.2 lists behaviors that may be subject to cultural differences and that should be considered by professionals in working with families from culturally diverse backgrounds.

Letitia Myers is a transition coordinator for the local high school. She is concerned about how to best work with the family of one of her students, Donnell. Donnell Anderson is a fifteen-year-old African American student who lives with his family in a low-income housing project. Donnell has mental retardation and needs limited supports. Although he may not be a good candidate for college, he has many skills to build on that would allow him to be employed in the community. Letitia also feels that he could live in his own apartment in the near future. The problem is that she does not know if Donnell's family shares her point of view about Donnell's potential. She has only met Donnell's mother (who is a single parent) one time at an open house at the school, and limited communication took place.

Letitia has contacted Donnell's mother to request that they meet, with Donnell, to begin to discuss his future. She wants to have an informal meeting so that information may be gathered prior to the formal IEP meeting. Donnell's mother reluctantly agrees to meet after school. Letitia schedules the use of a meeting room that will be somewhat comfortable for the three of them to talk. She decides to not use written information at this meeting, because it may not be conducive to open discussion, particularly because Donnell struggles with reading.

On the day of the meeting, Letitia greets Mrs. Anderson and Donnell warmly, but she notes to herself that Donnell's mother is, once again, a bit cold and unsmiling. Letitia reminds herself that this may reflect discomfort with the school setting or possible distrust of school personnel. As the discussion begins, Letitia says that she simply wants to help Donnell plan for his future; she specifically tries not to impose her own ideas on the Andersons until she has heard

TABLE 3.2   Behaviors Subject to Cultural Difference

- Eye contact
- Physical proximity
- Verbal and nonverbal interaction styles
- Comfort with reading written materials
- Valuing of postsecondary education
- Comfort with education professionals' language, dress, etc.
- Perception of people in authority
- Perception of the role of immediate and extended family in planning
- Perception of what constitutes success
- Perception of what contributes to success in one's community

their point of view. She listens respectfully to what Mrs. Anderson and Donnell say. Soon, the son and his mother are discussing the future, and it is clear that they are both very concerned and are unsure about what to do. To be more independent, Donnell wants to earn money on his own. He does not want to move out of his family's home at this time, but he does want to have his own apartment sometime in the future. Mrs. Anderson is skeptical about Donnell's ability to support himself financially in adulthood, and she does not feel that the school has helped him get ready for being an adult. She says she knows how hard someone has to work to make it in their neighborhood, and she does not want Donnell to fall into the drug subculture. Letitia listens, and makes a specific effort to not become defensive about Mrs. Anderson's comments. Letitia knows that she needs to build trust with this family, despite their differences in culture and experience. And she knows that listening is the most important first step.

Being aware of our own cultural biases is an important ingredient in efforts to work effectively with families of students with disabilities in transition. Above all, professionals should make every effort to respect a family's point of view, even if they are not in agreement.

Consider This!   What is your own cultural background and identity? Think about specific celebrations, ceremonies, foods, holidays, or family events that take place in your family and that reflect your cultural heritage. How would someone unfamiliar with your cultural background view these events? Could any behaviors of members of your family be misconstrued by those unfamiliar with your cultural heritage? How could you educate someone about your cultural heritage?

CHALLENGES TO FAMILY INVOLVEMENT IN TRANSITION PLANNING

As discussed above, there are multiple challenges to successful and productive family involvement in the transition planning process. This section will discuss some specific challenges that families may face.

Schedule Changes

One of the most immediate problems that families face is the potential change in their child's schedule during the day. For families in which caregivers work during the day, this can present a major problem. Often, families' choices about desired adult services programs are based primarily on this issue, and they may choose segregated or center-based programs over community-based services because these programs may be perceived (erroneously) as providing more safety and security.

Roberto's parents both work in the city. As long as Roberto has been in school, they have been comfortable knowing where he is during the day and that he is okay. A neighbor keeps an eye out for him during the hour and a half each day before Roberto's parents arrive home. Now, he needs a program to go to during the day. His parents cannot afford to pay someone to stay with him at home, and he cannot be left for long without supervision. They elect to apply for a placement in a sheltered workshop, even though Roberto's teachers feel that he could work in the community with support. Roberto's parents feel bad about not allowing him to try to work in the community, but above all they need to know that he is safe while they are at work, and they feel that the sheltered workshop will fulfill this need best.

Changes in Focus of the Program

Increasingly, students with disabilities are being educated in inclusive settings (Steere, Rose, & Fishbaugh, 1999), yet segregated adult service options continue to predominate. For some families, this presents a dilemma: is it better for the young person to be accepted to *any* adult service program, even if that program is segregated and is therefore not consistent with a belief in the value of inclusion? Should the family accept such a placement, or should they try instead to advocate for inclusive services such as supported employment?

Eliza's parents have pushed for inclusion throughout her educational career. Now, representatives from local agencies are telling them the only adult service options currently available are within center-based, segregated programs. They are informed that the service provider agency that provides most supported employment services in the area does not have an opening. Eliza's parents go home and discuss this challenge. They could simply accept placement in the sheltered workshop, and this would certainly help them with their dilemma about how to provide care and supervision for Eliza during the day. But, as they discuss the issue further, they know that this would not be in her best interests, and she clearly wants to work in the community. They are also knowledgeable about the protections afforded under laws such as the Americans with Disabilities Act, and they know that these protections help increase the chances for Eliza to work in the community. They refuse to go backward: they will have to advocate more strongly for supported employment services for their daughter.

Who to Trust?

One challenge posed by transition to adult life is that families' association with the schools come to an end. This transition to dealing with a new bureaucracy (Ferguson et al., 1988) means that families must develop new trusting relationships. This can be a challenge for families who have come to trust the school.

Leanna has a learning disability. She has been very successful in high school, and now she will be attending the local community college. Her parents are extremely happy and excited about her accomplishments and her next challenges. However, they are most concerned about not having someone to talk to about their daughter. Her transition coordinator has always been available to talk with them, and they have come to rely on her heavily. Now, they are unclear about who will be their contact at the community college. Will anyone fill this role? They have an uneasy feeling and a nagging doubt about how Leanna will do without someone they trust watching over her.

Where Is the Celebration?

For most young people and their families, graduation from high school is a time for celebrating their achievements. Students and their families eagerly look forward to graduation, and many young people prepare for their senior prom. For some families of students with disabilities, such celebrations may appear to be lacking. Certainly, their children have a right to participate in graduation, but it may seem like a graduation to an uncertain future.

Rashid has autism and mental retardation, and he is twenty-one years old. This is his final spring in special education. His family has been working with the school to ensure that Rashid has gained some work experience in the community, and they are arranging for him to receive services from a local rehabilitation agency that provides supported employment services. Despite these positive steps, Rashid's parents feel that this graduation is different from those of their friends' children. Their friends talk proudly of where their children are going to college and how well they have done. Rashid's parents are very proud of him, and they are looking forward to his obtaining paid work through supported employment. However, they find it difficult to talk about Rashid's transition with their close friends, and they feel in many ways that this experience with Rashid is very different from what is happening with their friends' children.

What Is Best for Our Child, and for Us?

A challenge that some families face is the tension or pressure to do what is best for their child while balancing this with what is best for the rest of the family. Sometimes, what seems to be best for the young person in transition may not also seem to be best for other members of the family. For example, a student may not want to move out of his family's house, while his mother and father may need a respite from continuous care responsibilities, and therefore would welcome their child moving to a residential program. Likewise, families may struggle with providing for their children with disabilities while also meeting the needs of their non-disabled children. These tensions or pressures can add to the difficulties of transition.

Ken's family has always provided for him, despite the severity of his disability due to traumatic brain injury (TBI). His physical and cognitive disabilities pose substantial challenges for his parents, and they feel that they may not have devoted enough time to Ken's younger sister. Therefore, they have begun to think about service options for Ken's adulthood that would get him out of the house and would provide him with supervision and training. They know that their decision is motivated less by what Ken may want than by what they feel is best for him—and for their daughter.

The previous examples highlight the many subtle and obvious challenges that may impede active and productive involvement of families in the transition planning process. In the next section we will discuss ways that professionals can try to address some of these challenges in order to better include families in transition.

CREATIVE STRATEGIES FOR BETTER INVOLVING FAMILIES IN TRANSITION PLANNING

The challenges that we have described thus far need not prevent families from active participation in transition planning. Professionals who are willing to be creative and proactive can make major contributions to the success of transition by helping families overcome the difficulties that are part of the process. Although specific strategies for enhancing the transition planning process are described in the next chapter, this section will provide an overview of ways to better involve families in transition. Specifically, we will discuss these important steps to take:

- build trust
- heighten awareness
- ask guiding questions
- provide information
- provide support and reassurance
- help identify family resources
- connect to sources of support

You should note that these steps can occur at any time: before, during, or following transition IEP meetings. The important thing is to have an ongoing collaborative relationship with the family that "keeps the door open" for further discussion about transition.

Build Trust

It is easiest to help families in transition if they trust you. Therefore, a first step to take is to establish that trust. Educators who work extensively with families know that trust is built upon being in constant communication with families and following through on commitments that were made to them. Frequent communication with families of students with disabilities is a first step. A note or email message may be more efficient than attempting to contact through a telephone call. Also, providing families with frequent "good news" communication is likely to make it easier and more motivating for them to be in contact with school personnel. It is important for professionals to always ask families about their preferred method of communication, how often they would like to be contacted, and what information will be most useful to them.

Heighten Awareness

Once trust is established, educators and other professionals can help raise families' awareness of the issues involved in transition planning. This does not mean that professionals should overwhelm families with too much information too quickly. Rather, the subject of transition should be broached to get families to begin to think about this issue. Surveys and questionnaires that include questions about the future are an excellent way to start the discussion of transition (Hutchins & Renzaglia, 1998). For some families who have a closer relationship with school personnel, a face-to-face meeting may be an appropriate time to begin to discuss transition to adult life. If possible, arrange to meet at the family home from time to time rather than expecting family members to always meet at the school building.

Ask Guiding Questions

Because transition is such a daunting challenge for many families, it may be best if they begin by addressing priority questions. This can be done in conjunction with surveys or meetings, described above. For example, questions such as "What is my son good at?" or "What interests has he shown?" may provide information about the best place to start. Teachers and other professionals who work with families can ask open-ended questions that get family members thinking about transition and about what their hopes, fears, and concerns are. Additional questions include:

- What chores does your child do at home?
- How does your child learn things most efficiently?
- What work experiences has your child had?
- What subjects or activities does your child enjoy most in school?

These questions may be organized according to domains of adult living (work, home life, community life, leisure, and recreation) to ensure that they cover the range of topics related to young people in transition. Hutchins and Renzaglia (1998) developed a survey form that provides an excellent way to help families begin to think about children's future employment options.

Provide Information

As indicated earlier in this chapter, families typically lack critical information. Professionals play a key role in providing this information. However, this is not accomplished by simply sending out stacks of brochures about adult agencies, because this information may be overwhelming and may not be read. Instead, professionals should use times of interaction with families to describe the adult service system and then to provide information about agencies that should be contacted. This can occur in individual meetings and interactions with families or through school-sponsored training events that are designed to provide information to families. Also, some coalitions of schools and adult service agencies have developed brochures and overview booklets that are designed to acquaint local families with transition services. Such materials are typically formatted in an easier to read, more concise manner, and they have the virtue of reflecting local transition services.

Provide Support and Reassurance

Families need to be reassured that they are going in the right direction. As indicated throughout this book, transition should be guided by students and their families, not solely by professional opinion. However, families do need professional support in knowing that steps that are being taken are going to help their children. Professionals who have developed a trusting relationship with specific families will find that open channels of communication make it easier to provide emotional support to families as well as information. Professionals should also commend and recognize families for taking active steps toward helping their children in the transition planning process.

Help Identify Family Resources

Families typically have resources that may be helpful in transition, but they may not be aware of these resources. For example, friends and extended family members are all potential sources of support for young people in transition. This is particularly important because most people find jobs through other people they know. Also, families may have connections to the community, that may be very important in the provision of assistance and support. For instance, for many families, their place of worship is an important community connection and support. Professionals should help families become more attuned to and aware of the resources that already exist and that may be helpful during the transition planning process.

Connect to Sources of Support

Finally, professionals should go beyond provision of information and help families to become connected to sources of support. This may involve providing specific names and contacts for families to seek out, or introducing families to other professionals who can assist. For some families, other parents who are going through the transition process or who are more experienced may be some of the best supporters. Some schools have started support and information groups for families in transition, and, if this is the case, professionals can encourage new families to attend these meetings. Also, families should be provided with information about training events and conferences that are presented by other family organizations or by adult service agencies.

CHAPTER SUMMARY

This chapter has introduced you to the critical role that families play in the transition planning process. Families are typically the most consistent source of support throughout students' lives. Families, not just students, experience and are affected by the transition process. As shown in Turnbull, Turnbull, Erwin, and Soodak's work (2006), families may be conceptualized as systems whose functioning is typically affected by major life events, including their children's passage out of the special education system. Families of students with disabilities face a number of substantial challenges during this period of their children's lives. Specifically, families are often poorly informed about the adult service system and steps that are necessary to take to help their children make a successful transition. School personnel and other professionals need to take a lead role in assisting families through the transition process by using their compassion and creativity to find ways for families to gain access to important information and to take a more active role in the planning process.

APPLICATION ACTIVITIES

The application activities listed below are essential for your continued learning and skill development in transition. Each of the activities will require your time and energy but will help you develop your professional skills in this area.

For Practice and Understanding:

Think back to your own transition from high school. Specifically, consider the many ways in which your family assisted you. Next to each of the aspects of adult living listed below, write what kind of help your family provided. (Note: these categories are based on an expanded set of outcome categories described by Wehman, 2001.)

- Employment
- Post-secondary education and training
- Independent living
- Community participation
- Recreation and leisure
- Social relationships
- Financial planning and money management
- Transportation and mobility
- Health and safety

What did your family do for you during this time of life? For example, some families provide assistance in helping young people find their first jobs, or provide rides to community events. Families often help their children by guiding them in learning about money, how to start a bank account, and how to be financially responsible. Also, some families help young people get started in their first dorm room or apartment. What did your family do to help?

Using Turnbull, Turnbull, Erwin, and Soodak's (1997) family systems model, describe the impact that major life events had on your family. These events may have been positive, such as the birth of a new child, a marriage, or a promotion, or perhaps not so positive, such as a divorce, loss of a job, or the death of a family member. How did the event you described have impact on your family system? Did the make-up or configuration of the family change? Were interaction patterns affected? Did the functions or who had to fulfill them change as a result of the event?

For Your Portfolio:

Begin a file of materials that you develop or that you come across that would help families whose children are in transition. These may include:

- family surveys or questionnaires
- descriptions of area adult service programs
- descriptions of what you teach and how the curriculum relates to success in adulthood
- descriptions of family support groups or information networks

If you are a teacher of students with disabilities, develop ways to recognize their achievements, particularly when these times are natural times of celebration for children without disabilities. The recognition does not have to be elaborate, but should serve to make it a positive event for students and for their families.

Develop a resource file of articles and other resources that provide information about different cultural backgrounds. Use this resource file to expand your knowledge about families and the many different cultural backgrounds they may represent.

If you are ambitious, consider starting a family support and information group at your local high school. This group should be a resource to families in transition. It is best to start with a nucleus of family members who are motivated and knowledgeable and who can provide inspiration to other family members.

RESOURCES AND WEBSITES

The following resources and websites will allow you to extend your knowledge about how to work most effectively with families of students in transition. Because each state typically has numerous organizations that can support and inform families, you should seek out those within your specific area. In particular, look up your state's *parent to parent program(s)*. Consider including these resources in your professional portfolio.

Beach Center on Disabilities

Information for families of people with disabilities. Includes national listing of Parent to Parent and other organizations in all states in the United States.
www.beachcenter.org

Partners in Policymaking

Training program for people with disabilities and their families, available in most states.
www.partnersinpolicymaking.com

AAMR

Information and advocacy regarding individuals with intellectual disabilities. Includes links to local chapters.
www.aamr.org

ARC of the United States

Information and advocacy regarding people with intellectual and developmental disabilities. Includes links to local chapters.
www.thearc.org

Council for Exceptional Children

Information about educational services for students with all exceptionalities. Includes links to local chapters. Also includes divisions that focus on students with specific exceptionalities and on specific issues, including the Division on Career Development and Transition (DCDT).
www.cec.sped.org

Learning Disabilities Association of America

Information and advocacy regarding citizens with learning disabilities.
www.ldanatl.org

National Alliance for the Mentally Ill

Information and advocacy about citizens with mental illnesses.
www.nami.org

TASH

Information and advocacy for people with disabilities, particularly severe and multiple disabilities. Includes links to local chapters.
www.tash.org

New Freedom Initiative's Online Resource

Federal interagency website to give access to information and resources for people with disabilities.
www.disabilityinfo.gov

REFERENCES

Blacher, J. (2001). Transition to adulthood: Mental retardation, families, and culture. *American Journal on Mental Retardation, 106,* 173–188.

Chambers, C., Hughes, C., & Carter, E. (2004). Parent and sibling perspectives on the transition to adulthood. *Education and Training in Developmental Disabilities, 39,* 79–94.

Cooney, B. (2002). Exploring perspectives on transition of youth with disabilities: Voices of young adults, parents, and professionals. *Mental Retardation, 40,* 425–435.

Featherstone, H. (1981). *A difference in the family: Living with a disabled child.* New York: Penguin Books.

Ferguson, P., Ferguson, D., & Jones, D. (1988). Generations of hope: Parental perspectives on the transition of their children with severe retardation from school to adult life. *Journal of the Association for Persons with Severe Disabilities, 13,* 177–187.

Gallivan-Felon, A. (1994). "Their Senior Year": Family and service provider perspectives on the transition from school to adult life for young adults with disabilities. *Journal of the Association for Persons with Severe Disabilities, 19,* 11–23.

Hanley-Maxwell, C., Whitney-Thomas, J., & Pogoloff, S. (1995). The second shock: Parental perspectives on their child's transition from school to adult life. *Journal of the Association for Persons with Severe Disabilities, 20,* 3–16.

Hutchins, M., & Renzaglia, A. (1998). Interviewing families for effective transition to employment. *Teaching Exceptional Children, 30,* 72–78.

Kraemer, B., & Blacher, J. (2001). Transition for young adults with severe mental retardation: School preparation, parent expectations, and family involvement. *Mental Retardation, 39,* 423–435.

Lehmann, J., & Roberto, K. (1996). Comparison of factors influencing mothers' perceptions about the futures of their adolescent children with and without disabilities. *Mental Retardation, 34,* 27–38.

Luft, P. (2005). Multicultural competence for working with families. In R. Flexer, T. Simmons, P. Luft, and R. Baer (Eds.), *Transition planning for secondary students with disabilities* (2nd ed.) (pp. 276–304). Upper Saddle River, NJ: Pearson–Merrill/Prentice Hall.

Rubin, S., Chung, W., & Huang, W. (1998). Multicultural considerations in the rehabilitation counseling process. In R. Roessler & S. Rubin (Eds.), *Case management and rehabilitation counseling: Procedures and techniques* (3rd ed.) (pp. 185–230). Austin, TX: Pro-Ed.

Steere, D., Rose, E., & Fishbaugh, M. S. (1999). Integration in the secondary school for students with severe disabilities. In M. Coutinho & A. Repp (Eds.), *Inclusion: The integration of children with disabilities* (pp. 333–365). Atlanta, GA: Wadsworth Publishing Co.

Thorin, E., Yovanoff, P., & Irvin, L. (1996). Dilemmas faced by families during their young adults' transitions to adulthood: A brief report. *Mental Retardation, 34,* 117–120.

Thorin, G., & Irvin, L. (1992). Family stress associated with the transition to adulthood of young people with severe disabilities. *Journal of the Association for Persons with Severe Handicaps, 17,* 31–39.

Timmons, J., Whitney-Thomas, J., McIntyre, J., Butterworth, J., & Allen, D. (2004). Managing service delivery systems and the role of parents during their children's transitions. *Journal of Rehabilitation, 70,* 19–26.

Turnbull, A., Turnbull, H. R., Erwin, E., & Soodak, L. (2006). *Families, professionals, and exceptionality: Positive outcomes through partnerships and trust* (5th ed.). Upper Saddle River, NJ: Merrill/Prentice Hall.

Wehman, P. (2001). *Life beyond the classroom* (3rd ed.). Baltimore: Paul H. Brookes.

Wehmeyer, M., Morningstar, M., & Husted, D. (1999). *Family involvement in transition planning and implementation.* Austin, TX: Pro-Ed.

Whitney-Thomas, J., & Hanley-Maxwell, C. (1996). Packing the parachute: Parents' experiences as their children prepare to leave high school. *Exceptional Children, 63,* 75–88.

CHAPTER 4

THE TRANSITION PLANNING PROCESS

CHAPTER OBJECTIVES

Upon completion of this chapter, you will be able to

1. conduct and implement transition plan activities.
2. ensure that the transition plan is effective in meeting students' desired postschool outcomes.
3. know the roles and responsibilities of team members in the transition planning process.
4. plan and write a quality IEP/transition plan with the collaboration from students, family, and professionals.

KEY TOPICS TO LOOK FOR IN THIS CHAPTER . . .

- Strategies for effective planning: In this chapter, look for the structure of effective transition IEPs and ways for planning teams to create these plans.
- The "results-oriented process": Note how the students' desired transition outcomes drive the planning process, if it is implemented correctly.

The goal of all special education programs for students with disabilities is to create an effective plan that complies with federal regulations and meets the spirit of IDEA. Yet school districts and special education programs have struggled to achieve this outcome (Grigal, Test, Beattie, & Wood, 1997; Powers, Gil-Kashiwabara, Geenen, Powers, Balandran, & Palmer, 2005). Perhaps school personnel, adult service personnel, students with disabilities, and families of students with disabilities have not fully appreciated the purpose of transition planning and its critical importance. Or perhaps these individuals have not been fully aware of the poor outcomes attained by students leaving the special education system. Another factor might be that schools have felt that it is their sole responsibility for helping students achieve the outcomes that would provide them with the opportunity for a "good adult life."

Despite the poor outcomes cited above, we do know that effective planning for transition and the delivery of quality educational services makes a positive difference. One study indicated that students with disabilities are 87 percent more likely to be employed after graduation if schools provided a job search and job attainment training component to their educational program (Rabren, Dunn, & Chambers, 2002). Carter and Wehby (2003) found that students with emotional and behavioral disorders have better outcomes if they are provided with training and awareness of what skills are important for acceptable job performance. Additionally, Durlak and Rose (1999) stated that students with learning disabilities have greater opportunities to go on to postsecondary education if they were taught skills of self-determination which will, in turn, allow them the possibility to attain greater economic success and personal well-being (Milson & Hartley, 2005). In general, students who exit high school where an effective transition program was provided have a greater potential for achieving their postschool outcomes and for an overall better quality of life (Kraemer, McIntyre, & Blacher, 2003). These studies will be discussed in greater detail later in this chapter.

These studies attest to the importance for students and families to be prepared to participate in the IEP meetings and to play an active role in their process. The fact that collaboration and a coordinated set of activities are essential elements of the law should help schools realize that no one entity can "do it all" for students. It is the intent of this chapter to provide you with the knowledge needed to create an atmosphere of collaboration, which allows equal participation of all the team members toward planning, developing, and writing an effective transition IEP.

SETTING THE STAGE: JAMES'S TRANSITION PLAN

James is a fifteen-year-old student with mild mental retardation who will be entering ninth grade in the fall. It was April and his annual IEP was being conducted for the next school year. James's mother, Mrs. Rose, had just received an invitation to attend his IEP. The letter of invitation indicated that transition would be discussed at this meeting and that other agencies were being invited to participate in this process. Mrs. Rose was confused because she was not sure what transition is or why these other agencies were being invited to attend her son's IEP meeting. So she called Mrs. Neff, James's teacher. Mrs. Neff explained to her that transition is something that will help prepare James for adult life after high school. Mrs. Rose's heart began to beat faster. She had not thought of James out of school or what he might do after he left school. In fact, she had hoped that he could stay in school for a long time, and, besides, hadn't they been preparing him all along? She asked who the other agencies are that were being invited. She was told that these would include the State Vocational Rehabilitation (VR) Department, the local Developmental Disabilities Department, and an adult service provider. She had no idea of what these agencies did or how they were going to help her son.

She hung up the phone and started thinking of James as a grown man, something she had never really done. James had always been a cute boy who smiled a lot and asked many questions. How could people think he would grow up and do adult things? She wondered if he could work or hold a job. Could he live by himself or would he have to live with other people like him? She had always expected that James would live with her and keep her company since Mr. Rose passed away. Perhaps he could live with his brother or sister? She trembled at the thought of his future and uncertainty. This is the first time anyone had mentioned life after school for James.

On the day of the meeting, Mrs. Rose was nervous. She wondered what questions to ask. She was not sure if she was prepared to discuss such important matters about James. When she arrived, James was sitting at the table with his teacher and several other people she had never seen before. She was a bit surprised to see James, since this was the first time that he had ever attended his IEP meetings. The school administrator, Mrs. Peak, welcomed Mrs. Rose and asked the participants to introduce themselves. There were two people she had never seen before present, one from the Vocational Rehabilitation Department and another from the Developmental Disabilities Department. Mrs. Rose was unsure whom these people represented and how they could help James. After participants introduced themselves, Mrs. Peak indicated the purpose of the meeting and the reason for the new faces around the table was that they would also discuss transition planning for James.

An attendance sheet was passed around for all to sign as being present at the meeting. Then Mrs. Peak turned the page of the IEP and said that, even though James was only fifteen years of age, it was time to start discussing transition planning. This was different from previous IEP meetings that Mrs. Rose had participated in, and her stress levels rose and a flash of warmth and nervousness quickly came upon her. Mrs. Peak asked Mrs. Rose if she knew what this meant. Mrs. Rose nervously asked, "It's about James's future?" "Yes," said Mrs. Peak, "that is exactly what this is about." Mrs. Neff, James's teacher, began to ask James a number of questions about what he thought he would like to do when he graduates. She asked James what type of work he would like to do and where he would like to live and what kind of things he likes doing for fun and recreation during his spare time. James began to respond to all of these questions, to Mrs. Rose's surprise. She had no idea that James had even thought about a career or where he would like to live other than at home with her.

The rest of the IEP meeting went as usual, discussing James's current rates of performance in school and his subject areas, but this time these were discussed in light of James's future aspirations. His strengths and needs in the various academic areas were discussed, as well as learning goals for the year. The goals identified particular behaviors that James would have to do under certain conditions and the certain levels he would have to achieve for the goals to be successful. Although this part of the meeting was very similar to others that she had attended, everything that was discussed now connected to the earlier discussion of James's future.

As the meeting concluded, Mrs. Rose thought about what jobs James might be able to do in the future. Could he really live in his own apartment? Does he know how to wash his clothes, cook for himself, or even clean up after himself? Was this realistic? Could they help him do these things? Would he really have a future beyond school?

RESEARCH ON TRANSITION PLANNING FOR STUDENTS WITH DISABILITIES

Before discussing the importance of transition planning and effective strategies to be used during the planning process, we will review some current and pertinent research in this area. In Chapters 2 and 3, we discussed student and family participation in transition planning, and you should refer to the material in those chapters as we discuss transition planning in greater detail in this chapter. As introduced in previous chapters, it is clear that transition plans that focus on the student's strengths, interests, and preferences meet the intent and spirit of the law and have a greater probability of helping the student achieve success after graduation from high school (Benz & Doren, 1997; Furney & Hasazi, 1997).

As discussed in the previous two chapters, an important consideration is how participants in transition planning perceive the planning process and the outcomes they feel will emerge from it. Chambers, Hughes, and Carter (2004) surveyed the perspective of eight parents and siblings of students with significant cognitive disabilities. In general, parents' and siblings' expectations were that their family members would work in sheltered workshops and have to live at home. These expectations are both somewhat disheartening and not completely surprising in light of long waiting lists for services in many states and the poor outcome data of transition programs nationally (Katsiyannis, Zhang, Woodruff, & Dixon, 2005). (These issues will be discussed in greater detail in Chapter 5.) Similar concerns about poor outcome concerns or low expectations have been raised about students with emotional and behavioral disorders (Carter & Wehby, 2003) and for students with learning disabilities (Dickinson & Verbeek, 2002; Durlak & Rose, 1999). As we stated in the last chapter, professionals must consider families' backgrounds when discussing the potential outcomes of transition planning. For example, Rueda, Monzo, Shapiro, Gomez, and Blacher (2005) point out that school personnel must be attuned to the cultural background of families and not impose their worldviews on students and their families during the transition planning process.

As discussed in Chapter 2, a major challenge school personnel face is determining student interest and preferences. Although there are many standardized systems for assessing student interests, one proven approach has been person centered planning (Mount & Zwernik, 1988), which was described in Chapter 2. Menchetti and Garcia (2003) studied the impact that person centered career planning and career choice had on employment outcomes in ninety-three individuals. Choice was measured by the degree of match between stated career preference and actual employment. Seventy-two out of ninety-three individuals (83 percent) had a high-to-moderate level of preference match. This study highlights the value that person centered planning can have on the success of an individual related to their expressed choice and participation in decisions.

In another study, Rojewski (2002) reviewed the literature regarding career assessment for adolescents with mild disabilities. It was recommended that an individual assessment plan be developed for students starting at age fourteen and that the plan be updated and revised regularly as students cycle through the career development phases of awareness, exploration, and establishment. This recommendation has major implications to transition planning since IDEA 2004 has eliminated the requirement to begin transition planning at age fourteen and has raised the age from fourteen to sixteen years for the required initiation of transition planning. Rojewski also suggested that the assessment process be guided by the following questions: (a) What do I already know about this student that would be helpful in developing postsecondary outcomes? (b) What information do I need to know about this student in order to determine postsecondary outcomes? (c) What methods will best provide this information? and (d) How will the assessment data be collected and used in the IEP process?

As we focus on student outcome achievement, we should also consider what program/service model will achieve the greatest benefit to students with disabilities. Clearly students with different disability characteristics may require different intervention approaches. Individuals with learning disabilities are more likely to be successful if provided with self-determination skill training (Durlak & Rose, 1999) and effective accommodations strategies to aid them in achieving postsecondary success (Milson & Hartley, 2005). In a study by Carter and Wehby (2003), forty-seven students with emotional and behavioral disorders and their supervisors, all working in different sites, were surveyed about (a) task-related social behaviors; (b) non–task-related social behaviors; (c) work performance behaviors; and (d) general work behaviors. Across all four of these domains, employers evaluated the students' performance levels lower than the students did for themselves. The employers also rated all four areas as more important than the students rated them. The implication of this study is that individuals with emotional and behavioral disorders, who tend to drop out at an unacceptably high rate and experience difficulty in obtaining employment, need more training and awareness of what skills are important or acceptable for job success, and will benefit from a program that includes social skills and emotional/behavioral support instruction. For students with mental retardation, community-based instruction may be the most appropriate option for success. Kraemer and colleagues (2003) examined the quality of life of 188 young adults with moderate and severe mental retardation. Students who had exited high school and had a community-based learning environment where employment training was provided had an overall better "quality of life" than those who were in sheltered workshops for adults. Rabren and colleagues (2002) examined employment status of 1,393 former special education students in Alabama from 1960 to 2000, representing 37 school districts. They found that there was an 87 percent probability that students would be employed one year after high school if they held a job at the time they exited school. Sitlington, Neubert, and Leconte (1997) describe the importance of an ongoing assessment process to support transition planning, starting no later than age fourteen, and that the assessment process must incorporate a variety of strategies, particularly those conducted in natural contexts. Held, Thoma, and Thomas (2004) reported on a participatory action research study of the transition planning process for a student with autism. Their strategy combined the use of the adapted Next S.T.E.P. curriculum with the Self-determined Learning Model of Instruction and the PATH planning process, which is a form of person centered planning. This study provides a good illustration of the need to adapt and individualize planning to meet students' unique needs.

Several studies have attempted to assess the quality of transition IEPs. Grigal and colleagues (1997) reviewed ninety-seven transition IEPs and found that, although they were generally in compliance with transition planning mandates (in other words, the required sections of the IEPs were filled in), the plans lacked specificity and reflected minimal student involvement. They found that many of the transition goal statements (outcome statements) were far too vague, and there was little evidence of changes in the transition plans. This is a particular concern when we consider that many young people may change their minds about future interests as they gain experience. Katsiyannis and colleagues (2005) conducted an analysis of the participation of students with mental retardation in transition planning and compared their participation to that of students with learning disabilities and with emotional/behavioral disorders. Concerns raised by this study included the findings that students with mental retardation were less involved and more likely to report no progress toward their transition outcomes than students from the other two groups. Also, a smaller percentage had postsecondary education as a goal (desired outcome) and most had sheltered or supported employment as transition outcomes. McMahan and Baer (2001) surveyed 186 people involved with transition planning, including parents and guardians, educators, and adult service professionals. Schools were reported to be generally in compliance, with the exception of the requirement to reconvene the IEP team when transition services could not be provided as needed. An important finding of this study was that, although plans were reported as being in compliance with requirements, many best practices, including students leading their meetings or the use of person centered planning, were reported as occurring infrequently. The strongest predictor of compliance and implementation of best practices was the presence of a school-based interagency planning team. Kraemer and Blacher (2001) conducted a study of the perceptions of 52 families of students with severe mental retardation about the transition planning process. When asked if their children had a transition plan while in high school, slightly over half (57.7 percent) reported yes, while 13.5 percent said no and 28.8 percent were unsure. The authors note that these findings are a concern because either plans were not in place or parents were not aware of them. Zhang, Ivester, Chen, and Katsiyannis (2005) surveyed 105 middle and high school teachers and 37 transition personnel in South Carolina about the transition planning process. Several areas of concern were raised by their findings:

- Special educators were reported as participating by 89 percent of respondents, far below the required 100 percent rate of participation.
- Parent and student participation was reported by 82 percent, far below the federal requirements and best practices recommendations.
- In 63 percent of districts, a transition coordinator or special education director had overall responsibility for coordinating transition planning. But in the remainder of the districts represented in the survey, this responsibility fell to teachers or other personnel who may lack the authority or knowledge to effectively coordinate planning.
- About half of the transition coordinators reported having responsibilities for facilitating the student assessment process.
- Community- and school-based work experiences were reported as occurring, but supported employment was one of the least reported vocational services.
- 94 percent of students had transition plans by age sixteen, but only 54 percent were reported as having transition plans by age fourteen.

The authors identified the several programmatic areas in need of strengthening, including the increased use of supported employment, increased advocacy and legal services, better medical services management, increased focus on transition to community residential life, and further development of approaches to teaching functional/life skills within the context of the state mandated curriculum standards.

Powers and colleagues (2005) reviewed 399 IEPs in two states in the western United States to analyze the quality of the transition components. They found that transition goal areas (outcome statements) mandated by IDEA 1997 were often not addressed or were inadequately detailed. Also, self-determination and career planning were not incorporated into most plans, and students were often found to have sole responsibility for implementing action steps that were discussed at their planning meetings. In addition, only 75 percent of plans showed student signatures, which raised questions about the degree of student participation. Thirty-three percent of transition goals (outcome statements) had no associated action steps to achieve them. Student interests or desires were noted for only 19 percent of the outcome statements. General educators and transition specialists were absent for a large percentage of meetings. Vocational rehabilitation counselors were present for only 1 percent of meetings. Finally, 56 percent of students participated in work experiences, only 7 percent of IEPs reflected self-determination training, and students with developmental disabilities were less involved than other students and their interests and employment goals were generally not reflected in their transition IEPs. The authors point out the irony that, although students were generally required to follow up on action steps toward their future aspirations, they had little training in self-determination. The authors conclude by stating that, although these results are sobering, the greater accountability mandated by IDEA 2004 may address these concerns to a degree.

Together, these studies highlight an important issue: those responsible for transition planning must strive to go beyond mere compliance with the law and meet the spirit of the law, as reflected in best practices. This calls for creativity and commitment by all involved to implement a transition planning process that is based on students' needs, strengths, preferences, and interests and that is dynamic and well coordinated. It is clear that an appropriate plan of service delivery will reap the greatest outcomes and benefit for students. Transition should be a seamless movement from school adult life. Studies such as those previously described make it clear that schools providing a program that is based on best practices will have a major impact on students' success as they transition (seamlessly) from school to adult life or postsecondary education, while those that do not implement best practices will perpetuate the challenge of poor outcomes.

THE IMPORTANCE OF EFFECTIVE
TRANSITION PLANNING

The case study you read at the beginning of this chapter has been replayed in the minds of parents of students with disabilities hundreds of times each year. Looking forward to adulthood has always been both exciting and stressful to parents and students alike. For most parents thinking of their son or daughter growing up and going to college or work, living in their own apartment, interacting and enjoying community life, are just some of the joys and stressors of parenthood. But for too many parents of children with disabilities it may be more stressful to think about than it is exciting.

For many students in America, looking forward to life after high school means going to college and/or work. For students with disabilities it may be more difficult to think about and is not always clear. Planning is often the key to a successful beginning and end of any journey. Personal life planning is critical and important for all students but perhaps it is even more critical for the student who is challenged by a disability. Students are often guided through a preparatory process by parents, teachers, guidance counselors, and friends. But far too many students with disabilities leave schools lacking some of the basic academic and functional skills needed for an adequate quality of life (Turnbull & Luckasson, 2001). The preparatory and learning process of students with disabilities may take many years to accomplish. Even though we know that *all* students need help unfolding and implementing their plans for the future, students with disabilities may require far more support and time to accomplish the same process. Early planning for students with disabilities is crucial. The more significant the disability, the more crucial this planning process becomes. Transition planning is designed to address and improve the postschool outcomes for students with disabilities, thus making it one of the most critical educational contributions to a student's future success.

Consider all of the people who are viewed as successful in our local communities, including doctors, lawyers, storeowners, repairpeople and people who own their own business. If they were asked how they had achieved their personal goals in their chosen vocation you might hear of the challenges they faced and the hard work it took to achieve their chosen careers. Their story may reveal all the people who helped them along the way and how they had to develop a long-term plan toward attaining their dreams of a successful profession. The stories told of hard work, planning, and acting on personal life goals and dreams are heard by many of these people we consider to be valued and successful members of our community. It is the same for people with disabilities except that the amount of support and guidance required to achieve their dreams may be more involved. In the remainder of this chapter we will explore the process of transition that includes identifying student's personal life goals, who should support the person in achieving these goals, who the members of the team are and their roles and responsibilities to the process, how to prepare students and parents to participate in the process, how transition planning is developed through the IEP, and how to ensure that the transition plan is effective in reaching the stated outcomes.

Dr. Edna Mora Szymanski, whose work was introduced in Chapter 1, has been a leader in our conceptualization of transition planning. A description of Dr. Szymanski's contributions is provided in Sidebar 4.1.

A CLOSER FOCUS ON TRANSITION

As introduced in Chapter 1, transition is the movement from school to adult life upon graduation or upon leaving school (when the student ages out of school at age twenty-one). Transition is not just the movement from school to no school. It is expected that the students have a specific idea of where they will be once they leave school. This

■ ■ ■ ■ ■ ▬▬▬▬▬▬▬▬▬▬▬▬▬▬▬▬▬▬▬▬▬▬▬▬▬

SIDEBAR 4.1
SPOTLIGHT ON HISTORY

EDNA MORA SZYMANSKI

Dr. Edna Mora Szymanski is currently Dean of the College of Education at University of Maryland, College Park. Prior to her current appointment, Dr. Szymanski was a professor in the Department of Rehabilitation Psychology and Special Education at the University of Wisconsin. While at the University of Madison-Wisconsin, she also held the positions of department chair, associate dean, director of the Rehabilitation Research and Training Center on Career Development and Advancement, and chair of the campus committees on retirement and disability. Dr. Szymanski has written and presented extensively about issues of career development for individuals with disabilities. Having had direct experience in the state Vocational Rehabilitation system, she has been a leader in advocating for quality services for people with severe disabilities. Her work on career development theories and their implications for transition planning has contributed to a broader and more longitudinal conceptualization of transition planning. In particular, she has helped us to see the connection between early childhood, elementary, and middle school experiences and subsequent success during transition from high school to adulthood. Likewise, her work has highlighted the importance of consideration of family culture in the planning process. Dr. Szymanski's work has appeared in numerous rehabilitation and special education publications, and she has received several national awards for her research, including three from the American Counseling Association, three from the American Rehabilitation Counseling Association, one from the American Association of Counselor Education and Supervision, and one from the National Council on Rehabilitation Education.

Source: Information taken from the website of the University of Maryland www.education.umd.edu.

requires planning, preparation, and the clear identification of postschool outcomes (Flexer, Simmons, Luft, & Baer, 2005; Wehman, 2004).

Although IDEA 2004 has changed the requirement for when transition must begin (that is, for students who are sixteen or older), we continue to recommend that transition planning should begin earlier, that is, no later than age fourteen. IDEA 2004 has raised the age for beginning transition planning from fourteen to sixteen years and emphasized that transition planning should be related to training, education, employment, and independent living skills (Johnson, 2005). This change directly reflects IDEA's outcome policy of "helping children with disability achieve equality of opportunities, full participation, independent living and economic sufficiency" and preparing them to lead "productive and independent lives" (Section 1400 ©(1), IDEA 2004). IDEA 2004 states that beginning no later than the first IEP, to be effective when the child is sixteen, the IEP must contain "appropriate measurable postsecondary goals, based on age appropriate transition assessments related to training, education, employment and, where appropriate, independent living skills," and "the transition service (including course of study) needed to assist the child in reaching those goals" (Johnson, 2005). Despite this regulatory change we continue to believe that for most students' transition the process of planning should begin as early as fourteen years of age. At this age, the IEP should reflect the relationship of the students' academics with the students' postschool goals (i.e., their desired adult outcomes). It is clear that the planning and preparation for the stated outcomes are the critical features of the transition planning process.

The transition plan lays out the path for a student's life beyond high school. It must reflect a student's choices, preferences, and needs in the areas of education and training, employment, adult living arrangements, and community experiences (Patton & Dunn, 1998; Wehman, 1995, 1998). Parents and students must be involved in all aspects of the planning and decision-making process. For parents and students to fully participate and become involved they must become familiar with the transition requirements and understand their role in this process. As for teachers and professionals, they too must fully understand the requirements and their role and responsibility for supporting students in the choices and preferences in the areas of education and training, employment, adult living arrangements, and community experiences. Parents, students, educators, and community service providers must work together to support students' planning and activities leading to the achievement of their personal adult life goals. Table 4.1 provides a section of the Individuals with Disabilities Education Improvement Act (IDEA 2004) language on transition.

As indicated in this section of IDEA, transition planning is a required service to students who qualify for special education. As discussed in Chapter 1 in greater detail, IDEA 2004 regulations contain several very important points.

- Transition is a **"coordinated set of activities."**
- The activities of transition are designed to be within a **"results-oriented process."**

TABLE 4.1 IDEA 2004 Language on Transition

Transition, as required under Individuals with Disabilities Education Improvement Act, Section 1401 (34) states:

Definition: Section 1401 (34) defines "transition services" to be "a coordinated set of activities" for a child with a disability that:
1) is "designed to be within a results-oriented process" and is focused on "improving" the student's "academic and functional achievement" in order "to facilitate the (student's) movement from school to post-school activities, including post-secondary education, vocational education, integrated employment (including supported employment), continuing adult education, adult services, independent living, or community participation";
2) is based on the individual student's needs, taking into account the student's strengths, preferences, and interests; and
3) includes—(i) Instruction; (ii) Related services; (iii) Community experiences; (iv) The development of employment and other post-school adult living objectives; and (v) If appropriate, acquisition of daily living skills and functional vocational evaluation.

- The transition process is focused on "improving" the student's "academic and functional achievement" in order to facilitate the student's **"movement from school to post-school activities that includes postsecondary education, vocational education, integrated employment, continuing and adult education, adult services, independent living or community participation."**
- The transition activities are based on the student's needs, **taking into account the student's strengths, preferences, and interests**.

This section of IDEA and the points discussed have been added to help alleviate the problems that exist in the poor preparation for adult life and the unusually high unemployment rate of students with disabilities leaving our schools (LaPlante, Kennedy, Kaye, & Wenger, 1996). For example, the term "outcome-oriented process" has been changed to "result-oriented process." This change was put into effect to make schools more accountable for the transition plan (Turnbull, Huerta, & Stowe, 2005). Adding this term reflects the importance of successful postschool employment or education as a measure of accountability for individuals with disabilities. Therefore, the impact of this regulation is critical to preparing students with disabilities to lead "enviable lives" (Turnbull & Luckasson, 2001) or any quality of life beyond school. Since 1990 up to the present 2004 Amendments, this aspect of IDEA is perhaps the single most important requirement that has attempted to functionally prepare students in special education for adult life.

THE TRANSITION PLANNING PROCESS

An effective transition planning program comprises two main functions, a planning process coupled with activities of preparation for attainment of identified postschool outcomes. These two functions are the basis of quality transition services. If attention is not placed on both of these functions, the process cannot be completely achieved. Planning without preparation and training will not lead to an outcome-oriented process and preparation without planning will not support the student's needs nor will it take into account the student's preferences and interests. Both are critical and important to meeting the spirit of the law as well as the student's specially designed instruction or related service needs. Let's discuss each of these two functions separately.

Transition Planning

Transition planning is simply the process of planning for a person's future from his or her high school years to adult life. In general, transition begins with the planning process, which means taking into consideration the student's hopes, dreams, desires, and career options. These become the student's focus for preparation and ultimately the student's course of study. Oftentimes, a person's interests, preferences, desires, and strengths are strong motivators for a person to accomplish everyday activities. It is from this basic perspective that we should view transition planning. An individual's desires should be the driving force in the planning process. Therefore, the planning of a student's future is not limited to any single area of a person's life. Although work is one of the goals for transition planning, it is only one. Stated another way, most people do not "live to work," rather they "work to live." Given that perspective, one might see that all areas of life, not just employment, are important to attaining a "good life." Therefore, the process of transition is a holistic approach that includes the various life domains that are identified by the person and his or her family as a need for preparation for life. Some of these life domain areas that must be considered and planned for are employment, postsecondary education and training, housing, medical care, transportation, recreation and leisure, and community participation. These life domains can be broad or narrow, based on a person's age and need for preparation. In keeping with IDEA's language, in this book we will refer to students' long-term goals in different life domains as "outcomes." We use this term specifically to distinguish these long-term aspirations from annual learning goals. As we will discuss later in this chapter, outcome statements should be clarified for transition-aged students in categories of employment, postsecondary education, residential or community living, recreation and leisure, and community participation.

As discussed in Chapter 2, identifying what they would like to do and be after leaving school is difficult for most young people, yet IDEA 2004 mandates active participation by the student in transition planning. As mentioned previously, this is a challenge when students are unsure about their future or have not even thought about or been asked about it. There are various approaches to understanding the future of students with disabilities where questions about hopes and dreams may never have been asked. As introduced in Chapter 2, person centered planning strategies can be useful in helping young people plan for the future (Miner & Bates, 2002). These planning approaches provide the needed information to understanding the future of people at any point in their lives. Person centered planning is designed to help individuals and students, families and professionals to identify what the "focus person" (student) wants out of life, to identify hopes, dreams, interests, preferences, and personal goals beyond the life of school (Mount & Zwernik, 1988). To develop an adequate transition plan, one must understand what the student wants his or her life to be like in the future. For teachers and school personnel, the focus is on what the student's life might look like after high school, and this requires school personnel to look beyond a single year. The process of identifying students' desired outcomes beyond high school can be a very challenging concept for school personnel, who are accustomed to thinking in terms of annual services.

Understanding the person centered approach means leaving behind preconceived ideas of programs and systems and, instead, attempting to look at the person's gifts, talents, and abilities rather than limitations, and then to identify what is possible. It might even be how we identify the student. Kunc (2004) discusses this point well, that if the student is identified primarily by his or her disability and limitations, it may be difficult to look beyond the student's "inabilities." But if the student is identified by his or her capacities and strengths, he or she may be seen as a person having potential and as one who will need supports. Person centered planning attempts to look at the person as having capacities that need to be discovered. It is also a way for students to begin to have more of a voice in their planning and in their lives. It is a way to help people and the focus person to create a vision for the future that is unique and personal. It is a journey and a process for planning one's own life.

Person centered planning teams, made up of people who are seen as crucial and important to the focus person, include family, relatives, friends, neighbors, teachers, and community members. These people are referred to as the Planning Team or Circle of Support. The team is facilitated by a person who understands the concept of person centered planning and can lead and guide the team in the process of searching for the person's strengths, talents, gifts, and capacities. In this way, the planning team develops a picture of the person in a way that is positive and helps the members understand and get to know the person on a very personal level. This process also helps those members of the team who need to get to know the person better, since they may be working with the student in the preparation stage of the transition process. This process can also help members of the team understand the person in terms of understanding the cultural and ethnic background that might help teachers to become better aware of the student's interactions within his or her environment.

Because person centered planning focuses all the attention on the student, it provides strategies for the student to take control of his or her life goals by discussing the kind of things he or she wants to do by creating a personal vision for the future. The focus of person centered planning is on the student's hopes, desires, and dreams. It means looking at the person's life with hope for the future while offering a sense of direction for the preparation process for the person. This process allows the person to become involved in planning for his or her life and developing skills toward self-advocacy and self-determination. It should be made clear that this process should be separate from any of the other planning activities that schools do. It is intended to supplement and complement the student's IEP by helping to establish outcome-based goals that are necessary in the transition section of the document. Together the IEP and person centered planning can provide a more comprehensive approach to the transition planning process.

Transition Preparation

Although IDEA 2004 requires that transition begin at age sixteen, we feel that it is preferable to begin by age fourteen. At age fourteen, a student is generally beginning the high school years, thus beginning the critical last four years of planning leading to graduation and perhaps postsecondary education. For the student who is not planning on continuing postsecondary education, it is the period of preparation for adult life training, work, and independent living. Therefore, we feel the preparation process should be viewed from two distinct points in a student's progress through school. One point begins at age fourteen and the second begins at age sixteen. At fourteen years of age, or younger if appropriate, the preparation process should be where schools identify students who will need transition services. In determining the need for transition service, schools can plan and consider the appropriate program designed to meet the student's needs when it is required at age sixteen. This process can then focus on the course of study that will better prepare students to attain their desired adult outcomes. For example, if a student's desired outcome is to secure a job, a transition service need might be to enroll the student in a career development class to explore options and specific jobs related to that career. This means that the educational experiences and all courses of study reflect the stated outcome. For a student with a significant disability, transition needs must be identified early and services begun as early as possible. This part of the plan can be seen as a multi-year plan that is updated at least annually. A checklist of what things need to be considered when transition planning begins at age fourteen is seen in Table 4.2 and after age sixteen in Table 4.3.

Beginning at age sixteen the IEP must contain a results (outcome)-related statement leading to the transition service plan, which includes, if appropriate, a statement of interagency responsibilities. This part of the preparation process begins to clarify how the coordinated set of activities will move students from school to adult life. This statement of needed transition service is based on students' needs, taking into account their strengths, preferences, and interests. It begins to coordinate the activities needed to help students attain successful adult outcomes. It does so by implementing strategies to improve students' academic and functional achievement to facilitate movement to postschool activities, including postsecondary education, vocational education, integrated employment, continuing adult education, adult services, independent living,

TABLE 4.2 Transition Planning Considerations When the Student Is Fourteen to Sixteen Years Old

- The student's interests and preferences have been identified and documented.
- Courses of study have been identified and relate to the student's postschool outcomes.
- Educational and community experiences have been identified and relate to the student's postschool outcomes.
- The various life domains have been assessed and the student's needs for learning have been identified.
- Options to explore the various interests and preferences chosen by the student are included in the IEP/transition document.
- The student is encouraged to make choices and decisions along the way, in planning and implementing his/her IEP goals.
- The student is learning self-advocacy and self-determination skills so that he/she can communicate needs in all domains of life.
- Accommodations and modifications are being explored as potential tools for accessing work, housing, and the community at large.
- The student is provided with opportunities for developing friendships and relationships in and out of school.
- The student is given opportunities for accessing transportation services, learning how to access public and private transportation.
- The student is being exposed to the concept of money management and purchasing power as a consumer.
- The student has acquired an identification card that contains personal information.
- The student is learning about practices of a healthy lifestyle and personal health and hygiene care.
- The student and family are actively exploring community resources that may likely support the student beyond school.

TABLE 4.3   Transition Planning Considerations When the Student Is Sixteen Years or Older

- Linkages with community services providers have been identified and made for services the student may likely need after graduation.
- Community services providers, VR, DD Services, Adult Service providers, have been invited to attend and participate in the IEP/transition meeting.
- The student and family have been provided with information about adult service agencies and have arranged visits and meetings with these identified linkages in the community.
- The student and family have completed necessary applications for services to determine eligibility of services requested beyond school.
- The student and family have determined the need for financial support such as Supplemental Security Income, Medical Assistance services, etc. and have gathered information and completed the appropriate application process.
- The student, with assistance as necessary, has developed a portfolio or résumé for employment and/or postsecondary education.
- The student is actively learning the skills needed for independent living.
- The student has identified a specific job choice and is taking the steps necessary to obtain the job upon exiting from school. Steps have been clarified and are being taken to secure the needed employment supports from an adult service provider.
- The student is learning responsible behavior that is necessary for success in employment and other community settings in adulthood.
- The student is taking the necessary steps to register to vote and to apply for selective services if appropriate.

or community participation. The coordinated activities can be provided and incorporated in the students' IEPs in the following ways.

- **Strategies in Instruction** are what the student needs in terms of modifications and/or accommodations that will benefit him or her to be successful in the curriculum.
- **Strategies in Related Services** are those services from which the student is benefiting, such as occupational, physical, and speech therapies, counseling and/or medical services. It should be noted that transportation is a related service that should be considered when discussing community-based options. Also, vocational counseling may be a related service. If the related services are needed beyond school, the IEP should identify linkages to adult service providers before the student leaves school as part of the transition plan.
- **Strategies in Community Experiences** are those activities provided outside the school building or in the community. These community experiences can include work experiences and job exploration as well as any other form of community-based education and training, such as travel training, shopping, and so forth, that the student might need to achieve postschool outcomes.
- **Strategies in Employment** are activities that may be related to career awareness, career exploration, and/or career preparation.

■ **Strategies in Adult Living** are activities that lead toward developing awareness, skills, and competencies in adult activities, such as voting, renting an apartment, being responsible, and so forth.

The transition services plan should address the above listed areas in terms of responsibilities and/or any needed linkages for the student. An important question to ask is: "How are we ensuring that the student is linked to the needed postschool services and supports?"

Consider This! If you are currently working with students of transition age (age fourteen and up), review the lists in Tables 4.2 and 4.3 and decide how many of these areas have been considered by and/or applied to your students. Have any of these steps been neglected? If so, what can you do to ensure that the necessary steps are being taken?

Now that we have a better understanding of some of the most important aspects of the transition planning process, let's apply it in the transition planning meeting.

THE IEP MEETING FOR TRANSITION PLANNING

The IEP meeting for transition planning works best when students and family members are actively involved and play an important role in the planning and preparation. Teachers, administrators, and support agencies must work with students and families to reach the long-range goals (outcomes) described in the IEP. Transition planning is a complex process that requires knowledge and understanding of the regulations as well as best practice in education and community-based services. No wonder Mrs. Rose was so stressed and intimidated at the IEP meeting for her son James in the opening scenario in this chapter. Participants on the IEP/transition planning team should be clear about their roles and responsibilities in order to achieve maximum effectiveness.

IEP/Transition Planning Team

The IEP/transition planning team is composed of many people who are there to assist the student in planning and preparing for adult life. Some members of the team are required by regulation to be present while others, although not required, may be helpful to the process in achieving the desired results. Members of the team that are required to attend are the Local Education Agency (LEA), teacher(s) (Special Education and Regular Education), evaluators (Psychologist, etc.), parents, and the student. Members of the team that are not required to attend and may be invited by the parents and/or student are family members or friends who know the student well, employers (potential employers or current), co-workers, community members who have interacted with the student, and/or parent advocates. Depending on the specific needs of students, other members of the team that must be invited by the school may include representatives of Vocational Rehabilitation, the local Developmental Disabilities or Mental Retardation Office, and/or community rehabilitation services providers. The specific agencies to be invited are selected based on students' specific needs and their desired future outcomes. (Note: more detailed descriptions of these various agencies are provided in Chapter 5.)

As previously stated, members of the IEP/transition planning team have important roles and responsibilities that can make them effective contributing members of the team and the process. The following provides a brief discussion of the roles and responsibilities of some of the key people in the planning process. Additional information regarding roles and responsibilities of the family and student were discussed in previous chapters in this book.

Students: The student, no matter what or how significant the disability may be, is the central member of the team. The student is the reason for this planning and the purpose for conducting the transition plan. The student is the reason for the meeting and should be the focus of the team. The student should be an active participant in all aspects of the transition process. The IEP team must specifically invite the student to attend any meeting in which the team will be considering transition services. The transition planning process is something that is done with the student, not *for* the student. The student's IEP/transition plan must be based on his or her individual needs, strengths, interests, and preferences that reflect needs for now and after school (NCSET, 2002). As discussed in Chapter 2, this is why the provision of self-determination skill training is an important educational ingredient of the planning process (Durlak & Rose, 1999). Preparing the student to participate is not a requirement of schools but if we expect students and parents to actively participate and be contributing members of the team, school districts should consider working with them in preparation for the IEP/transition meeting by implementing the steps listed in Table 4.4.

Consider This! We cannot assume that students will be ready to participate in planning without advanced preparation and support, as discussed in Chapter 2. What is currently being used in your school or district that prepares students to participate in the IEP/transition process? To what degree are students actually participating actively in their own transition planning meetings?

Parents: Along with students, parents are the most important members of the IEP/transition planning team. They know their children better than anyone else and will be their best advocates throughout their lives. They will be their children's primary case managers, social workers, and guides as they navigate through the educational and adult services system. Parents are often the key to making the transition from school to adult life a successful one. They bring information and knowledge about their children's interests, behaviors at home, and interactions in the community as well as pertinent medical histories. It is unfortunate that, sometimes, parents who are knowledgeable about their child and understand their legal rights are viewed negatively by schools and professionals. They challenge the school district, teachers, and professionals. But these parents should be welcomed and seen as an asset to the planning process. Through the active participation of families, schools can begin to better understand families' values about important issues that may affect the transition of students into adult life. The information shared may help teachers to better under-

TABLE 4.4 Steps to Take Before the IEP/Transition Meeting

Work with Students:

- Assist students to identify and determine their needs, preferences, and interests related to life after high school.
- Assist the student in creating a vision for him- or herself, a positive view of life based on interests and preferences, perhaps by creating a journal to write down their thoughts about the future.
- Role-play the IEP/transition meeting so the student knows what to expect.
- Meet with the student and help prepare a list of questions that will engage the student in the discussion and provide a basis for participation.
- Help the student in becoming a selfadvocate. Teach selfadvocacy and selfdetermination skills.
- Provide students opportunities to make choices daily in the classroom and out.
- Provide students with experiences that are broad and offer a varied view of the possibilities in life.
- Formally invite students to the IEP/transition planning meeting.

Work with Parents:

- Assist parents in identifying their child's needs, interests, and preferences with regard to life after high school.
- Assist parents in creating a vision for their son or daughter for life after high school. That is, what are the expectations for work, housing, community participation, etc. for their son or daughter?
- Provide information and explain the adult service world process (VR, DD, SSI/Medicaid, etc.), particularly with regard to the eligibility requirements of adult services.
- Assist parents in planning and meeting with those services that are likely to assist their child when he or she leaves school.
- Assist and prepare parents to develop specific questions regarding transition.
- Provide a written invitation to participate in the IEP/transition meeting, that includes that the purpose of the meeting will be to consider transition services, that the student will be invited, and that other agencies will be invited.

stand what services may be needed and necessary for the student beyond school. Parents, when invited to the IEP meeting, must be informed that transition will be discussed at the meeting so that they can be prepared to discuss outcome issues for their children. They should also be notified that, when their children reach the age of majority, certain rights transfer to the adult students and what that implies for future invitations to meetings. That is, when students reach the age of majority, they may choose not to invite their parents to their meeting.

Special Education and General Education Teachers: IDEA requires that at least one teacher who provides educational services to the student attend. Also, general education teachers who are knowledgeable about the general education curriculum must be in attendance. These professionals' knowledge of the student regarding classroom performance and needs, strengths, interests, preferences, likes/dislikes, and vision for life will be helpful to the process.

Local Education Agency Representative (LEA): IDEA requires that an LEA representative who knows about the availability of resources and services of the school attend the meeting. This person must be qualified to supervise the provision of special education services, including transition services. These representatives of the district will ultimately approve the financial cost of the services and the personnel who will support the activities and functions of the IEP/transition plan.

Other Agencies: When transition services are going to be discussed, agencies outside of the school district must be invited to participate. These agencies may be varied depending on the need, disability, and age of the student, but generally they are state vocational rehabilitation services, county mental health or developmental disabilities services, adult service providers, and/or postsecondary programs. The agencies that are the most critical to invite are those who will most likely be asked to pay for services when the student leaves school. It is important to note that many public and private agencies that offer adult services have eligibility criteria or waiting lists to receive services. School personnel, students, and parents should be made aware of what the eligibility criteria are and if there is a waiting list for the types of services the student may potentially need when he or she exits school. Some important questions to consider are: How long is the waiting list? What are the criteria that would qualify the student for the services needed? What are the choices in obtaining and/or purchasing the service needs? These are just a few of the questions that may help guide school personnel in determining how to proceed in the planning process. The procedures for services beyond school differ for different agencies and should be known by school personnel as well as by parents and students. There should be a clear understanding of how a student becomes eligible for services. Attendance and participation of adult service representatives at the IEP/transition planning meeting can provide some clarity to these issues. It should also be noted that some providers offer their services before the student graduates, which can provide a smooth transition from school to adult life. When outside agencies are invited but do not attend, school personnel should contact the agency representatives, solicit their ideas, and document the conversation. This ensures that these agencies were at least notified, were made aware of the student and his or her needs for future services, and that they were consulted on critical future issues.

When the members of the team can effectively play their part and participate in the IEP/transition planning team, a smooth transition will occur for the student from school to adult life. It is their collaborative efforts and this coordinated set of activities that will make the process successful.

THE PLANNING MEETING

As discussed in Chapter 1, transition planning is a process that evolves over the life span of the student's school career. Planning for adult life begins when students first begin school in pre-school and kindergarten. At this very early level they begin to understand the concept of personal responsibility, social skill development and begin to establish a work ethic. Along with the student's family, schools and teachers play an important role in developing these important values in life. But schools do not generally discuss transition for the preparation for adult life at these early stages in a student's school life. So we recommend that discussions about transition and preparation for adult life begin as early as fourteen years of age.

Although it may seem complicated to coordinate the various members of the team and the different roles that each has, and to work toward a common goal that prepares students for adult life, we must realize that the process of transition does not have to be an all-or-nothing process. That is, we do not have to wait for all the prerequisites and conditions to be in place before transition can be implemented. Transition can begin at any level simply by conceptualizing a process and a goal and working toward achieving that goal (Cavaiuolo, 1993). The IEP/transition team conceptualizes this process and develops a shared vision for the student that will help design a plan that leads to the desired outcomes for the student.

There are a number of steps that may be taken to ensure that the planning meeting is successful. These are described below.

Prepare for the Transition Planning Meeting

One of the key factors in making transition effective and successful is being prepared for the meeting. Prior to the meeting the team leader or facilitator should have information organized to keep everyone focused on the student, the outcomes being identified, and how those outcomes will be achieved. Being prepared means having information from the student's person centered plan, parent/guardian questionnaires (if they are available), and pertinent assessments and documents that are relevant to leading the team in furthering their discussion about the student.

Make Introductions and Clarify the Purpose

After the introductions, the purpose of the meeting should be stated so everyone understands that one of the major areas that will be discussed is transition. It should be made clear that the primary purpose is to discuss the student's and his or her family's vision for life after high school and how each member of the team will play a role and assist in achieving that outcome. It should be the hope of the team leader that each member of the team develop a common understanding of the expectations for the meeting and that their efforts be focused on those expectations. Members of the team should be encouraged to use their knowledge of their professional training to problem solve and develop solutions to issues that will lead to the stated outcomes of the student. As described in Chapter 2, students should take as active a role as possible in their meetings, including serving as facilitators who lead the meetings.

Sequence the IEP and Transition Discussion

Many states around the country have the option of designing their own IEP format to be used by school districts. That is, some state Department of Education Offices will design the IEP document whereas other states may allow individual districts to format their own IEP document. This creates much variation to the IEP document/forms. Unfortunately, many IEP forms are designed so that the transition section is located toward the back of the document. If this is the case, then the IEP meeting tends to begin with a discussion on the present level of performance of the student, leading to annual goals and objectives and then a discussion on transition. In most instances this is done simply because it follows the sequence and order of the IEP document as it is formatted. Figure 4.1 depicts this sequence of the planning meeting, which is counter-productive and is *not* recommended. The concern here is that if this order of sequence is followed, transition may become a secondary discussion in the IEP meeting and may lack the primary attention needed. That is, if the annual goals and objectives are completed before the transition section, which asks to identify the student's outcomes, then the IEP will lack the connection to the postschool outcomes.

Even though the order of the IEP document may be formatted in a way that transition is presented later in the document, it is recommended that the transition section be discussed *first*. Figure 4.2 depicts this recommended planning sequence.

As we have discussed throughout this chapter, the desired adult outcomes must be a driving force in transition planning from which other annual learning statements and services are derived (Steere & Cavaiuolo, 1999). Figure 4.3 shows the relationship of transition outcomes to annual goals and short-term objectives.

Thus, during the IEP planning meeting, the desired postschool outcomes are the starting point which should drive all of the other educational components of the IEP. Once this is done, the next discussion point should be the student's current abilities and the course of study that support the desired postschool outcomes. If the student is sixteen years of age (or younger), all of the components of the IEP that are related to transition are completed, including needed instruction, services, and linkages to adult service agencies that will provide needed services.

In order for this process to be effective and to realize the outcomes of a student in the most positive way, it is essential to follow the sequence shown above in Figure 4.2. Notice that in the sequence that schools often use but that is not recommended (Figure 4.1), the student's school outcomes are not discussed until later in the process. That means in this sequence the annual goals, and subsequent course of study, are developed first without considering the student's outcomes, therefore making the plan ineffective in addressing the student's postschool outcomes. If the student's outcomes

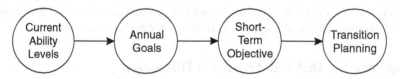

FIGURE 4.1   Sequence of the IEP/Transition Planning Process in Which Transition Outcomes Are Discussed Last (Not Recommended)

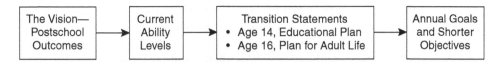

FIGURE 4.2 **Sequence of the IEP/Transition Planning Process in Which Transition Outcomes Are Discussed First (Recommended)**

are considered and discussed first, as shown in Figure 4.2, the annual goals and subsequent course of study are addressed and implemented within the context of the long-range transition plan, thereby increasing the likelihood that the student's postschool outcomes will be achieved.

Clarify Participant Responsibilities in an Action Plan

Once the student's needs and services have been identified, each member of the team should be allocated some responsibility to the transition process with the student. These responsibilities should be considered to be an action plan component, that is, specific steps to be accomplished, with timelines and responsibilities delineated. Although there is no one format for such an action plan, schools are encouraged to develop their own or adapt an existing format. For example, Wehman's Individualized Transition Plan (ITP) format provides a well-structured action plan that can serve as a useful addendum to the IEP document (Wehman, 1995, 1998, 2004). The responsibilities in the action plan should also include steps the student and his or her family may need to complete (as discussed in previous chapters). The service needs should be

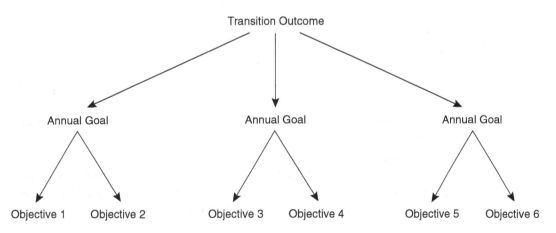

FIGURE 4.3 **Relationship of Transition Outcomes to Annual Goals and Short-Term Objectives**

Source: Adapted from Steere & Cavaiuolo, 1999.

prioritized and given to each member of the team to complete and report back on. The student and his or her family are encouraged to provide feedback and add other suggestions to what is being discussed. Throughout the meeting the student and his or her family should be asked for their input and opinions on the services and any other issues of concern.

Summarize the Meeting Results

At the conclusion of the meeting, the team leader/facilitator should summarize the postschool outcomes, the course of study or the activities that will lead to the stated outcomes, who will assist and be responsible for each of the priorities and services identified, and how each will report back on the progress being made. The members of the team should be reminded that their involvement and responsibility are the key for a successful outcome for the student. It is important that everyone understand how vital it is that everyone complete and follow through on their responsibilities.

For the team leader of the IEP meeting, the challenge is to keep everyone focused on the important areas of the plan. The team leader must be focused on ensuring that the student and parents are participating in the process, that the IEP/transition plan is meeting the spirit and legal aspects of the law, that the other members of the team understand and fulfill their roles and responsibilities, and that everyone leaves feeling positive about the process they were just involved in. Table 4.5 offers a list of things to remember during the IEP/transition meeting.

Consider This!   If you have the opportunity to participate in an IEP meeting for a transition-aged student, ask yourself these questions: What is the sequence of events at the meeting? What role do participants play in the meeting? In particular, what role does the student and his or her family play in the meeting? Are roles and responsibilities for follow-up activities clearly delineated?

In essence, the planning team should keep in mind the A-B-C's of transition planning:

> **A—Advocate** on behalf of the student and his or her family to think about life after high school.
>
> **B—Believe** and have faith in the student's desires and dreams that make up the postschool outcomes.
>
> **C—Collaborate** with community agencies on behalf of the student and his or her interests in life.
>
> **D—Design** school programs that offer experiences and provide the needed skills and training that will lead the student to the desired postschool outcomes.
>
> **E—Ensure** that linkages are made for the needed services on behalf of the student to achieve the desired postschool outcomes.

If these areas are considered and adhered to, services that are provided will have a greater chance to result in a smooth transition to adult life. But an effective planning

TABLE 4.5   Things to Remember During the IEP/Transition Meeting

- Transition and the postschool outcomes should drive the IEP process.
- Involve the student and his or her parents as equal partners of the planning team.
- If the student is age fourteen (strongly recommended) and no older than sixteen (required), complete a Statement of Needed Transition Services that:

  —is a long range plan
  —is based on the student's needs, strengths, interests, and preferences
  —includes a coordinated set of activities and strategies in the areas of:
  –Instruction
  –Related Services
  –Employment
  –Functional Vocational Evaluation
  –Post School Adult Living
  –Community Experiences
  –Daily Living Skills

- Make sure to include specification of linkages with adult service agencies, including contact information for each agency representative.
- Identify all the people who are responsible for supporting the activities listed on the transition IEP. Write down the steps that are to be taken along with timelines in the form of an action plan. Make sure to agree on a strategy for reporting on progress toward achieving these action plan steps.
- If the student is of the age of majority, make sure that the student has been informed of his or her rights. Likewise, ensure that the family has been informed of the student's rights when he or she turns the age of majority.
- Develop annual goals and short-term objectives that relate to the postschool outcomes.

meeting is not enough, as the transition IEP document itself must be clearly written. Since the IEP is a legal document, it must be written so that it meets the requirements as well as the student's needs. We discuss the writing of the transition IEP in the next section.

THE TRANSITION IEP

Before one articulates in writing a student's IEP/transition plan, the program must create a value and a common belief that supports the outcomes that lead to what Turnbull and Luckasson (2001) call "enviable lives." It is based on a clear understanding of the regulations as well as a clear philosophy of transition with regards to inclusion in the school, the community, and the world. This belief and philosophy must be articulated and put into practice. Therefore, schools must clearly define their values and vision for the implementation and follow-through of a student's IEP/transition program. This will create a common ground for all the members of the team to participate and design a plan that truly reflects a "results-oriented process."

The quality of an effective transition program is seen in both practice and in writing. As previously mentioned, it is not enough to adhere to IDEA's regulations and guidelines for transition planning, but they must also be reflected in the written IEP document. It is important to ensure that the document changes annually to reflect the student's changing desires, needs, and expectations for his or her future. It is not enough to simply say that a school is providing best practices in transition services and planning; it must also be well documented and written in a clear and coherent way in the IEP. While some consider the "transition plan" as a separate planning process from the IEP, it is important to remember that the IEP must contain sections that specifically address transition. The IDEA (Individuals with Disabilities Education Improvement Acts) of 1990, 1997, and IDEA 2004 (Individuals with Disabilities Education Improvement Act of 2004) specifically address what needs to be contained in the IEP, and there is no mention of a separate document called the "transition plan." There has always been only one planning document, which we will refer to as the transition IEP. IDEA 2004 describes the required transition IEP as: ". . . beginning not later than the first IEP to be in effect when the child is 16, and updated annually thereafter" and including ". . . appropriate measurable postsecondary goals based upon age appropriate transition assessments related to training, education, employment, and, where appropriate, independent living skills" and "the transition services (including courses of study) needed to assist the child in reaching those goals. . . ." (IDEA 2004, Sec. 614; Johnson, 2005).

States generally develop and design a format for their own transition IEP documents. In fact some states even go as far as giving that option to the individual school districts to develop and design the format of the transition IEP (e.g., New Jersey). Since we have determined earlier in this chapter that transition planning should be the driving force to the IEP, let's consider the components of an effective transition IEP.

As mentioned above, the transition IEP document may take on many different looks, depending on the format that each state adopts. Regardless of the many looks that the document may take on, the content of any document must contain the sections discussed earlier in this chapter. Therefore, the format that is presented in this book is just a sample of what you might see in your own state's IEP forms, specifically the sections that are relevant to transition planning. We provide a sample format for the transition sections of an IEP in Figure 4.4 and a completed example in Figure 4.5. An alternative format that may be used is shown in Figure 4.6.

If students are likely to need supports and services beyond graduation from high school, the transition IEP should identify the appropriate community agencies (typically referred to as *linkages*) that will assist them to continue to receive the needed supports and services in order to continue or maintain the desired postschool outcomes or to sustain an adequate healthy life. The transition IEP should contain a section that identifies the needed postschool supports and services, the name of the agency or organization that provides the support or service, and a contact person to the agency. These are shown on the second part of our sample transition section of an IEP in Figures 4.4 and 4.5. These community linkages may be critical for potential funding of supports and services or for health-related services. For example, the student may continue to need psychological counseling to address his anger and ex-

FIGURE 4.4   Transition Components of an IEP

(Note: Only the components that directly address transition planning are shown.)

Student:

D.O.B.:

Identify the student's needs, including strengths, preferences, and interests:

Student's Desired Postschool Outcomes (Vision for the Future):

Postsecondary Education:

Employment:

Community Participation:

Residential/Housing:

Recreation/Leisure:

Specific Skills To Be Learned in Order to Attain the Desired Outcomes:
Skills   *IEP Goal #*

Plan for Provision of Transition Services:
(These steps should include needed instruction, related services, community experiences, acquisition of daily living and other skills, or functional vocational evaluation.)
Service   *Timelines/Responsibilities*

Linkages with Adult Service Agencies:
Agency   *Contact Information*

---

plosive behaviors. A community agency that provides this service can be identified, a referral made to the agency, and a contact/intake visit arranged. (We will discuss the range of community rehabilitation agencies that may be important in transition planning in the next chapter.) It should be noted that, even though schools are ultimately responsible for the completion of transition IEPs, including inviting agencies

FIGURE 4.5 Sample Transition Components of an IEP

(Note: Only the components that directly address transition planning are shown.)

Student: *Shawn Tyrell*

D.O.B.: *7/8/88 (age 17)*

Identify the student's needs, including strengths, preferences, and interests:
Shawn needs specific services to help prepare him for entry into supported employment when he exits school. He needs to learn skills that will allow him to live semi-independently. Shawn likes to be outdoors so potential employment opportunities should be explored that include outdoor work. Shawn is a good visual learner and does best when pictorial/written directions are provided.

Student's Desired Postschool Outcomes (Vision for the Future):

Postsecondary Education: *Shawn will take adult courses through the county adult education program to further develop his skills in cooking and home finances.*

Employment: *Shawn will obtain a job working in a job that includes working outdoors some of the time. This job should be obtained through a supported employment service provider.*

Community Participation: *Shawn will be involved in his local community through his church, shopping at local stores, and through recreation and leisure activities, and will use public transportation to access these environments.*

Residential/Housing: *Shawn will live in a supported apartment with one or two other room mates.*

Recreation/Leisure: *Shawn will use community recreation and leisure activities, including the YMCA pool, the mall, and the park for hiking/walking.*

Specific Skills To Be Learned in Order to Attain the Desired Outcomes:

Skills   *IEP Goal #*
Appropriate interaction with others while working
Following more complex written directions
Cooking
*Home financial management (paying bills, use of
    checkbook, etc.)*
Grocery shopping
How to use the bus system

Plan for Provision of Transition Services:
(These steps should include needed instruction, related services, community experiences, acquisition of daily living and other skills, or functional vocational evaluation.)

(continued)

FIGURE 4.5 Continued

Service	Timelines/Responsibilities
Community-based work experience, once per week	*Start 9/05; Ms. Wu (teacher) and Mr. Watson (transition coordinator)*
Development of skills for home living	*Start 9/05; Ms. Wu, supported by practice at home (Shawn & Mr. & Mrs. Tyrell)*
Physical Therapy	*Start 9/05; Mr. Seimon (PT)*
Speech Therapy	*9/05; Ms. Rodriguez (speech therapist)*
Interest inventories and situational vocational assessment	*10/05; Mr. Watson & Shawn*
Community-based travel training	*10/05; Mr. Watson, supported by practice in the home community (Shawn and Mr. & Mrs. Tyrell)*

Linkages with Adult Service Agencies:

Agency	Contact Information
Office of Vocational Rehabilitation	*Lisa Renen (rehabilitation counselor)*
Office of Mental Retardation	*Sidney Addison (supports coordinator)*
Progressive Employment, Inc.	*Molly Sumner (Director of supported employment programs)*

(linkages), school personnel do not have to assume sole responsibility for contacting agencies. The responsibility for contacting organizations, arranging site visits, or even for completing referral forms can be, and perhaps should be, given to students and/or their families. For example, for many students, a particularly important linkage is the public Vocational Rehabilitation department. Even though the VR counselor is typically invited to attend the IEP meeting to discuss transition, the referral and any additional visits to the VR office can be arranged by students and their families. The school can simply follow up to ensure or encourage the follow through with the postschool linkages.

GENERIC TRANSITION PLANNING PRACTICES

Steere, Rose, and Gregory (1996) identified six "generic planning practices" as a guide for effective transition planning for students with diverse disabilities. These principles form a set of beliefs about the purpose and nature of transition planning.

FIGURE 4.6   Statement of Transition Service Needs

Beginning at age 14, or younger if appropriate, develop the long-range educational plan for the student's future.

Identify the student's needs, including strengths, preferences, and interests:

Student's Desired Postschool Outcomes (Vision for the Future):

Postsecondary Education: _____

Employment: _____

Community Participation: _____

Residential/Housing: _____

Recreation/Leisure: _____

List the student's course of study for the next four years while considering the desired postschool outcomes and the student's interests and preferences (Note: It is only required that the next year's course of study be listed, the additional years are projected which can be changed at the next IEP meeting.)

Grade 9: _____

_____

Grade 10: _____

_____

Grade 11: _____

_____

Grade 12: _____

Beginning at age 16, or younger if appropriate, develop a multi-year plan with a coordinated set of activities and strategies for the student that will promote the desired postschool outcomes while considering his/her interests and preferences.

FIGURE 4.6 Continued			
ACTIVITY/STRATEGIES	BEGINNING DATE	AGENCY OR PERSON PROVIDING SERVICE	RESPONSIBILITIES
Instruction:			
Related Services:			
Community Experiences:			
Employment or Other Postschool Objective:			
Daily Living Skills:			
Functional/Vocational Evaluation:			

Clarification of a Vision of Success to Guide Transition Efforts

Understanding and developing a clear path to the future is essential for effective transition planning. The vision of what students and their families see as postschool outcomes must be understood and become the driving force behind effective transition planning.

Close Collaboration and Support of Family and Significant Others

The effort to include the family and the student in the planning process is critical. It is important that school personnel and other professionals not overwhelm the student and/or family. Professionals should make it comfortable for the student and his or her family to participate in decisions and be equal partners in the process.

Dynamic Assessment Processes Based upon Relevant Questions

Questions should not be focused solely on whether the student has certain skills to participate in an activity or task but on the desired situations to which the student is best matched. Supports are then discussed as supplementary aids that will allow the student to participate successfully in the chosen activity or task in the natural environment. Assessment processes must be varied and must focus on students' future aspirations, current support systems, as well as skills, abilities, and aptitudes. These assessment processes must also be ecological, that is, include an analysis of the interaction of students with current and future community environments (Bates, 2002).

Reference of Curricula to Local Community Environments

Students are more likely to be prepared for adult life if their instruction is in settings that are functional and relevant to their learning. That is, the curriculum for teaching should be taught in "real" community-based settings. This requires that educators analyze current and future environments to which the student will transition and teach the student the skills needed to be successful in those environments (Falvey, 1989).

Individual Sequences of Assistance to Enhance Optimal Learning

This principle focuses on the need for instruction to be systematic and individualized. A thorough assessment of each student's learning styles should be conducted in order to identify and use effective teaching strategies. Learning should be made functional and relevant to the transition outcomes, with activities that lead to the desired postschool outcomes. Gold's philosophy that student learning is the responsibility of educators and is dependent on their skill, creativity, and commitment is a foundation for this principle (Gold, 1981).

Connections to Sources of Community Support

Connections to adult services and to natural community supports should be in place before students exit the special education system. Depending on students' specific needs, connections to adult services are generally made with Vocational Rehabilitation, Developmental Disabilities Offices, Social Security, and Medical Assistance Offices, and private nonprofit provider agencies. These agencies and organizations are typically potential sources of funding and support for students beyond high school. Students and families must be made aware that applying for services does not guarantee that services will be available. They should also be made aware that the aforementioned services are not entitlements as in the educational system but the student must meet certain eligibility criteria to receive and qualify for services. This is critical for students and families to understand, particularly where the state's fund is categorical in nature. That means that funding is made available for specific disability categories such as "mental retardation" and limited, if any at all, for other disabilities. They should be made aware of the potential waiting list for services, how long they may have to wait, and what the services are. One additional important point is that vocational rehabilitation plays a particularly important role in the transition planning process. Although rehabilitation counselors may be reluctant to open students' cases for services before they graduate from school, students should be able to apply for services and determine eligibility during their final year of school.

If these six generic practices are taken into consideration when writing the IEP/transition document, it will be an effective program in both practice and in writing.

CHAPTER SUMMARY

In this chapter we have discussed the transition planning process. The transition planning requirements of the Individuals with Disabilities Education Improvement Act of 2004 (IDEA 2004) were presented. We discussed how postschool outcomes might be obtained using a person centered planning approach. The roles and responsibilities of the members of the planning team were also presented. The critical point was made about the IEP meeting and the importance of attending to the transition outcomes first before developing the annual goals and objectives. Finally, we described the essential components of a transition IEP and discussed how it should be a clearly written working document that leads to successful postschool outcomes. It is our hope that this chapter has provided enough information for future and current teachers to be able to participate in or conduct an effective IEP/transition meeting,

TABLE 4.6 Questions to Guide Assessment of Transition Services

1. Is the student invited to the IEP/transition meeting?
2. How are the student's needs, strengths, interests, and preferences considered in the development of the IEP?
3. Are parents notified of the time and location of the meeting and are they made aware that transition will be discussed at the meeting?
4. Are community linkages invited to attend and participate in the IEP meeting?
5. If other agencies do not attend, does the school make an effort to obtain their input in the student's transition plan?
6. Was information about government funding sources, such as Developmental Disabilities, Vocational Rehabilitation, Social Security Administration, provided to the family or student?
7. Are the student's postschool outcomes clearly stated and specific to meeting the goals and objectives of the IEP?
8. If the student is sixteen years or older, does the IEP include a statement of needed transition services that are based on the student's needs, strengths, interests, and preferences?
9. Does the statement of needed transition services contain information on instruction, related services, community experiences, employment, and adult living objectives?

adhere to the requirements of the law, and provide a quality transition service to all students, regardless of their disability.

APPLICATION ACTIVITIES

The application activities listed below are essential for your continued learning and skill development in transition. Each of the activities will require your time and energy but will help you develop your professional skills in this area.

For Practice and Enhanced Understanding:

Identify how transition services are being conducted at your school or another school and determine how well they match the requirements of IDEA 2004. Is the school complying with the statements listed in Table 4.1?

Using the questions from Table 4.6, evaluate your school's or another school's compliance with the transition regulations. What areas of corrections would you recommend? How would these changes be implemented? How would you ensure continued compliance and effectiveness?

Using Tables 4.2 and 4.3 as guides, evaluate how your school is currently doing in implementing some of these important planning practices. Develop a checklist from these tables and determine how your school is preparing students at each stage of the process. What would be some of your recommendations for improving the process?

For Your Portfolio:

Using the information provided in Tables 4.4 and 4.5, develop at least two specific strategies to assist students and parents to participate more actively in the IEP meetings that focus on transition planning. Remember that many of these strategies to increase student and family participation can occur before actual meetings take place, while other strategies focus on improving how the meeting itself is conducted. What is currently in place in your school? What are some recommendations for change?

Conduct a record review of a student's IEP where transition was discussed. As you review the student's IEP, identify if the student's outcomes were discussed first as a starting point for determining the goals and objectives. Does the student's course of study reflect his or her long-term aspirations for adult life (outcomes)? Does the student have some responsibility in the process? Were linkages with community sources specified, and what role did these agencies play in the planning process?

RESOURCES AND WEBSITES

The following resources and websites will allow you to extend your knowledge about the transition planning process. Consider including these resources in your professional portfolio.

Transition Research Institute at Illinois

Research and training about effective transition practices. Includes list of model transition projects in each of the United States.
www.ed.uiuc.edu

National Longitudinal Transition Studies-2

Summaries of data from the NLTS2.
www.nlts2.org

NICHY National Dissemination Center

Transition Guidelines publication available.
www.nichcy.org

National Center on Secondary Education and Transition (NCSET)

Website about strategies for improving transition planning.
www.ncset.org

National Joint Committee on Learning Disabilities

Article available about strategies for effective transition planning for students with learning disabilities.
www.ldonline.org

AAMR

Information and advocacy regarding individuals with intellectual disabilities. Includes links to local chapters.
www.aamr.org

ARC of the United States

Information and advocacy regarding people with intellectual and developmental disabilities. Includes links to local chapters.
www.thearc.org

TASH

Information and advocacy for people with disabilities, particularly severe and multiple disabilities. Includes links to local chapters.
www.tash.org

New Freedom Initiative's Online Resource

Federal interagency website to give access to information and resources for people with disabilities.
www.disabilityinfo.gov

Institute on Community Inclusion

Supports the rights of children and adults with disabilities to participate in all aspects of the community. Conducts research and education about effective strategies for promoting the inclusion of people with disabilities.
www.communityinclusion.org

REFERENCES

Bates, P. (2002). Instructional assessment. In K. Storey, P. Bates, & D. Hunter (Eds.), *The road ahead: Transition to adult life for persons with disabilities* (pp. 25–45). St. Augustine, FL: Training Resource Network, Inc.

Benz, R. M., & Doren, B. (1997). School-to-work components that predict post-school success for students with and without disabilities. *Exceptional Children, 63,* 151–166.

Chambers, C., Hughes, C., & Carter, E. (2004). Parent and sibling perspectives in the transition to adulthood. *Education and Training in Developmental Disabilities, 39,* 79–94.

Carter, E., & Wehby, J. (2003). Job performance of transition-age youth with emotional and behavioral disorders. *Exceptional Children, 69,* 449–465.

Cavaiuolo, D. (1993). Systems change and its relation to transition from school to adult life: A collaborative process. *Transition from school to adult life for people with disabilities: Best practices and planning a process of transition into adult life.* New Jersey Department of Education Office of Special Education Programs Monograms.

Dickinson, L. D., & Verbeek, L. R. (2002). Wage differences between college graduates with and without learning disabilities. *Journal of Learning Disabilities, 20,* 175–185.

Durlak, C. M., Rose, E., & Bursuck, W.D. (1994). Preparing high school students with learning disabilities for the transition to postsecondary education: Teaching the skills of self-determination. *Journal of Learning Disabilities, 27,* 51–59.

Falvey, M. (1989). *Community-based curriculum: Instructional strategies for students with severe handicaps* (2nd ed.). Baltimore: Paul Brookes.

Furney, S. K., & Hasazi, B. S. (1997). Transition policies, practices and promises: Lessons from three states. *Exceptional Children, 63,* 343–356.

Flexer, R., Simmons, T., Luft, P., & Baer, R. (2005). *Transition planning for secondary students with disabilities* (2nd ed.). Upper Saddle River, NJ: Merrill.

Gold, M. (1981). *"Did I say that?": Commentaries on the Try Another Way System.* Champaign, IL: Research Press.

Grigal, M., Test, D., Beattie, J., & Wood, W. (1997). An evaluation of transition components of Individualized Education Programs. *Exceptional Children, 63,* 357–372.

Held, M., Thoma, C., & Thomas, K. (2004). "The John Jones Show": How one teacher facilitated self-determined transition planning for a young man with autism. *Focus on Autism and Other Developmental Disabilities, 19,* 177–188.

Johnson, D. (2005). Key provisions on transition: A comparison of IDEA 1997 and IDEA 2004. *Career Development for Exceptional Individuals, 28,* 60–63.

Katsiyannis, A., Zhang, D., Woodruff, N., & Dixon, A. (2005). Transition supports to students with mental retardation: An examination of data from the national longitudinal transition study 2. *Education and Training in Developmental Disabilities, 40,* 109–116.

Kraemer, B., & Blacher, J. (2001). Transition for young adults with severe mental retardation: School preparation, parent expectations, and family involvement. *Mental Retardation, 39,* 422–435.

Kraemer, B., McIntyre, L., & Blacher, J. (2003). Quality of life for young adults with mental retardation during transition. *Mental Retardation, 41,* 250–262.

Kunc, N. (2004, March). *The habits of inclusion.* Symposium: Common Solutions: Inclusion and Diversity at the Center. Syracuse University: Syracuse, NY.

LaPlante, M., Kennedy, J., Kaye, S., & Wenger, B. (1996). Disability statistics abstract, No. 11. Washington, DC: U.S. Department of Education, National Institute on Disability and Rehabilitation Research.

McMahan, R., & Baer, R. (2001). IDEA transition policy compliance and best practice: Perceptions of transition stakeholders. *Career Development for Exceptional Individuals, 24*, 169–184.

Menchetti, B., & Garcia, L. (2003). Personal and employment outcomes of person centered career planning. *Education and Treatment in Developmental Disabilities, 38*, 145–156.

Milson, A., & Hartley, M. (2005). Assisting students with learning disabilities transitioning to college: What school counselors should do. *Professional School Counseling, 8*, 436–442.

Miner, C., & Bates, P. (2002). Person-centered transition planning: Creating lifestyles of community inclusion and autonomy. In K. Storey, P. Bates, & D. Hunter (Eds.), *The road ahead: Transition to adult life for persons with disabilities* (pp. 7–24). St. Augustine, FL: Training Resource Network, Inc.

Mount, B., & Zwernik, K. (1988). *It's never too early, it's never too late: An overview of personal futures planning.* St. Paul, MN: Governor's Planning Council on Developmental Disabilities.

NCSET (2002). *Parent Brief: Promoting effective parent involvement in secondary education and transition.* National Center on Secondary Education and Transition.

Patton, J., & Dunn, C. (1998). *Transition from school to young adulthood: Basic concepts and recommended practices.* Austin, TX: Pro-Ed.

Powers, K., Gil-Kashiwabara, E., Geenen, S., Powers, L., Balandran, J., & Palmer, C. (2005). Mandates and effective transition planning practices reflected in IEPs. *Career Development for Exceptional Individuals, 28*, 47–59.

Rabren, K., Dunn, C., & Chambers, D. (2002). Predictors of post high school employment among adults with disabilities. *Career Development for Exceptional Individuals, 25*, 25–40.

Rojewski, J. (2002). Career assessment for adolescents with mild disabilities: Critical concerns for transition planning. *Career Development of Exceptional Individuals, 25*, 73–95.

Rueda, R., Monzo, L., Shapiro, J., Gomez, J., & Blacher, J. (2005). Cultural models of transition: Latina mothers of young adults with developmental disabilities. *Exceptional Children, 71*, 401–404.

Sitlington, P., Neubert, D., & Leconte, P. (1997). Transition assessment: The position statement of the Division on Career Development and Transition. *Career Development for Exceptional Individuals, 20*, 69–79.

Steere, D., & Cavaiuolo, D. (1999). Connecting outcomes, goals, and objectives in transition planning. *Teaching Exceptional Children, 34*, 54–59.

Steere, D., Rose, E., & Gregory, S. (1996). Generic practices to enhance transition to adult life for students with diverse disabilities. *Rehabilitation Education, 10*, 143–153.

Turnbull, R., & Luckasson, R. (Eds.). (2001). *Transition to adult life for people with mental retardation: Principles and practices.* Baltimore: Paul Brookes.

Turnbull, R., Huerta, N., & Stowe, M. (2005). *The individuals with disabilities education act as amended in 2004.* Upper Saddle River, NJ: Merrill-Prentice Hall.

Wehman, P. (1995). *Individual transition plans: The teacher's curriculum guide for helping youth with special needs.* Austin, TX: Pro-Ed.

Wehman, P. (1998). *Developing transition plans.* Austin, TX: Pro-Ed.

Wehman, P. (2004). *Life beyond the classroom: Transition strategies for young people with disabilities* (3rd ed.). Baltimore: Paul Brookes.

Zhang, D., Ivester, J., Chen, L., & Katsiyannis, A. (2005). Perspectives on transition practice. *Career Development for Exceptional Individuals, 28*, 15–25.

CHAPTER 5

INTERACTION
ACROSS AGENCIES

CHAPTER OBJECTIVES

Upon completion of this chapter, you will be able to

1. become familiar with the various community services available for individuals with disabilities.

2. identify the service needs of students, plan for those services, and prepare the student to access services prior to leaving school.

3. ensure that students are connected to the adult programs, supports, and services they need to achieve their desired postschool outcomes.

4. identify the various community options available to individuals with disabilities, be able to plan for them during the transition process, and assist students to access these services upon graduation from high school.

KEY TOPICS TO LOOK FOR IN THIS CHAPTER . . .

- Interagency Collaboration: IDEA 2004 defines transition as ". . . a coordinated set of activities. . . ." In this chapter, we will describe how this coordination can best be achieved.

- Self-determination: Students and their families must be empowered with the knowledge about different adult service agencies, the services that they offer, and how to best access these services.

The IDEA 2004 has defined transition as a "coordinated set of activities for a child with a disability, designed within a results-oriented process" (PL 108-446 (602(34)(A)). Implicit in this statement is the understanding that schools cannot and should not "do it alone." That is, since the goal is to "facilitate the child's movement from school to post school activities," adult agencies that are likely to support students, in terms of funding or services, must be part of the planning process. As the student is closer to graduation and/or leaving school, these adult agencies will not only be part of the planning process, but may also offer more of a funding and/or support service to the student. In this chapter we will discuss how adult service agencies interact with students with disabilities and how they play a critical role in the transition process.

One of our field's pioneers in the development of quality services, Dr. Gunnar Dybwad, is profiled in Sidebar 5.1.

SETTING THE STAGE, PART II: A RETURN TO JAMES'S TRANSITION PLAN

It had been a year since "transition" was introduced to Mrs. Rose, James's mother (introduced in Chapter 4). James was now sixteen years old, and his IEP meeting had just concluded. Transition was again brought up at the meeting and agencies from the community were present, including the Department of Vocational Rehabilitation (VR), the Department on Developmental Disabilities, and a local service provider agency called Greenway. Representatives from each of these agencies had described what they did and what they could offer to James once he leaves school. Although Mrs. Rose was still unsure what each of these agencies do and how they might help her son, she accepted their business cards, shook hands with them, and listened to their offers to discuss their services with her. She was still worried about James's future, but she was encouraged that agencies are available to help him.

At the meeting it was discussed that James should go to the Department of Vocational Rehabilitation (VR) office to meet with a counselor and apply for their services. Two weeks after the IEP meeting, they both went to the VR office to meet with Mr. Rodriguez, the VR Counselor. He introduced himself and began to explain what his office does and how they may be able to help James. He asked James what he hoped to do when he leaves school. He asked what careers and jobs he had had in the past and what his interests were for the future. James told him that he had tried out a few jobs at the local Wal-Mart, the Top Brand grocery store, and the Handy Man hardware store. In each of these places he had done mostly stock work. Mr. Rodriguez asked James if he liked working at these places. James said "yes, I guess," unsurely. Mr. Rodriguez told James that if he was not sure what he was interested in, he could arrange for assessments to be completed that might help produce some ideas. James became anxious because he hated taking tests in school and he never seemed to do as well as other students. Mr. Rodriguez then asked James if he had visited any of the adult service providers that were discussed at his IEP meeting. James was not sure what he meant, so Mrs. Rose answered for him. She told Mr. Rodriguez that they had not done so but that they were planning on it. She was not sure what the adult service providers could do but she knew that she had to find out.

Mr. Rodriguez now turned his attention to Mrs. Rose. She was given an application and was told that they needed to complete it and return it to him so that they could determine whether James was eligible for their services. She wondered what that meant. He had been receiving services from school all of these years without any questions, but now Mr. Rodriguez was telling her that James may not be eligible. He has

■ ■ ■ ■ ■ ▬▬▬▬▬▬▬▬▬▬▬▬▬▬▬▬▬▬▬▬▬▬▬▬▬▬▬▬

SIDEBAR 5.1
SPOTLIGHT ON HISTORY: GUNNAR DYBWAD

Gunnar Dybwad seemed to have spent his whole life as an advocate for persons with disabilities throughout the world. Along with his wife Rosemary, he was a tireless advocate for civil rights and self-determination for people with disabilities throughout the world. He is known as one of the founding fathers of Inclusion International.

Dr. Dybwad earned his doctorate in law in 1934 from the University of Halle, Germany. After relocating to the United States, he first worked for the penal system and then with juvenile delinquents in Indiana, New Jersey, New York, and Michigan. He graduated from the New York School of Social Work in 1939 and directed the child welfare program of Michigan State Department of Social Welfare from 1943–1951. He served as Executive Director of the Child Study Association of America, Executive Director of the National Association for Retarded Citizens, and Co-Director (with his wife Rosemary) of the Mental Retardation Project of the International Union for Child Welfare in Geneva. During the 1950s and '60s, he worked with the International League of Societies for Persons with Mental Handicap, now called Inclusion International. His work helped to influence the United Nations to write the United Nations Declaration of the Rights of the Mentally Retarded in 1971. Another of his major contributions during this period was to persuade the Pennsylvania Association for Retarded Citizens to file suit against the Commonwealth of Pennsylvania. This major case established the precedent for the rights of children with disabilities to a free and appropriate public education, which was subsequently mandated by the Education for All Handicapped Children Act (PL 94-142).

Beginning in 1967, Dr. Dybwad taught for more than thirty years at Brandeis University as the first director of the Starr Center on Mental Retardation at the Heller Graduate School. He also taught for twelve years at Syracuse University. In 1977 he became Professor Emeritus of Human Development at Brandeis. This is a position he held until his death in 2001. Dr. Dybwad was 92 when he died, and his beloved wife Rosemary passed away the following year.

Gunnar Dybwad was program chairman of the 1978 world congress of Inclusion International and was President of Inclusion International from 1978 to 1982. He served on the President's Panel on Mental Retardation for President Kennedy, and on the President's Committee on Mental Retardation for Johnson, Nixon, Regan, Ford, Carter, Bush, and Clinton.

Dr. Dybwad received many awards for outstanding service including the Kennedy Foundation Award, American Association on Mental Retardation, and the International Association for the Scientific Study of Intellectual Deficiency. He was one of our enduring pioneers of the rights of people with disabilities.

Source: Information retrieved from www.gunnardybwad.net

a disability, she thought, why would he not be eligible? She took the forms and thanked Mr. Rodriguez for his time and left with James. James was thinking about the assessments Mr. Rodriguez was talking about and Mrs. Rose was worried that, after all of this, James may not be able to receive any help from anyone. They were both very quiet driving home.

RESEARCH ON COLLABORATION AND INTERACTION ACROSS AGENCIES

Before discussing the importance and factors associated with interagency collaboration, we will provide a brief synthesis of some research about these practices. Currently, some of the best practices in transition from school to adult life are described as more than just identifying life goals and objectives, but also ensuring that students participate as equal members of the Individual Education Planning (IEP) team working toward a common goal with a focus on interagency collaboration. Interagency collaboration refers to key people from school personnel, family members, business, and human service agencies working together to promote successful postschool outcomes (Test, 2004). Research in the field supports the importance of collaboration and suggests that, without a concerted team effort, students with disabilities will not make successful transition to adult life (Aspel, Bettis, Quinn, Test, & Wood, 1999; Cozzens, Dowdy, & Smith, 1999; Dettmer, Dyck, & Thurston, 1999).

Problems with good collaboration among schools, families, and the community may be attributed to several factors, some of which are: (1) lack of knowledge of transition and of the community system that supports a positive transition outcome; (2) unclear roles by team members; (3) not being invited to participate in the transition plan process; (4) students' not being prepared for postschool activities; and (5) an ineffective collaboration model (or not having a model at all) to meet the needs of the transition team toward achieving the student's desired results. Several studies have highlighted these problems with collaboration.

Nuehring and Sitlington (2003) conducted a qualitative study of the transition process with students with autism. The results of their study pointed to several areas of the transition planning process that are in need of improvement. First, they concluded that more education and training about transition as a program focus and an IEP mandate is needed by teachers. In addition, more training was seen as needed for adult service providers regarding the nature and characteristics of students with autism and other challenging disabilities. Second, they highlighted the need for an effective assessment process as part of transition planning. Third, there is a need for increased communication among individuals (students) in transition, their families, school representatives, and adult service agencies. Last, schools' transition programs and adult service providers need to be better aligned and coordinated for successful transition to occur.

It appears that one of the challenges to optimal coordination is poor communication and collaboration among agencies. Despite the requirement for schools to invite community agencies to transition IEP meetings, Agran, Cain, and Cavin (2002) suggest that this may not be occurring as planned. These authors conducted surveys to better understand the level of involvement of rehabilitation counselors in the transition process. One survey sample was for special education teachers and the other was for rehabilitation counselors. The results of the study indicated that the involvement/ interaction of rehabilitation counselors was perceived as being inadequate, and this was exacerbated by the fact that counselors were not being invited to IEP meetings by school personnel. In addition, the perceptions of rehabilitation counselors were that students are often not adequately prepared for employment.

Despite these challenges, some researchers are demonstrating that effective collaboration can lead to improved outcomes for students in transition. For example, a study that reviewed a model of collaboration in California highlighted interagency resources and the expertise of three primary systems for people with significant support needs: public schools, Vocational Rehabilitation (VR), and Developmental Disabilities (DD) services, the latter two being potential government funding sources (Certo Mautz, Smalley, Wade, Luecking, Pumpian, Sax, Noyes, & Wechsler, 2003). There were two phases to this collaborative project. First, one year prior to the student exiting school, the school entered into a formal agreement with a "hybridized" agency funded by both VR and DD for community employment. Schools committed a teacher and funds equivalent to an instructional aid to support the activities (this teacher might be considered a Transition Coordinator). The teacher shared office space at the hybridized agency along with strategies and ideas. During the second phase, one year following the student exiting school, a policy management group made up of public school personnel and VR and DD representatives was convened to monitor employment of graduates. Outcomes of this collaborative model included the following: 63 percent of students who participated were competitively employed at graduation and 71 percent were competitively employed up to three years after graduation. This study is an important example of how shared collaboration among agencies can achieve significantly positive results.

Interagency teams can address policy differences and facilitate communication (Baer, Flexer, & McMahan, 2005). There are numerous advantages for schools to collaborate with adult service agencies during transition, as they (schools) lack in fiscal and/or personnel support to adequately develop student employment skills (Grossi, Schaaf, Steigerwald, & Mank, 2002). Collaboration is therefore an essential practice in transition programs. It is important to recognize that such collaboration can occur at multiple levels, including the individual student level through a transition IEP meeting, at the school level through a school-wide planning team, or at the local or community level through an interagency council or team.

Interagency collaboration is also essential for students who are making a transition to postsecondary education. Individuals with learning disabilities are more successful in life if they are able to go on to college (i.e., technical schools, 2- or 4-year colleges) (Dickinson & Verbeek, 2002). Many students with learning disabilities end up working in low-paying jobs with few benefits and little job security (Durlak, Rose, & Bursuck, 1994). However, if students with learning disabilities have clear transition IEPs that include collaborative activities through VR and local postsecondary institutions, this can open the door for future economic success, social power, and personal well-being for them (Milson & Hartley, 2005).

The interaction between members of the student's IEP team is important and the role they play in this process is viewed as one of the critical factors in the success of transition. For example, business and industry's role in employing people with moderate to severe disabilities is critical and becoming more evident (Wehman, Brooke, West, Targett, Green, Inge, & Kregel, 1998). Also, increased collaboration among service provider agencies prior to the student exiting the school system has been found to improve the transition process for students with disabilities (Noyes & Sax, 2003). Educators can influence the development of effective collaboration and interaction among agencies by ensuring that each member of the IEP team works toward a positive adult life outcome for students (Dettmer et al., 1999). Where transition from school to work is less successful, the literature suggests that, among several reasons for this poor success, one of the factors is the lack of effectiveness of interaction across agencies and coordination strategies between school and adult service and community professionals (Wehman et al., 1998).

COMMUNITY LINKAGES

For an effective transition to occur, community linkages must be established prior to students leaving school. These community linkages are seen as a continuation of the services the student may have needed while he or she was in school. Because these services were needed for the student to receive an appropriate education, they may also be necessary for the student to be successful in community life. For example, if a student was receiving mental health counseling for anger management in school, the student may need to continue to receive similar counseling from a community service provider when he or she leaves school. Therefore, a comparable service should be identified for the student in the community and a "connection" established as part of the transition program for the student when he or she exits school.

Community linkages may be any services that are needed by students to function fully within the community, including rehabilitative, housing, employment, medical, and/or mental health services. If a student was receiving therapeutic interventions while in school to meet his educational program, similar services are likely warranted as an adult. Community linkages could also be support services that students may need to allow them to live in their own homes or apartments. Support services might be necessary to help people find, keep, and maintain jobs in the community. Developing a connection to community linkages is one of the most critical components of the transition planning process. The efforts by the school to teach and provide opportunities to students may not mean a thing if students do not have some means to continue to receive the needed support and services that would allow them to work and live in the community.

There is a major difference between school-based services and those that the student may eventually access as an adult in the community. The key difference is that school services (e.g., physical therapy, occupational therapy, speech and language, etc.) are *entitlements* to students with disabilities, if such services are needed to ensure an appropriate education. That is, these services must be provided at no cost to students or their families. As students with disabilities leave school and enter the adult world, those entitlements are no longer available to the student. Students are now considered to be adults and must meet certain eligibility requirements to qualify for and receive services. Also, in the adult service system, an individual who is deemed eligible for a service may well have to wait for services to become available. Waiting lists for services are all too common. This fundamental shift from entitlement to eligibility is a major concern and a surprise for many families, as it was for Mrs. Rose (Hanley-Maxwell, Whitney-Thomas, & Pogoloff, 1995).

An additional difference between school-based services and community-based services for adults is who will pay for the service. For example, for medical needs, adult children usually become ineligible for their families' medical plans that may have covered them while they were in school. If adult children or their families cannot afford to pay for that type of continued coverage, they will need to apply for medical assistance and be deemed eligible before they can access that service. If they need support in housing or at work, they will need to apply for services from state agencies that potentially fund these services. Here again people must be deemed eligible before these services can be initiated. This is why it is so critical that community linkages and needs be identified and started early (14–15 years of age) in the IEP/transition planning process.

Transition planning teams must complete several steps in order to establish connections with adult service agencies for students with disabilities.

First, teams must identify students' needs regarding ancillary services in adulthood.

Second, they should identify the community providers that offer these comparable services.

Third, they must determine the process of applying for or determining eligibility for the service.

Fourth, they should encourage and support students to visit and select the agencies of their choosing.

Fifth, teams must be sure to invite the agency representatives to the IEP/transition meeting.

Sixth, the team should obtain student signatures to release pertinent information that will be needed by the appropriate adult service provider agencies.

Greater specificity about the implementation of these steps will be provided later in this chapter. The various services that might be needed by students in transition are discussed in the next section.

ADULT SERVICE OPTIONS

In this section you will be introduced to the various adult service providers that students with disabilities may need to sustain a successful community life. In the previous section we established the importance of helping students connect to the various supports and services upon leaving school. Usually, however, students and/or families are not aware of these supports and services unless someone helps. It is the responsibility of schools to identify service providers and establish linkages to needed supports and services in the community. Often, students and parents do not become aware of these services until they are introduced at the IEP/transition planning meeting. Therefore, it becomes critical for teachers and school personnel to have a clear understanding and awareness of adult service providers so they can better educate students and families in the process of identifying and selecting the supports and services that are most appropriate to meet students' needs as adults.

In general, the types of services that a person may receive from their community are varied and broad in scope. Adult services may be categorized according to the types of needs that each agency will support through service provision or funding. Table 5.1 provides a quick look at some of the services and disability categories that are typically available in most locations. (In order to find each of these types of agencies in your local area, refer to the websites at the end of this chapter, or investigate the websites of your state and/or county or local area. In addition, the Blue Pages in your local phone directory will typically list agencies that assist people with disabilities, along with local governmental offices.)

The agencies and services shown in Table 5.1 provide a variety of services through varied sources of funding. For example, medical services are generally provided by medical assistance, which is funded in part by state and federal initiatives. State and local Developmental Disabilities (DD) or Mental Retardation (MR) offices generally fund housing needs. For employment services, Vocational Rehabilitation (VR) generally provides initial funding for supported employment, which is usually followed by funding for the follow-along phase by the state's Developmental Disabilities (DD) or Mental Retardation (MR) office. As you can see, the funding for the potential services a student would need and utilize come from local, state, or federal initiatives. The common factor with all of these programs and services is that individuals must apply for and be deemed eligible based on specific criteria for these programs. The essence of the criteria for many of these programs is that an individual's disability is an impediment to employment and/or other life functioning activities.

FEDERALLY FUNDED PROGRAMS AND SERVICES

There are several federally funded programs that are available to people with disabilities. Among the programs most often accessed by adults with disabilities are the Vocational Rehabilitation and Social Security systems. These programs are described in the sections below.

Vocational Rehabilitation (VR)

While there may be several programs to assist individuals with disabilities to be employed, the primary program is the Vocational Rehabilitation program (OSERS, 2004). This program is overseen by the Department of Education and is available in every state in the United States. The original establishment of rehabilitation services came from the 1918 Soldier's Rehabilitation Act following World War I and the many subsequent amendments to the more current legislation under Title I of the Rehabilitation Act of 1973 and its amendments (OSERS, 2004; Parker & Szymanski, 1998; Rubin & Roessler, 2001).

The amended Act indicates that states receive federal grants to operate a comprehensive VR program. The VR program in each state is designed to assess, plan, develop, and provide rehabilitation services to eligible individuals with disabilities, consistent with their strengths, resources, priorities, concerns, abilities, capabilities, interests, and informed choices (OSERS, 2004). Each eligible individual is to have an Individualized Plan for Employment, or IPE. The eligibility requirements for the vocational rehabilitation program are provided in Table 5.2.

TABLE 5.1 Common Community Agencies and the Transition Services and Potential Funding They May Offer

AGENCY/PROGRAM* (PURPOSE AND FUNDING SOURCE)	EXAMPLE OF EMPLOYMENT SERVICE	EXAMPLES OF POST-SECONDARY EDUCATION SERVICES	EXAMPLES OF ADULT AND INDEPENDENT LIVING SERVICES
Vocational Rehabilitation: Assists persons with cognitive, sensory, physical, or emotional disabilities to attain employment and increased independence. Funded by federal and state money. VR agencies typically operate regional and local offices. VR services typically last for a limited period of time and are based on an individual's rehabilitation plan. If needed, an individual with disabilities can request services at a later time, and a new rehabilitation plan will be developed.	■ Vocational guidance and counseling ■ Medical, psychological, vocational, and other types of assessments to determine vocational potential ■ Supported employment, job development, placement, and follow-up services ■ Rehabilitation, technological services and adaptive devices, tools, equipment, and supplies	■ Apprenticeship programs, usually in conjunction with Department of Labor ■ Vocational training ■ College training toward a vocational goal as part of an eligible student's financial aid package	■ Housing or transportation supports needed to maintain employment ■ Interpreter services ■ Orientation and mobility services
Mental Health/Mental Retardation/Developmental Disabilities: Provide a comprehensive system of services responsive to the needs of individuals with mental illness, mental retardation and/or developmental disabilities. Federal, state, and local funding are used to operate regional offices; local funding is often the primary source. Services are provided on a sliding payment scale.	■ Supported and sheltered employment ■ Competitive employment, support for those who need minimal assistance		■ Case management services to access and obtain local services ■ Therapeutic recreation, including day activities, clubs, and programs ■ Respite care ■ Residential services (group homes and supervised apartments)

Agency			
Independent Living Centers: Helps people with disabilities to achieve and maintain self-sufficient lives within the community. Operated locally, ILCs serve a particular region. ILCs may charge for classes, but advocacy services are typically at no cost.	■ Information and referral services ■ Connecting students with mentors with disabilities	■ Advocacy training ■ Connecting students with mentors with disabilities	■ Advocacy training ■ Auxiliary social services (e.g., maintain list of personal care attendants) ■ Peer counseling ■ Housing assistance ■ Training in skills of independent living (attendant management, housing, transportation, career development) ■ Information and referral services ■ Connecting with mentors
Social Security Administration: Operates the federally funded program that provides benefits for people of any age who are unable to do substantial work and have a severe mental or physical disability. Several programs are offered for people with disabilities, including Social Security Disability Insurance (SSDI), Supplemental Security Income (SSI), Plans for Achieving Self-Support (PASS), Medicaid and Medicare.	Work incentive programs which may include: ■ Cash benefits while working (e.g., student-earned income) ■ Medicare or Medicaid while working ■ Help with any extra work expenses that individual has as a result of the disability ■ Assistance to start a new line of work	■ Financial incentive for further education and training	■ Medical benefits ■ Can use income as basis for purchase or rental of housing

*Name of agencies or programs may differ slightly from state to state.

TABLE 5.2   Eligibility Criteria for the State/Federal Vocational Rehabilitation System

According to the Rehabilitation Act of 1973 amendments, in order to be eligible for VR services, an individual must:

■ Be an "individual with a disability," meaning a person who (1) has a physical or mental impairment which constitutes or results in a substantial impediment to employment for the individual; and (2) can benefit from VR services to achieve an employment outcome.
■ Requires VR services to prepare for, secure, retain, or regain employment.

Individuals who receive Supplemental Security Income (SSI) and/or Social Security Disability Insurance (SSDI) benefits are presumed to be eligible for VR services leading to employment, *unless* there is clear and convincing evidence that they are too significantly disabled to benefit from VR services.

  The lists of services that can be obtained from the Vocational Rehabilitation Departments are broad, but they must lead to employment. According to Section 103(a) of the Rehabilitation Act of 1973, necessary services are those that an eligible individual may need in order to achieve his/her employment outcome. A list of services that the VR programs can provide is listed in Table 5.3.

Social Security

The Social Security Act Amendments were passed by Congress in 1956. The Amendments provided a financial allowance to individuals with disabilities (Rubin &

TABLE 5.3   Vocational Rehabilitation (VR) Program Services

■ Assessment for determining eligibility and VR needs.
■ Vocational counseling, guidance, and referral services.
■ Physical and mental restoration services.
■ Vocational and other training, including on-the-job training.
■ Maintenance for additional costs incurred while the individual is receiving certain VR services.
■ Transportation related to other VR services.
■ Interpreter services for individuals who are deaf.
■ Reader services for individuals who are blind.
■ Services to assist students with disabilities to transition from school to work.
■ Personal assistance services (including training in managing, supervising, and directing personal assistance services) while an individual is receiving VR services.
■ Rehabilitation technology services and devices.
■ Supported employment services.
■ Job placement services.

Roessler, 2001). This legislation provided a disability income allowance for any person who was deemed permanently disabled at age fifty and over and who was considered unable to return to employment (Erlanger & Roth, 1985). The office administering the programs from this Act is the Social Security Administration (SSA). The subsequent Amendments of the Social Security Act have a direct relevance to the federal-state vocational rehabilitation programs.

A major function of SSA is the management of two programs that provide cash benefits based on disability or blindness: the Social Security Disability Insurance (SSDI) program and the Supplemental Security Income (SSI) program that makes cash assistance payments to individuals who are aged, blind, and disabled (including children under age eighteen) and who have limited income or resources (SSA Pub. No. 64-030). These two programs are important to understand because individuals with disabilities who will need housing supports as an adult will need and use the income from these programs to supplement the state's contribution for residential housing and support (e.g., community living arrangements, supported living, etc.). Another important factor associated with this program is that an individual deemed eligible under this program is also eligible for medical assistance. People eligible for SSDI benefits are eligible for Medicare and those eligible for SSI are eligible for Medicaid.* Both SSDI and SSI define disability as the inability to engage in any substantial gainful activity (SGA) because of medically determinable physical or mental impairments (SSA Pub. No. 64-030). The eligibility requirements for these programs are listed in Table 5.4.

One of the highest priorities of the SSA is to help people with disabilities achieve independence by assisting them to take advantage of employment opportunities. But for years it has been a concern of people with disabilities that the earnings from employment would cause them to lose these benefits and consequently the medical benefits that would follow. Therefore, employment was seen as a disincentive. Many people with disabilities were reluctant to work toward gainful employment because there is a threshold which, if exceeded, results in the reduction or termination of benefits. More important were reductions in medical benefits because many people with disabilities often take medications for health stability. It is recommended that you obtain information from the state's Social Security Administration on Substantial Gainful Activity (SGA) limits for people with disabilities. Over the past fifteen years, SSA has acknowledged these disincentives in the regulations and has begun to make adjustments to SGA limits as well as introduce new initiatives, incentives, and programs to help people make employment a goal. Some of these employment opportunity initiatives are listed and briefly described in Table 5.5.

It should be noted that students of transition age who may be participating in a work development or trail work program and are being paid by an employer can begin to use SSA work incentives while still in school. Work incentives and linkages to community service providers do not just begin when the student graduates from high school, but may be accessed prior to leaving school. This will give the student a head

---

*Note that states may use different eligibility criteria for the medical assistance programs and it is recommended that you refer to your state's SSA to obtain a copy of the eligibility criteria.

TABLE 5.4   SSDI and SSI Eligibility Criteria

SSDI: To be eligible the worker must have worked and paid Social Security taxes for enough years to be covered under Social Security insurance. The person must

1. be the worker, or the worker's widow(er), or the worker's disabled adult child (among the requirements for a disabled adult child: the individual must be unmarried, is or was dependent on parents, age 18 or over, and the disability must have begun before age 22).
2. meet the definition of medically disabled.
3. not be working or working but not performing substantial gainful activity.

SSI: To be eligible based on medical condition, the person must

1. have little or no income or resources.
2. be a U.S. citizen or meet the requirement for non-citizens.
3. be considered medically disabled.
4. be a resident of one of the 50 states, District of Columbia, or Northern Mariana Islands.
5. file an application.
6. file for any and all other benefits for which the person is eligible.
7. accept vocational rehabilitation services, if referred.
8. not be working or working but not performing SGA, if the impairment is other than blindness, when the person applies.
9. be blind—then the first seven conditions apply.

start in the process, particularly if a Social Security employment initiative such as a PASS (plan for achieving self support) would offer some opportunities for the student toward self-sufficiency. In general, students can access the SSA work incentives while still in school. The next section will describe some of the work incentive options available through the Social Security Administration.

Work Related Options: The Social Security Administration has created several work-related options. The first option was previously mentioned with the increase in SGA. The increasing limit to SGA has been beneficial for people with disabilities to be gainfully employed and have a minimal effect on their lost income and medical benefits. In essence, even if the SSI or SSDI financial benefits are reduced substantially, the medical benefits are retained and continued, which has been the major barrier to employment for many people with disabilities. In the following section we will introduce additional major incentives and initiatives created to support the outcome of employment for individuals with disabilities.

Ticket to Work and Work Incentives Improvement Act of 1999 (P.L. 106-170): Under this program, people receive a ticket that they can take to an approved service provider of their choice to assist them in obtaining employment. It is a type of voucher where the provider is reimbursed after the services are provided and people receiving services are employed. In addition, this Act includes several improvements to

TABLE 5.5 Social Security Administration Employment Initiatives

SSI Employment Supports are:

- Impairment-Related Work Expenses (IRWE)
- Earned Income Exclusion
- Student Earned Income Exclusion
- Blind Work Expenses (BWE)
- Plan for Achieving Self-Support (PASS)
- Property Essential to Self-Support
- Special SSI Payments for People Who Work—Section 1619(a)
- Continued Medicaid Eligibility—Section 1619(b)
- Special Benefits for People Eligible Under Section 1619(a) or (b) Who Enter a Medical Treatment Facility
- Reinstating Eligibility without a New Application
- Continued Payment under a Vocational Rehabilitation Program

SSDI Employment Supports are:

- Impairment-Related Work Expenses (IRWE)
- Subsidy and Special Conditions
- Unincurred Business Expenses (Self-Employed Only)
- Unsuccessful Work Attempt
- Trial Work Period
- Extended Period of Eligibility
- Continuation of Medicare Coverage
- Medicare for People with Disabilities Who Work
- Continued Payment under a Vocational Rehabilitation Program

Medicare and Medicaid coverage that eliminates some of the barriers that required the person to choose between health care coverage and going to work.

The majority of people with disabilities want to work (Harris & Associates, 1987, 1994). Some of the barriers identified as reasons for not working have to do with the potential loss of benefits (e.g., SSI and/or Medicaid). As this may have been a real fear in individuals with disabilities in the past, current legislative initiatives have made it possible for people with disabilities who want to work to do so with less risk and potential loss of benefits (SSA Pub. No. 64-030). As shown in Table 5.5, there are many employment supports that a person can receive while working. Because the SSDI and SSI rules differ regarding their coverage, you should obtain specific information from the Social Security Administration in your area. We will discuss two of the most widely used employment supports, Impairment Related Work Expenses (IRWE)/Blind Work Expenses (BWE)* and Plan for Achieving Self Support (PASS).

*Note: IRWE and BWE are very closely related in terms of the deductible expenses, therefore they will both be covered together.

IWRE/BWE: Under the SSA rules, a person collecting SSI or SSDI is allowed to earn up to a specific amount before the benefit is significantly reduced or withdrawn. Both IWRE and BWE are ways to deduct the various impairment related costs and services that the person needs to be actively employed from the gross earning when deciding what is "countable income." That is, when calculating a person's earnings as a means to demonstrate Substantial Gainful Activity (SGA is the term used to indicate at what point a person's earnings are considered to be what a typical person could earn if he/she did not have a disability), these deductions will reduce what is considered countable earnings. This is somewhat similar to an itemized tax form in which deductions are used to lower a person's taxable income. The following are some examples of expenses that are likely to be deductible under SSA rules.

- Attendant care services
- Transportation cost
- Work-related equipment and assistants
- Prosthesis
- Routine drug and medical services

These are a few of the possible deductions that a person may receive, but you should refer to the SSA office for specific information of SSI and SSDI deductions.

PASS: PASS allows a person to set aside income for a specific time period for a work goal (SSA Pub. No. 64-030). This plan is available for people who receive SSI benefits only. Money could be set aside for education, vocational training (i.e., job coaching), or for starting a business. Income that is set aside under a PASS is not countable income when calculating the SSI cash benefit the person would receive. A PASS can help to establish or maintain SSI eligibility and can increase a person's SSI payment amount. A plan is developed that indicates a person's goals for what is needed to be self-sufficient. Then, it is determined what is financially needed to achieve the goals. A time period is established for saving the funds to get to the goal. The SSA office approves the plan; and then as the person works, an amount of money is deducted from the person's SSI benefit. The person's income is then calculated for a lower benefit amount. In general, the PASS allows a person to save money toward a plan that will allow the opportunity for self-sufficiency later in life. For a more detailed description of how the PASS works or what is required for a plan, contact your local SSA office.

STATE-FUNDED PROGRAMS AND SERVICES

Development Disabilities/Mental Retardation and Mental Health Offices

What we have just covered are some of the federal entitlement programs and services that are available to people with disabilities. Some of these programs require that states contribute a portion of funding to support the program activities. There are other programs, state operated solely through state funds, which we will describe in this section. First, you should be aware of the different titles used to identify the disability categories that state systems use. They are generally divided into two categories, states that serve the broad category of developmental disabilities (DD) and those that are specific in terms of their service category, for example, mental retardation (MR). Some states provide specific services to individuals with mental retardation and their service system may come under the Office of Mental Retardation, as in Pennsylvania. This type of service system leaves the majority, if not the total, funding for supports and services to that one specific disability group. A system that identifies developmental disabilities as a category has a much broader constituency base. Mental health (MH) services are typically a separate category from MR/DD services. The mental health service needs are generally funded through the medical assistance program with strict guidelines and criteria. In general, one of the main services often seen in schools from this program is known as the wraparound program (Turnbull, Turnbull, Shank, & Smith, 2004). As students become of adult age some of the services once obtained in school may continue as part of adult services, such as counseling and other forms of therapeutic intervention.

The importance of distinguishing which service category your state is under for serving students with disabilities is critical from the standpoint of planning for each student's future. Getting the state's MR or DD system involved as early as age fifteen should occur for the following reasons:

- Determining Eligibility: Early eligibility determination helps identify appropriate planning. If the student is determined ineligible for services upon graduation, the school district should design strategies that will address the student's future needs, knowing that the state's system will not be a source of support. If the student is determined eligible, the student can then be placed on that state's waiting list for future support. Since many states are experiencing funding problems, many have instituted waiting lists. That is, students and adults with disabilities who are not receiving support for any day programming due to the lack of funding are placed on a list by date of referral. Generally, a person only comes off the waiting list as people leave the service system. How long an individual has to wait for services is based on early determination. The earlier people are put on the waiting list, the greater the possibility that they can access services upon graduation.

- Vocational Services: States are generally responsible for the various vocational service programs that people with disabilities receive, such as Work Activity Centers (WAC), Adult Training Programs (ATP), and Supported Employment (SE). Again, states may vary in what titles are given to the various vocational services but, in general, they fall into facility-based services (WAC and ATP) and community-based services (SE). If it is expected that a student will need ongoing support in either a facility-based or a community-based program, this should be identified early and the appropriate state system should be invited to participate in the student's transition plan. It should be noted that there is a general agreement between VR and state MR/DD systems to work in concert to support those individuals who participate in supported employment. Usually VR pays for a person's initial on-the-job training and MR/DD picks up the follow-along (long-term) funding to continue to support the individual in their placement. The adult vocational service system will be described in greater detail in a later chapter.

- Housing Services: As previously mentioned, state systems not only financially support people in vocational settings, they also support them in their housing. People with disabilities who need support in community housing areas can be assisted by the state system's financial support. People with disabilities can generally be supported in various levels of need. For example, there are twenty-four hour supervised housing programs for those who require that level of care and attention. There is a supervised apartment level of care where a person would receive a range of support from twenty to forty hours, or more, a week. Another option is family living where a person would live with a family (foster family) and the person and the family would receive both personal and financial support. States may offer other hybrid options of housing, but generally individuals with disabilities may receive a level of care that falls into a range of twenty-four hours' intensive support to minimal hours of intermittent level support. In this area, too, a waiting list for receiving housing services most likely exists. Therefore, early identification of the student's need will aid in planning for needed housing services. A second result of this early identification is to again place the student on the state's waiting list to allow a better chance for accessing these services upon graduation.

- Social Services: State systems also offer social services to individuals as a way to access generic community services. Early identification and determination can allow the state's system to be active in supporting the student and his or her family to continue to learn beyond school, even if vocational and/or housing services are not requested at that time. The social services provided by professionals, called either case managers or supports coordinators, can help the individual and family to access generic recreational, leisure, and social services that can help in the continued community integration and assimilation.

These points make it critical for school personnel to plan early (as early as age fourteen) in determining eligibility and identifying vocational, housing, and social service needs. A school district's support in this area can only come with a clear understanding and knowledge of the state's system of supports and services for adults with disabilities.

LOCAL SERVICE PROVIDERS

When students with disabilities are identified as needing ongoing support beyond school, they will often receive support from adult service providers. These service providers are generally contracted to provide the various services that the state (MR/DD/MH) or federal systems (VR) fund (see previous section on these systems). Some of the activities or programs providers offer are supported employment, work activity centers, adult training programs, housing services, recreation services, case management and others. Vocational Rehabilitation is a funding source for vocational evaluation and supported employment services that adult service agencies provide. As students identify their desired postschool outcomes, they also identify which adult service provider can offer them the greatest opportunity to attain these transition outcomes. Local service providers are typically private, non-profit agencies. The names of such agencies, and the services that they provide, vary widely.

It becomes important for students and families to have a familiarity with the various functions of adult service providers in their area. They should have a clear understanding of the providers, their services, and how they can support the student to achieve his or her personal outcomes. Adult service providers should be invited to the student's IEP/transition meeting. Since not all adult service providers offer the full range of services (e.g., housing, vocational and/or recreational), more than one provider may need to be invited to attend the meeting. Adult providers should send a representative to participate in these meetings and maintain a record of students' preferences. Schools should also consider how they can assist students and their families to be better aware of the adult service system. For example, schools can hold a "provider fair" where local community service providers come in and meet with students and parents. Students and families can then begin to decide which provider they wish to work with and to invite to the students' IEP/transition planning meetings.

What we are covering here is information you will need to understand the complex world of human services and how they interact with students with disabilities. This is essential to our efforts to help students become successful adults and to help them achieve their desired outcomes. Some students will require more or less support than others. Teachers should be well informed and educate students and families to make the best choices that are available to them. In the next section, we will discuss what role each of these interagency linkages has in the lives of students with disabilities as they participate in the IEP/transition process.

Consider This!   Professionals in the education system are often confused by the workings of the adult services system. Conversely, adult service representatives may have little understanding of how schools operate. Clearly, both sectors need to understand the services and processes of their counterparts. Now, consider how confusing this can be to students with disabilities and their families. As discussed earlier in this book, the time of transition to adulthood is one of the most difficult for families of students with disabilities. It is incumbent upon us as professionals to do our utmost to understand the full spectrum of educational and adult services so that we can support students and their families during the transition process. The more you learn about the services in your local area and how and when to access them, the greater the likelihood that you will be able to provide needed help.

ROLE AND RESPONSIBILITIES OF ADULT SERVICE AGENCIES

"A coordinated set of activities" is the goal of any effective transition plan. The collaboration that occurs between members of the team is critical for achieving positive outcomes for students planning for the transition to adult life. Each member of the team has a role that must be carried out at each phase of the transition process. Each year of the planning process, beginning at age fourteen, is important, but we will identify three significant phases that are critical to the collaboration process. The first phase should begin no later than at age fifteen, but we recommend age fourteen. It is recommended that for some students it is more crucial to begin addressing transition needs earlier, as the risk of student dropout rates and long waiting lists for services are potential issues facing the special education system today. At this phase, Vocational Rehabilitation (VR), the state MR/DD of Mental Health system, and adult service providers play a consultation role in the process. That is, they will not participate in any major function but can provide technical assistance and consultation to the student, the family, and the school district personnel in the planning process. Table 5.6 provides a list of activities and the role that VR, MR/DD, and adult services may play at this phase.

It should be noted that students and families who are the center point of the transition plan must also play a major role and should have responsibilities, as do the other members of the team. Often, school district personnel do not see students as playing a role in the process, but, as described in Chapter 2, we feel that in order for students to practice self-determination behaviors they too must participate equally in the process and be given some responsibility toward achieving their own outcomes. Table 5.7 contains roles and responsibilities that students and families may have in the process in the three phases discussed here.

During the second phase of the interagency collaboration process, adult service agencies become more involved while still maintaining a consultation role. Here VR, MR/DD, and adult service representatives begin to discuss their services and determine the student's eligibility. The eligibility determination can occur in the first phase, but clearly it should be conducted no later than in this phase. This phase is

TABLE 5.6   Roles of VR, MR/DD, and Adult Services When Student Is 14 to 16 Years of Age*

1. Designates a representative to attend at least one IEP meeting between these ages.
2. Designee or representative explains the services and eligibility criteria for the service.
3. Designee or representative provides the family and the student with takeaway information which they can review after the meeting.
4. Designee or representative participates in some form of orientation to teachers explaining the nature of the services so that school personnel can more effectively guide students.
5. Designee or representative begins to develop a student file to follow the student through the transition years.
6. Designee or representative provides school personnel with current program eligibility criteria.
7. Designee or representative advises school personnel, student, and the family of additional assessment materials that may be needed to determine need, etc.

*This list represents minimum activities that should be accomplished by these service providers.

TABLE 5.7   Roles and Responsibilities of Students and Families at Each of the Three Phases of Transition

Transition Planning Activities Beginning by 14 Years of Age

- Identify educational courses and educational experiences in school and in the community that will help achieve postschool outcomes.
- Identify personal learning styles and accommodations needed to be successful as a learner and worker.
- Identify career interests and skills.
- Explore interests and options for postschool education and, if appropriate, postsecondary education/technical school admission criteria.
- Identify interest and options for future living arrangements and housing supports.
- Learn to effectively communicate personal interests, preferences, and accommodation needs.
- Learn and practice decision (choice) making skills.
- Determine assistive technology needs that may potentially increase community participation and inclusion.
- Explore community experiences and expanded friendships.
- Access and use public transition options.
- Assess money management skills and determine functional learning.
- Obtain a personal identification card.
- Assess and determine need for learning skills for independent living.
- Assess, learn, and practice personal health care skills.

Transition Planning Activities between the Ages of 16 and 20

- Identify adult and community support services that are potentially needed after graduation (i.e., Vocational Rehabilitation, State or Local MR/DD system, etc.).
- Invite adult service providers and significant personnel to the IEP meeting.
- Develop a long-range plan (desired outcomes) for postschool life.
- Ensure that the course of study matches up with career interests and skills needed for postschool success.
- Gather information from service providers and/or potential postsecondary school or technical programs.
- Determine health care plan needs beyond graduation, and how services or health care needs will be continued.
- Learn about sexuality and family planning issues.
- Determine the need for financial assistance beyond school, and apply for Social Security benefits, if appropriate.
- Learn and practice communication and social skills needed for job interviews, developing relationships and/or community participation.
- Develop and maintain a personal portfolio/resume.
- Participate in community-based skills for areas of independent living such as traveling, shopping, and daily living skills.

(continued)

TABLE 5.7 Continued

Transition Planning Activities in the Final Year of School

- Ensure all community linkages are established and all applications to these linkages have been made (ensure that eligibility has been determined).
- Identify potential postschool providers or postsecondary education programs for after graduation.
- Maintain skill development through community-based activities in all the needed areas including, transportation, daily living skills, recreation, employment, etc.
- Identify desired job interests and have paid employment with supports established upon graduation.
- Learn responsibility for personal well-being and needed work ethics.
- Register to vote and for the selective services if appropriate.

identified as the time the student is turning sixteen years of age, and all sections of the IEP related to transition planning are completed with the student's input. Some of the roles and responsibilities of adult service agencies during this phase are shown in Table 5.8.

The third and final phase of the process begins during the student's last year of school. For students who are on target to graduate alongside their peers, this could be at age eighteen. For some students, they will continue to receive educational services until they are twenty-one years of age, the legal limit for a student to be able to receive special education services by law. Therefore, depending on when the student is set to graduate, the final year will differ. During this final year, the role of the key players on the team is at the most involved level. At this phase, applications have been completed, eligibility has been determined, and supports and services have been identified and agreed upon. When the student exits school in June, it should be a smooth and seamless transition from school to adult life. It should be clearly more than a paper transfer, but a transfer of responsibilities and activities to the adult service community. Table 5.9 provides a list of activities that VR, MR/DD, and adult service providers might be responsible for during this last year of the transition process for students.

Consider This! The success of interagency collaboration rests in large part on the ability of team members to work together in an effective manner (Wehman & Target, 2004). This ability consists of a willingness to work toward a common goal, that is, the success of the student in transition. Team members who represent different agencies or aspects of the student's life need to understand and appreciate the roles that other members play in the planning process. Firsthand knowledge of and experience working with the other members of the team is usually helpful as well. Most important, clear communication among all members of the planning team is essential.

One of the issues in transition planning is how services and service providers are identified for students as they progress through the process. Generally, a student's IEP will offer a great deal of information with regard to the service needs of the student.

TABLE 5.8 Roles of VR, MR/DD, MH, and Adult Services When Student Is 17 Years of Age or Beyond (18, 19, 20, 21), Depending on the Year of Graduation for Student*

1. Designates a representative to attend the student's IEP meeting (it would be expected that this representative will be consistent throughout the student's transition year, if not, a transfer of information should be done to the new representative).
2. Designee or representative updates the services and eligibility criteria for the service.
3. Provides the family and the student with updated takeaway information which they can review after the meeting.
4. Develops a service plan, as required by each of the agencies.
5. Provides school district and teachers with information about the services.
6. Updates the student file that should follow the student through the transition years.
7. Provides school personnel with updated program eligibility criteria information.
8. Advises school personnel, student, and the family of additional assessment materials that may be needed to determine need, etc.

*This list represents minimum activities that should be accomplished by these service providers.

Another document that may offer information about potential service needs of a student is the student's Evaluation Report (ER). The ER summarizes an evaluation of the student and establishes the basis for the services needed at school. Therefore, school district personnel can begin to look at the student's needs based on his or her ER. In addition to the ER, school districts should also consider developing student profiles, such as those described in Chapter 2.

Adult service providers also have a way of identifying individual service needs for

TABLE 5.9 Roles of VR, MR/DD, MH, and Adult Services in the Student's Final Year of School*

1. A representative attends the IEP meeting for the student.
2. Has determined the student's eligibility and has recommended the student for the program.
3. Confirms funding status for any of the program services which the student is eligible.
4. Completes any service plan documents with the student and the family indicating the services he or she is requesting (for VR services, a completed Individual Plan for Employment [IPE]).
5. Provides the family and the student with any fees that may be required by the program.
6. Arranges, in cooperation with the school district, for the student to select service provider to obtain the recommended services.
7. Initiates employer outreach if employment is a desired outcome, or initiates outreach to technical schools or colleges.
8. Advises school personnel, student, and the family of additional assessment materials that may be needed.

*This list represents minimum activities that should be accomplished by these service providers.

their own planning purposes. Again, states may differ in what they call these documents, but for the purposes of this discussion we will call these planning documents Individual Service Plans (ISP). Providers use ISPs to identify a person's service needs, and then services are delineated into goals and objectives that are assigned to specific people, agencies, or providers of service. While a student is in the second phase of transition planning, adult service providers should begin to assist the school in the identification of the student's future service needs.

With the assistance of the adult service community, providers of services should be easily identified for students. As students approach graduation, the assistance and consultation of the adult service community becomes even more important. Most school personnel and families of students with disabilities are not always aware of the various providers of service that are available for individuals with disabilities in their communities. But working with case managers and support coordinators, who generally are aware of the community resources, can be beneficial. Case managers or support coordinators are usually employed by the state MR/DD or Mental Health (MH) systems and can make referrals on behalf of people with disabilities to the appropriate service providers. Therefore, inviting a case manager or support coordinator to the student's IEP/transition meeting will provide the needed personnel to offer this critical information. In some states the case manager or support coordinator may be an independent broker themselves. That is, they are not employed by the state system, but by an agency that contracts support coordination services. In either situation, the person can provide the information to identify the appropriate service providers in the community and aid the school, the student and the family in securing the services needed for the student after graduation.

School personnel play an integral part in this process. They, too, should be aware of the service system which students may likely need and use beyond school. This can be done in a very simple way. Many communities have resource guides that offer information about the various providers of service in that community. School personnel can familiarize themselves by obtaining a resource guide and learning about the various service providers in their community. This can be a helpful aid but it should be a complement to the assistance that one can receive by a good case manager or support coordinator.

STUDENT RESPONSIBILITY IN IDENTIFYING AND SELECTING SERVICE PROVIDERS

Throughout this book we have been supporting the idea of student-centered activities. That is, activities and decisions should be based on what is good for the student and what he or she chooses as an outcome. This also requires a self-directed approach for the student. We believe students should be more self-determined and take as much responsibility as possible for the learning activities and services identified in their IEP/transition plans. If possible, students should have the primary responsibility identifying and selecting their own service providers as a practice in the IEP/transition planning process.

For students to have a more active role in this process, they must become aware of the services and service providers available to them. This requires school personnel to provide the student with information and knowledge of the service providers in the community. This can be done in several ways. The following are a few possibilities:

- Give students assignments that require them to identify human service providers in their community and what their services are.
- Conduct community tours where students can visit service providers and get information as to what their services are.
- Bring speakers into classes to discuss the community system and what services they have to offer.
- Conduct "resource fairs" during a school open house where service providers can have displays and discuss with students and families their services individually.

These are a few examples of what schools can do to increase the student's awareness in the service system. This is followed by the selection of service providers. This is most difficult if the student has not had the opportunity to make choices and decisions in the past. Therefore, a student's ability to choose and select service providers comes from years of practice in self-determination. It comes from students being given choices and encouragement to make decisions about many things that occur to them in their lives. Schools and parents should encourage students to participate in their IEP/transition planning process and, if possible, to actually chair the meetings by the time they are attending high school. This is not something that is easily accepted by school personnel or some parents, but we must remember that students who are of adult age will be asked to make decisions as adults by the adult service community. Preparation and encouragement in this area is an important consideration.

POTENTIAL BARRIERS TO INTERAGENCY COLLABORATION AND/OR COMMUNITY LINKAGES

Despite the requirement by IDEA that transition is a collaborative process, collaboration seems to be difficult to achieve. Successful transition provides a smooth "handoff" of a student's service needs to service providers based in the community who will continue what school district personnel have identified as critical areas of need for the student. Usually the transition from school to adult life is smooth when the level of support provided equals that which the student needs to be successful in the community.

But a smooth transition does not always occur, and there are potential barriers to the transition from school to adult life. Barriers can be avoided when transition begins early (earlier for some where their needs are significant) and effective collaboration with agencies is achieved. Yet, some barriers may still exist, such as:

- lack of available funding to support the student after school, causing collaboration efforts to flounder;

- starting the transition and interagency collaboration process late causing delays in placing the student on a waiting list;
- schools not inviting agencies to the IEP meeting where transition planning will be discussed;
- not clearly identifying the student's potential needs beyond school and misinterpreting what the student will need for community living;
- not preparing the student to direct his or her own service options or to develop self-advocacy abilities;
- team members not having a clear understanding of their role and responsibility to the transition process;
- team members not focusing or agreeing on the student's personal goals, or team members having different expectations of the student that do not match up with those of the student; and
- poor communication between schools, students/parents, and community service providers.

Sue Anne and Mike

Sue Anne's transition to college was smoother because of interagency collaboration. Her high school guidance counselor knew what documentation she would need to be able to obtain needed accommodations at college. Likewise, the director of the Disability Support Services office at Sue Anne's college knew that the high school would do a good job ensuring that Sue Anne would have the necessary documentation. Arrangements were made for Sue Anne and her family to visit the Disability Support Service office before her graduation to ensure a seamless transition from high school to college. Because of repeated and effective collaboration between the high school and the college, students like Sue Anne would benefit from a smoother transition to adulthood.

Mike's intense and complex support needs resulted in the need for even more intense interagency collaboration. He applied for services from the Developmental Disabilities office in order to put him on a waiting list for residential services. His transition coordinator, who has an excellent relationship with both the local VR and DD offices, alerted these representatives that Mike is a likely candidate for supported employment services. It will be necessary to involve a local service provider agency that can deliver such services when Mike leaves the special education system. Many challenges will need to be faced, including ensuring that he is eligible for VR and DD services and that the best service providers are identified for him. These steps taken to help Mike and others like him to receive supported employment services are described in a later chapter.

CHAPTER SUMMARY

In this chapter we have discussed the various adult services that may be required by students in transition to adult life. We have discussed the community linkages that must be established to assist students beyond school. We have provided an overview of federal and state systems that can provide funding and services to students who qualify. We have discussed the importance of ensuring that practitioners, students, and families all become better aware of the possible services available to special education students after graduation. We have also discussed how student involvement in and their understanding and selection of these services are critical for self-determination and to ensure a "good life" as adults. The following activities will help you to further your understanding and awareness of this rather complex adult service system so that school personnel and human service professionals together can help students and families with the transition planning process.

APPLICATION ACTIVITIES

The application activities listed below are essential for your continued learning and skill development in transition. Each of the activities will require your time and energy but will help you develop your professional skills in this area.

For Practice and Enhanced Understanding:

Contact your local Mental Retardation or Developmental Disabilities (MR/DD) office and find out if a community services guide is available. Do the same for your local Mental Health (MH) office. As you review the service guide, what services are you familiar with? What providers are you familiar with that may be potential community linkages for your students going through the transition process?

Identify your state's service system (VR, MR/DD, and MH) and determine what services they offer and what their eligibility criteria are. Contact each of those local or regional offices and determine if there is a person assigned to work with transitioning students. Determine if there is a waiting list for individuals to receive their service and what the length of this waiting list is.

Interview a case manager or support coordinator from your local MR/DD or MH systems and find out what his or her role is in assisting individuals with disabilities and particularly students of transition age. When would he or she be likely to assist in the transition process for a student? What support or service could he or she provide prior to the student graduating from school? What is his or her understanding and relationship with the vocational rehabilitation system? Obtain an application and determine what the eligibility criteria are.

Interview a Rehabilitation Counselor from the VR system in your area and find out what his or her role is in assisting individuals with disabilities and particularly students of transition age. When would he or she be likely to assist in the transition process for a student? What support or service could he or she provide prior to the student graduating from school? What is his or her relationship with the MR/DD and MH systems? Obtain an application form and determine what the eligibility criteria are.

Many regions have transition coordinating councils. These are interagency councils that allow agency representatives to meet to discuss issues of mutual concern in developing quality transition services within a local area, for example, within a particular county or town. Determine in your area if there is a transition coordinating council and find out if they have a transition guide or if they have established some guidelines for your community to follow. If there is no transition coordinating council in your area, consider organizing one. List all of the potential members of this council and develop a mission statement for transition planning in your area.

Consider these additional activities:

- Help organize a resource fair where service providers can come together to discuss their services to students and families.
- Put together a packet that contains community linkage information for students and families to review to become better aware of the possible supports and services available to the student as an adult.
- Design a curriculum (or training module) for students to learn about the role and responsibility of becoming an adult.

For Your Portfolio:

Develop your own personal directory of adult service agencies. Use a large three-ring binder and insert dividers to create sections for each of the major types of agencies we have described in this chapter. As you gather information from the above activities, insert program descriptions, brochures, business cards, and other materials into the binder. Keep it well organized and current.

RESOURCES AND WEBSITES

The following resources and websites will allow you to extend your knowledge about how to work most effectively and collaboratively with agencies to benefit families and students toward an effective transition. There are numerous organizations and Internet sources that can provide information and best practice ideas; therefore, you may need to do an extensive search to obtain information on your specific area. Consider including these resources in your professional portfolio.

For information about your local MR/DD or MH systems, or about local service provider agencies, refer to the websites of your state and/or county/local government, or refer to the Blue Pages in your local phone directory.

Rehabilitation Services Administration (RSA) Website

Provides a list of all VR agencies for each of the states.
www.ed.gov/about/offices/list/osers/rsa/resources-sta.html

Administration on Developmental Disabilities (ADD)

Provides a list of the Governor's Council on Developmental Disabilities and the Protection and Advocacy systems for each of the states.
www.acf.hhs.gov/programs/add/

Social Security Administration (SSA)

Social Security Online Office Locator
Provides information about local Social Security Offices.
http://s3abaca.ssa.gov/pro/fol/fol-home.html

Website on Centers for Independent Living

Provides a list of Centers for Independent Living for all of the states.
www.jik.com/ilcs/html

National Center on Secondary Education and Transition (NCSET)

Website about strategies for improving transition planning.
www.ncset.org

Virginia Commonwealth University Research and Training Center on Workplace Support and Job Retention

Provides research, training, and technical assistance.
www.worksupport.com

Transition Coalition Homepage

The Transition Coalition provides online information, support, and professional development on topics related to transition.
www.transitioncoalition.org

PACER Center (Parent Advocacy Coalition for Educational Rights)

National center dedicated to expanding opportunities and to enhance the quality of life for children and young adults with disabilities and their families. Emphasis is on families helping other families.
www.pacer.org

REFERENCES

Agran, M., Cain, H., & Cavin, M. (2002). Enhancing the involvement of rehabilitation counselors in the transition process. *Career Development for Exceptional Individuals, 25*, 141–155.

Aspel, N., Bettis, G., Quinn, P., Test, D. W., & Wood, W. M. (1999). A collaborative process for planning transition services for all students with disabilities. *Career Development for Exceptional Individuals, 22*, 21–42.

Baer, R., Flexer, R., & McMahan, R. (2005). Transition models and promising practices. In R. Flexer, T. Simmons, P. Luft, & R. Baer (Eds.), *Transition planning for secondary students with disabilities* (2nd ed.) (pp. 53–82). Upper Saddle River, NJ: Merrill Prentice Hall.

Certo, N., Mautz, D., Smalley, K., Wade, H., Luecking, R., Pumpian, I., Sax, C., Noyes, D., & Wechsler, J. (2003). Review and discussion of a model for seamless transition to adulthood. *Education and Training in Developmental Disabilities, 38*, 3–17.

Cozzens, G., Dowdy, C., & Smith, T. (1999). *Adult agencies: Linkages for adolescents in transition: Transition series*. Austin, TX: Pro-Ed.

Dettmer, P., Dyck, N., & Thurston, L. (1999). *Consultation, collaboration and teamwork for students with special needs* (3rd ed.). Boston: Allyn and Bacon.

Dickinson, L. D., & Verbeek, L. R. (2002). Wage differentials between college graduates with and without learning disabilities. *Journal of Learning Disabilities, 20,* 175–185.

Durlak, C. M., Rose, E., & Bursuck, W.D. (1994). Preparing high school students with learning disabilities for the transition to postsecondary education: Teaching the skills of self-determination. *Journal of Learning Disabilities, 27,* 51–59.

Erlanger, H. S., & Roth, W. (1985). Disability policy: The parts and the whole. *American Behavioral Scientist, 23*(3), 319–346.

Grossi, T., Schaaf, L., Steigerwald, M., & Mank, D. (2002). Adult employment. In K. Storey, P. Bates, & D. Hunter (Eds.), *The road ahead: Transition to adult life for persons with disabilities* (pp. 101–120). St. Augustine, FL: TRN Publishers.

Hanley-Maxwell, C., Whitney-Thomas, J., & Pogoloff, S. (1995). The second shock: Parental perspectives on their child's transition from school to adult life. *Journal of the Association for Persons with Severe Disabilities, 20,* 3–16.

Harris, L., & Associates (1987). *The ICD survey II: Employing disabled Americans*. New York: Author.

Harris, L., & Associates (1994). N.O.D./Harris survey of Americans with disabilities (Study No. 942003). New York: Author.

Milson, A., & Hartley, M. (2005). Assisting students with learning disabilities transitioning to college: What school counselors should do. *Professional School Counseling, 8,* 436–442.

Noyes, D., & Sax, C. (2003). *Changing systems for transition: Students, families, and professionals working together*. Unpublished manuscript.

Nuehring, M., & Sitlington, P. (2003). Transition as a vehicle: Moving from high school to an adult vocational service provider. *Journal of Disability Policy Studies, 14,* 23–35.

Office of Special Education and Rehabilitative Services. (2004). www.ed.gov/print/about/office/list/osers/rsa/faq.html.

Parker, R., & Szymanski, E. (1998). *Rehabilitation counseling: Basics and beyond* (3rd ed.). Austin, TX: Pro-Ed.

Rubin, S. E., & Roessler, R. T. (2001). *Foundations of the vocational rehabilitation process*. Austin, TX: Pro-Ed.

Social Security Administration. (2001). *2001 Red book on employment support*. Publication No. 64-030.

Social Security Administration, Office of Research, Evaluation and Statistics. (2002). Quarterly report on SSI disabled recipients who work: March 2002, Washington, DC: Author.

Test, D. W. (2004). Invited commentary on Rusch and Braddock (2004). One person at a time. *Research and Practice for Person with Severe Disabilities, 29,* 248–252.

Turnbull, R., Turnbull, A., Shank, M., & Smith, S. (2004). *Exceptional lives: Special education in today's schools* (4th ed.). Upper Saddle River, NJ: Merrill.

Wehman, P., & Targett, P. (2004). Principles of curriculum design: Road to transition from school to adulthood. In P. Wehman & J. Kregel (Eds.), *Functional curriculum for elementary, middle, & secondary age students with special needs* (2nd ed.) (pp. 1–36). Austin, TX: Pro-Ed.

Wehman, P., Brooke, V., West, M., Targett, P., Green, H., Inge, K., & Kregel, J. (1998). Barriers to competitive employment for persons with disabilities. In P. Wehman (Ed.), *Developing transition plans: Transition series* (pp. 5–24). Austin, TX: Pro-Ed.

CHAPTER 6

INTERACTING
WITH BUSINESSES

CHAPTER OBJECTIVES

Upon completion of this chapter, you will be able to

1. contact local employers in an effective manner.
2. complete a full compatibility analysis between a student with a disability and a specific job or career.
3. conduct a comprehensive job analysis.
4. analyze the culture of a workplace and identify important sources of natural support.
5. work with local businesses to create employment and training opportunities for students with disabilities and/or assist students in job development activities.

KEY TOPICS TO LOOK FOR IN THIS CHAPTER . . .

- Focus on Capacity: In this chapter, we discuss using students' profiles of their strengths, abilities, and capacities to guide the job seeking process.
- Collaboration: The business and industry community is a key collaborator in our efforts to help young people with disabilities achieve successful transition outcomes.
- Adaptation and Accommodation: In this chapter, notice how professionals need to be creative in making adaptations and accommodations that allow workers with disabilities to succeed in the workplace.

As introduced earlier in this book, employment in the community is one critical aspect of a satisfying and fulfilling adult life. Although transition planning is guided by several categories of desired postschool outcomes (employment, postsecondary education, community living, and community participation), employment is in many ways the linchpin upon which the other areas of successful living depend (Kraemer, McIntyre, & Blacher, 2003; Wehman, 2001). As shown in Table 6.1, successful employment can contribute to one's sense of fulfillment, self-definition, and self-esteem, or even sufficient income to use to enjoy other aspects of living. Work is, therefore, a central component to adult living.

TABLE 6.1   Potential Impact of Employment on Other Aspects of Adult Living

Financial Stability and Security:

- Greater independence due to financial security
- Greater sense of control over one's destiny
- Increased sense of security that future financial challenges will be met

Self-esteem and Self-definition:

- A sense of pride on one's profession
- A sense of oneself as a contributing member of the local community
- A sense of one's immediate or future impact on society

Participation in Community Life:

- Ability to use community resources for recreation and leisure
- Ability to travel safely within the community
- Ability to take vacations

Home Living:

- Ability to have a home that is safe, comfortable, and enjoyable
- Ability to improve one's living conditions

Challenge and Advancement:

- Opportunity to find fulfillment through facing challenges
- Opportunity to advance within one's chosen profession

For this reason, it is essential that professionals within special education programs at the secondary level develop skills in working with business and industry. In many ways, this presents new responsibilities and challenges for school personnel, who may not be used to working with local businesses. Without these skills, however, educators are unable to help young people with disabilities to start on the right career path. It should be noted that although employment training, work experiences, and job development are often seen as a programmatic need for students with mental retardation or more significant challenges, employment as an outcome is an expectation for all students, regardless of disability. One of the major goals of public education is for students to become self-sufficient adult members of society, and this means obtaining employment. Therefore, every student receiving special education services should have some exposure to opportunities that exist for them. For some students with milder disabilities, this may be a matter of career awareness and matching their skills with the appropriate career path, while for those students with greater needs it means actual job training and job development services as part of their special education program (Hutchins & Renzaglia, 2002).

In this chapter, we will describe the role that employment and employment training play in the transition process. We will also describe successful ways for school programs to contact and then collaborate with local business and industry representatives in order to develop jobs and training opportunities for their students. We will also describe how to use the compatibility matching process to help predict students' potential successes in certain types of employment. We will describe how to conduct a thorough job analysis, including an analysis of the workplace culture and natural support systems. Finally, we will review guidelines for establishing community-based employment training sites that conform with Department of Labor regulations while providing optimal job training and exploration opportunities. First, we will provide a brief overview of some research related to these topics.

RESEARCH RELATED TO INTERACTING WITH BUSINESSES

A focus of study related to interacting with businesses has been the comparison of different approaches to developing jobs for people with disabilities. Williams, Petty, and Verstegen (1998) compared the cold-call method of job development with the referral method. In the cold-call method, the job developer makes initial contact with a potential employer without the intercession of an intermediary, while the referral method relies on other community members and business representatives to serve as intermediaries. Data were gathered through four rehabilitation agencies in Tennessee over an eight-month period. The referral method resulted in fewer rejections and required fewer contacts than the cold-call method. Nietupski, Verstegen, Hamre-Nietupski, and Tanty (1993) described five benefits of the referral model of job development: (1) it adds credibility to the services of a rehabilitation agency; (2) it uses a "time-honored" approach in business; (3) it allows access to higher level decision makers; (4) it saves time and effort in job development; and (5) it can lead to greater success in job development. Brady and Rosenberg (2002) described the importance of assessing the "goodness of fit" between the characteristics of potential employees with disabilities and the requirements of jobs and job environments. Callahan and Garner (1997) contrasted the labor market approach to job development with the individualized approach. In the labor market approach, the needs of specific employers are assessed and then potential employees who can meet those needs are identified and matched to specific jobs. In the individualized approach, a comprehensive profile of an individual is developed and then potential employment opportunities are created through consultation to employers so that the individual's unique characteristics are viewed as contributions of assets to specific workplaces. Callahan and Garner (1997) point out that, although the labor market approach has been successful with people with moderate to mild disabilities, the individualized approach is necessary for those with severe and complex disabilities who typically do not succeed when competing for existing jobs. Unger and Simmons (2005) described several options for job development for students in transition, including customized employment, supported self-employment, competitive employment with supports, the use of business advisory councils, the use of job clubs, and mentoring approaches for job seeking and retention. Steere, Ellerd,

Sampson, and Barry (1997) stressed the importance of person centered planning and the use of a business advisory council in finding jobs for individuals with severe disabilities. Menchetti and Garcia (2003) also stressed the utility of person centered planning in helping to develop jobs that matched people's career aspirations as closely as possible. Carey, Potts, Bryen, and Shankar (2004) described the importance of using personal networks to locate potential jobs. In their qualitative study of users of augmentative and alternative communication devices, they found that, although members of personal networks who were considered to have strong ties to the focus person (e.g., family and close friends), the use of "weak ties" (acquaintances from the community) opened up new avenues for job development. Finally, Griffin and Hammis (2003) described self-employment as a potential option that can meet the needs of some individuals with disabilities while still resulting in community integration.

Several authors have investigated ways of collaborating more closely with employers and with corporations in the job development and design processes. Wehman (1998) stressed that supported employment professionals must view both people with disabilities and employers as their customers and that marketing efforts must focus on assessing and meeting the needs of both of these constituent groups. The theme of focusing on employers' needs and viewing them as collaborative partners has extended to job development efforts within major corporations. Zivolich and Weiner (1997) described the success of their collaboration with Pizza Hut, which resulted in numerous job placements over a six-year period. They extended this collaborative approach to job development to United Studios of Hollywood and reported successful placement of sixteen people with severe disabilities (Weiner & Zivolich, 1998). A key feature of the United Studios project was a focus on natural support strategies within the workplace. In another example of collaboration with business and industry, Donovan and Tilson (1998) described the work of the Marriott Foundation's "Bridges . . . From School to Work" program in seven communities across the United States. The program involved job development and matching, followed by a paid internship experience with support, and finally placement in a competitive job. Over three thousand individuals participated in the program from 1990 to 1996, with 84 percent of them completing internships, and 84 percent of those individuals being placed into competitive jobs. Weiner and Zivolich (2003) reported on the use of a consultant model of natural supports that enlisted supervisors and co-workers throughout the employment process. Their collaborative work with a country club work environment resulted in longitudinal success for the individuals with disabilities who worked there. In addition, the employer requested more additional applicants with disabilities than could be referred by the local developmental disabilities agency. These studies highlight the critical importance of enlisting employers as collaborators in the job development process.

Finally, research has been conducted to determine the perceptions of employers toward hiring people with disabilities. Kregel and Unger (1993) conducted interviews with forty-six employers and found that they had generally favorable views toward employees with disabilities and toward the services of supported employment providers. Supported employment services were not viewed as disruptive or overly intrusive, but concerns were expressed about the potential of supported employment to address the job turnover needs of employers. Morgan and Alexander (2005) surveyed employers with and without experience in hiring people with disabilities. Both groups of employers had generally favorable attitudes, but those with experience in hiring people with disabilities were better able to identify benefits to such hiring. In addition, 97 percent of those employers with experience in hiring people with disabilities reported that they would do so again, while 80 percent of those without experience indicated that they would be willing to hire employees with disabilities. This finding suggests that, if the job development and placement process is successful and employers are satisfied, then they are more likely to hire people with disabilities again. Smith, Webber, Graffam, & Wilson (2004a) surveyed 656 employers in Australia and found that employers' perceptions of the job matching process were important determinants of their degree of satisfaction with the performance of employees with disabilities. This suggests that the approaches that schools and rehabilitation agencies use in the job development process can have substantial impact on how employers view new employees with disabilities. In a related study, Smith, Webber, Graffam, & Wilson (2004b) found that employers from the same survey had specific concerns about employees with disabilities and how they fit into the workplace climate. The authors suggest that employers may be particularly sensitive about the work and social behavior of employees with disabilities.

Together, these studies highlight the importance of working collaboratively with business and industry representatives to find or create employment opportunities for young people with disabilities. If job development efforts are conducted in a systematic and professional manner, and if they build on the abilities and strengths of students with disabilities, employer perceptions can be very positive and can influence their future hiring decisions. Considering that satisfied employers can become referrals for placements with other employers, this is indeed important for job developers to keep in mind.

THE ROLE OF BUSINESS AND INDUSTRY IN TRANSITION PROGRAMS

Effective transition programs cannot operate without close collaboration with local business and industry. Transition programs in schools gain many benefits from working with business and industry:

- Businesses provide information and experiences that allow students to make informed choices about career options and preferences.
- Businesses provide information about skills and abilities that students will need to develop in order to be successful within the working world.
- Businesses can provide training sites to allow students to develop work and work-related skills within a naturalistic setting.
- Businesses allow students to demonstrate their abilities to adult service agencies prior to graduation, thereby increasing the likelihood that these agencies will view the students as employable.

For these reasons, school personnel who are involved in developing transition programs for students with disabilities must view local employers as partners and allies in the transition planning process.

Likewise, local businesses benefit from working closely with the schools:

- By working with the schools, businesses are able to identify students who would make promising employees once they leave the school system.
- Businesses benefit from working with the schools because they will be viewed as contributing members of the local community who are concerned about all community members, including those challenged by a disability.
- By collaborating with the local schools, local business leaders have the opportunity to have a positive influence on the local education system by informing the schools about important skills, abilities, and attributes of successful employees.

For these reasons, successful collaboration between local education agencies and local businesses can be mutually beneficial. In order to initiate this collaboration, school personnel must develop skills in identifying, contacting, negotiating with, and working with local businesses. Consider how collaboration with businesses helps Sue Anne and Mike.

Sue Anne

Sue Anne's exposure to the world of work started during her intermediate and high school years, primarily her volunteer work at the daycare center, her church's preschool program, and her numerous babysitting jobs. These experiences convinced her to pursue an early childhood education degree in her postsecondary education program. While at the college, she had the opportunity to develop skills early in her program at the college preschool program, first as an observer and then as a student intern. In addition, she had specific field-based assignments through her education courses, and these further exposed her to the field of early childhood education. Finally, her skill development continued at a more advanced level in her student teaching experience during her final year at the college. These longitudinal experiences helped Sue Anne to find a career path and to develop and refine her professional skills to the point where she was a competitive applicant for teaching positions.

Mike

As discussed in Chapter 2, Mike's team reached the important conclusion that he very much needed a community-based work experience. Working with the school's transition coordinator, Mike's teacher arranges for Mike to go out to visit several community work sites. These visits are not initially intended as in-depth training opportunities, but to provide Mike with some exposure to different types of work places and employment activities. Arranging these visits is both time and labor intensive for the transition coordinator, but the team is committed to providing Mike with the experiences he needs to start to make an informed choice about what kind of work he might enjoy. Fortunately, the school has a positive relationship with several area businesses that have allowed their work sites to be used for job exploration and training. Mike is able to experience jobs that include custodial work in an office setting and dishwashing/kitchen work in a food service setting. These experiences, and his reactions to them, will provide valuable information that Mike's team needs to help him plan an effective transition to supported employment.

DEVELOPING COMMUNITY-BASED TRAINING EXPERIENCES

It is important for schools to find and enlist potential employers for two reasons: first, so that students can experience jobs and be exposed to a variety of job situations while enhancing their skills; and second, to secure and obtain jobs for students once they graduate from school. Both reasons are vital for the development of appropriate and effective transition programs. Yet, the enlisting of employers for these purposes has been difficult for school personnel to achieve. Throughout this chapter, we will look at strategies that will be beneficial for schools to consider when enlisting employers for their transition programs.

First, let us look at how to create and develop community-based opportunities for students. As mentioned above, community-based work opportunities provide important exposure to the world of work. For example, if students are not able to articulate to their transition teams their interests with regard to employment, the teams may want to expose these students to potential jobs to discover their interests. The team may want to find out what the student's strengths in specific work sites might be, or they may want to enhance skills or develop particular attributes in students. These are a few of the reasons for creating community-based options. It should be mentioned that community-based options are not only for the discovery of job interests, but they can also provide a way to discover other interests for a student, such as recreation and community life activities. They can provide valuable information to school personnel on other critical areas related to transition in a broader sense, such as housing, community participation, and recreation/leisure activities. For the purpose of the discussion in this chapter, we will focus our attention on employment and enlisting employers in order to create community-based options.

It should also be noted that career exploration is not limited to students with significant disabilities or even those in special education. Students exiting schools who do not have clear career paths for themselves can benefit from such opportunities as well. Being exposed to a variety of career options through community-based exposure may prove beneficial in aiding a variety of students in identifying a career path.

Steps in Developing Community-Based Training Experiences

The following process should be used to develop job-training sites in which students can experience and be exposed to work opportunities. Transition coordinators who are attempting to establish new or more extensive community-based options are encouraged to follow these steps in developing their programs.

1. **Identify the types of jobs to secure from the local community:** This requires an understanding of what jobs students are interested in and from which they would benefit. One of the key aspects of this first step is to gain insight from students as to what their interests are. This will guide the direction for securing potential job sites in the community. In the instance where students are unable to articulate or provide specific information about their interests, it would be advisable to solicit information from family members or people who know the students the best. This may offer a direction, but it may also be a "search and discovery mission" on behalf of the student. Conducting a person centered plan is an excellent strategy for obtaining this information, particularly for students with more severe disabilities (Mount & Zwernick, 1988). Also, the use of surveys and interest inventories is an additional way to gain information about students' interests (look back to Chapter 2).

2. **Identify businesses with specific jobs targeted from step one:** Once the types of jobs are identified, the businesses that provide those jobs are targeted for development. A key point here is to try to locate job sites that project a positive image. That is, jobs or settings that are valued and will enhance the value of a person's image should be the priority. The image factor may be in terms of location (e.g., upscale vs. run down area) or type (e.g., desirable vs. undesirable jobs); these are important considerations to keep in mind when developing a business connection. These considerations, which relate to the acceptance of people with disabilities by the community and their value within society, build on the principles of Social Role Valorization (Wolfensberger, 1983).

    Identifying potential businesses can be done in various ways. For example, transition coordinators may obtain personal contacts and connections from colleagues and teachers, from the student's parents and relations, from the Chamber of Commerce, from business advisory boards or from contacts provided by adult service agencies that offer employment services. The personal connection method is generally an effective strategy for identifying potential business (Griffin & Targett, 2001). Business advisory councils have also been found to be effective in providing direction for job development efforts and in brokering contacts with other area businesses (Simmons & Whaley, 2001; Steere et al., 1997).

3. **Contact the business:** The next step in this process is to contact the business and express the school's interest for developing community-based sites. Letters to the business or a visit describing the purpose of your request and the value that the business could offer to the school and the student are often all that is needed to make a positive connection. The use of brochures and other marketing materials that describe the school's transition program is also a valuable strategy. Third, as suggested earlier, using other community members or leaders as referrals can be extremely effective and can result in improved opportunities to meet with local business owners. Local businesses are generally willing to par-

ticipate in school-sponsored programs as a community service, if they are approached in a professional manner.

4. Identify and analyze the appropriate jobs to be conducted as part of the work site experience: This requires a complete analysis of the job site and the jobs to be used for the purpose of the experience. Ecological inventories are required to fully analyze job sites in order to design an assessment system for collecting data about the student's potential participation and involvement in this site. Job analysis will be discussed in detail later in this chapter.

5. Schedule time for the community-based experience: Scheduling the community-based experience depends on many factors, including transportation, the student's school academic schedule, or when the experience is to be conducted. Other factors that are critical to consider are how long the student has left before graduation or how much information is needed to make decisions about specific outcomes, and so forth. It is our belief that as the students' classmates/peers approach graduation, the greater percentage of time students should be spending in community-based experiences. That is, if the transition student is eighteen years of age and all of his or her classmates/peers have left school (for higher education, technical school, or work), and if the student is expected to continue in school until twenty-one years of age, the more time the student should spend in community experiences. So, if at age eighteen the student is spending 50 percent of the time in community-based experiences, then by the time the student is twenty to twenty-one years of age he or she should spend 90 to 100 percent of the time in community-based experiences. This concept corresponds with the typical student's schedule of graduation and moving on to postschool activities.

6. Collect data on the experience: The final step in this process is to collect information and data on the experience so as to have documentation of the student's interests as well as other important factors. A system for collecting specific information and data should be developed.

This point may be common sense, but it is so important that it must be emphasized here: when looking for environments in order to develop community-based options, it is also important to look for environments that are attitudinally and physically accessible. First, the environments should be inviting and present an expression of acceptance which acknowledges diversity. Second, it would be foolish of us, as special educators and rehabilitation professionals, or as advocates for the rights of people with disabilities, to consider an environment that is not physically accessible, even if the student does not seemingly need a barrier-free environment. Additional factors to consider in creating community-based options can be found in Table 6.2.

DEVELOPING JOBS FOR ADULTHOOD

The second purpose to enlist employers and businesses is to secure jobs for students so that when they graduate high school they will have successfully transitioned into a com-

TABLE 6.2   What to Look for in Developing Community-Based Options

- A positive workplace culture: A job setting that values and demonstrates respect for all of its employees.
- A site with a variety of job types: Settings that offer opportunities to experience and be exposed to a variety of job types and situations.
- Availability of a flexible schedule: A setting that can accommodate a flexible time schedule so that the student can be assessed working at various times during the day.
- Jobs within the business that are representative of jobs found in other businesses in the community: This is referring to a business that is not seen as an "exclusive" type of business where jobs can only be obtained in that company.
- Job types that are representative of the student's choice: Community experiences should be based on what the student is interested in and desires to be exposed to.

munity-based job. Job development for this purpose is perhaps the most challenging function that any transition specialist or rehabilitation professional will have. Although there have been many small and large companies who have participated with local schools to utilize their work settings for the purpose of providing experiences to students (i.e., large department store chains and regional super market chains), the development of community-based opportunities for special education students continues to be a challenge for transition programs, despite the evidence of its worth and effectiveness. It is unclear why the development of community-based employment sites is difficult for school professionals, but it may relate to a poor understanding of the business world, to the minimal training professionals receive in job development, or professionals' belief that this is not one of their responsibilities. Whatever the reason, job development has clearly been a difficult function for transition professionals, as evidenced by the poor employment outcomes experienced by students graduating from special education programs nationally. And yet, one of the key indicators of an effective transition program is whether a student is working after he or she graduates from school.

There are many strategies for conducting job development. One of these strategies popularized early during the initial inception of the supported employment model was the "market survey" approach (Wehman, 1981). This approach was designed to generally identify within a community those jobs that are considered to be most readily available with respect to the high turnover rate. Once these jobs were identified, there would be a matching process to secure those jobs for people. Although, initially this was an excellent approach to securing jobs for people with disabilities, one of the criticisms was that it did not consider the person's interests sufficiently. Therefore, as any new concept, there has been an evolution to the strategy of job development. Current practice in job development has taken on a business approach and has acknowledged that job development should have a marketing consideration. First there should be an attempt to make the business community aware that a transition program exists and that graduates will be a potential workforce for them and, secondly, that the program will produce students with the necessary skills that employers need to fill their positions. Therefore, marketing should describe the services to be provided and the ability of the students who are looking to be employed.

Developing jobs necessitates the establishment of relationships with businesses and ensuring that these relationships will be mutually beneficial to schools and students and to businesses. A study regarding this relationship indicated that job developers who focused on establishing personal, trusting relationships with employers rather than filling a job opening were the most successful (Hagner & Daning, 1993). In doing so, the job developer can basically take three approaches: assess the student's skills and then find a job that maximized those skills; assess the needs of a business and match it to the student's skills; or a combination of the first two approaches. A generally accepted approach to job development has been determining what a student's interests are regarding a particular job or career choice while also assessing their skills and then finding the businesses that will offer those possibilities for the student to be successful.

We have already determined that the first step to effective job development is to create a marketing plan that includes brochures and other professional materials and activities that will raise awareness and inform business of the school's transition program. These marketing materials should be highly professional in appearance and accurately portray how the transition program instructs students in order to meet the demands of the employment world. These materials should also show how students and community businesses benefit from collaboration. Now, we need to take that professional behavior and apply it to secure jobs for students in transition programs.

As discussed previously, one of the most effective means for becoming aware of and obtaining jobs is generally referred to as the "personal networking" approach. This refers to obtaining job leads from sources that are personally known to the job developer and/or job seeker. Witt (1992) reported that as many as 80 percent of jobs are filled without ever coming to the attention of the public. That means that these jobs were obtained by a referral or knowing about the open position from some personal connection. Individuals with disabilities might be considered to be at a disadvantage when conducting a job search. Obtaining job leads through personal connections may offset this disadvantage and create the opportunity the person may need to secure a job. The personal network approach means that the student's family members, friends, and relations be asked to make referrals for potential jobs. These personal connections can provide the job developer with a "foot in the door," often needed when developing jobs for this population. Other networking approaches might be through Business Advisory Councils who come together to strategize and help create opportunities for employment for students in transition programs. Another interesting networking approach involves the use of *advocate referrals*. These are simply business people who are considered advocates or as ones who embrace the idea that people with disabilities can work and should be given the opportunity for community integrated employment. These advocate referrals use their personal business connections to advocate and provide access to these business contacts.

All of these ideas are proven strategies for job development. The job developer needs to find their comfort level and the strategy that best fits his or her personality and go with it. The personal connection methods though, should be generally used in connection with other strategies. Additional job development approaches to consider are responding to recruitment advertisements, contacting businesses that are not advertising by making "cold calls" (finding employers and simply contacting them for a potential job), or using the state job services or vocational rehabilitation agencies to obtain job leads.

Once a job lead is obtained, the job developer must present a case for why it is a good idea for the employer to hire the person. As one prepares for this process, a script should be developed that will clearly elaborate and present the reason for the visit, the nature of the meeting, and why it is a good idea for the employer to hire the person. There is no way to predict in advance which employers will be receptive to hiring people with disabilities and, although decisions are often based on a number of factors, one factor that is important is the job developers professionalism and the quality of the presentation. Some critical factors in creating a professional presentation are listed below (Griffin & Targett, 2001).

- Appearance: Dress professionally and in a manner appropriate to the business.
- Positive Attitude: Focus on developing relationships instead of getting a job lead.
- Business Meeting Guidelines: The presentation should be clear, concise, and no longer than ten to fifteen minutes.
- Set the Stage: At the start of the meeting, explain what you would like to achieve.
- Address Concerns and Questions: Anticipate questions and be prepared to answer without hesitation.
- Wrap Up: At the close of the meeting indicate what it is you want—a job for the student!

Job development is a difficult activity for anyone in the field helping people with disabilities secure jobs in the community. Those people just getting started should talk to job developers and shadow them to obtain pointers and ideas. Job developers should not get frustrated when they are not successful in the first or even the tenth attempt in securing a job for someone. With practice, perseverance, and patience, the job developer will get results. Developing a marketing plan, designing a script that describes the program and your expected outcomes, and practice are the key ingredients for success.

Consider This!   Several authors have suggested that job developers conduct a job market screening in order to determine potential employers who may be willing to hire individuals with disabilities (Moon, Goodall, Barcus, & Brooke, 1986; Nietupski, Verstegen, & Petty, 1995). The employment opportunities that result from such an analysis can then be pursued, based on the individual interests of specific students (Parent, Cone, Turner, & Wehman, 1998). The following questions can be used to guide this job market analysis.

- Who are the major employers in this community?
- What are the most prevalent types of jobs that are available?
- What businesses have a strong track record of hiring people with disabilities?
- What jobs have a higher turnover rate, and why?

■ Are there seasonal employment opportunities that exist within this community?

■ What new businesses are projected to open or what existing businesses are planning on expansions?

Now, looking back over this list of questions, try to provide answers to them for your local community. If you do not know the answer to one of the questions for your local community, investigate your local job market more closely by reading the papers, contacting the Chamber of Commerce, or checking one of the One-Stop Centers that provide information about the local job market. Once you have gathered this information, keep a file on your local job market, and then add to the file as you come across new information about new businesses that open or expand, or other changes in the job market. In conducting this activity, you will find that the local newspaper, including the local and business sections, provide a wealth of valuable information.

COMPATIBILITY MATCHING

As school personnel develop employment-training opportunities for students in transition, it is important to help students make choices about types of jobs or even careers to which they may be best suited. Although there are many strategies and tools that may be used to guide students' career decision making, one effective and flexible strategy is *compatibility matching* (Moon et al., 1986; Powell, Pancsofar, Steere, Butterworth, Itzkowitz, & Rainforth, 1991). Compatibility matching does not tell students what job or career to pursue, but it does provide a direction for job search and development efforts.

Compatibility matching is based on the concept that people tend to be more successful and stay longer in jobs to which they are best suited or matched. Several theories of career advancement and work adjustment, such as the Minnesota Theory of Work Adjustment (Dawis & Lofquist, 1984), are based on this concept of congruence between the attributes and needs of the worker and the requirements or demands of the employer and job. The concept is that satisfaction for both the employee and employer are increased when congruence is high, which can lead to longer job tenure and increased productivity. In this section, we present a simple and flexible use of the compatibility matching process that can be adapted to different types of students and different careers or jobs.

Table 6.3 shows the steps of using the compatibility matching process. First, the job developer develops a list of factors to be used in comparing the student to a particular job and to assess the quality of the match between the student and job. Factors are any consideration that should be taken into account in making decisions about whether or not a person could potentially succeed at a particular job. Table 6.4 provides a list of potential factors that a job developer may wish to use in assessing the quality of a match between a student and a job. Note that these factors are not the same as job duties or essential functions of the job. Rather, they are aspects of the job that tend to influence someone's success at that particular job. For example, some jobs require employees to have excellent hygiene skills and to dress neatly (a bank employee), while other jobs do not (a groundskeeper). Readers should note that there are

TABLE 6.3   Steps of the Compatibility Matching Process

1. List all potential factors that could provide information in assessing the quality of the match between the individual and the potential job.
2. Analyze the job and record information about it in relation to each factor that was selected in step #1. This should focus on the demands of the job and how a successful employee ought to be able to perform on the job.
3. Describe the individual in question in relation to the same set of factors that were used to describe the job.
4. If any information is missing regarding either the job or the individual, additional steps should be taken to find this information.
5. Once information is known about both the job and the individual in relation to each factor, the quality of the match between the person and the job should be assessed on each factor. It is helpful to use a Likert scale to indicate the quality of the match: for example, 3 = very well matched, 2 = moderately well matched, 1 = poorly match, 0 = very poorly matched.
6. For any factors that indicate a less than optimum match, list supports and accommodations that would improve the quality of the match on that factor.
7. When all of the above information has been gathered, assess the quality of the match overall and decide whether or not to pursue that job opportunity further.

Source: Powell, Pancsofar, Steere, Butterworth, Itzkowitz, & Rainforth, 1991.

almost limitless numbers of different factors that might be considered in comparing a person to a potential job.

Once the job developer has listed all potentially important factors, then the job is analyzed and is described according to these factors. For example, Table 6.5 shows a section of a compatibility analysis of supermarket checkout clerk's job. Simultaneous with this step, the job developer completes the section of the compatibility analysis that describes the individual on the same set of factors. This information may come from observations and interactions with the student, from the student himself or herself, or from the family. If person centered planning has been used, then the profile section will provide a great deal of this information. Clearly, the more well developed

TABLE 6.4   Potential Factors to Be Used in Assessing Person-to-Job Matches

■ Appearance	■ Orienting ability
■ Attention to details	■ Rate of work
■ Dress	■ Reading skills
■ Endurance	■ Schedule/availability
■ Hygiene	■ Strength
■ Interactions with customers	■ Stress tolerance
■ Interactions with co-workers	■ Tolerance for environmental conditions
■ Interactions with supervisors	■ Transportation/location
■ Math skills	■ Writing ability
■ Mobility/accessibility	

TABLE 6.5 Section of a Compatibility Analysis of a Supermarket Checkout Clerk's Job

FACTOR	DESCRIPTION OF THE JOB
Appearance	Must be well dressed and well groomed
Hygiene	Must be very neat and clean
Strength	Must be able to lift about 20 pounds
Endurance	Must be able to be on one's feet for entire shift
Attention to detail	Must be able to locate prices on some items; must be able to determine savings on current coupons
Math skills	Must have strong math skills; must have strong money use skills
Equipment use	Must be able to use a cash register. Must be able to use a flat scanner and hand-held scanner for price identification and inventory according to bar codes
Customer interaction skills	Must be very personable and have excellent customer interaction skills

the profile of the student, the easier it is to complete this aspect of the compatibility analysis. Table 6.6 shows this section of the compatibility analysis for a student with emotional disturbance. Once the job and the student have been described relative to each factor, the job developer and team assess the quality of the match on each factor.

TABLE 6.6 Section of a Compatibility Analysis of a Supermarket Checkout Clerk's Job—Student Assessment

FACTOR	DESCRIPTION OF THE STUDENT
Appearance	Is typically well dressed and well groomed
Hygiene	Is typically very neat and clean
Strength	Very strong
Endurance	Appears to have adequate endurance
Attention to detail	Is attentive to detail if interested in the topic; otherwise, requires prompting to notice details
Math skills	Has strong math skills (on grade level); computer use skills are strong; adequate money use skills
Equipment use	Has no experience with cash registers or scanners
Customer interaction skills	Has difficulty when corrected and may become sarcastic or angry if confronted

TABLE 6.7   Section of Compatibility Analysis for a Supermarket Checkout Clerk

Key: 3 = Excellent match   2 = Good match   1 = Marginal match   0 = Very poor match

FACTOR	DESCRIPTION OF THE JOB	STUDENT	QUALITY OF MATCH
Appearance	Must be well dressed and well groomed	Is typically well dressed and well groomed	2
Hygiene	Must be very neat and clean	Typically neat and clean	2
Strength	Need to lift 20 pounds	Very strong	3
Endurance	Must be able to be on one's feet for entire shift	Adequate endurance ability	2
Attention to detail	Must be extremely attentive to details in price, coupons, etc.	Is attentive to detail if interested in topic; otherwise, needs prompting to attend to details	1
Math skills	Must have excellent math skills; money skills important	Has strong math skills (on grade level) and has good computer use skills; adequate money use skills	2
Equipment use	Must be able to use a cash register and flat and hand-held scanners	No experience	0
Customer interaction	Must be very personable and have excellent customer interaction skills	Has difficulty when corrected and may become sarcastic or angry if confronted	0

Table 6.7 shows this comparison and assessment for the above-mentioned student and job. Supports and accommodations that may improve the quality of poor or marginal matches are then brainstormed. These supports and accommodations are not guaranteed to overcome all poor matches, but some may substantially improve the quality of the match on certain factors. Table 6.8 provides an example. Once all of the preceding steps have been completed, the team assesses the overall quality of the match and decides whether or not to proceed with trying to develop this job opportunity further for the student in question. There is no formula for how to determine the overall quality of the match; instead, members of the team need to use their best judgment in deciding whether or not this particular job opportunity has sufficient potential to warrant further efforts to secure it for the student.

It should be noted that compatibility matching is just one aspect of a broader job analysis, including the strategies that are discussed in the next section. This strategy does provide an indication to the student, family, and to the team whether or not specific jobs, or even certain types of jobs or careers, are worth pursuing. In the next section, we will describe additional strategies for analyzing jobs in greater detail.

TABLE 6.8 Section of Compatibility Analysis for a Supermarket Checkout Clerk

Key: 3 = Excellent match   2 = Good match   1 = Marginal match   0 = Very poor match

FACTOR	DESCRIPTION OF THE JOB	STUDENT	QUALITY OF MATCH	SUPPORTS
Appearance	Must be well dressed and well groomed	Is typically well dressed and well groomed	2	
Hygiene	Must be very neat and clean	Typically neat and clean	2	
Strength	Must lift 20 pounds	Very strong	3	
Endurance	Must be able to be on one's feet for entire shift (8 hours)	Adequate endurance ability	2	
Attention to detail	Must be extremely attentive to details in price/coupons	Is attentive to detail if interested in topic; otherwise, needs prompting to attend to details	1	Co-worker or supervisor reviews throughout the day; written self-prompting form at workstation.
Math skills	Must have excellent math skills; money use skills important	Has strong math skills (on grade level) and has good computer use skills; adequate money use skills	2	
Equipment use	Must be able to use a cash register and scanners	No experience	0	Training in use of cash register and scanners should be sufficient
Customer interaction	Must be very personable and have excellent customer interaction skills	Has difficulty when corrected and may become sarcastic or angry if confronted	0	Training in customer relations/interactions; anger management training with role playing

JOB ANALYSIS

Job analysis is conducted after a site or employment has been secured for an individual student. There is some debate as to *when* and *how* a job analysis should be conducted. The issue here is related to the *image* and *message* that is being sent to the employees of the worksite and potential co-workers. Some employment specialists prefer to conduct the job analysis prior to the person with disability being placed or employed at the jobsite while others prefer to conduct the job analysis as the person is learning the job skills. The issue and controversy here is that when a professional comes into a worksite and conducts this analysis the image of the person who will be placed there may be diverted from one of competence to one of incompetence. That is, co-workers and employees may perceive the person who will be placed there as having a "significant problem" and that is why the training specialist must come before the person. This issue is one that requires judgment on the part of the transition team and employment specialist, and this comes with experience. The critical factor here is that a job analysis be conducted in order to determine the best *fit* of the job for the individual student.

An effective job analysis requires several important factors to be identified and considered. The process that we describe here is adapted from recommendations by early leaders in the area of systematic instruction and job development for individuals with disabilities (Bellamy, Horner, & Inman, 1979; Rusch & Mithaug, 1980; Wehman, 1981). (A profile of one of these leaders, Marc Gold, is provided in Sidebar 6.1.)

The following points are critical factors to be considered: (1) schedule and work routine/task sequence; (2) job duties; (3) task analysis; and (4) potential job accommodations. Each of these are described below.

1. Schedule and Work Routine/Task Sequence: Identifying the work routine is the initial activity for the training specialist. Figure 6.1 provides a sample form for obtaining information on a work schedule and routine. This includes what time the person should arrive, take breaks, lunch, leave or report for specific responsibilities. This also includes task functions the individual is required to perform at specific times of the day.
2. Job Duties: This is a list of the main responsibilities and duties of the job that the person will be required to perform. This is not a reiteration of the task sequence but should contain a list of the main job responsibilities that the person is expected to perform as part of the job. A sample job duties form is in Figure 6.2.
3. Task Analysis: Once all of the job duties have been identified, the person should be allowed to begin to learn what is expected of him or her. The job duties or responsibilities that are the most challenging to the person, that is, that require intensive instruction, will need to be taught. Some employment specialists prefer to run through the job to allow any prior learned work behaviors to appear. If the person is able to quickly learn the job it will reduce the amount of time and effort on the part of the teachers to conduct the training. This action will also provide teachers with a baseline of data that will help to identify at what level teaching must occur for each of the job areas. So in essence, not all job tasks need to be analyzed but those that will need to be taught to the person should be. A task analysis (Gold, 1985) is a job or activity that is broken down into teachable steps. The size of the step is based on the person who will be instructed in that task. A task analysis is important for teaching the individuals who find it difficult to learn. It provides the teacher with a clear teaching approach (combined with systematic instruction), based on the person's level of learning and offers a way to collect data at the same time. A sample of a Task Analysis is found in Figure 6.3.
4. Potential Job Accommodations: As teachers and training specialists begin to conduct their instruction with students, there may be aspects of jobs that some

SIDEBAR 6.1
SPOTLIGHT ON HISTORY: MARC GOLD

Well before the passage of the Education for All Handicapped Children Act (now called the Individuals with Disabilities Education Improvement Act), Marc Gold was teaching children with significant disabilities in East Los Angeles, California. The time was the late 1960s and the prevailing belief was that these individuals couldn't learn much at all let alone relevant and productive job skills. Against this belief, Gold thought that his students had far more potential than the "experts" in the field believed. He also believed that individuals with disabilities should have the opportunity to live lives of their choosing and that they could learn so much more if we could find better ways to teach them. Following his beliefs, Gold entered doctoral studies at the University of Illinois, Champaign-Urbana and by the early 1970s was teaching at the university. His research was based on developing a systematic method of teaching skills to individuals with severe disabilities, in particular individuals with mental retardation. Unlike many methodologies of the day, Gold's system incorporated the values he believed necessary to advance the lives of people with disabilities: greater opportunity to lead mainstream lives and accountability on teachers to learn and use innovative methods so their students could learn the level of skills needed for greater independence in the community and in the workplace.

To get his message and methods to a broader audience, Marc Gold put together a three-day workshop to train teachers, job trainers, and rehabilitation specialists in the approach he called, "Try Another Way" (TAW). At one of his workshops in California, Ed Roberts (see Chapter 7), then Director of Vocational Rehabilitation for the state was in the audience. He was so impressed with TAW, he contracted with Gold to teach the system to staff persons throughout the state. This was the first of many large scale trainings and led Gold to form a company, Marc Gold & Associates (MG&A).

In 1982, after completing major projects in Mississippi and Ohio, Gold convened members of the company to discuss a major shift in how they would do their work. In essence, they would de-emphasize the complex analysis of tasks, promote the learning of marketable skills in integrated settings, and emphasize the need for what we now call job coaches, personal care assistants, and peer coaches. Three months later, cancer would take Gold's life. Members of MG&A met to consider whether or not the company should go on. A few of the members decided to obtain the rights to run the company and continued to work on evolving the training in systematic instruction in natural settings. Today, the company and philosophy of Marc Gold lives on and provides consulting and training to groups and organizations that embrace the MG&A model. The significant advances in the community integration of persons with mental retardation and severe disabilities during the 1980s and 1990s can be traced back to the seminal work and belief system espoused by Marc Gold ten to twenty years earlier.

students may not be able to perform due to the complexity of the tasks and other factors. It should not be automatically assumed that the student would not be qualified to perform that aspect of the work. The question should be asked: could the student perform, or otherwise be qualified for the job, if it were accommodated? Special education teachers are very familiar with instructional accommodations in the classroom and the concept of work accommodations is not

FIGURE 6.1 Schedule and Work Routine

Employee/Student: <u>Mike Franks</u>
Employer/Site: <u>North Star Guitar Company</u>
Address: <u>333 Anywhere Road</u>
<u>Metroplace, USA 10001</u>
Telephone: <u>(555) 555-5555</u>
Job Title: <u>Packaging</u>   Department: <u>Strings</u>

Work Schedule:
Circle/underline days required for work:
<u>Mon</u>   <u>Tues</u>   <u>Wed</u>   <u>Thurs</u>   <u>Fri</u>   Sat   Sun
  Arrive: <u>8:00 am</u>
  Break: <u>10:00–10:15 am</u>
  Lunch: <u>12:00 pm</u>
  Break: <u>2:00–2:15 pm</u>
  Quit: <u>3:30 pm</u>

Major Duties:
1) Count strings and sets of completed envelopes
2) Form cartons for packaging
3) Close and seal cartons
4) Replenish work supplies

FIGURE 6.2 Job Duties

Employee/Student: <u>Mike Franks</u>
Employer/Site: <u>North Star Guitar Company</u>
Address: <u>333 Anywhere Road</u>
<u>Metroplace, USA 10001</u>
Telephone: <u>(555) 555-5555</u>
Job Title: <u>Packaging</u>   Department: <u>Strings</u>
Hours: <u>8:00 am–3:30 pm</u>   Days: <u>Monday–Friday</u>
Supervisor Name/Title: <u>James Biggs, Production Manager</u>
Salary Rate: _____
General Functions: 1) Packaging pre-coiled strings into a cardboard envelope.
          2) Packaging 12 cardboard envelopes into a carton.

Major Duties and Responsibilities:
1) Correctly count "3" strings to a packet
2) Place packet into a cardboard envelope and secure envelope with its tab into the slot
3) Count out four sets of "3" enveloped strings for placement into box
4) Form box
5) Correctly package "12" enveloped strings into box
6) Close the box correctly (without damaging it)
7) Correctly place finished product into final carton
8) Take finished/loaded carton to end of station
9) Replace needed supplies

FIGURE 6.3 Task Analysis

Name: <u>Mike Franks</u>
Employer: <u>North Star Guitar Company</u>
Task/Job: <u>Packaging</u>
Instructor:

1. Obtain required supplies
2. Count "3" in a packet
3. Discard any other number ("1", "2", or "4")
4. Envelope packet into a paper pouch
5. Place "3", "3", "3", "3" paper pouches correctly into the adaptive device
6. Form dozen box
7. Place "12" paper pouches correctly into dozen box
8. Close dozen box
9. Place dozen box correctly into 24P box
10. Take finished 24P box to end of station
11. Request more work after 24P box is at final station

that much different. It simply requires teachers to look at the situation in the context of the circumstances. This aspect of the job analysis will be further discussed in the next section.

ADAPTING JOBS AND DESIGNING REASONABLE ACCOMMODATIONS

Section 504 of the Rehabilitation Act of 1973 and the Americans with Disabilities Act of 1990 state that a person cannot be found unqualified for a job without first considering whether a reasonable accommodation would otherwise render the individual qualified. In essence, this statement is an attempt to "level the playing field" so that individuals with disabilities will have equal access to jobs and job opportunities. But identifying and designing reasonable accommodations and job adaptations can be a very difficult part of the job of the transition specialist or any rehabilitation professional. In light of this challenge, it might be advisable to obtain the aid and assistance of professionals whose background and discipline can offer this type of assistance, specifically Occupational Therapists (OT). Since the role of an OT is to assist individuals with physical and cognitive difficulties to function with the greatest amount of independence with the use of adapted equipment, their knowledge and expertise in this area may offer huge benefits to teachers who need adaptations in community job settings. In addition to OTs, another discipline that has recently come to surface is Rehabilitation Engineering. Rehabilitation engineers have recently played an important part of state vocational rehabilitation (VR) services systems. In the 1986 Amendments of the Rehabilitation Act, one of the amendments offered the use of rehabilitation engineering services as a service of the state VR system. With this amendment, the vocational rehabilitation service system can be a potential source for evaluation and assistance in designing and creating adaptations and accommodations for students.

Adaptations and accommodations are sometimes viewed as two separate things. An adaptation is something that will change *how* something gets done but does not change the expected outcome. For example, if someone is using a manual stapler (one that has to be pushed together by hand) to attach documents together, an adaptation to this is an electric stapler that will automatically attach documents together by simply pushing the documents into the stapler slot. The outcome of the job has not been changed but how it gets done has. This adaptation may be useful for someone who has limited strength and vitality. This person may not be able to perform the task with the manual stapler but once the task is adapted, the person is able to perform the task. An accommodation is something that does not change how something gets done but will allow greater *latitude* or *flexibility* as to how it gets done. Using the example above with the stapler, if a person with a disability could not perform the stapling task as quickly as one without disability, and the employer does not consider this an important factor in the job performance of this person, then the employer is consequently providing greater latitude and flexibility to the job.

The concept of universal design is an important consideration in designing job adaptations. The Center for Universal Design states that the purpose of universal design is "to simplify life for everyone by making products, communications, and the building environment more usable by as many people as possible at little or no extra cost" (2004). Clearly, adaptations in the workplace that benefit not only workers with disabilities but all employees can benefit entire businesses. With this in mind, job developers should look to design adaptations that will go beyond the immediate needs of workers with disabilities and simplify or improve performance of other employees as well. In fact, one clear benefit of job analysis for businesses is the discovery of ways to make all employees more efficient.

Reasonable accommodations are any modification or adjustment to a job or the work environment that will enable a qualified applicant or employee with a disability to participate in the application process or to perform essential job functions. Reasonable accommodations also include adjustments to assure that a qualified individual with a disability has rights and privileges in employment equal to those of employees without disabilities. Examples of reasonable accommodations are:

- Making facilities used by employees readily accessible to and usable by an individual with a disability
- Modifying equipment
- Providing qualified readers or interpreters
- Appropriately modifying examinations, training, or other programs
- Reassigning a current employee to a vacant position for which the individual is qualified, if the person is unable to do the original job because of a disability even with an accommodation.

These are just a few possible accommodations that can be provided. Note that employers are required to make reasonable accommodations only after having been notified by the individual with the disability. In essence, adaptations and accommodations are evaluated once the person is on the job. Some adaptations can be easily done, while others may require more extensive evaluations by professionals qualified to determine the extent of the need and identify how to accommodate it. What is important to note here is that teachers and practitioners should not assume that a person with a disability is not qualified to do a job or perform certain tasks without first considering if an accommodation would otherwise qualify the person. Teachers should understand the requirements of the law to ensure that students have equal opportunities to the same jobs as the general population, despite a perceived disability that may be seen as an inability.

TEACHING STUDENTS TO DEVELOP THEIR OWN JOBS

Up to now, we have discussed strategies that may be used by school personnel in developing employment and job training opportunities for students with disabilities. As introduced in Chapter 1, however, self-determination is an essential ingredient to success in transition planning. To review briefly, self-determination is a combination of the skills, knowledge, and attitudes or beliefs that allow people to take greater control over the course of their lives. This applies to all areas of a student's transition, including employment. As with other aspects of adult life, the more that young people are able to analyze potential jobs, assess the quality of their match to a job, and then apply for and obtain jobs, the greater the likelihood that they will be able to apply these skills to future jobs or career advancement opportunities. Conversely, students who must rely on others to develop and secure jobs for them are in a much more dependent role.

In this section, we describe several steps that students can take to increase their abilities to develop their own jobs in the future. These steps are described below.

Develop and Update One's Own Résumé

Students who have the ability to do so should be active participants in the development of their own résumé and marketing materials. With guidance from teachers and family members, they can develop and then update résumés that highlight their skills and contributions to the school and to their home community. Relevant coursework, employment training experiences, and extracurricular activities are important components of a résumé. Students should also learn how to develop an application letter and to fill out a job application.

Develop a Network of Support

Because family, friends, and acquaintances are a very important source of employment opportunities, students should be taught to identify a network of potential supporters. Students should then be taught to contact these people in order to alert them to the fact that they may be called on to assist the student in finding employment. As with other job development skills, this involves correspondence, email, and telephone skills. An effective strategy is to have students send out a letter of introduction and a resume to all people whom they feel are potential allies in the job search process.

Practice Interviewing Skills

Like many skills, interviewing skills improve with practice. Students who are just starting the employment search process benefit from additional practice in role-playing and rehearsal situations. Teachers can invite specific employers to contribute their time to provide opportunities for students to practice and then give them feedback on how to improve their interviewing skills.

Analyze Jobs and Assess the Quality of the Match

Finally, students can be active participants in each of the strategies introduced earlier in this chapter. Depending on their abilities, they can be taught to complete the steps of a job analysis and then to assess the quality of the match between themselves and specific jobs. In fact, the more they participate in these activities for initial jobs, the greater the likelihood that they will be able to assume control of these activities for subsequent jobs.

DEVELOPING COMMUNITY-BASED EMPLOYMENT TRAINING SITES THAT MEET DEPARTMENT OF LABOR GUIDELINES

In this chapter, we have been discussing strategies that are used to identify, analyze, and obtain jobs for individuals with disabilities. These strategies may be used to secure jobs while students are still receiving special education services or to help them obtain jobs upon exiting school. The focus of our discussion so far has primarily been on obtaining paid community employment, and we have emphasized the contribution that paid employment makes to someone's overall quality of life.

Many students, however, benefit from unpaid training opportunities as part of their special education curriculum, as suggested earlier in this chapter. There are numerous benefits to such unpaid training opportunities, as shown in Table 6.9. Because of these many potential benefits, it is important for professionals in transition programs to understand the steps necessary to establish community employment training sites that comply with the Fair Labor Standards Act of 1938 (Pumpian, Fisher, Certo, Engel, & Mautz, 1998). At the heart of the issue here is that there is a significant difference between an employment relationship, in which the worker is paid, and a training relationship, in which the trainee is not paid. The Fair Labor Standards Act was created to protect workers in the United States and to ensure fair payment for employment. It protects workers, including those with disabilities, from being exploited by being underpaid or being asked to "volunteer" when, in fact, they should be paid under law.

TABLE 6.9   Benefits of Training in Community-Based Employment Training Sites

- Allows students to explore different types of employment, different work environments, and different types of supervision styles
- Contributes to a more complete profile of students' interests and abilities
- Allows for more in-depth assessment of students' skills and abilities in relation to particular types of work
- Allows students to be exposed to the actual cues that exist within particular work environments
- Allows for more in-depth assessment of students' skills and abilities with work-related skills, such as use of public transportation, social skills, etc.
- Helps students and their teams to revise and refine the desired postschool outcome statements on their transition IEPs

This issue can create uncertainty for school personnel who want to provide students with functional skill development in actual community-based work environments but who are not sure whether a student should be paid. The U.S. Departments of Education and Labor (in an excellent example of interagency collaboration at the federal level) adopted guidelines to assist school programs in dealing with this issue (U.S. Department of Education, 1992). They prefaced their guidelines with this statement of purpose and principle:

> The U.S. Departments of Labor and Education are committed to the continued development and implementation of individual education programs, in accordance with the Individuals with Disabilities Education Act (IDEA), that will facilitate the transition of students with disabilities from school to employment within their communities. This transition must take place under conditions that will not jeopardize the protections afforded by the Fair Labor Standards Act to program participants, employees, employers, or programs providing rehabilitation services to individuals with disabilities. (U.S. Department of Education, *Guidelines for Implementing Community-based Educational Programs for Students with Disabilities*, p. 1).

These guidelines included a set of criteria for determining whether or not a training relationship exists (versus a paid or employment relationship). These criteria are shown in Table 6.10.

School transition programs that are attempting to establish community-based employment training sites are strongly urged to consult these guidelines and to contact the local Department of Labor office if they are uncertain about whether or not students should be paid.

WORKPLACE CULTURE AND NATURAL SUPPORTS

Amendments to the Rehabilitation Act (1992) (P.L. 102-569), included "natural supports" as a possible source of ongoing and extended services as a function of supported

TABLE 6.10   Guidelines for Implementing Community-Based Educational Programs for Students with Disabilities (U.S. Department of Education, 1992)

(Note: All criteria must be met for a training relationship to exist.)

■ Participants will be youth with physical and/or mental disabilities for whom competitive employment at or above the minimum wage level is not immediately obtainable and who, because of their disability, will need intensive ongoing support to perform in a work setting.
■ Participation will be for vocational exploration, assessment, or training in a community-based placement worksite under the general supervision of public school personnel.
■ Community-based placements will be clearly defined components of individual education programs developed and designed for the benefit of each student. The statement of needed transition services established for the exploration, assessment, training, or cooperative vocational education components will be included in the student's Individualize Education Program (IEP).
■ The information contained in a student's IEP will not have to be made available, however, documentation as to the student's enrollment in the community-based placement program will be made available to the U.S. Departments of Labor and Education. The student and the parent or guardian of each student must be fully informed of the IEP and the community-based placement component and have indicated voluntary participation and the understanding that participation in such a component does not entitle the student-participant to wages.
■ The activities of the students at the community-based placement site do not result in an immediate advantage to the business. The U.S. Department of Labor will look at several factors.
  1. There has been no displacement of employees, vacant positions have not been filled, employees have not been relieved of assigned duties, and the students are not performing services that, although not ordinarily performed by employees, clearly are of benefit to the business.
  2. The students are under the continued and direct supervision by either representatives of the school or by employees of the business.
  3. Such placements are made according to the requirements of the student's IEP and not to meet the labor needs of the business.
  4. The periods of time spent by the students at any one site or in any clearly distinguishable job classification are specifically limited by the IEP.
■ While the existence of an employment relationship will not be determined exclusively on the basis of the number of hours, as a general rule, each component will not exceed the following limitation during any one school year:

Vocational exploration	5 hours per job experienced
Vocational assessment	90 hours per job experienced
Vocational training	120 hours per job experienced

■ Students are not entitled to employment at the business at the conclusion of their IEP. However, once a student has become an employee, the student cannot be considered a trainee at that particular community-based placement unless in a clearly distinguishable occupation.

employment. Since its introduction into the field of supported employment, the concept of natural support has had major impact on approaches to job development for individuals with disabilities (Nisbet & Hagner, 1988). In this section, we will discuss some of the most critical features of natural supports and how teachers and practitioners can begin to look at this strategy and incorporate it in their programs.

Natural supports have been defined in several ways in the literature (DiLeo & Luecking, 1995; Butterworth, Hagner, Kiernan, & Schalock, 1996), but here we will use the definition developed by Rogan, Hagner, and Murphy (1993):

> Any form of assistance which allows a person to secure, maintain, and advance in a community job of their choosing in ways which correspond to the typical work routines and social actions of other workers, and which enhance their work and non-work social relations with other employees.

This definition contains several key ingredients of the concept of natural support. One of the key ingredients contained in this definition is that obtaining a job for a student and instructing the student in that job should be done in the most *typical ways*. This means that, rather than a teacher or job coach being the active participant in instructing and teaching the skills to the student, the employer becomes the active participant in the job training. For example, if employers typically use co-workers to train new employees on the job, which is considered the typical routine, this work routine is also followed when the student receives job training. Teachers and/or job coaches are there to support the training and provide the support to both the student and the person doing the training. The main reasons for using this approach are: (1) it helps to get the employer quickly invested in the hiring of the student, (2) it allows opportunities for greater social interaction between co-workers and the student, and (3) it provides the opportunity to fade from the site more quickly (Hagner, 1992; Mank, 1996; Rogan, 1996).

The second part of the definition that distinguishes this strategy from others is the enhancement of work and non-work social relationships. Clearly, one of the biggest challenges facing students and adults with disabilities is the development of social relationships among all members of the community, including those without disabilities. The natural support concept clearly invests much effort in trying to establish and enhance these social relationships in work and non-work activities. Again, the literature is abundant in the areas of social relationships being established through the natural supports model (Hagner, 1992; Mank, 1996). Now, let's review briefly some of the key components of natural supports and how this concept is incorporated into the job analysis and job development processes.

Job Development

The approach is characterized by developing jobs based on the person's interests and career goals so that the individual has a greater opportunity to fit into the social structure (culture) of the workplace. Involving the individual in creating a career plan and developing jobs based on that career plan, rather than on availability of jobs, is a major characteristic of the natural supports concept. A job developer would consider employers that have a good stable workforce where perhaps there is little turnover. The consideration here is that if a job is obtained in a site where there is a low turnover rate and the workforce is stable, the person will work in an environment that is consistent and cohesive with the potential to develop positive long lasting relationships, not to mention that the job might offer a great deal of satisfaction. One way of looking at this is through an *analysis of the workplace culture*. In analyzing the workplace culture, the teacher and/or job coach considers critical factors that will distinguish the worksite as one that is open and accepting of differences. Table 6.11 offers some factors to be considered when analyzing a workplace culture.

Job Training

As previously mentioned, one of the key ingredients of natural supports is that typical job training methods are used, and the manner in which the employer trains typical new employees is what is encouraged. The rationale for this point has been discussed, but one added activity that teachers and/or job coaches can do during this stage is to provide consultation to employers and employees of the jobsite. This might be an opportunity to form an alliance with the employer, to continue to enhance the positive image of the student and all people with disabilities, and to offer ideas and strategies that might aid the trainer and help improve the student's work performance. Such

TABLE 6.11   Analyzing the Workplace Culture

- Non-Spoken Rules and Social Customs—Informal rules that guide interactions, what goes on in areas such as the break room or work areas, not working faster than everyone else, productivity, keeping busy, etc.
- Key People Who Exert Power and Influence—Who has the greatest influence over the workplace, either formally or informally; who is good to know that will provide job stability?
- Identify Routines—What people do when coming into work and taking lunch and breaks.
- Social Activities—Where people go after work, hang out and enjoy each other's company.
- Gathering Places—Where people gather to talk and informally socialize.
- Celebrations—Birthdays, holidays, etc. How do they celebrate? Do people share bringing in cakes for birthdays or cards for each other?
- Do's and Don'ts—Knowing the difference between serious joking comments and when to realize it is enough.
- Workspace—How do people react to their personal workspace or where their personal things are kept?
- Supervisor Interaction—How do supervisors interact with and direct employees? Is the supervision style friendly or businesslike?
- Image—Are employees required to dress a certain way, not necessarily a uniform but a code of appearance?
- Open vs. Closed Groups—Do employees interact with each other based on cultural background or common interests, or are they an inclusive group? Are there any language barriers?

consultation may also provide the employer with strategies that will help other, non-disabled employees improve their performance.

Follow-Along

Traditionally employment for individuals with disabilities has been looked at in standards of longevity and earnings. Although these factors are important, other factors are considered to be of equal or greater importance, including job satisfaction and career advancement. Questions that are asked include (a) is the student content, happy or satisfied with the work, the jobsite and the people around him or her? and (b) is there an opportunity for the student to advance or learn new skills that will allow more and different opportunities? These questions were not often asked fifteen years ago, but today it has become critical as we view students and adults with disabilities differently.

It should also be noted that the degree of use of natural supports varies depending on the needs of individuals with disabilities. That is, for some students whose disability does not significantly affect them in terms of job performance, it might be expected that the teacher or job coach can expect a great deal of involvement by employers and co-workers in each of the components of job acquisition and training. On the other hand, if the student has a more significant disability, the teacher or job coach may be expected to be more involved in each of the components of job acquisition and training. This discussion involves creating a balance between the needs of the individual based on his or her disability and how closely it will correspond to the natural support strategies. In some cases, because the individual will require an experienced teacher who has the ability to teach complex skills to someone who finds it difficult to learn, the training may look like typical job coach training, but that might be the balance required for this particular student.

In closing this section, it is important to emphasize that natural supports is a concept that requires a keen understanding of business, teaching, and consultation. This concept requires professionals within transition programs to understand the motivations and desires of the students that they serve, as well as the culture and organization of workplaces. This concept also requires a change of role for transition coordinators and requires them to develop skills in consulting with business and industry. Most important, the concept of natural supports helps to create employment situations in which individuals with disabilities are most likely to find success.

CHAPTER SUMMARY

This chapter has introduced you to strategies for investigating, analyzing, and then securing jobs for students and adults with disabilities. As we have discussed, work is a central aspect of a successful and satisfied adult life. Transition personnel in special education programs typically have to learn a new set of skills, as described in this chapter, in order to work effectively with the business community and to create employment and training opportunities for their students. The development of these skills, and the establishment of a strong network of supportive employers in the local community, takes both time and sustained effort. As a final note, we emphasize once again that students themselves should take an active role in the job search process and that the skills they develop in doing so will serve them throughout their working lives.

APPLICATION ACTIVITIES

The application activities listed below are essential for your continued learning and skill development in transition. Each of the activities will require your time and energy but will help you develop your professional skills in this area.

For Practice and Understanding:

Select a community job with which you are familiar, and then conduct a full job analysis as described in this chapter. Make sure to include an analysis of the workplace culture: unwritten rules, informal "history" of the workplace, rituals and other signs of acceptance into the workplace culture. Use forms such as those shown in Figures 6.1, 6.2, and 6.3 as you conduct your analysis.

For Your Portfolio:

Develop a compatibility analysis form to be used to assess the quality of the match between students and particular job opportunities. Include a comprehensive list of factors to be used in matching a particular student (or your son or daughter) to a particular job.

Begin a "job file" that lists area employers by category (for example, service or manufacturing) and by sub-category (restaurants, banks, etc.). Include information about each business, such as their size, number of employees, location, and so forth, and then add to this database as you accumulate additional information.

If you work for a transition program in a school, consider starting a business advisory council to provide input into the development of your community-based employment training programs, your school-based training programs, and your employment-related curricula. We suggest that you start by inviting employers who you know and with whom you have a good relationship, including those who have demonstrated a willingness to hire people with disabilities. Such business advisory councils not only provide valuable input into the design of transition programs, but they also can be a source of leads for employment or training opportunities.

RESOURCES AND WEBSITES

The following resources and websites will allow you to extend your knowledge about how to assist people with disabilities to obtain employment in the community. Consider including these resources in your professional portfolio.

APSE—The Network on Employment

Organization dedicated to the improvement and expansion of integrated employment opportunities through advocacy and education.
www.apse.org

Virginia Commonwealth University Research and Training Center on Workplace Support and Job Retention

Provides research, training, and technical assistance.
www.worksupport.com

Employment and Disability Institute

Focus on advancement of knowledge, policies, and practices that enhance the opportunities of people with disabilities in all aspects of life.
www.ilr.cornell.edu

Job Accommodation Network (JAN)

Consulting service designed to increase the employability of people with disabilities.
www.janweb.icdi.wvu.edu

UCP

Information about employment and other services for people with disabilities.
www.ucp.org

Marc Gold & Associates (MGA)

Training and technical assistance to enhance the community participation of people with significant disabilities.
www.marcgold.com

New Freedom Initiative's Online Resource

Federal interagency website to give access to information and resources for people with disabilities.
www.disabilityinfo.gov

Institute on Community Inclusion

Supports the rights of children and adults with disabilities to participate in all aspects of the community. Conducts research and education about effective strategies for promoting the inclusion of people with disabilities.
www.communityinclusion.org

REFERENCES

Bellamy, G. T., Horner, R. H., & Inman, D. (1979). *Vocational training of severely retarded adults.* Austin, TX: Pro-Ed.

Brady, M., & Rosenberg, H. (2002). Modifying and managing employment practices: An inclusive model for job placement and support. In K. Storey, P. Bates, & D. Hunter (Eds.), *The road ahead: Transition to adult life for persons with disabilities* (pp. 121–136). St. Augustine, FL: Training and Resource Network.

Butterworth, J., Hagner, D., Kiernan, W., & Shalock, R. (1996). Natural supports in the workplace: Defining an agenda for research and practice. *Journal of the Association for Persons with Severe Handicaps, 21,* 103–113.

Carey, A., Potts, B., Bryen, D., & Shankar, J. (2004). Networking towards employment: Experiences of people who use augmentative and alternative communication. *Research and Practice for Persons with Severe Disabilities, 29,* 40–52.

Callahan, M., & Garner, B. (1997). *Keys to the workplace: Skills and supports for people with disabilities.* Baltimore: Paul Brookes.

The Center for Universal Design. (2004). Retrieved from the World Wide Web: http://www/design/ncsu.edu/cud/.

Dawis, R., & Lofquist, L. (1984). *A psychological theory of work adjustment.* Minneapolis: University of Minnesota Press.

DiLeo, D., & Luecking, R. (1995). The risks of misapplying natural supports in the workplace. *Supported Employment Infolines, 6*(8), 4–5.

Donovan, M., & Tilson, G. (1998). The Marriott Foundation's "Bridges . . . from School to Work" program—A framework for successful employment outcomes for people with disabilities. *Journal of Vocational Rehabilitation, 10,* 15–21.

Fair Labor Standards Act, 29 U.S.C. 201 *et seq.* (1938). U.S. Department of Labor, Employment Standards Administration, Wage and Hour Division.

Gold, M. (1985). *Try another way training manual.* Champaign, IL: Research Press.

Griffin, C., & Hammis, D. (2003). Guest editorial: Is self employment a cop-out? *Journal of Vocational Rehabilitation, 18,* 143–144.

Griffin, C., & Targett, P. M. (2001). Finding jobs for young people with disabilities. In P. Wehman (Ed.), *Life beyond the classroom: Transition strategies for young people with disabilities* (3rd ed.), (pp. 171–209). Baltimore: Brookes.

Hagner, D. C. (1992). The social interactions and job supports of supported employees. In J. Nesbet (Ed.), *Natural supports in school, at work, and in the community for people with severe disabilities* (pp. 217–239). Baltimore: Paul Brookes.

Hagner, D., & Daning, R. (1993). Issues in career decision making for workers with developmental disabilities. *Career Development Quarterly, 38,* 148–158.

Hutchins, M., & Renzaglia, A. (2002). Career development: Developing basic work skills and employment preferences. In K. Storey, P. Bates, & D. Hunter (Eds.), *The road ahead: Transition to adult life for persons with disabilities* (pp. 65–95). St. Augustine, FL: TRN.

Kraemer, B., McIntyre, L., & Blacher, J. (2003). Quality of life for young adults with mental retardation during transition. *Mental Retardation, 41,* 250–262.

Kregel, J., & Unger, D. (1993). Employer perceptions of the work potential of individuals with disabilities: An illustration from supported employment. *Journal of Vocational Rehabilitation, 3,* 17–25.

Mank, D. (1996). Natural supports in employment for people with disabilities: What do we know and when did we know it? *The Journal of The Association for Persons with Severe Handicaps, 21,* 174–177.

Menchetti, B., & Garcia, L. (2003). Personal and employment outcomes of person centered career planning. *Education and Training in Developmental Disabilities, 38,* 145–156.

Moon, M. S., Goodall, P., Barcus, J. M., & Brooke, V. (1986). *The supported work model of competitive employment for citizens with severe handicaps: A guide for job trainers.* Richmond: Rehabilitation Research and Training Center, Virginia Commonwealth University.

Morgan, R., & Alexander, M. (2005). The employer's perception: Employment of individuals with developmental disabilities. *Journal of Vocational Rehabilitation, 23,* 39–49.

Mount, B., & Zwernick, K. (1988). *It's never too early, it's never too late: A booklet about personal futures planning.* (Publication No. 421-88-109). St. Paul, MN: Metropolitan Council.

Nietupski, J., Verstegen, D., Hamre-Nietupski, S., & Tanty, S. (1993). Leveraging community support in approaching employers: The referral model of job development. *Journal of Vocational Rehabilitation, 3,* 38–45.

Nietupski, J., Verstegen, D., & Petty, D. M. (1995). *The job development handbook: A guide for facilitating employer decisions to hire people with disabilities.* Knoxville: University of Tennessee.

Nisbet, J., & Hagner, D. (1988). Natural supports in the workplace: A reexamination of supported employment. *Journal of the Association for Persons with Severe Handicaps, 13,* 260–267.

Parent, W., Cone, A., Turner, E., & Wehman, P. (1998). Supported employment: Consumers leading the way. In P. Wehman & J. Kregel (Eds.), *More than a job: Securing satisfying careers for people with disabilities* (pp. 149–167). Baltimore: Brookes.

Powell, T., Pancsofar, E., Steere, D., Butterworth, J., Itzkowitz, J., & Rainforth, B. (1991). *Supported employment: Developing integrated employment opportunities for persons with disabilities*. White Plains, NY: Longman.

Pumpian, I., Fisher, D., Certo, N., Engel, T., & Mautz, D. (1998). To pay or not to pay: Differentiating employment and training relationships through regulation and litigation. *Career Development for Exceptional Individuals, 21*, 187–202.

Rehabilitation Act Amendments of 1992, P.L. 102-569. (June 24, 1992). Federal Register, vol. 52, no. 122, pp. 28432–28442.

Rogan, P. (1996). Natural supports in the workplace: No need for a trial. *The Journal of The Association for Persons with Severe Handicaps, 21*, 174–177.

Rogan, P., Hagner, D., & Murphy, S. (1993). Natural supports: Reconceptualizing job coach roles. *Journal of The Association for Persons with Severe Handicaps, 18*, 275–281.

Simmons, T., & Whaley, B. (2001). Transition to employment. In R. Flexer, T. Simmons, P. Luft, & R. Baer (Eds.), *Transition planning for secondary students with disabilities* (pp. 416–438). Upper Saddle River, NJ: Merrill.

Smith, K., Webber, L., Graffam, J., & Wilson, C. (2004a). Employer satisfaction, job match, and future hiring intentions for employees with a disability. *Journal of Vocational Rehabilitation, 21*, 165–173.

Smith, K., Webber, L., Graffam, J., & Wilson, C. (2004b). Employer satisfaction with employees with a disability: Comparisons with other employees. *Journal of Vocational Rehabilitation, 21*, 61–69.

Steere, D., Ellerd, D., Sampson, M., & Barry, M. (1997). Enhancing and expanding supported employment in a large rural state: Montana's Projects with Industry. *Rural Special Education Quarterly, 16*, 3–10.

Unger, D., & Simmons, T. (2005). Transition to employment. In R. Flexer, T. Simmons, P. Luft, & R. Baer (Eds.), *Transition planning for secondary students with disabilities* (2nd ed.) (pp. 360–387). Upper Saddle River, NJ: Merrill Prentice Hall.

United States Department of Education (1992, September). *Guidelines for implementing community-based educational programs for students with disabilities, OSEP 92-20*. Washington, DC: Office of Special Education and Rehabilitative Services.

Wehman, P. (1981). *Competitive employment: New horizons for severely disabled individuals*. Baltimore: Paul Brookes.

Wehman, P. (1998). Editorial. *Journal of Vocational Rehabilitation, 10*, 1–2.

Wehman, P. (2001). *Life beyond the classroom: Transition strategies for young people with disabilities* (3rd ed.). Baltimore: Paul Brookes.

Weiner, J., & Zivolich, S. (1998). Universal access: A natural support corporate initiative at Universal Studios Hollywood. *Journal of Vocational Rehabilitation, 10*, 5–14.

Weiner, J., & Zivolich, S. (2003). A longitudinal report for three employees in a training consultant model of natural support. *Journal of Vocational Rehabilitation, 18*, 199–202.

Williams, I., Petty, D. M., & Verstegen, D. (1998). The business approach to job development. *Journal of Vocational Rehabilitation, 10*, 23–29.

Witt, M. (1992). Job strategies for people with disabilities. Princeton, NJ: Peterson's Guides.

Wolfensberger, W. (1983). Social role valorization: A proposed new term for the principle of normalization. *Mental Retardation, 21*, 234–239.

Zivolich, S., & Weiner, J. (1997). A national corporate employment initiative for persons with severe disabilities: A ten year perspective. *Journal of Vocational Rehabilitation, 8*, 75–87.

CHAPTER 7

TRANSITION TO POSTSECONDARY EDUCATION

CHAPTER OBJECTIVES

Upon completion of this chapter, you will be able to

1. describe the differences between high school and postsecondary education institutions.

2. describe the differences in laws that protect the rights of students with disabilities in the K–12 system and the postsecondary education system.

3. describe the importance of self-determination in the education of students with disabilities and a procedure to select and implement self-determination instruction for students who will transition to postsecondary education.

4. discuss the important elements of an academic program and an independent living program for students who will transition from high school to postsecondary education.

5. discuss the expanding importance of assistive technology and universal design for the success of students with disabilities in postsecondary education.

6. assist students with disabilities in making the transition from high school to a postsecondary education campus.

KEY TOPICS TO LOOK FOR IN THIS CHAPTER . . .

- Changes in laws and regulations: Students moving from the K–12 system to postsecondary education also move from a very comprehensive act that addresses their educational and social needs while at school to multiple acts that cover educational accommodations, accessibility, and their civil rights. Look for a discussion of these differences and how you can help students and their parents understand them.

- Self-determination as a key developmental process. Critical to the success of students with disabilities in postsecondary education is their knowledge of their rights and responsibilities under the laws enacted for adults with disabilities. But, knowing one's rights is not enough. Students must be able to advocate for themselves to ensure they will receive the services and accommodations for which they are eligible. Look for ways you can work with students to make informed choices, set goals, and not let unnecessary barriers stop them from achieving their goals.

- Independent living: An important topic related to all forms of transition planning and education is independent living. Look for our discussion on preparing students for the "temptations" of college life and critical issues related to safety and self-discipline.

- Technology: An important feature in almost everyone's life these days is the influence of technology. One of the most promising areas is assistive technology and the opportunities it is providing for individuals with disabilities to lead more accessible lives. Look for examples of how assistive technology is helping students with disabilities demonstrate their learning and how it has helped create a universal design that makes communities more inclusive.

Sue Anne had a dream. She wanted to be a college student and learn to become an early childhood teacher. She was concerned that she might not make it to college if her grades weren't good enough. And, oh those state exams! She didn't perform well on standardized tests with time limits. Most, but not all, of her high school teachers were easy to work with when it came to providing reasonable accommodations for her learning disability. Some were reluctant to give her extended time on tests thinking it was unfair to other students. Sue Anne's special education teacher and guidance counselor were supportive when it came to explaining her rights under the law and negotiating accommodations during her freshman year, but at that point they began to work with Sue Anne on self-determination skills because learning how to advocate for herself would be critical to her success in college. As with all students who have disabilities and want a postsecondary education, she would have to learn more and work harder than students without disabilities.

Sue Anne's goal of attending college was well founded. Several researchers have noted the improved prospects of obtaining better-paying jobs with benefits after earning a college degree (Benz, Doren, & Yovanoff, 1998; Blackorby & Wagner, 1996; Field, Sarver, & Shaw, 2003; Reis, Neu, & McGuire, 1997). But the postsecondary education experience is very different from that of high school (Brinckerhoff, McGuire, & Shaw, 2002; Dalke, 1993; Field et al., 2003). The latter is a highly structured educational experience with a time schedule for classes, breaks, and lunch. Administrators and teachers make sure the school schedule is followed and parents will often see to it that time is set aside for homework on evenings and weekends.

A residential college, on the other hand, requires a great deal of self-discipline. No parent is around to roust you out of bed and fix breakfast before classes. Typically, professors do not take roll and expect students to find out and understand what went on in class on their own if they fail to show up. There is more than one textbook to read and quite often fewer exams, which account for a higher percentage of the grade. In other words, college students are pretty much on their own to learn course material and manage the many distractions that accompany the college experience.

From a legal standpoint, children with disabilities cannot be excluded from elementary and secondary schools. In fact, IDEA ensures there will be a "zero reject" of students with disabilities no matter how severe the condition. Higher education, on the other hand, is voluntary and campuses can set their own standards for acceptance, retention, and graduation. Such standards essentially preclude attendance by students who do not have the intellectual capacity to meet the academic and performance criteria at most two-year and four-year colleges. Nevertheless, there are laws that protect postsecondary education students with disabilities from discrimination while also protecting the quality and integrity of undergraduate and graduate degree programs (Sitlington, 2003; Wolanin & Steele, 2004). These laws will be discussed later in the chapter.

In a 1999 study by the National Center for Education Statistics, 428,280 postsecondary undergraduate students identified themselves as having a disability and represent an estimated 6 percent of all students on college campuses. The disabilities reported in the student sample are as follows:

Learning disabilities	45.7%
Mobility or orthopedic impairments	13.9%
Health impairments	11.6%
Mental illness or emotional disturbance	7.8%
Hearing impairments	5.6%
Blindness and visual impairments	4.4%
Speech or language impairments	0.9%
Other impairments	9.1%

(From An Institutional Perspective on Students with Disabilities in Postsecondary Education, National Center for Educational Statistics, Postsecondary Education Quick Information System, August 1999.)

The U.S. Department of Education has suggested that the number of students who identify themselves as disabled (including those with learning disabilities) has increased from 3 percent in 1973 to nearly 10 percent in 2000 (Carlson, 2004; Wolanin & Steele, 2004). As the awareness about students with disabilities grows among college faculty and administrators and the availability and use of assistive technology and universal design for instruction become more prevalent, these percentages may increase even more.

The increase in students with disabilities on postsecondary campuses is due, in great measure, to their protection from discriminatory practices. As often happens in the history of social movements and civil rights activism, there is at least one individual who stands out for his or her courage, conviction, commitment, and creativity. When it comes to the rights of students with disabilities on college campuses, there is no more inspiring figure than Ed Roberts. (See Sidebar 7.1).

Consider This!   Think back to your first year in college.

- Did you live on campus? Why or why not?
- How did you meet your roommate(s)?
- After attending the first month of classes, was there one class you really wanted to drop? If so, why and, did you?
- How many tests and written assignments did you have that first semester?
- Did you have enough time to get from one class to another or have time between classes for lunch?
- Did you have to work a part-time or full-time job to help pay for your tuition, room, and books?

■ What was the most difficult adjustment you had to make that first year of college?

BEYOND IDEA: LAWS AND REGULATIONS FOR ADULTS WITH DISABILITIES

One of the benefits of IDEA is that as a single law, it comprehensively addresses the legal rights of students with disabilities in K–12 education and lays out a process for eligibility and reasonable support services in all areas of school activity from the classroom to after school events. But, the provisions of IDEA end when a student leaves the K–12 system and other laws take its place in protecting the rights of adult individuals (age eighteen and over) with disabilities. To make sure students and their families understand their rights and which laws protect those rights, special education teachers, administrators, and counselors must make sure they can facilitate the transition from IDEA to the laws in effect in postsecondary education.

The Rehabilitation Act of 1973, Section 504

In 1977, after a delay of four years which sparked protests by people with disabilities, including a takeover of a government building in San Francisco (Shapiro, 1994), the former Department of Health, Education, and Welfare (currently the Department of Education) established regulations for implementing Section 504 of the Rehabilitation Act of 1973 (PL 93-112, § 504, 29 U.S.C. 794). The regulations stated that individuals with disabilities must be provided an equal opportunity to achieve the same result, earn the same benefit, or to attain the same level of achievement, in the most integrated setting that fits the individual's needs. Section 504 was the first Congressional action to mandate that individuals with disabilities could not be discriminated against or denied benefits solely on the basis of being disabled by any program (or activity) receiving federal funding (§ 504, 29 U.S.C. 794).

Subpart E of the regulations addressed postsecondary education and established that institutions of higher education must adapt academic requirements and methods of evaluation that discriminate against individuals with disabilities. However, postsecondary education institutions do not have to modify requirements that are vital to the integrity of a program or course of study and that are directly related to licensing or accreditation requirements, or that change the concentration or processes that are necessary to assessing the performance of individuals (*Southeastern Community College v. Davis*, 1979). And importantly, postsecondary education schools cannot establish practices that restrict the participation of students with disabilities. Thus, where appropriate to the individual's disability, reasonable accommodations must be provided such as extended time on examinations, the use of note-takers and tape recorders in classes, course materials provided in large print or recorded formats, and sign language interpreters (*Guckenberger v. Boston University*, 1997). Section 504 means that today's college students with disabilities do not have to fight groundbreaking battles for admission, accessibility, and accommodations like Ed Roberts did in the early 60s. See Table 7.1 for more examples of academic accommodations and auxiliary aids and services.

SIDEBAR 7.1
SPOTLIGHT ON HISTORY: ED ROBERTS

Independence [is] measured not by the tasks one [can] perform without assistance but by the quality of one's life with help (Shapiro, 1994).

In 1962, Ed Roberts entered the University of California at Berkeley. What was remarkable about his enrollment was that Roberts had contracted polio at age fourteen and needed the use of an 800 pound iron lung for up to eighteen hours a day. His mobility was a wheelchair that he was unable to navigate himself. Although the university was willing to admit him, they had no formal office of services for students with disabilities, nor did they understand reasonable accommodations for such individuals. For example, no dormitory was available to support the size and weight of the iron lung, but Roberts was undeterred and was eventually offered a room in a wing of the University's hospital (Rothman, 2003; Shapiro, 1994).

Prior to entering UC Berkeley, Roberts attended San Mateo Community College where he had found a supportive environment. However, the California Department of Rehabilitation would not pay for attendants and other supports to help him continue his education at Berkeley because they considered him "infeasible" to ever be employed. It took officials from San Mateo CC going to a local newspaper with the story and the accompanying negative publicity before the department relented (Shapiro, 1994; Disability Rights and Independent Living Movement, 2004).

With money from the Department of Rehabilitation, Roberts was able to hire attendants to push his wheelchair and carry him up and down stairs. Eventually other "crippled" students joined him in the hospital wing making it the first dormitory for students with physical disabilities. These students formed the first disabled student group, calling themselves the "Rolling Quads." The Rolling Quads had an impact beyond the campus. Unable to get the growing number of motorized wheelchairs over the curbs of Telegraph Avenue, the Rolling Quads advocated for curb cuts at the Berkeley City Council and in 1970 their demand was met (Rothman, 2003; Shapiro, 1994).

In 1970, Roberts and John Hessler started the Physically Disabled Students Program (PDSP) at UC Berkeley. The program was run by disabled students for disabled students and served many academic and social needs. It was so popular that students with other types of disabilities and nonstudents with disabilities began requesting services. The students staffing the PDSP did not want to turn anyone away, but they could not keep up with the demand.

For some time, Roberts, Hessler, and others had been discussing the need for a new service model that would support disabled individuals based upon the person's own preferences. They came up with the idea for a Center for Independent Living (CIL). The revolution they started in disabled student services on the Berkeley campus spread into the community and eventually nationwide (Rothman, 2003; Shapiro, 1994; Disability Rights and Independent Living Movement, 2004).

In an ironic twist of fate, Governor Jerry Brown named Roberts director of the California Department of Rehabilitation in 1975. Thus, he came to head the very agency that had once refused him funding for college because he was deemed unemployable (Shapiro, 1994). Ed Roberts passed away in 1995.

TABLE 7.1   Frequently Requested and Used Accommodations among Students with Disabilities in Postsecondary Education

Generally, there are two basic types of accommodations—academic adjustments and auxiliary aids and services. Academic adjustments are modifications to the academic program, such as its requirements or method of delivery, to accommodate the needs of a student with a disability. Some examples are:

- substituting courses that do not pose disability-related barriers for those required for a degree, such as a foreign language sequence;
- lengthening the time for degree completion;
- scheduling classes and other activities to provide adequate time for a student with mobility problems to get from class to class on time, for a student to get necessary medical or psychological treatment, or for a student to adequately rest and recuperate between academic activities;
- extending the time for examinations;
- offering examinations in alternative locations, such as a place that is quieter and has fewer distractions than the regular examination location; or
- providing examinations in alternative formats, such as oral instead of written.

Auxiliary aids and services are accommodations to meet the needs of students with disabilities who have impaired sensory, manual, or speaking skills, or other challenges. These may include:

- priority access to course registration;
- a special parking space for a persons with, for example, a chronic medical problem such as kidney disease that makes walking distances difficult;
- a notetaker or tape recorder for a person with impaired vision or hearing or a learning disability;
- Braille calculators, printers, or keyboards;
- interpreters or real-time captioning for the deaf;
- reaching devices for library use;
- readers and scribes for testing;
- academic, personal, and vocational counseling;
- wheelchair-accessible desks and tables;
- calculators or keyboards with large keys; and
- materials provided in alternative media such as large print.

The Americans with Disabilities Act (ADA)

The Americans with Disabilities Act (PL 101-336), signed into law in 1990, extended the reach of Section 504 to cover all programs and services whether they receive federal funding or not (Sitlington, 2003). The ADA clarified that methods or other criteria for programs of study may be subject to reasonable accommodations without altering the integrity of programs or courses. In other words, institutions of higher education do not have to modify the structures and requirements of degree programs, but they do have to allow students with disabilities the opportunity to utilize reasonable accommodations to meet the criteria for passing courses and earning degrees.

Reasonable accommodations are determined by the student and designated officials of the postsecondary education institution. Students initiate the process by identifying and documenting their disability(ies) and by requesting specific reasonable accommodations within a workable timeline. The designated officials, usually staff personnel in an office of services for students with disabilities, then determine the eligibility of the student and the "reasonableness" of the requested accommodation(s). Reasonable accommodations include the variety of assistive technology available and variations in use of technology.

The Family Educational Rights and Privacy Act (FERPA)

FERPA (20 U.S.C. § 1232g; 34 CFR Part 99), also known as the Buckley Amendment, is a federal law that protects the privacy of student education records. Schools receiving funds from federal programs must comply with FERPA regulations. The law gives parents certain rights with regard to their children's educational records. These rights transfer to children when reaching the age of majority (eighteen years) or when they attend an educational institution beyond that of high school. When the rights have been transferred to an individual at the age of eighteen, he or she is referred to as an "eligible student." At this point, parents no longer have the right to request their child's educational records without the permission of their child.

Parents or eligible students have the right to inspect and review the individual's education records kept by the school. Schools are not required to provide copies of records unless, because of great distance or hardship, it is impossible for parents or eligible students to review the records at the school. Schools may charge a reasonable fee for copies.

Parents or eligible students have the right to request that a school correct records which they believe to be inaccurate or misleading. If the school decides not to amend the record, the parent or eligible student then has the right to a formal hearing. After the hearing, if the school continues its position not to amend the record, the parents or eligible student has the right to place a statement in the records declaring his or her view about the contested information.

In general, schools must have written permission from the parent or eligible student in order to release any information from a student's education record. However, FERPA allows schools to disclose those records, without consent, to various parties or under the following conditions (34 CFR § 99.31):

- Other schools to which a student is transferring;
- School officials with legitimate educational interest;
- Specified officials for audit or evaluation purposes;
- Appropriate parties in connection with financial aid to a student;
- Organizations conducting certain studies for or on behalf of the school;
- Accrediting organizations;
- To comply with a judicial order or lawfully issued subpoena;
- Appropriate officials in cases of health and safety emergencies; and
- State and local authorities, within a juvenile justice system, pursuant to specific law.

Additionally, schools may disclose, without consent, "directory" information such as a student's name, address, telephone number, date and place of birth, honors and awards, and dates of attendance. However, schools must tell parents and eligible students about directory information and allow parents and eligible students a reasonable amount of time to request that the school not disclose directory information. Schools must notify parents and eligible students annually of their rights under FERPA. Eligible students who seek assistance from vocational rehabilitation agencies or other adult services organizations while attending a postsecondary education school should check to see if FERPA regulations apply to the disclosure of their educational records and whether or not they must provide written permission.

SELF-DETERMINATION AS AN ORGANIZING CONCEPT FOR THE TRANSITION TO POSTSECONDARY EDUCATION

It is unknown to this author whether or not Ed Roberts ever used the term self-determination in his thinking and work to gain greater independence for individuals with disabilities. Many of his ideas came from his own experiences and his education in community organizing on how to put pressure on systems and bureaucracies more interested in regulations than people (Shapiro, 1994). Certainly, his activism and that of others set the stage for our current knowledge that self-determination is a vital part of student success in postsecondary education and adult life (Field et al., 2003; Malian & Nevin, 2002; Wehmeyer & Palmer, 2003; Wehmeyer & Schwartz, 1997).

Defining Self-Determination

According to researchers at the Beach Center on Disability at the University of Kansas (2004):

> self-determination refers to the concept that a person with a disability should have the opportunity to choose what happens to the person, to receive education that enables the person to make a choice, to have support to make a choice and to carry out the choice, and, consistent with law governing the age of majority and competence/incompetence, to be assured that those people already in the person's life will heed the choice.

In this sense, the definition follows the IDEA Amendments of 1997 that transition planning must include "taking into account the student's preferences and interests." However, as Field and colleagues (2003) note, many secondary schools are lax on this requirement and tend to rely primarily on the preferences of parents and teachers. This, in turn, is poor preparation for students who will attend postsecondary education programs because their rights are governed by Section 504 and the ADA, which assume the individual as the initiator of services/accommodations, not parents or others (Sitlington, 2003). Thus, it is critical that high school teachers, paraeducators, counselors, and certainly parents understand the essential differences between Section

TABLE 7.2 Four Essential Characteristics of Self-Determination

1. <u>Autonomous</u> if a person acts according to his or her own preferences, interests, and/or abilities, and independently, free from undue external influence or interference.
2. <u>Self-regulated</u> if a person makes decisions about which skills to use in a situation; examine the task at hand and his or her available repertoire; and formulate, enact, and evaluate a plan of action with revisions when necessary.
3. <u>Psychologically empowered</u> if a person acts based on the beliefs that he or she has the capacity to perform behaviors needed to influence outcomes in his or her environment and, if he she performs such behaviors, anticipated outcomes will result.
4. <u>Self-realized</u> if a person uses a comprehensive, and reasonably accurate, knowledge of himself or herself and his or her strengths and limitations to act in such a manner as to capitalize on this knowledge in a beneficial way.

Source: Wehmeyer & Schwartz, 1997.

504, the ADA, and the IDEA. Additionally, parents must understand that under the regulations of FERPA, they cannot be given information about their adult sons and daughters without their permission. Occasionally, some parents will become exceedingly frustrated over this regulation in the law after spending years advocating for their child's special needs.

Teaching the Skills of Self-Determination

Wehmeyer and Schwartz (1997) identified four salient characteristics of self-determination as being (1) autonomous action, (2) self-regulated decision making, (3) psychologically empowered initiation, and (4) self-realizing manner. These characteristics are described in Table 7.2. It is important for students, teachers, and parents to understand and agree upon the characteristics or components of self-determination for the purposes of teaching and learning. Even when the components are agreed upon, strategies for teaching the components will vary depending on the outcomes desired. For example, Sue Anne might identify the need to learn self-determination skills for high school academics and social functions, college academics and social life, employment, and community living/adult life. Mike would perhaps choose to learn self-determination skills for daily living, employment, transportation, and community living/adult life. Both of them must learn to transfer the skills of self-determination they learn to multiple environments when needed (Durlak, Rose, & Bursuck, 1994; Malian & Nevin, 2002).

Browder, Wood, Test, Karvonen, and Algozzine (2001) created a mapping system for teachers to learn about self-determination through a conceptual resources path and to choose strategies for teaching the skills of self-determination through an intervention resources path. The first path, conceptual resources, helps teachers work through definitions of self-determination and identify teachable components. The authors also point out five potential pitfalls that can occur when selecting a conceptual framework of self-determination. Among the pitfalls are

- assuming that what I value is what you value
- ignoring cultural differences
- neglecting collaboration with families
- requiring prerequisites for self-determination
- ignoring the social environment.

These potential pitfalls remind teachers that the aim of self-determination is to promote the individual's preferences, not those of the teacher. Educators need (a) to understand and respect definitions of self-determination based upon the cultural norms of the student and family; (b) to realize that many children with disabilities want to involve their families in decision making and that can be an expression of their preference; (c) to not put up barriers that will impede the development of self-determination skills and the outcomes that happen from them; and finally (d) to ensure that students have the opportunity to practice the skills of self-determination in authentic environments and situations.

The second path, intervention resources, aids teachers in discovering ways to include self-determination on IEPs and Transition Plans, and make it a part of students' educational programs. Browder et al. (2001) present five questions for teachers to consider in guiding which self-determination strategies or programs they might select.

- Does the resource have research-based support?
- Can the resource be used in developing IEPs?
- What teaching strategies are described?
- Can an environment be created that promotes self-determination?
- Will the resource make me a more self-determined teacher?

In answering these questions, teachers are encouraged to think about reasons for teaching the skills of self-determination and the strategies or programs that best fit their students and themselves.

Malian and Nevin (2002) conducted a comprehensive review of the literature on self-determination for practitioners. They described model programs and curricula, research on the effectiveness of self-determination training, model/program evaluations, and research on instructional strategies developed or conducted between 1992 and 1999. Malian and Nevin (2002) came to a number of conclusions suggesting that self-determination is:

- a developmental phenomenon that changes over an individual's lifetime and includes concurrent areas of development such as communication and social and emotional behaviors;
- an ecological phenomenon that develops through interactions with the environment and is, in turn, shaped by the environment's response;
- a process that is teachable and can be modeled and transferred to various life and educational situations;
- a desirable skill or valuable competency that increases the likelihood of success in adult life whether in education, employment, or community activities;
- a psychological phenomenon that is not a fixed characteristic, but rather an adaptable set of skills depending on conditions or environment;

- a predictor of successful transition to adult life, which therefore should be included in IEPs and Transition Plans as a strategic goal for all children with disabilities; and
- a skill that is made stronger in collaboration with parents and family, teachers, and friends insofar as they support the right of the individual to make choices and pursue personal interests.

These conclusions make clear that teachers, parents and family members, and friends should begin stressing the development of self-determination skills as early as possible and make self-determination a continuing goal on IEPs and Transition Plans. Self-determination appears to be every bit as important as academic prowess for success in postsecondary education.

As cited above, a number of authors have developed or described instructional models for teaching self-determination behaviors (Agran, 1997; Field, 1996; Field, Martin, Miller, Ward, & Wehmeyer, 1998; Malian & Nevin, 2002; Martin, Marshall, Maxson, & Jerman, 1996; Test, Karvonen, Wood, Browder, & Algozzine, 2000; Ward & Kohler, 1996; Wehmeyer, 1999; Wehmeyer, Agran, & Hughes, 1998). Durlak and colleagues (1994) studied the effects of a model to teach the skills of self-determination to students with learning disabilities who hoped to transition from high school to institutions of postsecondary education. These authors identified four components of instruction, including (a) the awareness of one's academic and social strengths and challenges and the compensatory strategies most useful in these areas, (b) the ability to communicate this awareness to faculty/staff and service providers, (c) an awareness of services and reasonable accommodations, and (d) the ability to request information, assistance, and accommodations when appropriate and necessary. The latter component requires that students understand their basic rights under the protection of Section 504 and the ADA and can communicate this to others.

In the Durlak and colleagues' (1994) model, high school students with learning disabilities were brought together and, through direct instruction, taught seven skills that fit the components delineated above. These skills covered the ability to (a) ask for clarification of lecture/instructional material from classes, (b) make an appointment to inform a teacher that the student has a learning disability and how it affects the student's learning, (c) make an appointment to discuss instructional needs and/or accommodations, (d) make a request to tape record a lecture, (e) request permission to have another student take notes or to copy another student's notes, (f) request assistance from a librarian, and (g) make an appointment to meet with a resource person (other than a teacher) and request academic assistance.

Using a direct instruction format (Carnine, Silbert, & Kameenui, 1990), instructors described the specific skills to be learned and demonstrated the skills through role playing. Students were then given the opportunity to ask questions and request repeated demonstrations. This was followed by the students rehearsing the skills with one another with feedback from instructors and their peers until all skills were mastered. This instructional phase was followed by a maintenance phase and then a generalization phase where the students initiated the skills in settings with teachers, librarians, and resource persons throughout the high school.

Durlak and colleagues (1994) demonstrated that this model was successful in teaching the self-determination skill set to a majority of the students, but this research was just a snapshot in time and given a longer period of instruction on these and other skills of self-determination, the effects should increase. Keep in mind, this is but one model for teaching self-determination and there are other models covering more content and different instructional strategies. Refer to Browder and colleagues (2001), Malian and Nevin (2002), and other references cited above.

Alberto's family own and operate an automobile repair and tire shop. From the time he was ten years old, Alberto would help around the shop, cleaning and running errands. As he grew into his teenage years, he began to learn the business of tuning automobiles and became rather good at it. His dream was that he and his older brothers, Roberto and Manuel, would take over the business when their father retired. Alberto's parents were concerned about him graduating from high school. Alberto was easily frustrated when he experienced difficulty in learning academic subjects, which would lead to acting out, leaving the classroom without permission, or, occasionally, skipping school altogether. His older brothers had graduated and were no longer around to calm him down and get him back to his classes. Alberto had spent some time in classes for students with learning and behavior disorders, although he was presently included in all general education courses for academics. He also saw the speech therapist because he had a mild stuttering condition. Three times per week, Alberto would meet with a small group of students who had learning or behavioral disabilities to learn and practice self-determination skills. His special education teacher thought Alberto would benefit from learning to communicate his academic needs in positive ways, minimizing his frustration and the tension that increased his stuttering. The group also worked on identifying things they wanted to do in their lives after high school and how they might go about making that happen through their IEPs and Transition Plans.

In the spring of Alberto's junior year, he and his parents met at the high school for an IEP/Transition Planning meeting. Alberto's parents were surprised by his active involvement in the meeting. This was quite a switch from his former sullen disinterest. And they were amazed by his primary goal for his senior year. Alberto explained that the local community college had an automotive program that high school students could attend and earn credit toward graduation and earn credits in the college program as well. Alberto had already visited the community college with other students and because of his experience and abilities in working on automobiles, the college would accept him into the program with his parents' permission. The teachers and the college program advisor attending the meeting assured Alberto's parents that the program courses would count toward high school graduation and after finishing high school, Alberto could move seamlessly into the community college and begin taking the other courses needed for an associate degree in automotive technology. Alberto closed the meeting by saying he felt he now had a real motivation for graduating high school and moving on to work he truly enjoyed.

As you can see, self-determination is a critically important component of an education for students with disabilities and should begin as soon as possible. By the middle school years, students should be active participants in the development of their own IEPs and preparing to lead IEP/Transition Planning meetings when they reach high school. This fosters greater attention in the student to matching interests with possibilities, which enables parents and teachers to think about supports, resources, and experiences necessary to help the student succeed (Price, Wolensky, & Mulligan, 2002). Such a process meets both the spirit and the letter of the law in IDEA and creates a bridge to knowing and using the regulations of Section 504 and the ADA.

Consider This!   Think about some of the times when you had to practice self-determination.

- Have you ever had to speak to a professor about needing more time to complete an assignment? If so, how did you handle the situation and what was the professor's response?
- Have you ever had to speak with a teacher or professor about a grade you were given that you thought was unfair? If so, how did you handle the situation and what was the response?
- Have you ever been made to feel you probably couldn't accomplish a goal you set for yourself? If so, how did you handle the situation? Did you succeed, fail, or modify the goal so you could succeed?

PLANNING THE TRANSITION TO POSTSECONDARY EDUCATION

The academic performance of students with disabilities in elementary and secondary education has increased over the past several years. According to the U.S. Department of Education (2002), 56 percent of these students graduated with a standard diploma in 1999–2000, a significant increase from just a few years earlier. Additionally, the percentage of disabled students who drop out has concurrently declined. See Table 7.3 for quick facts on students with disabilities in postsecondary education.

Wolanin and Steele (2004) have reported that the single most important reason in a four-year college's decision to accept or reject a candidate for admission is his or her high school academic record. The academic progress made by students with disabilities in the last twenty years is estimated by the increased percentage of college freshmen reporting a disability. That figure has gone from approximately 3 percent to nearly 10 percent or somewhere around 1.3 million (Carlson, 2004). Nevertheless, students with disabilities drop out of high school at twice the rate as non-disabled students and in 1999, 85 percent of high school dropouts reported some form of disability (National Council on Disability, 2003).

Thus, it is critical that IEP/Transition Planning Teams see to it that students who show an interest in two-year and four-year colleges be scheduled into courses that will help them qualify for admission and prepare them to succeed in the academic world of postsecondary education. Even if the student is interested in a technical program rather than a purely academic program, there is a level of literacy and numeracy students must achieve or they will not meet the criteria for the program degree or certificate. A watered-down curriculum with low expectations will surely have

TABLE 7.3   Quick Facts on Students with Disabilities in Higher Education

- In 2001, 78 percent of adults with disabilities reported that they had a high school diploma compared to 91 percent of the general population.
- Only 57 percent of youth with disabilities received standard high school diplomas.
- By 2000, 73 percent of high school graduates with disabilities enrolled in some form of postsecondary education compared to 84 percent of their peers without disabilities.
- However, students with disabilities who were highly qualified academically enrolled in four-year colleges at the same rate (79 percent) as their peers without disabilities.
- Approximately 10 percent of the total student population had some kind of disability, and of those with disabilities roughly half have more than one disability.
- Learning disabilities appear to be the most common disability type at the secondary school level, and among first-time, full-time freshmen at four-year colleges.
- Minority students (other than Asians) and low-income students are more likely to have a disability than other groups.
- Although the gap in achievement is improving between those with disabilities and their peers, students with disabilities are underrepresented among those graduating from college due to a variety of factors: low high school graduation rates, inadequate preparation, and unique challenges with transition to college.

Source: Wolanin & Steele, 2004.

an adverse effect on the student's ability to become college-qualified and may delay or end the goal of a postsecondary education (President's Commission on Excellence in Special Education, 2002).

As stressed earlier in this chapter, academic preparation alone will not be enough to put students in a strong position to succeed in college programs. Skillfulness in (1) self-determination behaviors along with (2) academic performance and (3) a basic understanding of laws and regulations that protect the individual's rights are key components (see the Beyond IDEA section above). A fourth component is a strong set of independent living skills such as shopping for items like books, school supplies, music, clothes, and food items. Other skills include housekeeping, laundry, grocery shopping (if living in an apartment or sharing a house), and transportation (e.g., independent driving with or without vehicle modifications, use of regular mass transit, city or county specialized transport, taxi, or car pool). This milieu for independent living during the college years is complex and yet it is too often considered to be a naturally occurring development. Cobb (2004) has summarized a top ten list of things to think about as individuals with disabilities prepare for the transition to adulthood. This list can be found in Sidebar 7.2.

Independent Living Skills—Start Early, Teach Often

Although formal transition planning is not mandated until at least age sixteen, children with disabilities should be given household chores whenever they are at a point to learn how to perform them. (Refer back to the work of Szymanski, which was introduced in Chapters 1 and 4). Typically, children at very young ages can learn to put away their toys when they are finished playing. Setting and clearing the table at meal-

■ ■ ■ ■ ■

TOP TEN THINGS TO THINK ABOUT AS YOU PREPARE FOR YOUR TRANSITION TO ADULTHOOD

Summer provides a perfect opportunity for students with disabilities to evaluate progress made over the past school year toward their academic goals and to explore new strategies for continued success. Many such students have recently left the structure and security of secondary education and are venturing out into postsecondary education and employment and the increasingly independent realm of adulthood. For young adults with disabilities, this transition is the culmination of a lot of hard work, many obstacles overcome, a roller coaster full of emotional ups and downs, and countless IEP meetings. To be best prepared for the journey ahead, students should be closely involved with their own transition planning and also recognize that considerable planning and preparation remains to be done.

We offer the following Top Ten list to help transitioning students focus on areas that they can control to ensure success and to get them started on the journey with solid footing.

1. Know Your Disability.

If you are a transitioning student with a disability you will have to become your own resident expert on everything about your disability, the ways it impacts your activities, and the ways you have learned to overcome it. This expertise can be the key to your future success, for if you can identify your strengths and challenges you will also likely be able to identify your needs and limitations. Knowing the areas in your life that are limited due to disability puts you in the driver's seat for your future. To practice sharing your expertise about your disability, consider preparing an Elevator Speech. This is simply a concise, plainspoken, and direct explanation of the exact nature of your disability (it's called an elevator speech because, while informative, it should also be relatively brief, no longer than it might take you to reach your destination in an elevator).

2. What Are Your Needs?

Every transitioning student needs to be able to answer this question before commencing postsecondary education. Integral to identifying needs is understanding which of your life functioning skills require accommodation. Do you have an auditory processing deficit that requires you to use books on tape? Does accommodating your disability require that you sit in the front of the classroom where you won't be as distracted by others and where you can concentrate more fully on the professor? Having the answers to these sorts of questions will help you to define the arrangements you need to make before the semester begins. Reviewing your transition plan and your IEP with teachers and parents can help you anticipate the specific accommodations that will need to be arranged.

3. Postsecondary Choices—Weigh Your Options.

There are so many options out there for the transitioning youth that it can be very easy to make the wrong choice. The key here is to remember that you, the student, have to live with the choices—not your parents, teachers, or advisors. Thus, you need to be an active participant in any planning or discussion about your postsecondary options and you need to consider all of the options before making a choice.

With members of your transition team, evaluate what will be the best direction to take after high school. College is a great option: it can provide important opportunities for independent growth, and provide a wealth of encounters with new people and ideas that can enrich the rest of your life. But for many students who have to manage their disabilities, the sudden freedom that college affords can be too much. Don't overlook the community college option. It may be perfect if you aren't sure you know what you want to study, if you want to get the hang of arranging for accommodations before heading off to a bachelor degree program, or if you'd like an opportunity to learn better daily living skills before living away from home. You can always transfer to a four-year college when you feel more prepared. And the school of record that appears on your diploma is the one where you finish.

Other options for postsecondary study include vocational and technical schools, which are great places to learn a trade and embark on a career. Employment is also an appropriate postsecondary path. Some students with disabilities make this choice because they are already working as a result of a placement while still in high school. For the student who likes to work and is thriving and enjoying such independence, this may be a good situation at this time. Frequently, the desire to excel in a job or profession dictates that additional schooling be obtained later on.

The point is, it's your life and these choices directly affect you. Therefore, it's wise to consider ALL of your options, carefully weighing the pros and cons of each.

4. College Entrance Exams.

Many postsecondary programs require standardized testing for consideration of admissions. The most common of these are the SAT and the ACT. It's important to get an early start on planning for the SATs and ACTs. Requests for accommodations may take some time to be processed as they are reviewed on a case-by-case basis. Also, pay particular attention to the documentation requirements of any testing for which you are seeking accommodations: your request will not be considered if your documentation is deemed incomplete. You should also seriously consider taking the PSAT in the spring of your junior year in high school—it's good practice for the SATs or ACTs to come and allows you plenty of time to retake the test in your senior year if needed.

It is also preferable if you can demonstrate precedence for testing accommodations. In other words, you have needed accommodations all through high school and therefore there is still a need for accommodations during these scholastic aptitude exams. Taking ownership of the process of arranging for accommodations on these exams is a great way to hone the self-advocacy skills that you will need in your postsecondary endeavors. The following websites will get you started on arranging for testing and accommodations:

> www.ets.org/disability
> www.collegeboard.com/disable/students/html/indx
> www.act.org/aap/disab/index.html

5. Documentation.

The documentation of your disability needs to be current and complete and you need to know exactly what documentation your next school or training program will require if you are seeking accommodations or services on the basis of disability. The two most important questions you can ask of any of the postsecondary programs you are considering are "What documentation is needed for me to receive accommodations?" and "How old can it be?" Most schools will ask that the documentation not be over three years old.

If new documentation is requested, you may need to find a provider that can perform the necessary evaluations. If you are eligible for or already receive state vocational

(continued)

rehabilitation (VR) services, inquire with your local VR office about testing and evaluation. In some cases, if your documentation is not too old, the evaluator can make an amendment to the current documentation and provide an updated statement about the disability and what accommodations are recommended. Stay involved in this process—the better you understand your documentation, the better able you will be to identify your needs and to ask for the help that will give you a chance to do your best.

6. Self-Advocacy.

This is the whole game right here, and we've alluded to it in each of the previous points. It is never too early to become your own advocate and it is never too late to learn. As early as possible, begin asking questions at your IEP and Transition Planning meetings—such active engagement will pay off in all aspects of your later life when you have to self-advocate for services, identify your disability, and articulate your needs to function successfully.

If you haven't been as actively involved in your transition planning, fear not. There are a lot of things you can do right now to become more involved and that will invariably make you a more resourceful, articulate self-advocate. Begin by gathering the information required to take the SAT or ACT exams or other entrance exams with accommodations. Or, research the requirements for documentation in order to receive services at various postsecondary programs. And familiarize yourself with your civil rights and the laws that protect them, in particular Section 504 of the Rehabilitation Act (1973) and the Americans with Disabilities Act (1990). Visit various websites and consult your reference librarian for other sources of information.

7. Vocational Rehabilitation Services.

A good practice drill in self-advocacy is going to the local Vocational Rehabilitation Services office to determine what services may be available to you. Vocational Rehabilitation may be able to help you to attend a particular trade school, and in some instances, has been known to pay for two- and four-year college coursework. To locate the Vocational Rehabilitation office nearest you, go to http://janweb.icdi.wvu.edu/SBSES/VOCREHAB.HTM.

8. Living Space Issues.

As your transition plan comes together you may have to make some decisions regarding your living space. Your living arrangements can be enormously important to your chances for postsecondary success. Do you welcome the opportunity to live in a small space with other roommates? Are you confident that you have, or can quickly develop, the social and independent living skills needed to survive with one or more roommates? Consult with your parents and teachers for input and advice. Living space issues are frequently ignored prior to admission, only to surface after the student encounters difficulty. If you and your family and advisors agree that you might require special housing, such as a single room, discuss your concerns with the disability service coordinator at the school or program. Specific accommodations may be required to get the arrangements you need but it should be addressed well in advance of the semester, and perhaps even prior to admission, as there may be limitations on the availability of housing options within a particular program.

9. Time Management.

Are you a good manager of your time? Not many people leaving high school are, regardless of disability. But many postsecondary experiences, be they technical school or college level learning or employment, will challenge your ability to manage time. If you haven't mastered these important time management skills yet, start practicing them now. Are you in the habit of using a calendar to keep track of your appointments, classes, and social obligations? Are you good at estimating how much time a particular task might require? Will you need to schedule time with a tutor? Are all of your classes nearby or does it take longer to get to some than to others? So much of adult life requires an ability to plan for and juggle multiple tasks. Any improvement you make in managing your time will serve you well throughout your adult life.

10. Mistakes Are NOT the End of the World.
Students who approach this next phase of their lives with reasonable expectations are often the best prepared to face many new challenges. Know that there will be days when note takers do not show up; when wheelchair ramps are not cleared; when proctors are not available; when professors do not understand; when plans and strategies do not work out. But that is OK and to be expected. Reacting coolly and acknowledging that many such hiccups happen to everyone—not only you—is an important part of learning to adapt and to compensate. Overcoming such inevitable pitfalls will only make you stronger and better prepare you to deal with the next bump in the road. Review these ten topics occasionally to ensure that you are anticipating the necessary steps to a successful transition. Be sure to seek guidance from family and counselors whenever questions arise: doing so helps you to hone your self-advocacy skills and to become increasingly confident that you can achieve your goals for postsecondary education.

Source: Joyanne Cobb, MS, CRC, CRP, The George Washington University, HEATH Resource Center.

---

time is a traditional chore as is washing dishes during the adolescent years. To assume such skills will be learned by observation is a mistake (Dacy & Travers, 1994; Woolfolk, 1998). Teachers often have classroom tasks for students, like putting away art supplies, emptying trash receptacles, and cleaning desks. For children with physical disabilities, working with an occupational therapist can produce options for their participation in household chores and learning to become more independent.

During the adolescent years, learning to manage money has become even more important as credit and debit cards become more ubiquitous and targeted toward younger consumers. Running up large debts without the means to pay them off can be the beginning of a bad credit rating (difficult to overcome from the young adult years onward). While advanced courses in mathematics are important in building academic credibility for postsecondary education, "practical math," like balancing a checkbook and creating and following a monthly budget, are essential for students who will be living away from home.

Certainly, a big issue is transportation. An expected right of passage during the teenage years is learning to drive a car and getting a driver's license. While this will be possible for some students with mild or no cognitive disability, it will not be possible for those with more severe cognitive involvement, those who have low vision or are blind, and those who have severe and multiple physical disabilities. Cost is another factor. While it is possible for some individuals with physical disabilities to drive modified vehicles, such modifications are expensive and may preclude a low-income family from outfitting such a vehicle unless they qualify for assistance. Thus, it is important that individuals with disabilities learn to use other forms of transportation available to them. It is important to remember that not every college student owns a car and some colleges do not allow resident freshmen to have a car on campus. Many campuses have their own bus system for transporting students on and off campus to residential locations and shopping areas. This is a service that students and parents should investigate when choosing a postsecondary education institution.

Likewise, learning the techniques of meal preparation and good nutrition is important. A sure way for undergraduate students to put on unwanted weight and tax their health is to subsist largely on "junk" food because it is readily available and inexpensive. Although most high schools offer at least one course in health and well being, many students do not take such a class unless it is required for graduation and those who do may not retain the most practical information. Parents should ensure that all their children, but especially those with disabilities, learn how to prepare simple nutritious meals or, if they cannot participate in the preparation, know what to shop for or to order/request. Most dining halls on college campuses now offer healthy, low-fat and low-carbohydrate selections, but it is up to the individual to choose.

On the topic of health, one cannot ignore the use of alcohol and drugs (including tobacco) on college campuses. Newspapers and magazines are filled with stories of binge drinking, "club drugs," and the occasional story of the tragic death of a student who succumbed to overdosing, individually or through peer pressure. Students with disabilities who have not engaged in drug and alcohol use during the high school years because of parental controls may be tempted into experimentation as a way of meeting new friends or be pressured to try them by peers (Woolfolk, 1998). The danger is all the more prevalent if the student is taking medications due to a physical or mental health condition. Students with mental health issues tend to be more prone to suicide attempts if they engage in illegal drug use (All Info About Healthy Living, 2004). Specific attention must be given to this topic by parents and teachers and it should be considered part of self-determination training.

On college campuses, sexual activity is often associated with alcohol and drug use. This is an uncomfortable topic for many parents and school personnel, but it is a very important subject to cover. The rise in sexually transmitted diseases (STDs) among young adults cannot be ignored. Recent data show that fifteen to twenty-four-year-olds, who represent one-quarter of sexually active Americans, accounted for half of newly diagnosed STDs; over nine million cases in 2000 (Allan Guttmacher Institute, 2004). Sexual activity may be encouraged through individual or peer pressure. The use of alcohol or drugs can lead to faulty judgment rather than a well-thought-out choice. It is not clear if the number of date rapes is increasing or increasingly being reported, but it is a serious issue on college campuses. While some would counsel abstinence as the only safe choice until marriage, we know this will not be the choice of many young adults. Thus, it is important that beyond any health course students with disabilities may enroll in, discussions about safe sex practices with parents and professionals must take place. Again, self-determination training can be helpful in teaching students with disabilities to follow their own instincts rather than those of an individual or a group. Learning to say "no" to unwelcome advances and pressure situations is a necessary skill.

Academic Planning

As previously stated, academic performance is particularly important for those students who plan to apply to four-year colleges and universities (Wolanin & Steele, 2004). That means the IEP/Transition Planning Team must be aware of the courses colleges look for when considering applicants. For example, most four-year colleges look for success in course sequences of English, mathematics, the sciences, social studies, and foreign languages. They also look for specializations in the visual or performing arts, communication skills, computer science, and the like. They pay attention to volunteer work and community service, participation in athletics, and clubs (e.g., debate). And of course, there is the traditional essay.

Starting in the freshman year of high school, an academic schedule should be developed for all the years in high school. This includes not only the recommended sequence of required courses, but alternate plans for retaking courses in summer school if the grades earned during the regular school year are too low. Students should begin using their self-determination skills to request accommodations in their high school courses, which might include tutoring in some of the more difficult courses. Plans should also be made for preparing to take the PSAT and SAT or ACT tests according to a schedule that would allow for retaking the test if necessary. Prior to that, requests and documentation for extended time, the use of assistive technology, or other accommodations on these tests must be submitted by specified deadlines.

Most high schools have at least one designated counselor who helps students prepare for the college application process and this individual should participate in transition planning meetings early on and from time to time. This counselor can be very helpful in not only discussing the academic requirements of colleges, but in informing students and parents about campus services for students with disabilities and other student services highly relevant to their college experience. For students and parents who plan on visiting one or more campuses before applying, they should call ahead to set up an appointment with the director or an associate in the Office of Services for Students with Disabilities and likewise in housing or residential services. The purpose of such a visit is to clarify the college's eligibility requirements for services under Section 504 and the ADA and to become knowledgeable about the types of accommodations, supports, and services available.

Credit-Based Transition Programs

Sue Anne knew early on that she wanted to attend a four-year college and her transition plan was designed accordingly. Her parents were both college graduates, her sister was attending college and her brother was just a year away from doing the same. Alberto was losing interest in school and was not sure if he would graduate high school even though his parents wanted him to do so. His oldest brother had enlisted in the Navy hoping to eventually attend college on the GI Bill. His other brother was finishing an Associate of Arts degree at the local community college and was planning on transferring to a state university campus. Then, one of Alberto's special education teachers suggested he enroll in a credit-based transition program at the local community college. The program described in Alberto's story is referred to as a "dual credit program" (Bailey & Karp, 2003). There is some evidence that students enrolled in dual credit programs are better prepared for postsecondary education, enroll in two-year colleges at greater rates, and are more successful in their program courses (Bailey & Karp, 2003; Windham, 1997).

Bailey and Karp (2003) have described the current types of credit-based transition programs around the country. Dual credit programs between high schools, community colleges, and some four-year colleges have been established for some time. Courses are usually taken at a college or technical school and count toward high school graduation and a degree or certificate program at the college. In some small rural high schools where courses in specific foreign languages or mathematics at the level of calculus are not offered, students can take these courses from a two-year or four-year college and transfer them directly into that college or another college willing to accept the credits. Over the past several years, new forms of credit-based transition programs have been developed. Two of those forms are referred to by Bailey and Karp (2003) as singleton programs and comprehensive programs. Singleton programs are typically set up for advanced students to provide a greater academic challenge than the typical high school curriculum because they are taking college level courses. Advanced Placement (AP) programs are a good example. Students in singleton programs are able to begin their college career before graduating high school. Courses may be offered on a college campus, the high school campus, or online from an accredited college.

Another credit-based transition program is the Comprehensive Program. Again, this type of program is oriented toward the high achieving student. They are called comprehensive programs because students must commit themselves to all of the program's offerings during the last year or two of high school (Bailey & Karp, 2003). All courses completed in the program are credit-based and may include other aspects of college preparation in addition to academic courses (e.g., entrance examination preparation, college application assistance, etc.). International Baccalaureate (IB) programs are comprehensive programs as are some Tech Prep programs.

The last of the newer credit-based transition programs is the Enhanced Comprehensive Program and they are the most intensive type of credit-based transition programs (Bailey & Karp, 2003). These programs were created to prepare students for college through rigorous academic instruction, and by offering a wide range of services such as counseling, assistance with college applications, mentoring, and basic personal support. Enhanced comprehensive programs attempt to cover all aspects of the high school to postsecondary education transition. Due to their intensity and orientation to student-teacher relationships, these programs are far less common than singleton and comprehensive programs. However, their strength is in serving the needs of nontraditional college students and their potential to move middle or low achieving students into postsecondary education.

The most common type of enhanced comprehensive program is called the middle college high school (MCHS). In addition to academically challenged students, enhanced comprehensive programs also focus on students who are socially or economically disadvantaged. They are more likely to be located on college campuses than other credit-based transition programs, but many are also located at high schools. As Bailey and Karp (2003) suggest, little research has been conducted on the outcomes of these programs, but enhanced comprehensive programs appear to have many elements that would benefit students with disabilities who want to make the transition to higher education.

Some Practical Matters Affecting Choice

The choice between a two-year and four-year program should take into consideration what appears to be the best prospects for future employment and career. As we emphasize throughout this book, employment rates for individuals with disabilities are much worse than individuals without disabilities (Blackorby & Wagner, 1996). Likewise, underemployment is a serious condition of disability and often linked to a lack of postsecondary education preparation (Blackorby & Wagner, 1996; Bursuck & Rose, 1992; Hart, Mele-McCarthy, Pasternack, Zimbrich, & Parker, 2004). The prospect of employment is also of interest to state vocational rehabilitation agencies, which may provide funding for postsecondary education based upon prospects for employment. (Recall the initial decision of the California Department of Rehabilitation for Ed Roberts.)

Personal finances are also an important factor. Community colleges are far less expensive than even state colleges and universities, especially with tuition costs increasing steadily. In addition to saving on tuition and fees, the community college student can live at home saving residence costs and usually meal costs. Transportation may also be more accessible and the opportunity to find a part-time or full-time job while attending classes may be more realistic. In cases where students will need financial aid, transition planning should include resources for the students and their parents by the end of the junior year in high school so there is ample time to understand the requirements of the Free Application for Federal Student Aid (FAFSA). The application can be filled out on a World Wide Web site hosted by the U.S. Department of Education, but it can be complicated for first-time users and some training on navigating the website is advisable. There are a number of services available from the website including pages for college planning and college selection (see http://studentaid.ed.gov/).

A deciding factor in choosing a two-year or four-year college may be maturity. There are many students with disabilities who can handle the academic rigor of a four-year college, but lack the confidence and maturity to be successful. Along with training in self-determination, maturity matters and an additional year or two at home can be beneficial for some students. Additionally, most community colleges have learning resource centers that provide tutoring and other academic services that are more comprehensive than those on most four-year colleges (Brinckerhof et al., 2002; Bursuck & Rose, 1992; Bursuck, Rose, Cowen, & Yahaya, 1989; Rose, 1991). Remember, there is no sure thing and a small but steady percentage of "college qualified" nondisabled students fail each year for a myriad of reasons. That is why IEP/Transition Planning teams should leave as little to chance as possible when preparing a disabled student for postsecondary education.

ASSISTIVE TECHNOLOGY
AND UNIVERSAL DESIGN

Assistive Technology

With the growing numbers of students with disabilities on postsecondary education campuses and their interaction with more sophisticated and personalized technology (Center for Applied Special Technology, 2004), there may be a growing trend away from traditional program-based support services to individually based or person centered supports (Weir, 2004). Most students attending colleges today have participated in on-line homework chat rooms where the participants share ideas and knowledge to answer questions and develop projects. The availability and affordability of scanners makes it possible to share notes and resources, and, unfortunately, term papers and tests.

Voice activated software for operating systems and word processing are becoming more sophisticated and accurate. Sound systems in new and redesigned classrooms include wireless earphones for students who are hard of hearing or are easily distracted by secondary noises. Adaptive hardware makes software programs accessible and navigable for individuals with physical disabilities. And, of course, search engines such as Google and Yahoo! have made it possible to find more information than anyone can typically digest and use.

With so much technology available and in use by students with and without disabilities, it is only a matter of time until more creative options for accommodations and supports will be designed by developers and by the very students who need them. Nevertheless, students with disabilities should consider campus support services a collaborator in their quest to earn a degree or certificate and consider carefully whether or not they can succeed without such assistance (Scott, McGuire, & Shaw, 2003; Weir, 2004).

As with all aspects of transition planning and implementation, students should learn to use assistive technologies in the most updated form possible while in middle school and high school. An excellent source of information about assistive technology products, their uses, quality, and affordability is the website for ABLEDATA.Com (http://www.abledata.com/). Students, parents, and teachers can assess the possibilities of assistive technologies through this comprehensive website. See Table 7.4 for an example of information that can be retrieved from ABLEDATA.Com.

Universal Design

The term universal design has been around for over 30 years. It was originally used by Ronald Mace, a professor in the School of Design at North Carolina State University. Mace was a polio victim and therefore knew firsthand about the issues of accessibility in the built environment. The purpose of universal design (UD) is "to simplify life for everyone by making products, communications, and the built environment more usable by as many people as possible at little or no extra cost" (Center for Universal Design, 2004). In 1989, Mace started the Center for Accessible Housing, which is now known as the Center for Universal Design. The Center has produced designs for accessible homes, office buildings, parks, museums, and

TABLE 7.4   An Example of Assistive Technology Product Information from ABLEDATA.Com

Brand Name
INFOSCAN

Description
The InfoScan is a hand-held scanner designed for use by individuals with learning, neurological, or physical disabilities. Completely portable, this pen-style scanner enables the user to scan and transfer printed text directly into a PC or to scan, store and transfer up to 500 pages of printed data to a PC, laptop, PDA or any Windows application via Infrared or serial port. The InfoScan recognizes 6 to 22 point font sizes, including text that is bold, italicized, underlined, or inverted. This scanner can be set for right- or left-handed use. An Opticard and built-in Character Bar enables text that cannot be directly scanned to be manually input. The InfoScan comes equipped with a CD-ROM with desktop and pen software and documentation, a communications cable, and a protective carrying case. COMPATIBILITY: For use with IBM and compatible computers. Mac compatibility is available only with Virtual PC. SYSTEM REQUIREMENTS: Windows 95/98/NT/2000/ME/XP, CD-ROM drive for installing Desktop Applications and available communications port if serial connection is desired. POWER: Uses 2 triple-A batteries (included). OPTIONS: USB connection. DIMENSIONS (L×W×H): 6 × 1.5 × 1 inch. WEIGHT: Three ounces.

Price
119.95 to 99.99

Price Date
March 2004

Available from
Manufacturer or Local

Manufacturer Information
WizCom Technologies Inc.
257 Great Road
Acton, MA 01720
888-777-0552 (toll free), 978-635-5357 (in state)
978-929-9228 (Fax)

Manufacturer's Website
www.wizcomtech.com

Manufacturer's Email
usa.sales@wizcomtech.com

Distributor(s) Name and Phone Number
6816 Secrest Resources Ltd. at 604-228-8920 or 604-228-1134 Fax (British Columbia, Canada)
6817 1Click2Computers.com at 905-238-8037 (Ontario, Canada)

(continued)

TABLE 7.4   Continued

6658 Aroga Group, Inc. at 800-561-6222, 604-431-7997, or 604-431-7995 Fax (British
   Columbia, Canada)
6819 L.E.S. Inc. at 418-841-0816 (Quebec, Canada)
6827 CompUSA at 800-266-7872 (TX)

Distributor(s) Website
www.1click2computers.com
www.aroga.com
www.compusa.com

Distributor(s) E-mail
stuible@telus.net
sales@1click2computers.com
sales@aroga.com
lexibook@ccapcable.com

Comments
The manufacturer recommends the following brands of rechargeable batteries for those
preferring to use rechargeables: Radio Shack NI-Cadium and GP Ni-Me-Hydride. Ship-
ping and handling charges are not included in the purchase price listed.

<u>Indexing Terms</u>
Identifiers
UNIVERSAL
COMPUTERS
HARDWARE
Input
General Input Interfaces
EDUCATION
INSTRUCTIONAL MATERIALS
Instructional Materials General

Generic Term(s)
LEARNING DISABILITIES
NEUROLOGICAL DISABILITIES
SEVERE PHYSICAL DISABILITIES
PRICE 101 TO 500
SCANNER
EDUCATIONAL AID

shopping centers. It has also produced many policy and technical papers that have
guided government regulations on accessibility standards in the ADA and the Fair
Housing Amendments of 1988 (Center for Universal Design, 2004).

Recently, researchers have been extending the concept of universal design to the
areas of teaching and learning (Scott et al., 2003). The Center for Applied Special
Technology (CAST) and the Universal Design for Instruction Project at the University of Connecticut have been applying the principles of UD to the design of class-

room environments and the design of lessons for instruction in all subject areas. As the numbers of students with disabilities continue to grow on college campuses and the diversity of students in general continues to grow, postsecondary education faculty will be faced with students who do not learn well in the traditional lecture format. Additionally, regional accreditation boards, state boards of higher education, and the general public have begun to pay more attention to the teaching mission of colleges.

Thus, more colleges are providing professional development opportunities for faculty to work together to design courses that make learning more accessible to all students. This is an important issue because faculty willing to work collaboratively with students on accommodations and supports has been identified as one of the most critical factors in whether or not students with disabilities succeed in earning a degree or certificate in postsecondary education (Wolanin & Steele, 2004; Rose, 1993). Just as curb cuts and ramps have benefited a larger population of people than those who use wheelchairs, UD for teaching and learning has the potential to improve the academic experience for students, faculty, and student services professionals in postsecondary education.

CHAPTER SUMMARY

Sue Anne's dream seems simple enough, but there is a great deal of complexity involved. She must learn that attending a college and living in a college community are very different from living at home and following the scheduled routines of high school. She will also have to learn that her rights as a person with a disability are covered by laws other than IDEA. Having a single law regulating how she has been served from elementary school through high school will seem easy compared to learning the protections available to her under Section 504 of the Rehabilitation Act of 1973, the Americans with Disabilities Act of 1990, and the Family Educational Rights and Privacy Act Amendments of 1997.

Thus, she must learn to advocate for herself. To accomplish this, she will study and practice the skills of self-determination to increase her potential to be an independent person who makes good decisions while she is away at college. The temptations will be many. There are many social distractions available to young college students including some that are unhealthy and unwise. Alcohol, drugs, and sexual activity are decision points for every young person, but they are especially challenging decisions for individuals with disabilities who want to be in step with their peers. Learning to protect oneself from harmful activities is essential.

To accomplish her dream of earning a degree in early childhood education, Sue Anne will have to enroll in challenging courses while in high school. To be successful in these courses she will have to be self-determined and advocate for her right to reasonable accommodations. She should work with her IEP/Transition Planning Team to consider options for credit-based transition programs offered by her high school and a local college and she must begin working with the pre-college counselor to learn the ropes for applying to colleges that accommodate both her academic and disability needs.

During her junior year, Sue Anne will have to discuss with her parents which campuses she will want to apply to and visit during the fall semester of her senior year. A campus that fosters independence in its students and is supportive of their needs will likely be her choice. In addition, she will be looking for a college that provides the kind of technological support she is used to and has a faculty that is committed to her learning. It is a tall order, but it is possible and that is the stuff of dreams.

APPLICATION ACTIVITIES

The application activities listed below are essential for your continued learning and skill development in transition planning. Each of the activities will require your time and energy, but will help you develop your professional skills in this area.

For Practice and Enhanced Understanding:

Make an appointment to interview the director of services for students with disabilities on your campus. Ask about the procedures used to qualify an individual for accommodations and/or supports at your campus.

Make an appointment to speak with a high school counselor who assists students in putting together applications for public and private colleges. Ask about the advice and training the counselor gives to students with disabilities and why.

Interview a student and his or her parents about plans for a postsecondary education and how that education will be used.

Interview a faculty member from your college about how he or she feels about providing accommodations for students with disabilities and why he or she feels that way.

For Your Portfolio:

Make an appointment to interview your Vice President for Student Affairs and ask about the policies in place to deal with drug and alcohol use, date rape, and discrimination against persons with disabilities.

Investigate the assistive technology resources on a local college campus and the procedures to become qualified to use them.

Shadow a person with physical disabilities around your campus to assess the accessibility to classrooms, offices, residences, and athletic/entertainment venues.

Interview a student with a disability and ask about the accessibility to courses and programs and the kinds of accommodations he or she requests. Find out how much he or she must use self-determination skills to get the accommodations he or she has a right to receive.

Study the websites for the Association on Higher Education and Disability (AHEAD, http://www.ahead.org/), CAST (http://www.cast.org/udl/), and the Center for Universal Design (http://www.design.ncsu.edu/cud/). What can they tell you about the present and the future of postsecondary education for students with disabilities?

RESOURCES AND WEBSITES

The HEATH Center at George Washington University

The top clearinghouse on individuals with disabilities and postsecondary education. www.heath.gwu.edu/

LD Online

A rich resource for students with learning disabilities planning the transition to post-secondary education.
www.ldonline.org/ld_indepth/postsecondary/index.html

Kid Source

Provides articles on transition to postsecondary education and information on legislation for parents of children with learning disabilities, ADD, ADHD, and other disabilities.
www.kidsource.com/kidsource/content3/college.planning.LD.html

U.S. Department of Education

Comprehensive information on laws related to the civil rights of individuals with disabilities in postsecondary education.
www.avila.edu/info/disability/downloads/knowrightstest.pdf

Wrights Law

Provides a single resource to many websites on rights and responsibilities, preparation for college, and the keys to a successful college experience.
www.wrightslaw.com/flyers/college.504.pdf

Americans with Disabilities Act, Section 504

Q & A website and postsecondary education from the PACER Parents Center.
www.pacer.org/pride/504.htm

Virginia Board for People with Disabilities

A college planning guide.
www.vacollegequest.org/

ThinkCollege

Focuses on students with cognitive disabilities.
www.thinkcollege.net/programs/index.php

Andrea M. Ketchum from Pittsburgh, Pennsylvania has created a website based on her research of the most wheelchair-accessible college campuses in the United States.
www.geocities.com/ketchum4/index.html

Information on supplemental security income (SSI), financial aid, and other programs to help fund a college education can be found at:
ici.umn.edu/products/impact/151/over3.html

REFERENCES

Agran, M. (1997). *Student-directed learning: Teaching self-determination skills*. Pacific Grove, CA: Brooks-Cole.

Allen Guttmacher Institute. (2004). *Sexually transmitted diseases among young Americans call for realistic approach.* Retrieved from the World Wide Web: www.guttmacher.org/media/nr/2004/02/24/

All Info About Healthy Living. (2004). *Suicide and college students.* Retrieved from the World Wide Web: http://healthyliving.allinfo-about.com/suicide.html.

Americans with Disabilities Act of 1990, PL 101-336, 42 U.S.C. §§ 12101 *et seq.*

Bailey, T., & Karp, M. M. (2003). *Promoting college access and success: A review of credit based transition programs.* New York: Community College Research Center, Teachers College/Columbia University.

Beach Center on Disability, University of Kansas, Lawrence, KS. *Definition of self-determination* www.beachcenter.org/?act=view&type=General%20Topic&id=10 (accessed 2004).

Benz, M., Doren, B., & Yovanoff, P. (1998). Crossing the great divide: Predicting productive engagement for young women with disabilities. *Career Development for Exceptional Individuals, 21,* 3–16.

Blackorby, J., & Wagner, M. (1996). Longitudinal postschool outcomes of youth with disabilities: Findings from the National Longitudinal Transition Study. *Exceptional Children, 62,* 399–413.

Brinckerhoff, L., McGuire, J., & Shaw, S. (2002). *Postsecondary education and transition for students with learning disabilities.* Austin, TX: Pro-Ed.

Browder, D. M., Wood, W. M., Test, D. W., Karvonen, M., & Algozzine, B. (2001). Reviewing resources on self-determination: A map for teachers. *Remedial and Special Education, 22*(4), 233–244.

Bursuck, W., & Rose, E. (1992). Community college options for students with mild disabilities. In F. Rusch, L. Destefano, J. Chadsey-Rusch, L. A. Phelps, & E. Szymanski (Eds.), *Transition from school to adult life: Models, linkages, and policy.* Sycamore, IL: Sycamore Publishing Company.

Bursuck, W., Rose, E., Cowen, S., & Yahaya, M. A. (1989). Nationwide survey of postsecondary education services for students with learning disabilities. *Exceptional Children, 56*(3), 236–245.

Carlson, S. (2004). Left out online. *The Chronicle of Higher Education,* June 11, 2004.

Carnine, D., Silbert, J., & Kameenui, E. (1990). *Direct instruction reading.* Columbus, OH: Merrill.

Center for Applied Special Technology (2004). *Universal design for learning.* Retrieved from the World Wide Web: http://www.cast.org/.

Center for Universal Design. (2004). Retrieved from the World Wide Web: www.design.ncsu.edu/cud/.

Cobb, J. *Top ten things to think about as you prepare for your transition to adulthood.* Information from HEATH, a quarterly newsletter. The George Washington University HEATH Resource Center, April 2004.

Dacy, J., & Travers, J. (1994). *Human development across the lifespan* (2nd ed.). Madison, WI: WCB Brown & Benchmark.

Dalke, C. (1993). Making a successful transition from high school to college: A model program. In S. Vogel & P. Adelman (Eds.), *Success for college students with learning disabilities* (pp. 57–79). New York: Springer-Verlag.

Disability Rights and Independent Living Movement. (2004). Retrieved from the World Wide Web: http://bancroft.berkeley.edu/collections/drilm/collection/items/roberts_edward.html

Durlak, C. M., Rose, E., & Bursuck, W. D. (1994). Preparing high school students with learning disabilities for the transition to postsecondary education: Teaching the skills of self-determination. *Journal of Learning Disabilities, 27,* 51–59.

Family Educational Rights and Privacy Act Amendments of 1997.20 U.S.C. § 1232g; 34 CFR Part 99.

Field, S. (1996). Self-determination instructional strategies for youth with learning disabilities. *Journal of Learning Disabilities, 29,* 40–52.

Field, S., Martin, J., Miller, R., Ward, M., & Wehmeyer, M. (1998). *A practical guide to teaching self-determination.* Reston, VA: Council for Exceptional Children.

Field, S., Sarver, M. D., & Shaw, S. (2003). Self-determination: A key to success in postsecondary education for students with learning disabilities. *Remedial and Special Education, 24*(6), 339–349.

Guckenberger v. Boston University, 974 F. Supp. 106 (D. Mass. 1997).

Hart, D., Mele-McCarthy, Pasternack, R., Zimbrich, K., & Parker, D. (2004). Community college: A pathway to success for youth with learning, cognitive, and intellectual disabilities in secondary settings. *Education and Training in Developmental Disabilities, 39*(1), 54–66.

Individuals with Disabilities Education Act Amendments of 1997, Public Law 105-17, 20 U.S.C. 1400.

Malian, I., & Nevin, A. (2002). A review of self-determination literature: Implications for practitioners. *Remedial and Special Education, 23*(2), 68–74.

Martin, J., Marshall, L., Maxson, L., & Jerman, P. (1996). *Self-directed IEP*. Longmont, CO: Sopris West.

National Council on Disability (2003). *People with Disabilities and Postsecondary Education*, Washington, DC: Author.

President's Commission on Excellence in Special Education (2002). *A New Era: Revitalizing Special Education for Children and Their Families*, Washington, DC: Author.

Price, L., Wolensky, D., & Mulligan, R. (2002). Self-determination in action in the classroom. *Remedial and Special Education, 23*(2), 109–115.

Rehabilitation Act of 1973, PL 93-112, § 504, 29 U.S.C. 794 *et seq.*

Reis, S., Neu, T., & McGuire, J. (1997). Case studies of high-ability students with learning disabilities who have achieved. *Exceptional Children, 63*, 463–479.

Rose, E. (1993). Faculty development: Changing attitudes and enhancing knowledge about learning disabilities. In S. Vogel & P. Adelman (Eds.), *Success for college students with learning disabilities*, (pp. 131–150). New York: Springer—Verlag.

Rose, E. (1991). Project TAPE: A model of technical assistance for service providers of college students with learning disabilities. *Learning Disabilities Research & Practice, 6*(1), 25–33.

Rothman, J. C. (2003). *Social work practice across disability*. Boston: Allyn and Bacon.

Scott, S., McGuire, J., & Shaw, S. (2003). Universal design for instruction: A new paradigm for adult instruction in postsecondary education. *Remedial and Special Education, 24*(6), 369–379.

Shapiro, J. (1994). *No pity*. New York: Three Rivers Press.

Sitlington, P. (2003). Postsecondary education: The other transition. *Exceptionality, 11*(2), 103–113.

Southeastern Community College v. Davis, 442 U.S. 397 (1979).

Test, D., Karvonen, M., Wood, W., Browder, D., & Algozzine, B. (2000). Choosing a self-determination curriculum: Plan for the future. *TEACHING Exceptional Children, 33*(2), 48–54.

U.S. Department of Education. (2002). *Twenty-fourth annual report to Congress on the implementation of the Individuals with Disabilities Education Act*, Washington, DC: Author.

Ward, M., & Kohler, P. (1996). Teaching self-determination: Content and process. In L. Powers, G. H. S. Singer, & J. Sowers (Eds.), *On the road to autonomy: Promoting self-competence for children and youth with disabilities* (pp. 275–290). Baltimore: Brookes.

Wehmeyer, M. (1999). A functional model of self-determination: Describing development and implementing instruction. *Focus on Autism and Other Developmental Disabilities, 14*, 53–61.

Wehmeyer, M., Agran, M., & Hughes, C. (1998). *Teaching self-determination to students with disabilities*. Baltimore: Brookes.

Wehmeyer, M. L., & Palmer, S. B. (2003). Adult outcomes for students with cognitive disabilities three years after high school: The impact of self-determination. *Education and Training in Developmental Disabilities, 38*(2), 131–144.

Wehmeyer, M. L., & Schwartz, M. (1997). Self-determination and positive adult outcomes: A follow-up study of youth with mental retardation or learning disabilities. *Exceptional Children, 63*(2), 245–255.

Weir, C. (2004). Person-centered and collaborative supports for college success. *Education and Training in Developmental Disabilities, 39*(1), 67–73.

Windham, P. (1997). *High school and community college dual enrollment: Issues of rigor and transferability*. Tallahassee, FL: Florida State Board of Community Colleges. ERIC Document ED 413 936.

Wolanin, T., & Steele, P. (2004). *Higher education opportunities for students with disabilities: A primer for policymakers*. Washington, DC: The Institute for Higher Education Policy.

Woolfolk, A. (1998). *Educational psychology* (7th ed.). Boston: Allyn and Bacon.

CHAPTER 8

MOVING OUT OF THE FAMILY HOME TO COMMUNITY LIVING

CHAPTER OBJECTIVES

Upon completion of this chapter, you will be able to

1. describe the steps that should be taken to help connect individuals with developmental and other disabilities to adult residential services.

2. design curricular content that will assist students with disabilities in living in their own apartments or homes after leaving their families' homes.

3. identify specific residential service providers within your local community.

4. collaborate with students and their families in helping them take the steps necessary to assist them in making the transition to their first home or apartment away from home.

5. assist students with disabilities in taking the steps to move into homes outside of their families' homes.

KEY TOPICS TO LOOK FOR IN THIS CHAPTER . . .

- Self-determination: In this chapter, self-determination is discussed within the context of individuals with disabilities making decisions about where and how to live in the community. Notice particularly how the supported living philosophy incorporates the concepts of self-determination.

- Options for Adulthood: In this chapter, look for the range of options that may be available for young people once they leave their families' homes. Also, consider how desirable each of these options might be and whether or not young people could come to consider them as real homes.

You might remember the day you found yourself in your own dorm room, apartment, or home. This memory often stays with us because the move out of one's family home is one of the most defining aspects of independence. This aspect of transition to adult life is closely tied to the overall success of the transition planning process (Blacher,

2001; Cooney, 2002; Knoll & Wheeler, 2001). Although transition is a process that takes place over a span of several years, as described in Chapter 1, the move out of the family's home for the first time is a significant moment or event in that process.

It is important to establish our intent in this chapter. We are concerned with helping students with disabilities make a successful transition to a home or apartment of their choosing, not simply to a residential program. A home, whether it is our family's home or our own home or apartment, is a unique place that offers safety, comfort, relaxation, privacy, and the opportunity for personalization (O'Brien, 1994; Steere & Burcroff, 2004). As with successful employment, securing a "happy home" is closely tied to overall satisfaction and improved quality of life. O'Brien described a home as being characterized by these three key dimensions:

- a sense of place that allows comfort and personalization;
- a sense of control over where to live and with whom to live; and
- a sense of security that results from being a homeowner or a tenant who controls the terms of a lease.

Given these characteristics, effective transition programs will prepare students to find home living options that meet these key dimensions. In this chapter, we will describe the steps that need to be taken to assist young people with disabilities in making the transition from their family's home to their own first home. We will describe the skills that students need to develop in order to live as independently as possible in the community and how these skills can be addressed within the secondary-level curriculum. We will also discuss the range of options for community living, with a focus on the supported living philosophy. Finally, we will discuss the potential impact of the move into the community on both students and their families.

Consider This!   What really is the difference between an apartment or house and a *home*? If you are currently living in an environment that you consider to be your home, what makes it feel this way? In what ways do you personalize your home and make it uniquely yours? What personal spaces do you have within the home, and what spaces are shared with others? In what ways does your home make you feel safe, secure, and comfortable?

John and Connie Lyle O'Brien have been leaders in helping professionals and typical citizens develop the capacity to be responsive to the choices of people with disabilities and to help them to be included in all aspects of local community life. See Sidebar 8.1 for their story.

OVERVIEW: WHEN TYPICAL YOUNG PEOPLE MOVE AWAY FROM HOME

As introduced above, moving out of one's family's home and taking the steps to find a new home is a major step in the process of growing up and making the transition from school to adulthood. For typical young people who do not experience a disability,

■ ■ ■ ■ ■

SIDEBAR 8.1

SPOTLIGHT ON HISTORY: JOHN AND CONNIE LYLE O'BRIEN

John and Connie Lyle O'Brien have been innovative leaders who have helped professionals think differently about their role in supporting people with disabilities. The focus of their work has been to help local networks of people build the capacity to support individuals with disabilities within inclusive community environments. Working through Responsive Systems Associates and in conjunction with the Center for Human Policy at Syracuse University, they have pioneered innovative practices related to supported living and person centered planning. All of their work has been characterized by the need for professionals to better listen to people with disabilities and their families and to respond to their choices. Their work has expanded beyond to the United States to Australia, Bosnia, Canada, England, Ireland, the Netherlands, New Zealand, Scotland, Spain, and Wales.

Source: Taken from Website of the Center for Human Policy at Syracuse University www.thechp.syr .edu

there are several options for a first place to live away from home. These are shown in Table 8.1. Notice that not all of these options will be perceived as "home-like." Some may be a step or one in several steps that young people may take toward finding a true first independent home in which they can experience privacy, comfort, and safety. In fact, it is fairly typical for a young person to live in a series of different places as they progress through the longer transition from being a recent graduate to an established adult.

Note that for many young people with milder disabilities, such as Sue Anne, the more typical options (apartment, dorm room, own home) will be sufficient. These individuals will not typically need the intensity or longevity of supports that people with severe disabilities will need. However, students with milder disabilities will need to master the skills discussed in the next section, and some of the same learning challenges they experience with academics may also affect their ability to learn these critical skills. It is for this reason that the Division on Career Development and Transition (DCDT) of the Council for Exceptional Children (CEC) published a position statement in which the authors asserted that all young people with disabilities,

TABLE 8.1 Possible First Places to Live upon Leaving Home

■ College dorm room
■ Military barracks
■ Apartment
■ Summer camp
■ Relative's home
■ Purchased home

not just those with more severe disabilities, need to learn functional life skills that are needed in adulthood (Clark, Field, Patton, Brolin, & Sitlington, 1994).

Developing Skills for Independence

During transition, young people must learn several important skills that are associated with home living and with increased adult independence. These skills are listed in Table 8.2. Often, parents or other family members have completed some of these activities for their children while they lived at home. Once young people move away from home, however, they must assume the responsibility of completing these tasks on a daily or regular basis. It is also important to recognize that the necessity of taking responsibility for the consistent completion of these activities typically comes at the same time that young people are also assuming other increased or new responsibilities, such as a new job, new college courses, or new training programs.

Clearly, experience in learning these many skills before young people move out of the home is beneficial. As with many other aspects of transition to adult life, this is an area in which the family plays a central role. Szymanski (1994, 1995) indicated that chores and other responsibilities within the home not only help young people learn important skills for adult living but also contribute to the development of a work ethic and sense of responsibility.

An additional issue concerns the necessity for independent performance of these tasks. That is, completing chores within the family's home under the guidance of parents is different from initiating and completing these activities without external prompts or reminders. Self-management skills such as self-initiation, self-monitoring, self-correction, and self-reinforcement take on importance once young people move into their own first place to live away from home.

Impact on Young People and Their Families

When young people without disabilities move out of their families' homes, this event has a different impact on each member of the family. Table 8.3 shows some potential reactions by each member of the family to a young person's move out of the home. As shown in Table 8.3, the move away from home can be an emotional event and is certainly one that affects the entire family, not just the young person who is transitioning.

THE RANGE OF OPTIONS FOR COMMUNITY LIVING FOR YOUNG PEOPLE WITH DISABILITIES

Thus far in this chapter, we have discussed the transition out of the family home for typical young people who do not experience disabilities. In this section, we will discuss the range of options for home living for individuals with disabilities. As we discussed in Chapter 1, the intent of transition planning is to help young people with disabilities achieve satisfied and fulfilled adult lives, not simply access to program placements. In terms of home living, this means that our intent is to help people with

TABLE 8.2 Skills That Young People Must Start Performing When They Leave Home

SKILL AREA	SPECIFIC ACTIVITIES
1. Planning and preparing meals	Planning a menu Preparing meals Using cooking equipment Storing food safely
2. Self-care, bathing, and hygiene	Showering or bathing Caring for hair, nails, teeth Toileting Washing hands and face Medication use
3. Cleaning and care of the home	Vacuuming Dusting and wiping surfaces Neatening and organizing
4. Cleaning and care of clothing	Washing and drying clothes Changing clothes as needed Folding and storing clothes
5. Home finances and services	Arranging for services such as phone, water, electricity and heat to be provided Paying bills on a timely basis Maintaining a checkbook
6. Telephone/email use	Calling for appointments or services Calling friends and acquaintances Calling in emergencies Answering calls from others Using email
7. Leisure activities	Watching television Listening to music Performing hobbies Entertaining visitors Internet Video games
8. Safety procedures	Calling 911 in an emergency Evacuating during a fire Responding to smoke detectors Using a fire extinguisher Calling an ambulance or doctor if one becomes very sick or injured Safely answering the door
9. Time management and scheduling	Adhering to a daily schedule of responsibilities Using and following calendar Using alarm clocks

TABLE 8.2 Continued

SKILL AREA	SPECIFIC ACTIVITIES
10. Negotiating with others, self-advocacy	Negotiating responsibilities with roommates
	Negotiating communal versus personal property and areas within the home
	Negotiating with neighbors regarding issues such as noise, external lights, and so on
	Speaking up to ensure that important responsibilities are carried out by roommates or others
	Speaking up on one's behalf to ensure that needed supports are obtained

Source: Adapted from Steere & Burcroff, 2004.

disabilities find places to live that meet O'Brien's (1994) dimensions of "home," described earlier. Some options will allow young people to attain the characteristics of a quality home, while others may never allow people to perceive where they live as their home. Consider these two individuals:

Lisa is thirty-two years old and has multiple disabilities, including cerebral palsy, mental retardation, and a seizure disorder. She requires extensive supports in taking care of herself, including toileting, eating, and other aspects of self-care. When Lisa exited the special education system, no suitable residential options were found for her. Her family attempted to care for her for several years, but the strain was too much physically and emotionally. Three years ago Lisa was placed in a nursing home. She now spends her days in the day hall or in her room, alongside people who are decades older than she. Although she cannot communicate her feelings verbally, she knows that this is not her home.

TABLE 8.3 Potential Impact on Members of the Family of a Young Person's Move Out of the Home

	POSITIVE IMPACT	NEGATIVE IMPACT
Young Person	<ul><li>Increased independence</li><li>Greater control over one's schedule and activities</li><li>Pride in accomplishments</li></ul>	<ul><li>Loss of support or assistance</li><li>Increased responsibility</li><li>Missing family interactions</li></ul>
Parents	<ul><li>Pride in child's maturity</li><li>Increased space in home</li><li>Increased freedom to pursue own interests</li></ul>	<ul><li>Missing child's presence</li><li>Loss of child's contributions to home chores, etc.</li></ul>
Siblings	<ul><li>Increased attention</li><li>Access to new areas of home</li></ul>	<ul><li>Missing sibling's interactions</li><li>Increased responsibilities for chores</li></ul>

Juanita is a survivor of traumatic brain injury (TBI) and has characteristics similar to Lisa's. Unlike Lisa, however, Juanita was fortunate to have the option of moving to a community home with support from an area rehabilitation agency that specializes in helping people with disabilities live and participate in their local communities. Her home is accessible, and she lives there with one other individual with disabilities, with whom she gets along well. Each has her own bedroom, and staff members are always available to assist with their many needs. Like her roommate, Juanita is supported in personalizing her home with favorite items and photographs of her family. Although it took some time for her to adjust to her new living arrangements, Juanita seems to be happy in her home. Like Lisa, she cannot communicate in a typical manner, but her behavior indicates that she is happy in her new home.

Table 8.4 shows the various types of living arrangements that may be used by people with disabilities. Community-based residential programs that are designed for people with disabilities include group homes and supported living arrangements. These options allow people with disabilities to be part of their local communities, while institutions and nursing homes segregate people with disabilities to a greater degree. Group homes and supported living arrangements are typically administered and staffed by private service provider agencies. Some such agencies specialize in residential services, while others provide a wider range of employment and residential services. Residential programs are typically funded by the state Developmental Disabilities/Mental Retardation office/department or by the state Mental Health

TABLE 8.4   Residential Options for People with Disabilities

Typical Options

- Family home
- Own home (ownership of the property)
- Apartment (holds lease)
- Dorm room
- Barracks or camp

Specialized Living Arrangements

- Supported apartment or home:
  —support provided only as necessary
  —person chooses where to live
  —person chooses with whom to live
  —person controls supports to maximum extent

- Group home
  —various numbers of co-residents
  —varying intensities of staff support patterns

Most Restrictive and Least Desirable Options

- Nursing homes
- Institutional placements

office/department. Staffing patterns in community-based residential programs vary by agency and by the individuals who are served by the programs.

As indicated by the two profiles above and by Table 8.4, some options are far more desirable than others as homes for people with disabilities. Consequently, it is not easy helping young people and their families make decisions about where and with whom to live. In general, the trend has been toward the development of smaller, more home-like living situations in which people with disabilities exert greater choice and control over their living conditions. When helping people with disabilities plan the transition to a new home, a simple rule of thumb to consider is to ask yourself: "Would I be happy or comfortable living in this home?" If the answer is "No," then the question arises: "Why would this person with a disability want to live here any more than I do?"

Consider This!   Pretend for a moment that you are an individual with a disability who has just been "placed" in a new group home. You have only visited there once, and you did not understand that you were going to live there permanently. You did not choose to live in this place, but now you are here, and the staff tells you . . . . *"Welcome! You have been selected to live in one of this agency's community residences, and we know that you will be happy here. You will be living with five other people (you have not met these people before) and you will be sharing a room with one of them, because there are only three bedrooms within the house. The typical daily schedule is this:*

> *Up at 6:00 A.M. for dressing and breakfast*
> *Clean-up at 7:30*
> *Depart for the day program at 8:00*
> *Return home at 4:00*
> *Group leisure activity until 5:30*
> *Dinner at 6:00*
> *Clean-up at 7:00*
> *Evening group leisure activity or community outing at 7:15*
> *Get ready for bed at 10:00*

The weekend schedule revolves around a community outing each day. Otherwise, the schedule is similar to that shown above. We are so glad that you are with us, and we know that you will like it here!"

How would you react to a move to this new home? Why would you react in this way? In what ways would your freedom, privacy, control, choice, and ability to personalize your home be compromised by a move to this residential program?

Supported Living Philosophy and Approach

In the wake of the deinstitutionalization movement, the development of group homes was a major step in helping people with disabilities, especially developmental disabilities, live within the local community. However, as the focus on self-determination and choice have increased during the past decade, the concept of supported living

(O'Brien, 1993; Racino & Walker, 1993; Racino, Walker, O'Connor, & Taylor, 1993) has had a major impact on the process of helping people with disabilities find homes outside of their families' homes. The hallmark of the supported living philosophy is a separation of the concepts of housing (where, with whom, and how one lives) and support (the assistance one requires to live successfully). Instead of people being placed in residential programs that have sufficient staffing already available, individuals choose where they want to live, with whom they want to live, and how they live. This approach helps to address several serious concerns about the typical continuum of residential options for people with disabilities (Racino, Taylor, Walker, & O'Connor, 1993). These concerns have focused on lack of choice and control that people with disabilities have had in where and how they live. For example, Taylor (1988) raised these criticisms in his analysis of the typical continuum of residential options for people with disabilities:

- Where someone lives is confused with the degree of support they need. That is, people with more intense support needs are typically required to go to residential placements where such support is already available, thereby removing individuals' choices of where to live.
- People have to move as their support needs change, which disrupts relationships and connections within the community.
- People with severe disabilities rarely get to move "up the continuum" to less restrictive options.
- The opinions and choices of people with disabilities are subordinate to those of professionals.

In using the supported living approach, support is arranged or made available, only as needed, to allow individuals to follow through on their wishes. People with disabilities assert maximum control over their own home living. This approach has several advantages:

- People with disabilities have greater choice and control in their living arrangements.
- People with disabilities can develop greater stability and predictability in their living arrangements.
- People can develop connections to and relationships within their local community.
- Creativity can be used to design support systems that are responsive to individual needs and that incorporate natural supports such as families, friends, and neighbors.

The Reality of Waiting Lists

Despite the efforts of preparing individuals for living in a home in the community, the reality for most students graduating from school who will require some kind of support is that it may not happen as they exit school. For individuals with more significant disabilities who may require extensive support in adulthood, a waiting list for residential services is a real problem and the wait is usually lengthy. A discussion on waiting lists can be found in Chapter 4. In many states, waiting lists for group homes or other community placements may be years long, and those individuals who are not considered to be a priority in terms of urgency of need may have a longer wait. The issue of where their children will live is one of major concern to many families of people with mental retardation and other more significant disabilities (Cooney, 2002; Ferguson, Ferguson, & Jones, 1988; Thorin & Irvin, 1992). The best way to address this issue is for professionals to help the family to understand the urgency of this situation and to encourage them to apply for services from the state Developmental Disabilities/Mental Retardation office or other appropriate funding agency as early as possible. This should occur well in advance of the student exiting school and leaving special education services. This planning and preparation begins as early as fourteen years of age or sooner. School personnel should encourage families to decide early about their children's future housing needs, help them identify who (agency or funding source) to contact and assist them in the application process if necessary. Families that are apprehensive in discussing their children's future housing needs should at least be encouraged to apply for services and have their child placed on the waiting list until they feel more comfortable facing this important step.

RESEARCH RELATED TO COMMUNITY LIVING
FOR INDIVIDUALS WITH DISABILITIES

As indicated above, residential options for people with disabilities have ranged from more restrictive or segregated options, such as institutions, to living in one's own apartment or home with minimal or no specialized supports. For many individuals with disabilities, group home placements and more intensive community-based residences that are operated by community residential service providers have been the primary options. Taylor, Bogdan, and Racino (1991) noted that the trend in the mid-1980s into the early 1990s was toward supporting people in their own homes or with their families as opposed to placement in group homes. These authors also described several characteristics of agency-operated residential facilities that they consider to be drawbacks:

1. These facilities or group homes are typically agency-owned or -rented, and are not owned or leased by the individuals who live there.
2. These facilities are licensed or certified by funding and other state agencies, which tends to limit choices made by residents, as decisions are made primarily by people who do not live in the facility.
3. These facilities are staffed by agency personnel, who are accountable to the agency management, not necessarily to the residents to whom they provide support.

4. Staff ratios are based on groups of residents, not on individual support needs.
5. Certain facilities are designed to provide support to those with greater or lesser support or service needs; in essence, where one lives is inextricably linked to the support that one requires.
6. Core funding from agencies is typically tied to the facility and not to the individual resident. Thus, if a person chooses to move, funding for services may not follow.
7. The relationship between funding and individual service planning has often been weak.

These potential challenges associated with agency-operated, community-based residential facilities has led to the aforementioned trend toward smaller, more personalized living arrangements. Rosenau (2004) questioned the "myth" that people with chronic and complex support needs require ". . . a special kind of building to live in and to share with others with similar complex needs . . ." (p. 8). This author goes on to suggest that a minute by minute analysis of what actually happens in a more restrictive facility be conducted, and that such an analysis would reveal that anything that happens in a more restrictive facility could be replicated and/or improved upon in a home setting that is controlled by the person who lives there. Kennedy (2004) provided a personal perspective on living in agency-operated residential programs and concluded that living "outside the system" was preferable because he was better able to make choices and decisions without the control of staff and was better able to choose and hire his own support staff members.

The trend toward smaller, person-controlled homes as opposed to agency-operated facilities has raised important issues of choice, control, and quality of life. Howe, Horner, and Newton (1998) compared supported living and traditional residential services in Oregon. In their study, a matched comparison was conducted using twenty people in supported living arrangements and twenty in traditional residential services. Their results indicated that those in supported living had more variety in community activities, engaged in community activities more frequently, engaged in preferred community activities more frequently, and interacted or engaged with a greater number of people. They also found that these benefits were obtained for similar costs as traditional residential services. Stancliffe, Abery, and Smith (2000) measured personal control in seventy-four adults living in community living settings in Minnesota. Their study revealed that those individuals living semi-independently through supported living had greater personal control than those living in settings funded through Home and Community-Based Waiver (HCBW) funding, and that those in HCBW-funded programs, in turn, had greater personal control than those living in residences funded as Intermediate Care Facilities for the Mentally Retarded (ICF-MR). In essence, this study suggests that residential settings that provide more intensive programming and services also tend to restrict personal control of those who receive the services. Stancliffe (1997) analyzed the relationship between the size of residences and choice-making for people with disabilities living in Australia. In his analysis, residences of one to five residents were analyzed on dimensions of choice-making, and the results indicated that greater choice was available in smaller residences and that increased choice was possible in settings with longer periods without support staff being present. Duvdevany, Ben-Zur, and Ambar (2002) compared the levels of self-determination among adults with mild and moderate mental retardation living in either their parents' homes or in group homes in Israel. Those living in group homes scored lower on measures of self-determination. The authors suggest that current residential programs are overly structured and overprotective and that they do not place enough emphasis on providing opportunities for people to make meaningful choices. These studies reflect the continuing efforts to help people with disabilities find homes that afford them the comfort, personalization, and control that non-disabled citizens typically desire in a home. However, despite this trend, it should be reiterated that a range of residential options continues to be used and that waiting lists continue to be a chronic challenge for people with disabilities and their families. Thus, although people with disabilities want optimal home living situations, they are often in a position in which they are fortunate to obtain a less-than-optimal residential program.

Other studies have addressed the impact of the move from families' homes to residential placements on people with disabilities and their families. Baker and Blacher (2002) studied family adjustment following the placement of individuals with mental retardation. Although families reported both pros and cons of residential placement out of the home, more than 90 percent of the respondents reported that the placement was positive overall for the family and the individual. Advantages of such placement for the families were reported as being peace of mind, greater freedom, and reduced stress. Disadvantages described were the child being absent from family life and the emotional responses of the child and the family. Seltzer, Krauss, Hong, and Orsmond (2001) conducted a longitudinal study of families of adults with mental retardation. Four-hundred sixty-one families from Massachusetts and Wisconsin were interviewed over the years between 1988 and 1999, with eight interviews being conducted with each family. The results of the study suggest that the "launching stage" of residential relocation out of the family home is typically delayed for adults with mental retardation due to family preferences and to the lack of residential options. The authors also found that aging mothers continued to be highly involved with their children after placement out of the home, that mothers became increasingly satisfied and less worried over time, and that contact with their children decreased over time. They also found that siblings reported improved relationships with their siblings with disabilities and that they tended to feel less pessimistic about the future. Chambers, Hughes, and Carter (2004) conducted a study of the perspectives of eight parents and eight siblings of high school students with significant cognitive disabilities. The respondents indicated that, despite their feelings that their children's/siblings' future employment and independent living were important, their expectation was that they would work in a sheltered workshop setting and continue to live in the family home. The authors speculate that these pessimistic perspectives may indicate a lack of knowledge of options by families as well as their concern for what they perceived to be safe environments for their child/sibling.

It is likely that future research will continue to emphasize the degree to which different options for community living afford the highest degrees of personal choice and autonomy for people with disabilities who leave their families' homes. It is equally likely that students in transition to adult life will continue to face challenges associated with limited residential options and the restrictions associated with current funding and regulatory policies.

ACQUIRING SKILLS FOR COMMUNITY LIVING

Table 8.2, shown earlier in this chapter, lists key skill areas that are important for living on one's own in the community. As indicated previously, many of these skills are learned at home longitudinally, under the guidance of parents and other family members. Many of these skills, however, can also be learned in school, either through participation in courses that can specifically address the skills needed or in naturally occurring situations such as in community-based learning. Table 8.5 lists courses or classes that are available in many high schools in which home living skills might be addressed. This list highlights two very important issues; first, that students in special education get access to the full range of the curriculum available in schools, and second, that students have the opportunity for inclusion. Table 8.6 lists naturally occurring opportunities at the high school level in which home living skills might be practiced or learned.

Schools have a responsibility to teach students what they need to know in order to survive in the community. This is an appropriate component of the IEP and, for some students, it is one of the most important skill areas that they need to learn. In

TABLE 8.5 High School Level Courses/Classes That May Focus on Home Living Skills

SKILL AREA	COURSES/CLASSES THAT ADDRESS THE SKILL AREA
1. Planning and preparing meals	Family and Consumer Science
2. Self-care, bathing, and hygiene	Health
3. Cleaning and care of the home	Family and Consumer Science Parenting Skills Classes
4. Cleaning and care of clothing	Family and Consumer Science Parenting Skills Classes
5. Home finances and services	Consumer Math
6. Telephone/email use	Technology/Computers
7. Leisure activities	Technology/Computers
8. Safety procedures	Health
9. Time management and scheduling	Required for success in all classes
10. Negotiating with others, self-advocacy	Required for success in all aspects of high school

TABLE 8.6 Naturally Occurring Opportunities to Practice Home Living Skills at the High School Level

SKILL AREA	NATURALLY OCCURRING OPPORTUNITIES
1. Planning and preparing meals	Lunch
2. Self-care, bathing, and hygiene	Gym, extracurricular sports
3. Cleaning and care of the home	Maintaining locker
	Cleanup in shop and other classrooms
4. Cleaning and care of clothing	Gym, extracurricular sports
5. Home finances and services	Math classes; cafeteria
6. Telephone/email use	Technology/Computers
7. Leisure activities	Lunch
8. Safety procedures	Fire and other drills
9. Time management and scheduling	Throughout the day to meet classes
10. Negotiating with others, self-advocacy	Throughout the day

essence, schools prepare all students to function in the community, including those with and without disabilities. For students with more significant disabilities this need becomes more of a priority. Therefore, how schools teach the necessary skills is critical to students' future success in the community. Teaching of such skills may occur in a simulated setting in the school itself or it may occur in a more natural environment. Because students with disabilities have difficulty transferring or generalizing learned skills to new environments they were not previously introduced to, it is better to teach skills in as many natural environments as possible (Horner, Sprague, & Wilcox, 1982; Steere, 1997; Stokes & Baer, 1977). This becomes difficult to accomplish when teaching students home living and daily living skills. Some school programs rent actual apartments to be used for instruction of home living skills. Not only is this an excellent way to teach these critical skills, but it initially aids teachers in assessing students' ability levels so that they can receive the most effective instruction. This is one very effective way to address this critical and important challenge in a more natural setting.

In addition to what schools can do to assist students in learning needed community living skills, it cannot be overemphasized how important the family is for the successful acquisition of home living skills. Many of these skills are learned cumulatively and increase in complexity (for example, home financial skills), and the family is typically in the best position to teach some of these skills. The family also has the advantage of being able to teach home living skills through repeated modeling of the use of the skills within a natural environment, that is, the home.

Steere and Burcroff (2004) pointed out that many home living skills must be performed in varied or multiple ways in order to be functional. For example, paying bills is an important skill, but the ability to do so is only functional when one can interpret and pay any bill that comes into the home and also distinguish between bills and junk mail. Likewise, reading recipes is a skill that is typically done in multiple ways. Table 8.7 shows skills that are typically performed in multiple ways.

TRANSITION PLANNING FOR COMMUNITY LIVING

Home living is one of the major categories of postschool outcomes that are contained in transition IEPs. It is therefore essential that transition planning teams support students and their families in looking to the future to decide where students will live after leaving home. For some students who intend to pursue postsecondary education, the plan may focus on living in a dorm room during the first year or two of college. For other students, moving out of the home may not be as high a priority as obtaining paid employment, and they may want to live at home for the foreseeable future. For students with more severe disabilities, planning needs to begin years before exiting special education to apply for services that may have extensive waiting lists.

Regardless of the situation, it is important that this aspect of transition planning not be neglected and that this section of the IEP (home living or residential outcome statement) be completed during the IEP development process, even if the student will

TABLE 8.7   Home Living Skills That Are Performed in Multiple Ways

SKILL AREA	ACTIVITIES PERFORMED IN MULTIPLE WAYS
1. Planning and preparing meals	Reading recipes
	Using stoves/ovens
2. Self-care, bathing, and hygiene	Using faucets and other bathroom appliances
	Shaving
3. Cleaning and care of the home	Use of vacuum cleaners
	Use of cleaning products in different containers
4. Cleaning and care of clothing	Use of washing machines, dryers
5. Home finances and services	Reading bills
6. Telephone/email use	Using different types of telephones
7. Leisure activities	Using different TV remotes
8. Safety procedures	Responding to different smoke and carbon monoxide alarms
9. Time management and scheduling	Using different types of calendars
10. Negotiating with others, self-advocacy	Negotiating with roommates versus neighbors

not be leaving the family home for several years. As with all areas of transition planning, advanced planning and preparation are the best strategies. Also, there are many steps that students and their families, as well as professionals who support them, can take to increase the effectiveness of transition planning in this area. These are shown in Table 8.8.

COMMUNITY INVOLVEMENT AND PARTICIPATION

A home, whether it is a house, apartment, supported apartment, or group home, exists within the context of a broader community. Ultimately, an important aspect of having a satisfying and secure place to live is to feel comfortable within one's home and within the community in which the home is located. A sense of community membership is also increased and enhanced when connections to different people and places in the community are strengthened (Mount & Zwernik, 1988). Therefore, it is important for students in transition to make a successful move to a new home community outside of their families' communities.

When people relocate to new homes, they typically have to reestablish important connections within this new home community. These connections involve important goods and services that are needed for success. For example, Table 8.9 lists important community connections that are usually established upon moving to a new home in a new community. These connections are established at two levels. First, initial establishment is made, for example, starting a bank account, visiting a doctor for the first time, or locating a local movie theater. The second level is established when individuals use these community resources with such regularity that they are recognized to some degree as local community members. There are several (sometimes

TABLE 8.8   Steps to Increase Effectiveness of Transition Planning for Home Living

Steps for Students and Families to Take

- Visit and tour dorm rooms at colleges
- Visit and tour area group homes or supported living programs
- Ensure that students are steadily increasing their responsibilities for completion of chores and other home living skills
- Start a checking or savings account for the student and teach home finance skills

Steps for Professionals to Take

- Provide students and families with information about residential service providers and programs
- Provide students and families with information about how to apply for services and how to get on waiting lists
- Help students learn important skills while in school through targeted classes or through naturally occurring opportunities

TABLE 8.9 Community Connections to Be Established When Moving to a New Community

Health Care Services

- Physician (general practitioner or specialists, if needed)
- Dentist

Financial Services

- Bank for checking and/or savings accounts
- Local ATM machines for cash withdrawals

Postal Services

- Local post office
- Local mail carrier

Self-Care Services

- Hair stylists
- Heath or exercise club

Food and Other Services

- Grocery stores/supermarkets
- Hardware store
- Convenience stores
- Department stores

Entertainment Services

- Library
- Video store
- Restaurants
- Movie theaters

Religious Services

- Church
- Synagogue
- Mosque
- Temple

subtle) indicators of when an individual becomes a "regular" and is therefore recognized within local community environments:

- People in the community recognize the person's face and say "Hi."
- People in the community remember the person's name.
- People in the community ask "How have you been?"
- People in the community anticipate a person's request.
- People in the community wave to the person from a distance.

O'Brien (1987) described the importance of community presence and participation. It is helpful to distinguish between these two concepts. Community presence means sharing community locations with others who do not have disabilities, while community participation implies reciprocal interaction with other members of the community. In helping young people make a transition to adult life, it is important to continue to assess to what degree they are both present and participating in their new home communities.

Although it is beyond the scope of this chapter, it should be noted that there are many possibilities for students to live in a home with people of their choosing. Sometimes, if they or their families can afford to do so, individuals with disabilities can own their own homes and have people with or without disabilities sharing the expenses. There are also many government subsidized options for individuals with disabilities to rent or purchase a home through the Federal Housing and Urban Development (HUD) program. For more information on these options go to the HUD website where these and other options are described (www.HUD.gov). These and other issues related to housing and community living are things that schools and teachers seldom attend to and perhaps it may even be beyond the realm of their role and responsibility, but knowing that there are many options, teachers can help ask the right questions and perhaps advocate for the student with community agencies and Case Managers who do have the expertise in this area.

SUE ANNE AND MIKE

Sue Anne

When Sue Anne started college, one of the biggest challenges she faced was getting used to living on her own. At first, she was bewildered by the entire process: getting a campus identification card, locating the cafeteria and figuring out how to charge meals to her meal plan, finding where to do laundry in the dorm, and so on. She was also somewhat lonely for her family, which made the first weeks of her freshman year more difficult. Over time, however, these activities became second nature. It was also new for Sue Anne to have to live in a dorm with a total stranger. Fortunately, she got along fairly well with her assigned roommate, although they would not be close friends. Sue Anne did find someone else in her dorm, however, with whom she did strike up a friendship during her freshman year.

During her sophomore and subsequent years of college, Sue Anne opted to live in an apartment off campus with her friend. This involved learning additional skills, including paying the rent on time, paying for heat and electricity, and making sure that the apartment was secure at night or when they were away at class. She and her friend still got along, but they had to negotiate some sharing of duties and responsibilities for keeping the apartment clean and for shopping. They now had to go out into the community to do their laundry, so this took more time and effort. They both had cars, and this meant paying for gas and insurance. Sue Anne had to work at a local restaurant in order to pay for all of this, which took even more of her time. Between school, work, and keeping up with these other responsibilities, she found that there was little time for relaxing.

Mike

Mike's circle of support had been meeting regularly throughout the past several years, which has been an enormous support for Mike's family. He is now twenty years old and is beginning his last year in special education. A major part of his curriculum involves working in a community-based employment training site, with support from a job coach who works for the school. The vocational rehabilitation counselor attended one IEP meeting at the end of last year, and it was agreed that Mike is an excellent candidate to receive supported employment services from a local service provider agency upon graduation. So the work aspect of his life seems to be coming together, although there is still a long way to go.

In terms of community living, Mike's family cannot agree if he is ready to move out of their home. Mike's father is concerned that he will be hurt or that others will simply not understand him and what makes him happy. This has been a point of contention within the family, as Mike's mother thinks it would be good for him to move out while his father is still very reluctant. Fortunately, Mike's parents trust Ellen, the school's transition coordinator, and she has convinced the family to at least apply for services from the Developmental Disabilities office so that, should the time come that they are ready for him to move out, the wait will be lessened. In the meantime, they continue to increase Mike's responsibility for completing chores within the home. He now sets the table, helps stack dirty dishes in the dishwasher, picks up his room, and helps his mother with washing and drying clothes. He continues to make progress with these tasks, although he still requires prompting.

As Mike's father watches him doing the dishes one evening, he thinks to himself that his son is indeed growing up and will someday have to move out on his own. On the one hand, this is a frightening thought for Mike's dad, but, on the other hand, he does not want to deny Mike the option of experiencing life, including adulthood, as fully as possible.

CHAPTER SUMMARY

This chapter has focused on the move from one's family home to community living. This is a pivotal event and one of the most defining moments during the transition process. It may take several moves after leaving the family home before students with disabilities find their first real home. All young people, both those with and without disabilities, need to learn many skills in order to learn to live more independently. Young people with more severe disabilities will require longitudinal support in order to live in the community as independently as possible. This support should be provided in accordance with the tenets of supported living in order to provide these individuals with as much choice and control over their own living conditions. Because one lives in a community and not just a home, it is important for young people with disabilities to take the steps to become more connected to (that is, present and participating in) their local communities. Finally, the essential role of the family in helping young people be prepared for adult community living cannot be overemphasized.

APPLICATION ACTIVITIES

The application activities listed below are essential for your continued learning and skill development in transition planning. Each of the activities will require your time and energy, but will help you develop your professional skills in this area.

For Practice and Enhanced Understanding:

Using a typical week as a guide, list all of the community locations that you visit during the week. Note how often you go to each location, and why you go there. In which of these locations are you recognized or considered to be a "regular"?

Think back to when you first left home, and then make a list of as many apartments or houses you have lived in since that time. How many of these really felt like your "home"? Why did you move from one place to another?

For Your Portfolio:

If you are currently working with students of transition age, research your local community and develop a directory of service provider and funding agencies that assist people with disabilities to live and participate in the local community. Find out about the types of community residences that these agencies help to operate. How are these programs staffed? What is the process for applying for services?

Research local colleges or universities to find out what residential services they provide for students, particularly during freshman year. If you know people who are in college, ask them about what living in the dorms is like and what the advantages and disadvantages of living on campus are. Consider this question: why do many colleges require students who do not commute from home to live on campus during their freshman year?

RESOURCES AND WEBSITES

The following resources and websites will allow you to extend your knowledge about how to assist people with disabilities move into their own homes in the community. Consider including these resources in your professional portfolio.

Beach Center on Disabilities

Information for families of people with disabilities. Includes national listing of Parent to Parent and other organizations in all states in the United States.
www.beachcenter.org

Federal Housing and Urban Development

www.HUD.GOV

AAMR

Information and advocacy regarding individuals with intellectual disabilities. Includes links to local chapters.
www.aamr.org

ARC of the United States

Information and advocacy regarding people with intellectual and developmental disabilities. Includes links to local chapters.
www.thearc.org

TASH

Information and advocacy for people with disabilities, particularly severe and multiple disabilities. Includes links to local chapters.
www.tash.org

New Freedom Initiative's Online Resource

Federal interagency website to give access to information and resources for people with disabilities.
www.disabilityinfo.gov

World Institute in Disability

www.lid.org

Syracuse University Center on Human Policy

Look for monographs and information about supported living.
www.thechp.syr.edu

Institute on Community Integration (University of Minnesota)

Information on ways to improve the community services and social supports available to individuals with developmental and other disabilities, as well as their families.
www.ici.edu

Institute on Community Inclusion

Supports the rights of children and adults with disabilities to participate in all aspects of the community. Conducts research and education about effective strategies for promoting the inclusion of people with disabilities.
www.communityinclusion.org

Center for Housing and New Community Economics (CHANCE)

Mission is to improve and increase access to integrated, affordable, and accessible housing that is coordinated with, but separate from, personal assistance and supportive services.
www.alliance.unh.edu

Independent Living Institute

Promotes self-determination through independent living.
www.independentliving.org

Independent Living USA

This site lists all Centers for Independent Living across the United States.
www.ilusa.com

REFERENCES

Baker, B., & Blacher, J. (2002). For better or worse? Impact of residential placement on families. *Mental Retardation, 40*, 1–13.

Blacher, J. (2001). Transition to adulthood: Mental retardation, families, and culture. *American Journal on Mental Retardation, 106*, 173–188.

Chambers, C., Hughes, C., & Carter, E. (2004). Parent and sibling perspectives on transition to adulthood. *Education and Training in Developmental Disabilities, 39*, 79–94.

Clark, G., Field, S., Patton, J., Brolin, D., & Sitlington, P. (1994). Life skills instruction: A necessary component for all students with disabilities: A position statement of the Division on Career Development and Transition. *Career Development for Exceptional Individuals, 17*, 125–134.

Cooney, B. (2002). Exploring perspectives on transition of youth with disabilities: Voices of young adults, parents, and professionals. *Mental Retardation, 40*, 425–435.

Duvdevany, I., Ben-Zur, H., & Ambar, A. (2002). Self-determination and mental retardation: Is there an association with living arrangement and lifestyle satisfaction? *Mental Retardation, 40*, 379–389.

Ferguson, P., Ferguson, D., & Jones, D. (1988). Generations of hope: Parental perspectives on the transitions of their children with severe retardation from school to adult life. *Journal of the Association for Persons with Severe Handicaps, 13*, 177–187.

Horner, R. H., Sprague, J., & Wilcox, B. (1982). General-case programming for community activities. In B. Wilcox & G. T. Bellamy (Eds.), *Design of high school programs for severely handicapped persons* (pp. 61–98). Baltimore: Paul Brookes.

Howe, J., Horner, R., & Newton, S. (1998). Comparison of supported living and traditional residential services in the state of Oregon. *Mental Retardation, 36*, 1–11.

Kennedy, M. (2004). Living outside the system: The ups and downs of getting on with our lives. *Mental Retardation, 42*, 229–231.

Knoll, J., & Wheeler, C. (2001). My home: Developing skills and supports for adult living. In R. Flexer, T. Simmons, P. Luft, & R. Baer (Eds.), *Transition planning for secondary students with disabilities* (pp. 499–539). Upper Saddle River, NJ: Merrill.

Mount, B., & Zwernik, K. (1988). *It's never too early, it's never too late: A booklet about personal futures planning*. Mears Park Centre, MN: Metropolitan Council.

O'Brien, J. (1987). A guide to lifestyle planning: Using the Activities Catalog to integrate services and natural support systems. In B. Wilcox and G. T. Bellamy (Eds.), *The Activities Catalog: An alternative curriculum design for youth and adults with severe disabilities* (pp. 175–189). Baltimore: Paul Brookes.

O'Brien, J. (1993). *Supported living: What's the Difference?* Decatur, Georgia: Responsive Systems Associates, Inc.

O'Brien, J. (1994). Down stairs that are never your own: Supporting people with developmental disabilities in their own homes. *Mental Retardation, 32*, 1–6.

Racino, J., Taylor, S., Walker, P., & O'Connor, S. (1993). Introduction. In J. Racino, P. Walker, S. O'Connor, & S. Taylor (Eds.), *Housing, support, and community: Choices and strategies for adults with disabilities* (pp. 1–30). Baltimore: Paul Brookes.

Racino, J., & Walker, P. (1993). "Whose life is it anyway?": Life planning, choices, and decision making. In J. Racino, P. Walker, S. O'Connor, & S. Taylor (Eds.), *Housing, support, and community: Choices and strategies for adults with disabilities* (pp. 57–80). Baltimore: Paul Brookes.

Racino, J., Walker, P., O'Connor, S., & Taylor, S. (1993). *Housing, support, and community: Choices and strategies for adults with disabilities*. Baltimore: Paul Brookes.

Rosenau, N. (2004). "But aren't there some people . . . ?": Dispelling the myth. *TASH Connections, 30,* 8–10.

Seltzer, M., Krauss, M., Hong, J., & Orsmond, G. (2001). Continuity or discontinuity or family involvement following residential transitions of adults who have mental retardation. *Mental Retardation, 39,* 181–194.

Stancliffe, R. (1997). Community living-unit size, staff presence, and residents' choice-making. *Mental Retardation, 35,* 1–9.

Stancliffe, R., Abery, B., & Smith, J. (2000). Personal control and the ecology of community living settings: Beyond living-unit size and type. *American Journal on Mental Retardation, 105,* 431–454.

Steere, D. (1997). *Increasing variety in adult life: A general-case approach (Innovations, issue # 10).* Washington, DC: American Association on Mental Retardation.

Steere, D., & Burcroff, T. (2004). Living at home: Skills for independence. In P. Wehman & J. Kregel (Eds.), *Functional curriculum for elementary, middle, & secondary age students with special needs* (2nd ed.) (pp. 293–316). Austin, TX: Pro-Ed.

Stokes, T., & Baer, D. (1977). An implicit technology of generalization. *Journal of Applied Behavior Analysis, 10,* 349–367.

Szymanski, E. (1994). Transition: Life span and life space considerations for empowerment. *Exceptional Children, 60,* 402–410.

Szymanski, E. (1995). *Transition from school to adulthood.* Presentation at the Statewide Conference on Transition from School to Work, Montana State University-Billings.

Taylor, S. (1988). Caught in the continuum: A critical analysis of the principle of least restrictive environment. *Journal of the Association for Persons with Severe Handicaps, 13,* 41–53.

Taylor, S., Bogdan, R., & Racino, J. (1991). *Life in the community: Case studies of organizations supporting people with disabilities.* Baltimore: Paul Brookes.

Thorin, G., & Irvin, L. (1992). Family stress associated with the transition to adulthood of young people with severe disabilities. *Journal of the Association for Persons with Severe Handicaps, 17,* 31–39.

CHAPTER 9

MODELS FOR INTEGRATED COMMUNITY EMPLOYMENT

CHAPTER OBJECTIVES

Upon completion of this chapter, you will be able to

1. describe the supported employment process and the various models of supported employment.

2. describe how supported employment works as an effective program for individuals from mild to severe disabilities.

3. use assessment strategies to help students and their families identify program options that best meet the students' interests and level of need toward the most effective vocational outcome.

4. have a greater understanding of the various adult vocational models currently used by community vocational service programs to assist individuals with disabilities in obtaining paid employment in the community. You will also have a greater understanding of strategies for assisting students with disabilities in the selection of the most appropriate options to meet their needs.

KEY TOPICS TO LOOK FOR IN THIS CHAPTER . . .

- Self-Determination: As you read this chapter, notice how consumer choice is a key ingredient to successful employment in the community. As with other aspects of adult life, the more that students can take charge of their own career development process, the more successful they will be.

- Community Inclusion: This chapter is about helping people with disabilities find jobs within integrated community environments. Thus, a key element of supported employment is social inclusion through work.

- Career Advancement: Most people don't just want a job, they want a satisfying career. In this chapter, look for the difference between vertical career development and horizontal career development.

- Models of Supported Employment: In order to best meet the needs of people with diverse and severe disabilities, different approaches or models of supported employment have been developed. What are the differences between these models, and what are the relative advantages and disadvantages of each?

MIKE WANTS TO WORK

Mike is nearing graduation. He is in his last year of school, and his mother would like to see him be gainfully employed, but she is not sure how this could be done or even if it is possible, given his physical and cognitive challenges. As described in Chapter 6, Mike's team had already arranged for him to be exposed to work experiences in a custodial capacity in dishwashing and kitchen work. In the past, some members of the team assumed that, because of the severity of his disability, Mike would have to go to an adult training facility, which is generally a non-vocational day program. However, the team is now unified in its commitment to help Mike find paid community employment, and they feel that segregating him as an adult in a training program would be a major step back in his continued growth toward a fulfilling adult life. The team has contacted an adult service provider agency that has a reputation for working with individuals with severe disabilities by providing supported employment services. The agency program manager, Mr. Peters, has agreed to attend and participate in Mike's IEP meeting at the high school.

The school had prepared Mike for vocational options by providing him with the work exposure opportunities described above. It seems that Mike does best while working with a small group of students since they can share the responsibilities of the work. In addition, Mike seems to enjoy these work experiences. His mother is also pleased with these experiences and feels that they will prepare him well for similar types of work after he graduates. The adult services program manager, Mr. Peters, agrees that these experiences seem to be appropriate and that there are opportunities for Mike to work in similar types of job programs as an adult once he graduates. Mr. Peters suggests a vocational assessment to clarify Mike's abilities and to determine how he might be matched up with one of their program options. The vocational assessment is discussed as something the service provider could do as part of the preliminary steps to supported employment. Since a Vocational Rehabilitation (VR) representative is present, Mr. Peters asks if that state agency would be willing to pay for the vocational assessment that was discussed. As this is the last year of Mike's transition from school to adult life, the vocational rehabilitation representative agrees to this plan and to pay for the service.

The focus of the discussion returns back to the school and how the school program will help Mike achieve his employment outcome. The school personnel clearly need to collaborate with these adult service agencies and continue to work on preparing Mike for integrated work. With such collaboration, paid employment in the community is a viable and attainable option.

Mike's situation reflects the experiences of many school districts and the vision of many parents for their children. Many parents today are requesting this outcome for their children who have moderate to severe disabilities. How schools react to this decision is often the source of either a family's struggle or satisfaction with their district.

Although transition from school to adult life focuses on several life domains, employment may arguably be one of the most important. Work for many people in society provides a sense of identity and self esteem (Balser, Harvey, & Hornby, 1991). For some it is a source of satisfaction and for most of us it is a source of income and support for family and ourselves. Being employed gives people independence and purchasing power, which makes them contributing members of society with a greater potential of being seen as valued citizens. These same factors should also be a consideration for individuals with disabilities, and it is paramount to focus on paid, integrated employment as an outcome for transition planning. This chapter will discuss and describe options for community-based employment in integrated settings. It should be noted that the previous chapters on interacting with adult service agencies (Chapter 5) and interacting with business (Chapter 6) provide information that is relevant to this chapter.

RESEARCH ON THE DEVELOPMENT OF INTEGRATED EMPLOYMENT OPPORTUNITIES

As introduced in Chapter 1, a key role of the educational system is to prepare *all* children for success in society, that is, to become productive citizens who can contribute to the American workforce. However, this has been an elusive outcome for so many individuals with disabilities. High unemployment rates for people with disabilities have been and continue to be a major concern (Hanley-Maxwell, Pogoloff, & Whitney-Thomas, 1998; Harris Interactive, 2002). In addition, there are general concerns that poor employment and academic outcomes exist for students with specific disabling conditions, including mental retardation (Katsiyannis, Zhang, Woodruff, & Dixon, 2005), emotional and behavioral disorders (Carter & Wehby, 2003), and learning disabilities (Dickinson & Verbeek, 2002).

In general, the response for most educational programs has been to prepare students to enter an adult service system that is based on the continuum of services. As we discussed in Chapter 5, and will discuss in this chapter, adult day programs are becoming difficult for individuals with disabilities to enter but, more important, they are seen as inappropriate when it is expected that most people with disabilities can and should learn to work productively in community settings (Wehman, 1992, 1999). The continuum model of adult vocational services, in which people with disabilities must "earn" their way through a series of steps toward integrated employment, has been seriously questioned (Buckley & Bellamy, 1985; Murphy & Rogan, 1995; Taylor, 1988; Wehman, Brooke, & Inge, 2001). In particular, this criticism has focused on the poor track record of sheltered workshops and adult day programs in helping people with disabilities find and maintain community employment (Michaels, 1999). In addition, the level of productivity in facility-based programs has been questioned. For example, Reid, Parsons, and Green (2001) observed 100 congregate community and institutional program sites in six states. They noted that only about half of the consumers' time was spent in purposeful activity, 75 percent of which was age appropriate activity. In 20 percent of the sites, most of the activity was age inappropriate. One of the recommendations offered by the authors in light of these findings was to increase consumers' opportunities to participate in supported employment. Pendergast and Storey (1999) compared Individualized Program Plans (IPPs, or formal planning documents) of people in integrated versus segregated employment settings, using a set of best practice indicators for comparison. These best practices included the use of age-appropriate materials, a focus on functional and critical skills, and a focus on teaching across settings and materials and in natural settings. Significant differences were found in the quality of program plans for people in integrated versus segregated employment settings, with those from integrated employment showing closer adherence to the best practice indicators.

Because of these criticisms of the continuum of adult vocational options, supported employment has expanded from a modest beginning during the early 1980s (Wehman, 1981) to a major program that serves people with diverse disabilities (Wehman, West, & Kregel, 1999). A major benefit of the supported employment approach is the attainment of an improved quality of life for adults with disabilities as a result of increased income and social inclusion. For example, Kraemer, McIntyre, and Blacher (2003) examined the quality of life of 188 young adults with moderate and severe mental retardation. Students who had exited high school and had obtained community-based employment had a higher overall quality of life than those who were in sheltered workshops. Since its introduction, the effectiveness of supported employment has been demonstrated repeatedly (Conley, 2003; Wehman, Revell, & Kregel, 1998; Wehman et al., 2001).

More recently, the concept of natural supports has been incorporated into practices for implementing supported employment (Mank, 1996; Murphy & Rogan, 1995). Storey and Garff (1999) conducted a study on the effect of co-worker instruction on the transition of youth to competitive employment. Interventions for co-workers without disabilities included teaching them instructional skills and then having them demonstrate these skills by teaching students with disabilities a new task. In general, all students who participated in this study increased the frequency of interaction and all showed an overall increase in social inclusion as measured by the Vocational Integration Index. This is one example of a natural support concept being applied with good results. In a related study, Mank, Cioffi, and Yovanoff (2000) looked at the effect the presence a job coach had on the "typicalness" of the employment site for an individual with disability. In general, increases in direct support (job coach presence) reduced the "typicalness" or "naturalness" of employment, while the use of natural supports tended to increase integration. The study was based on results of a survey of thirteen agencies in eight states. Although this finding suggests that employment specialists can impede the social inclusion of workers with disabilities, the authors also found that, even with a higher level of direct employment specialist intervention, wages and integration outcomes can be increased *if* there is co-worker training. Studies such as these suggest that the success of supported employment can be enhanced if intervention efforts focus not only on skill acquisition by workers with disabilities but also on increasing co-worker and supervisor skills and responsibilities in working with them. The role of the employment specialist in working with co-workers and supervisors is therefore a critical ingredient for success (Hagner & Cooney, 2005).

Overall, supported employment, with the addition of the natural supports concept, has shown great promise and effectiveness in promoting integration in employment for persons with disabilities. Yet an important factor in any job placement is the completion of a comprehensive profile of a student so as to properly match the student's interest with that of the job. In Chapters 2 and 4 we discussed the importance of person centered planning in learning about students' interests and aspirations. Menchetti and Garcia (2003) investigated the impact that person centered career planning had on career choice and employment outcomes of eighty-three supported employees. Choice was measured by the degree of match between stated career preferences and actual employment. In all, seventy-two (83 percent) of the people had a high to moderate level of preference match. This finding supports the implication that person centered planning can provide an effective strategy for supported employees to express their choice and participate in decision making. In a related study, Brady and Rosenberg (2002) focused on "goodness of fit" in the job selection process, based on the characteristics of the worker (i.e., aptitude, behavior, interests, skills, etc.) and the requirements of the job and the employment setting. Five types or categories of modifications and supports were identified that increased the quality of the match and what the authors called "goodness of fit." These categories were: (1) change the task and/or adaptive materials to allow better performance of the task; (2) restructure the complexity of the job into a single-task job; (3) use direct instruction; (4) use self-management strategies; and (5) add natural support strategies. These ideas demonstrate the possibilities that can be considered in developing a good job match. This also shows the skill that an instructor or employment specialist must have in order to create an optimal job match.

Despite the successes of supported employment in helping people with significant disabilities enter the competitive workforce, the use of segregated adult service programs is an ongoing concern, while, at the same time, the growth of the supported employment approach has "stalled." Butterworth, Metzel, Boeltzig, Gilmore, and Sulewski (2005) reported that 74 percent of people with developmental disabilities received services in sheltered workshops, day habilitation programs, and non-work community integration programs, as opposed to community-based integrated employment programs. These authors concluded that there is ample room for improvement and growth of integrated employment. Rusch and Braddock (2004) reported that the rate of growth of segregated services continues to exceed the growth of supported employment, and that the percentage of adults with developmental disabilities participating in supported employment has leveled or slowed. They also reported that funds expended on segregated services were approximately four times the amount spent on supported employment services. In response to these sobering findings, these authors recommend that *all* students should leave high school into competitive community employment or postsecondary education, and that no students should exit high school into segregated services.

Studies such as these make it clear that schools and adult services together will need to focus additional energy on the goal of all students having the opportunity to leave school and enter the competitive workforce. Too often, educators and adult service professionals, and even families, have made the assumption that students with more severe disabilities will need to transition into facility-based day programs, and this assumption has severely limited the options for these students to work in the community. Instead, as suggested by Rusch and Braddock (2004), the assumption should be that all students can and should work in integrated, paid community jobs. However, the attainment of such employment is a significant challenge, and to meet that challenge, several programmatic elements need to be in place: (1) family and student involvement and participation (Roessler, Shearin, & Williams, 2000); (2) a career plan that is based on individual needs (Rojewski, 2002); (3) a school-based interagency and collaborative transition team (McMahan & Baer, 2001); and (4) a school-based program that ensures that the postschool outcomes are realized. When schools are committed to providing paid work experiences while students are in school, there is a greater chance that they will be employed once they leave school (Rabren, Dunn, & Chambers, 2002). Families of people with disabilities and professionals alike should continue to advocate strongly for the continued growth of adult service strategies, such as supported employment, that result in integration of people into the competitive workforce.

THE ROLE OF EDUCATION IN PREPARING FOR EMPLOYMENT

Schools have several purposes for education, but perhaps one of the major goals of education is to prepare all students for a career and employment. Whether students go on to college or technical schools, their education is preparing them for a job and potential career in their chosen field. For those students who do not go on to college, work may be a reality earlier in life. The schools' preparation may come from courses students take or from the training received from district vocational technical centers. Such preparation is viewed not as an end but as a beginning for many students, leading toward a possible career.

Transition from school to work for students with disabilities is an attempt to create the same possible outcomes as for students without disabilities. Many students with disabilities and their families might desire employment as a postschool option if they were encouraged and if they felt that their children were receiving adequate preparation for employment. As described in Chapter 1, too many people with disabilities are not working (Harris Interactive, 2002). Those individuals who are working are often in low paying jobs with few opportunities for advancement (Curl, Hall, Chisholm, & Rule, 1992; Harris Interactive, 2002; Hood, Test, Spooner, & Steele, 1996; Shafer, Revell, & Isbister, 1991). To avoid many of these pitfalls for students with disabilities, schools must make a commitment to supporting the notion of employment for *all* students, including those who are in special education programs. Schools should design programs that support the employment preparation, based on a student's interests and preferences, and that foster collaboration with community organizations to ensure a seamless transition from school to adult life. Consequently, vocational planning needs to be a central theme for the IEP/transition plan. As we plan for vocational opportunities, one model that has proven to be effective is the *supported employment* model. We begin this chapter by focusing on this vocational option and introduce several variations of this model that can potentially lead to employment for individuals with disabilities. As we discuss each aspect of this model, we will also describe best practices in the field for finding, getting, and keeping employment for individuals with disabilities.

SUPPORTED EMPLOYMENT

Although supported employment was introduced in Chapter 5, this chapter will provide a more detailed discussion. As previously mentioned, employment for people with disabilities, particularly for those with severe disabilities, has been an elusive outcome (Harris Interactive, 2002). Our society has an expectation for people to be productive, to work and make their own way. Without the opportunity to work people will always be economically dependent on family or governmental subsistence (Bishop & Falvey, 1989). It should be clear that we believe that work should be considered for all individuals, regardless of the severity of the disability, not just for students who are seemingly "able" or "employable." It is up to educators, service providers, and businesses to be creative and broaden their view of competence of individuals with disabilities and help create opportunities.

Early pioneers in the field of disability (Bellamy, Horner, & Inman, 1979; Gold, 1972) demonstrated that individuals with severe disabilities could perform complex vocational tasks with appropriate instruction. Other leaders in the field expressed and demonstrated the value and benefits of individuals with severe disabilities to be in integrated settings (Brown et al., 1984; Strain, 1983). The combination of these two factors contributed to the introduction of and growth of supported employment (Wehman, 1981). Although the intent of this chapter is not to focus solely on students with severe disabilities, this research and the demonstrations that individuals with severe disabilities can work is included to ensure that these students are not excluded from the *opportunity* to work. In fact, supported employment was designed specifically for individuals with severe disabilities, but it has also proven effective for individuals with a wide range of disabilities that require assistance in searching for, obtaining, and retaining employment (Wehman, 1981).

Sidebar 9.1 shows a profile of Dr. Paul Wehman who, perhaps more than anyone else within the field of rehabilitation, has demonstrated that people with severe disabilities can work through supported employment.

Consider This!   People with severe disabilities have often been relegated to segregated rehabilitation programs in which they received training to "get them ready" for employment. Unfortunately, many of these people are never deemed to be ready enough and, consequently, they are never allowed to experience real work in the community.

Now, consider your own work history and your readiness to fulfill your job responsibilities. Focus particularly on when you first started on certain jobs. How ready were you really to fulfill all of your professional responsibilities? How many skills did you have to learn *on the job*, not before starting the job? The point we want to make is that *all people* learn a substantial amount on the job, and virtually no one is entirely or fully ready on the day that they begin work. Why, then, should we expect people with severe disabilities to be job-ready prior to starting work?

Defining the Elements of Supported Employment

Supported employment assists people with disabilities in the challenge of competing for a job in the community. The model is characterized by four key functions: job development/placement, on-the-job instruction, ongoing assessment, and follow-along. These four functions will be described later in this section. An *employment*

■ ■ ■ ■ ■

SIDEBAR 9.1
SPOTLIGHT ON HISTORY: DR. PAUL WEHMAN

Dr. Wehman is Professor of Physical Medicine and Rehabilitation at Virginia Common-wealth University, with joint appointments in the Department of Curriculum and Instruction and Department of Rehabilitation Counseling. Dr. Wehman is also Director of the Rehabilitation Research and Training Center on Workplace Supports and Chairman of the Division of Rehabilitation Research. Dr. Wehman has been a pioneer in the development of supported employment since the early 1980s, and his work has contributed directly to the employment of thousands of individuals with diverse disabilities. Since that time, he has been a tireless champion of the goal of paid, integrated employment for people with disabilities. Dr. Wehman and his colleagues were also among the first to describe the need for effective transition planning for students who are leaving the special education system and entering the workforce. He has written over 150 articles, 24 book chapters, and authored or edited 33 books on topics that include supported employment and transition from school to adulthood. He is a recipient of the Joseph P. Kennedy, Jr. Foundation International Awards in Mental Retardation, was a Mary Switzer Fellow for the National Rehabilitation Association in 1985, and received the Distinguished Service Award from the President's Committee on Employment for Persons with Disabilities in October 1992. Dr. Wehman is currently Editor-in-Chief of the *Journal of Vocational Rehabilitation*, and he has been the Principal Investigator of over 24 million dollars worth of federal grants since his employment at VCU.

Source: Information taken from website of the Department of Physical Medicine and Rehabilitation of VCU, www.pmr.vcu.edu.

training specialist or a *job coach* is usually the title given to a person who performs these functions. A title more recently adopted and used to describe this position is *employment consultant*, which reflects the natural supports concept of supported employment. Supported employment is also known as a "place and train" model as compared to a "train and place" approach (Gardner, Chapman, Donaldson, & Jacobson, 1988). The difference between these approaches is critical: in the place and train (supported employment) approach, there are no conditions or prerequisite skills required for an individual to participate in work, as is the condition for traditional vocational programs, such as sheltered employment. Consequently, individuals in supported employment are placed in job positions that best meet their aptitudes, abilities, and interests and then training occurs *on the job*. In the traditional vocational approach, people have to learn and develop specific skills *before* employment is introduced, which typically results in prolonged participation in segregated programs, where it is hoped they would gain the skills for employment. Because of this, the traditional approach, also known as the continuum of service model, has proven ineffective in securing paid community employment for people with disabilities, particularly those with more severe disabilities (Bellamy, Rhodes, Mank, & Albin, 1988). It is for this reason that sheltered workshop placement was eliminated as an option for successful job placement by the Vocational Rehabilitation (VR) system under the Rehabilitation Act and the term "employment outcome" was clarified as "an individual with a disability working in an integrated setting" (Federal Register, 2001). Therefore, with this policy change, employment outcomes in nonintegrated or sheltered work settings were no longer eligible to receive funding through the state Vocational Rehabilitation system.

As defined by the Rehabilitation Act Amendments of 1986, supported employment is "for persons with developmental disabilities for whom competitive employment is unlikely and who, because of their disabilities, need intensive, ongoing support to perform in a work setting." In addition to this definition, the Office of Special Education and Rehabilitation Services (OSERS) has offered several guidelines for the implementation of supported employment (Jackson & Associates, 1985):

1. Employment—work in a typical workplace at minimum wage or above for at least 20 hours a week.
2. Integration—frequent daily social interaction with non-disabled co-workers.
3. Ongoing Support—ongoing support provided at the worksite for the purpose of sustaining paid employment.
4. Severe Disabilities—supported employment is intended for persons with severe disabilities who require a range of support services to maintain employment.

In addition to these guidelines, the Virginia Commonwealth University's Rehabilitation Research and Training Center on Workplace Supports, a leading research and training center in the development of supported employment and arguably one of the most prolific sources of research on the subject, offered nine core values critical to the model (Brooke, Inge, Armstrong, & Wehman, 1997; Wehman & Targett, 2002):

1. the belief that all people can work and have a right to work;
2. the idea that this work should occur within regular local businesses;
3. the value that people should choose the support they want;
4. the right to equal wages and benefits;
5. a focus on abilities rather than disabilities;
6. the importance of community relationships;
7. personal determination of goals and supports;
8. challenging traditional service systems which do not emphasize a consumer driven perspective; and
9. the importance of both formal and informal community connections

These core values not only support the definition of supported employment from the Rehabilitation Act of 1986, but provide a clear direction for the future of supported employment and for the movement toward greater self-determination. Although supported employment was originally designed and demonstrated with people with mental retardation and developmental disabilities, people with traumatic brain injury, mental illness, autism, and other disabilities have benefited from this approach.

Key Components of Supported Employment

As described above, there are four major components of the supported employment model: job development/placement, on-the-job instruction, ongoing assessment, and follow-along (see Table 9.1) (Wehman & Kregel, 1984). Although we are presenting the model as it was designed in the mid-1980s, we are also describing some minor variations to each component to reflect some of the more current approaches and ideas. As with many new approaches that are introduced, supported employment has undergone a process of evolution and improvement since its initial development.

Job Development/Placement.   Job development begins with a thorough assessment of the individual's interests and strengths. (This assessment process is described in greater detail later in this chapter.) This information is then used as a basis for doing the job search for the person. Potential community job sites are identified and analyzed, and their acceptance of diversity and natural supports is assessed. Both assessments, the assessment of the individual and the analysis of potential worksites, are then compared for their compatibility. This compatibility matching (previously discussed in Chapter 6) helps to match the potential jobs with the person. There are many factors that are considered in the compatibility matching, but one of the more important is transportation. Transportation is usually one of the most critical barriers to employment for people with disabilities and should be a priority in the planning process. Therefore, one of the areas to consider during the matching process is whether the job is on a public transportation route and if the individual is able to use public transportation or whether there are other means for the individual to get to the job site. Another important factor in job development is the person's interest in a specific occupation they desire. Keeping this aspect in mind, it may take a longer period of time to place an individual, since the job search process is narrowly based on the specific category of opportunities. When the job development process is complete, the process of negotiating for the job placement for the person begins. A thorough discussion on job development and interacting with business was provided in Chapter 6.

On-the-Job Instruction.   Originally, the job coach was considered to be responsible for all areas of job site training and instruction. Although this responsibility is still true,

TABLE 9.1   Key Elements of Supported Employment

- Job Development/Placement
- On-the-Job Instruction
- Ongoing Assessment
- Follow-Along

how it is implemented has changed since the initial development of supported employment. With the concept of natural support in mind (Murphy & Rogan, 1994), it is now expected that the employer and co-workers take a greater role in the job training and instruction. Most employers will already have a new employee training procedure, and, because the person with disability is considered a new employee, the expectation should be that the person will follow the same typical training procedure. For example, if the training procedure uses a mentoring approach to introduce the job, the job coach takes on a different role. Rather than being responsible for teaching the job duties to the employee with disabilities, the job coach may be more involved in supporting and mentoring the co-workers who will be responsible for the initial training. Because of this rethinking of the function of job coaches, they are now frequently referred to as *employment consultants*. This reflects the notion that the employment consultant is an advocate for the individual with a disability but also acts as a mentor to the employer or co-worker doing the job training process. By involving employers and co-workers early in the process, they will be more invested in the placement and are likely to solve problems and create successful jobs for people with disabilities.

Since many natural support practices have been implemented and more clearly understood (Mank, Cioffi, & Yovanoff, 1997), several questions have arisen regarding how employers respond to these practices, particularly with people with severe disabilities. The concept of natural supports must be understood in terms of a balance between what individuals' needs are and how effectively and efficiently work places can meet those needs without compromising the businesses' "bottom line" (Callahan & Garner, 1997). We must consider the individuals' physical and cognitive characteristics and the extent to which employers are capable of providing training and support (natural supports) before the support personnel (employment consultants) provide a more intense intervention (see Figure 9.1). This carefully applied strategy ensures the balance of natural support in the work environment.

The implementation of natural supports in supported employment has had significant impact on the field of vocational habilitation (Murphy & Rogan, 1994; Mank et al., 1997). With the concerns of funding long-term placements, waiting lists, and other issues related to the economics of supported employment, natural supports has been seen as necessary strategy for successful employment for people with disabilities. However, this concept is not a panacea, but one of many possible solutions to the problems we face in securing and retaining employment for people with disabilities.

Since the introduction of supported employment, service providers have tended to place individuals with mild disabilities more so than people with severe disabilities, as was originally intended (Shafer et al., 1991). Perhaps one of the reasons for this shift has been the difficulty of maintaining a long-term commitment to individuals with severe disabilities on the job, which some current funding streams have limited. Natural supports have some expectation to offset some of these problems by recruiting and infusing the features of natural supports in the workplace (Murphy & Rogan, 1994; Mank et al., 1997).

Educators may see a limited role for themselves in natural supports, but it is critical for educators to introduce the concept of natural supports to employers and students alike. Educators can also assist students and families in considering natural

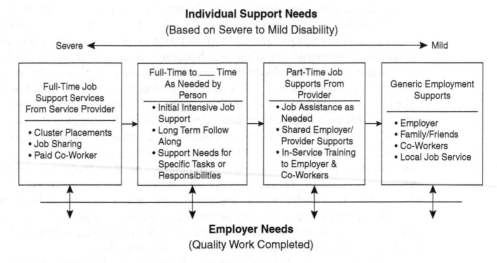

Individual Support Needs
(Based on Severe to Mild Disability)

Severe ◄─────────────────────────────────► Mild

| Full-Time Job Support Services From Service Provider ──────────── • Cluster Placements • Job Sharing • Paid Co-Worker | Full-Time to ___ Time As Needed by Person • Initial Intensive Job Support • Long Term Follow Along • Support Needs for Specific Tasks or Responsibilities | Part-Time Job Supports From Provider • Job Assistance as Needed • Shared Employer/ Provider Supports • In-Service Training to Employer & Co-Workers | Generic Employment Supports ──────────── • Employer • Family/Friends • Co-Workers • Local Job Service |

Employer Needs
(Quality Work Completed)

FIGURE 9.1   Intensity of Support and Natural Support Options Necessary to Meet Employer Needs

supports in their decisions and choices about adult service programs. The willingness of vocational programs to incorporate this concept within their service procedures should be one of the factors to consider when evaluating and selecting a program to work with.

Ongoing Assessment.   The assessment of a person on the job is an ongoing process. The original idea of this component was to assess both the new employee and the employer on a regular basis. Addressing the person's satisfaction with the job, his or her performance, and the employer's perception of work accomplishments are also a part of this component. Any problems identified would be corrected and adjustments made to ensure the long-term placement of the person. This idea has not necessarily changed over time, except that we have acknowledged that, as we assess individuals on the job, we must also assess the culture of the workplace to determine how natural supports can best be arranged.

Follow-Along.   This component assures that employees with disabilities receive ongoing assistance when needed, throughout the duration of their employment. Ongoing assistance is critical for long-term success for most people with disabilities, particularly severe disabilities. During this phase of supported employment, a job coach would generally conduct periodic visits to the job site or make calls to the employer to inquire how the individual is doing. This phase of the process does not begin until it is determined that the individual is stable in the job, which is defined as when the person receives 20 percent or less of intensive job site training. During this phase of the process the amount of on-site training generally indicates whether the placement is a success or not. This phase generally requires long-term financial support for the person to continue to receive the follow-along supervision by agencies, which often requires a commitment by both the funding source and the agency.

For the reasons just mentioned, follow-along has been an area of concern by funding sources and agencies. The major commitment needed to sustain a placement has challenged the system and providers alike. A possible solution to this issue comes from the natural supports model of supported employment. In the traditional supported employment approach, the job coach tended to take on the majority of the responsibilities for follow-along support. In our current system, it is imperative to recruit and solicit co-worker support as part of the follow-along support and supervision. As indicated above, the process of natural supports begins with the premise that the employer assumes the role of supervisor as soon as the person begins work. This is appropriate, as most employers consider themselves to be their employees' supervisor anyway. When supported employment was first developed, the job coach was generally considered to be the supervisor and mediator of problems to the person with disability. Today, the employer assumes typical responsibility and a more normal role of supervision. This is perhaps one of the most important natural support functions to help sustain a placement.

An additional issue that arises during follow-along is that of career development and advancement. For many American workers, a career is often considered moving up the ladder of success. This concept of a career ladder holds true for many people with disabilities. For other people, however, a career ladder may be more horizontal in nature (laterally mobile), as shown in Figure 9.2.

A lateral career move may offer different job options, perhaps with an increase in income, variations in job duties and responsibilities, or simply a change in the work environment and co-workers. This is not to say that a person with a disability cannot be upwardly mobile and move up the career ladder. However, this approach presents options for people with disabilities when making allowances for physical and cognitive limitations that may narrow the possibilities of choices. Career advancement is an important aspect of job satisfaction, either through vertical or horizontal career changes.

We have emphasized how the concept of natural supports has been infused into the original model of supported employment to help you understand how it has evolved into an approach that requires unique and creative strategies. The use of natural supports in employment services is a critical factor since it attempts to recruit and establish a network of supports that may not always require an agency's intervention. This includes a network of supports and services that are typically found in our communities and that can help support people with disabilities in settings and situations. This point is paramount for the future of community inclusion of people with disabilities. The reliance on government funding has actually become a barrier to community inclusion, as less and less funding is available to human service programs for the long-term supports that so many people with disabilities need. Since the funds are scarce for long-term supports, parents are often reluctant to have their adult children participate in community work programs and instead ask for segregated adult services, which they perceive to be more "secure," even though these services are not likely to

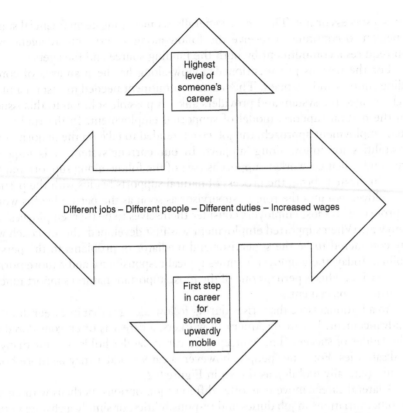

FIGURE 9.2   Career Ladder Choices for People with Disabilities

result in placement into integrated employment. Also, this is a double-edged sword, for there is also a scarcity in funding for segregated adult programs, as evidenced by the long waiting list for their services. Parents, therefore, must choose between waiting for an opening in a segregated program or opting for an *integrated* employment option, where the funds are also limited but are better through vocational rehabilitation (VR) services, previously discussed in Chapter 5. In light of this challenge, it is imperative that we assist students and families in establishing a network of natural supports so that, upon graduation, they will have a greater chance of success in their communities.

Models of Supported Employment

In this section we will discuss the various models of supported employment. Supported employment has generally been identified as having four different program models (see Table 9.2) (Wehman & Kregel, 1984). These four models are not the only models considered, and, in fact, the literature has offered up to seven types of supported employment (Bellamy et al., 1988; Gardner et al., 1988). As we move forward to improve our supports for people with complex disabilities in community-integrated settings, it becomes imperative that we think creatively in our approach to working with individuals with disabilities. Therefore, it is important to see supported employment as a base from which models of supports and services can be adapted and modified to best fit the individual and the unique challenges they pose.

An important consideration is to view these models as options to best fit individuals' unique abilities and needs. For many people with disabilities in our communities, the severity or their behavioral challenges is often the major barrier to integration. These challenges should not exclude people from employment opportunities. If we believe that we must change the person's behaviors or improve (develop) the person's work characteristics before giving them an opportunity, then we are likely to exclude them from community-based employment. This has been the premise of the traditional "readiness" model of service. This traditional approach focused on trying to ameliorate behaviors or challenges, leaving some practitioners feeling that individuals need to "get ready" before being included or employed. In other words, this approach attempted to "fix" people with disabilities rather than trying to find the best "fit" for them (O'Brien, 1987). When this happens, the person is typically deemed to be in need of "pre-vocational" or readiness training in segregated settings with little hope for advancement to community-integrated activities or employment (Bellamy et al., 1988). On the other hand, if we consider individuals' characteristics and find a situation or a model that best fits their needs and abilities, we create the opportunity for success. This is not to say that we feel that every student leaving our special education programs will be employed or integrated within our society. However, we are convinced that if skilled and creative people make a concerted effort, employment and community inclusion can be made a reality *for far more people.*

The following is a description of several models of supported employment and, depending on individuals' support needs, one of these models may be a best fit for a particular person. A few of the major differences in these models involve the level of support, the supervision provided, the opportunity for social integration and wages being earned. Each will be discussed with regard to these differences. As you review each of these models, keep in mind our previous discussion of the components of supported employment, and try to understand and incorporate the functions discussed earlier while also considering the natural support functions.

TABLE 9.2   Common Models of Supported Employment

- Individual Placement
- Enclaves in Industry
- Mobile Work Crews
- Entrepreneurships

Individual Placement Model.   This model is perhaps the most popular and is based on a one-to-one service approach. A job coach or employment specialist works to place one person in a job setting and arranges for the needed supports and services to that person alone. After the individual begins to perform the job duties independently, the job coach begins to fade supervision from the site. Follow-along services begin after the job coach's supervision has met a specific criterion. The person placed in a job would earn at least minimum wage, work alongside nondisabled co-workers and have ample opportunities for social integration.

This model has some possible limitations for people with the most severe disabilities. Oftentimes, such individuals will need ongoing supervision and support that, without natural supports, would essentially be financially prohibitive. Usually persons with more severe disabilities can learn and perform the job but when it comes to the follow-along phase, in which they require ongoing support, the resources are generally limited. In a situation where ongoing support is a concern and where natural supports are not available for the person to sustain employment, another model of supported employment might be a better option.

Group Placements in Industry.   This model may be implemented in two different ways. The first is the *enclave model*, and the second is the *mobile work model* (Gardner et al., 1988; Wehman & Bricout, 1997). Each is discussed below.

Enclave Model.   The enclave model is characterized as a group of people (five to ten) with disabilities who work alongside nondisabled co-workers in a business or industry. Note that the smaller the number of people in the enclave, the easier it tends to be to promote social inclusion with nondisabled co-workers. The group can be directly employed by the employer and supervised by the employer, or an adult service agency may contract with the employer to bring a group of workers to the industry and be supervised by the staff member of the agency. Given the two possible options, the former approach is preferred because the employer will have greater investment in the success of the employees. The benefit of either approach is that there is ample opportunity for social integration, but if the employer hires the group of workers there is the opportunity for them to earn commensurate wages and receive benefits. The latter approach differs in that if an agency contracts with the employer, there is a possibility that the workers with disabilities will be paid on a piece-rate basis, which would usually be below minimum wage, which is allowed under their sub-minimum wage certification by the Department of Labor. In addition, the workers would most likely not receive benefits. Of course, the former is preferred but employers are more likely to contract with providers if given the choice. It should be noted that earning a wage may not be the critical feature to some people, and social integration may be equally or more important.

The enclave model, if available to people with disabilities, may have several benefits for those considered more challenging or for whom the individual placement model may not be viable. First, there would be a qualified instructor to teach and supervise the group of people. For those individuals considered too challenging or too disabled, this group placement model has a greater potential to solve this concern. A second benefit is for someone who requires more consistent or long-term, ongoing support. The employer or staff person both understand the need for continuous on-going support. A third benefit is the issue of transportation. If the employer agrees to contract with the agency, it may be easier to transport a small group to one location as opposed to transporting individuals to several different locations. A fourth benefit has to do with financial resources. The cost of having a group of people placed in one setting reduces the cost of individualized training and the long-term support for them. The final benefit may be related more to the employer than to the person with disability. Where employers may be reluctant to hire people with disabilities, this approach offers the employer an opportunity with only minimal risk. This model may be appropriate for people with disabilities who would benefit from this type of support and supervision.

Mobile Crew Model.   The mobile crew is made up of four to five individuals who usually perform work such as lawn care, janitorial work, or various cleaning-type jobs that may require moving from one job site to another. Crews may be established as an operation that provides a single service to its customers or vary depending on the weather conditions and needs of the geographical area. Usually a manager is responsible for several crews with each crew having its own supervisor. This type of model is very functional for rural areas where businesses and industry is scarce. It may also be appropriate for urban areas where lawn care and janitorial work is available.

The model is not appropriate for some individuals whose mobility is a problem. It may also not be good for those who have behavioral challenges that may be difficult to handle by a supervisor. It is appropriate for individuals who prefer gross-motor-type work and enjoy moving around from job site to job site. It is also good for people who like being outdoors, if the work is of that nature. Conversely, the same things that some people may like about the work others may find difficult to handle, such as changing work environments and moving from site to site. One other drawback is that if the work is generally outdoors, in some areas of the country it would be seasonal work and may be dictated by the weather conditions of the day. The benefits are that it offers the opportunity for community participation and the potential for social integration as well as the opportunity to earn commensurate wages and participate in meaningful work. This model is different from the previous two models discussed but one that may be a good fit for some individuals.

Entrepreneurships.   Millions of Americans are self-employed and own their own businesses. Until recently, people with disabilities have rarely been considered as potential business owners (U.S. Department of Labor, 2004). This option may only be a consideration for some individuals with disabilities but should be considered wherever it seems a possibility. Supported self-employment is a type of individual placement that is receiving attention in the field of rehabilitation (Rizzo, 2002).

With the appropriate supports and guidance, some people with disabilities can develop and operate (with supports) their own business (Hagner & Davies, 2002; Rizzo, 2002). The support and guidance might involve assistance in conceptualizing the business type, developing a business plan, or in securing grants and funds for initial startup costs. Vocational rehabilitation (VR) has and continues to be supportive of consumer-owned business and has offered assistance for business development and training as well as providing for some startup costs. In addition, there are grants and small business loans that are available for individuals who meet certain criteria for initial startup costs for small business (Hagner & Davies, 2002). It is important for teachers, vocational rehabilitation counselors, and other practitioners to keep an open mind about the possibilities that some students with disabilities may be able to be self-employed and own their own business.

ASSESSMENT FOR COMMUNITY EMPLOYMENT

In this chapter, as well as in Chapters 5 and 6, we have provided an overview of how to find, get, and keep a job. In this section we will provide more detail on assessment processes in supported employment. As was mentioned earlier in this chapter, job development begins with a thorough assessment of an individual's interests, preferences, and strengths. The following is a brief introduction to assessment that will assist teachers and other professionals to help students get a good start toward a potentially enriching career or job. Please note that this is only intended to be an introduction on conducting an assessment.

In this chapter, we have discussed the possibilities and options that students with disabilities can have toward starting a career or a job. The options discussed are based on many factors associated with the student characteristics and ability levels, as well as an understanding of their interests and preferences toward a job and/or career. Other factors may include functional abilities, the level and need for supervision, the compatibility of the individual's abilities to the job requirements, and accessible transportation to and from work and/or the ability to use public transportation. These factors should be some of the most important to be considered when assisting a student with disabilities to decide on a job/career path. In order for these factors to be fairly and clearly assessed, an appropriate vocational evaluation should be conducted. Next we will discuss our ideas of the most appropriate and useful assessment strategies to assist students and teachers to determine what the "best fit" is for the individual in terms of paving a potential career path.

Vocational Assessment and Planning

Vocational assessment and planning is critical to understanding students' strengths and to securing appropriate career options. We believe that vocational assessments must be based on the values that all people with disabilities have the potential for gainful employment. In addition, the goal is to achieve an integrated employment outcome by discovering the student's capacities and strengths, not by highlighting the person's deficiencies and weaknesses. Not only does the vocational assessment help practitioners learn about the person, but it is also a way for the person to learn about themselves. A vocational assessment should provide a unique understanding of the person, his or her interests, abilities, and motivating characteristics.

There are generally three types of vocational assessments: formal (standardized instruments), informal (interviews and observations), and situational (job site analysis). It is our general view that formal assessments are less valuable in helping to understand the compatibility of work to the student with disabilities (Callahan & Garner, 1997; Pancsofar & Steere, 1997). Such instruments tend to provide insufficient information about the person's competencies and capacities, and they generally provide deficit-based information based on comparison to a norm group (Callahan & Garner, 1997). The purpose of these evaluations has typically determined the vocational "potential" of individuals and has resulted in the exclusion of people with more severe disabilities from the opportunity of being employed (Callahan & Garner, 1997). We are assuming that most students with disabilities have vocational "potential." In fact, the Rehabilitation Act of 1992 (PL 102-569) indicates that an evaluation that documents rehabilitation "potential" be replaced by a "presumption of ability" (Button, 1992). Therefore, we consider the informal types of assessment more functional and useful and recommend that assessments be conducted using informal and/or situational assessment methods.

The informal, or situational assessment, method gathers information in a functional way that offers concrete data that can be used to determine what is needed to assist an individual in becoming successful on a job. This assessment format assumes employability. The role of an informal vocational assessment is to accomplish the following outcomes:

1. To link the individual to job development efforts.
2. To paint an accurate picture of the person.
3. To offset any of the negative deficit-based assessments that were conducted.
4. To empower the individual and others closest to the person toward a network of connections.
5. To obtain information that reflects personal preferences, employment goals, gifts and talents (Callahan & Garner, 1997).

Informal Assessment.   The informal assessment process is a series of activities that leads to a profile of the person, similar to the concept of person centered planning (Callahan & Garner, 1997). Although we are discussing employment, it should be noted that an individual profile is extremely useful in assessing areas such as community living, recreation, and community accessibility skills. For the purpose of this discussion we will focus on the vocational profile.

Vocational Profile.   Obtaining a vocational profile on a person is akin to getting a "snapshot" of the life of the individual. It is a process that strives to obtain specific information that will lead to a clear outcome. It is a guide that asks questions in order to discover detailed information about the person, his or her life, important relationships, and experiences that can help to establish a direction to employment. In essence, it provides the facilitator of the assessment with an understanding and insights into the life experiences of the person (Callahan & Garner, 1997). Information is gathered by getting to know the individual, interviewing friends, neighbors, and relatives and reviewing pertinent sources of information. Much of this may be gathered through the process of person centered planning or it can be done specifically for a vocational purpose. When the vocational profile does not give enough information with regards to skills, abilities, and performance measures on specific job areas, a situational assessment can supplement the process in order to further explore the potential career options of the student.

Situational Assessment. A situational assessment is also considered to be a functional approach and is sometimes referred to as a functional assessment. Since it is functional, it represents a meaningful, practical, and useful way to evaluate and assess the student's experiences. A situational assessment describes and defines the skills within the student's repertoire that will allow him or her to participate in a wide variety of integrated community activities and environments, including employment (Falvey, Rosenberg, & Grenot-Scheyer, 1982). Understanding that a situational assessment is functional and practical, it is defined as a way to determine an individual's strengths, interests, and support needs in a variety of areas in the community. One of the major characteristics of the situational assessment approach is that it focuses on identifying personal strengths and capacities of an individual. (Refer to Table 9.3 for additional characteristics of situational assessments.)

Situational assessments are conducted in real community-based environments. Since we are focusing our attention on employment, we will discuss how a situational assessment is developed and implemented in local businesses. Again, we are only providing a brief introduction to this valuable concept, and we recommend that you further investigate this approach and determine how it might be used in your setting. (For a more complete discussion of the situational assessment process, refer to Pancsofar & Steere, 1997.) The following steps should be taken in developing a situational assessment. Note that these steps incorporate strategies described in Chapter 6.

1. Identify the types of jobs to look for in the local community: Here you will locate several job types and sites that have been identified as preferred by students from initial discussions through the vocational profile questions or from person centered planning meetings.

TABLE 9.3   Characteristics of Situational Assessments

Situational assessments seek to determine . . .

- Interests (use important person centered information)
- Strengths
- Capacities
- Learning styles
- Adaptation and modification needs
- Level of ability—Where to begin (baseline learning level)
- Proper environmental match

2. Locate the available jobs in the local community appropriate for the students, that is, those specific jobs identified in step one.
3. Identify the businesses with the target jobs. Research the local business community, utilizing resources such as the Chamber of Commerce, business advisory boards, and departments of labor and rehabilitation services.
4. Contact the targeted businesses, either through a letter or phone call. Introduce yourself, the purpose of your program, and how the businesses can be part of a collaborative effort to enhance a student's education.
5. Identify and analyze the jobs in those businesses. A thorough analysis of the jobs must be conducted, including a task analysis of the job, the duties, requirements, and responsibilities associated with the work.
6. Schedule the situational assessment. Identify the best times to conduct the assessment with the student and employer. Request at least four consecutive hours for each assessment and provide a copy of the schedule to the employer.
7. Conduct the situational assessment. Collecting data on the performance of the student is critical in this step.
8. Generate a report based on the data collected during the assessment. This report should provide information about the student's performance, interest in the work, areas in which he or she worked independently, and where support is needed.

The process of gathering information may require both a vocational profile and a situational assessment.

INITIATING CAREER DEVELOPMENT: HOW IT ALL COMES TOGETHER

Choosing a career is difficult for anyone but more so for someone challenged by cognitive difficulties and/or physical disabilities. We should not assume that the establishment of a clear career path occurs during or immediately after high school (Szymanski, 1994). Careers can be established at virtually any point in a person's life. In fact, it is estimated that a person changes careers several times during a lifetime. So, for people with disabilities, jobs may begin after high school but perhaps careers may not be established until several years later. But what we do know about helping people with disabilities get jobs is that in order to help students become successful in the employment world, we must have high expectations and believe that they have potential and can accomplish great things. Teachers who are creative and understand the broad scope of their responsibilities, which includes working with the business community and students alike, are more likely to be successful in helping students achieve positive outcomes. Creating a network of supports and a sense of collaboration with students, teachers, parents, employers, businesspeople and community leaders to sustain a possible career for the student with disabilities is critical. Creating this opportunity for success begins with offering experiences to students. Perhaps an appropriate statement with which to close this section is: *realistic career choices come from the opportunity for realistic experiences.*

We believe that a commitment to integrated employment must drive the unified efforts of the school, teachers, parents, students, vocational rehabilitation personnel, disability services offices, and adult providers of services. It all comes together when the key people involved in the transition planning and implementation process work together on a common goal. There is no question that success comes from the efforts and creativity of all those people involved in the planning team. So, it begins with having the shared commitment to the same values.

The second action that must be taken is good planning. Planning is critical and must be based on gathering relevant information that will help understand the person's personal history and that will clarify the student's hopes and dreams for the future. Planning should also serve to develop the network of supports that will be needed to achieve the desired outcomes for the student.

Finally, the third action is to provide the needed experiences and opportunities for worthwhile and positive experiences, that is, community based, real life, and meaningful experiences. As mentioned earlier, realistic career choices come from the opportunity for realistic experiences.

CHAPTER SUMMARY

In this chapter, we have discussed the concept of supported employment and introduced the various options and models. We presented information about natural supports and how each of the supported employment components can be adapted in light of this concept. We discussed how to assist students in identifying the best "fit" or compatibility to the various options, as well as how to obtain an individual profile and conduct situational assessments. It is our hope that the values that guide students through transition programs are based on opportunities and choices, as presented in this chapter.

APPLICATION ACTIVITIES

The application activities listed below are essential for your continued learning and skill development in transition. Each of these activities will require your time and energy but will help you develop your professional skills in this area.

For Practice and Enhanced Understanding:

Visit local provider agencies in your area to learn more about the supported employment services that they provide. As you learn about these services, compare what they tell you to the key programmatic elements described in this chapter. In particular, are services available for individuals with more severe disabilities who are not able to benefit from other approaches to rehabilitation?

Interview an individual with disabilities who has participated or is participating in supported employment services. How has this individual's quality of life been affected by working in the community?

Identify how each of the components of the supported employment process can be accomplished using natural supports, as defined and discussed in this chapter.

>Job Development
>Job Training
>Ongoing Assessment
>Follow-Along

List some of the benefits and/or outcomes that are associated with each of these natural support activities other than what might be considered obvious.

For Your Portfolio:

Visit the website of the organization APSE, formerly the Association for Persons in Supported Employment (www.apse.org). APSE was founded in 1989 as a professional organization concerned with the expansion and enhancement of supported employment services in the United States and abroad. Consider joining APSE national as well as the state chapter where you live. You will find that their publications and training events are extremely valuable in helping you to continue to learn about supported employment.

RESOURCES AND WEBSITES

The following resources and websites will allow you to extend your knowledge about how to assist people with disabilities obtain employment in the community. Consider including these resources in your professional portfolio.

APSE—The Network on Employment

Organization dedicated to the improvement and expansion of integrated employment opportunities through advocacy and education.
www.apse.org.

Virginia Commonwealth University Research and Training Center on Workplace Support and Job Retention

Provides research, training, and technical assistance.
www.worksupport.com

Employment and Disability Institute

Focus on advancement of knowledge, policies, and practices that enhance the opportunities of people with disabilities in all aspects of life.
www.ilr.cornell.edu.

Job Accommodation Network (JAN)

Consulting service designed to increase the employability of people with disabilities.
www.janweb.icdi.wvu.edu

AAMR

Information and advocacy regarding individuals with intellectual disabilities. Includes links to local chapters.
www.aamr.org

ARC of the United States

Information and advocacy regarding people with intellectual and developmental disabilities. Includes links to local chapters.
www.thearc.org

TASH

Information and advocacy for people with disabilities, particularly severe and multiple disabilities. Includes links to local chapters.
www.tash.org

New Freedom Initiative's Online Resource

Federal interagency website to give access to information and resources for people with disabilities.
www.disabilityinfo.gov

Institute on Community Inclusion

Supports the rights of children and adults with disabilities to participate in all aspects of the community. Conducts research and education about effective strategies for promoting the inclusion of people with disabilities.
www.communityinclusion.org

REFERENCES

Balser, R., Harvey, B., & Hornby, H. (1991). *A focus on job coaching: The untapped potential.* Hospital Industries Program: Department of Rehabilitation Medicine Maine Medical Center.

Bellamy, G. T., Horner, R. H., & Inman, D. P. (1979). *Vocational habilitation of severely retarded adults: A direct service technology.* Baltimore: University Park Press.

Bellamy, G. T., Rhodes, L. E., Mank, D. M., & Albin, J. M. (1988). *Supported employment: A community implementation guide.* Baltimore: Paul H. Brookes.

Bishop, K. D., & Falvey, M. A. (1989). Employment skills. In M. Falvey (Ed., 2nd ed.), *Community-based curriculum: Instructional strategies for students with severe handicaps* (pp. 165–187). Baltimore: Paul H. Brookes.

Brady, M., & Rosenberg, H. (2002). Modifying and managing employment practices: An inclusive model for job placement and support. In K. Storey, P. Bates, & D. Hunter (Eds.), *The road ahead: Transition to adult life for persons with disabilities* (pp. 121–136). St. Augustine, FL: TRN Publishers.

Brooke, V., Inge, K. J., Armstrong, A. J., & Wehman, P. (Eds.) (1997). *Supported employment handbook: A customer driven approach for persons with significant disability.* Richmond: Virginia Commonwealth University Rehabilitation Research and Training Center on Supported Employment.

Brown, L., Shiraga, B., York, J., Kessler, K., Strohm, B., Rogan, P., Sweet, M., Zanella, K., Van Deventer, P., & Lomis, R. (1984). Integrated work opportunities for adults with severe disabilities. *Journal of the Association for Persons with Severe Handicaps, 9*, 262–269.

Buckley, J., & Bellamy, G. T. (1985). *National survey of day and vocational programs for adults with severe disabilities: A 1984 profile.* Unpublished manuscript, Johns Hopkins University, Baltimore.

Butterworth, J., Metzel, D., Boeltzig, H., Gilmore, D., & Sulewski, J. (2005). Employment outcomes: Room for change. *TASH Connections, 31,* 4–6.

Button, C. (1992, October–November). P.L. 102-569: A new season for the Rehabilitation Act. *Word from Washington.*

Callahan, M. J., & Garner, B. G. (1997). *Keys to the workplace: Skills and supports for people with disabilities.* Baltimore: Paul H. Brookes.

Carter, E., & Wehby, J. (2003). Job performance of transition-age youth with emotional and behavioral disorders. *Exceptional Children, 69,* 449–465.

Conley, R. (2003). Supported employment in Maryland: Successes and issues. *Mental Retardation, 41,* 237–249.

Curl, R. M., Hall, S. M., Chisholm, L. A., & Rule, S. (1992). Coworkers as trainers for entry-level workers: A competitive employment model for individuals with developmental disabilities. *Rural Special Education Quarterly, 11*(1), 31–35.

Dickinson, L. D., & Verbeek, L. R. (2002). Wage differential between college graduates with and without learning disabilities. *Journal of Learning Disabilities, 20,* 175–185.

Falvey, M., Rosenberg, R., & Grenot-Scheyer, M. (1982). Strategies for assessing students with multiple handicapping conditions. In S. Ray, M. J. O'Neill, & N. T. Morris (Eds.), *Low incidence children: A guide to psychoeducational assessment* (pp. 245–273). Natchitoches, LA: Steven Ray Publishing.

Federal Register (2001, January, 22). 66(14), 7249–7258.34 CFR 361.

Gardner, J. F., Chapman, M. S., Donaldson, G., & Jacobson, S. G. (1988). *Toward supported employment: A process guide for planning change.* Baltimore: Paul H. Brookes.

Gold, M. (1972). Stimulus factors in skill training for the retarded on a complex assembly task: Acquisition, transfer and retention. *American Journal on Mental Deficiency, 76,* 517–526.

Hagner, D., & Cooney, B. (2005). "I do that for everybody": Supervising employees with autism. *Focus on autism and other developmental disabilities, 20,* 91–97.

Hagner, D., & Davies, T. (2002). "Doing my own thing": Supported self-employment for individuals with cognitive disabilities. *Journal of Vocational Rehabilitation, 17,* 65–74.

Hanley-Maxwell, C., Pogoloff, S. M., & Whitney-Thomas, J. (1998). Families: The heart of transition. In F. Rusch & J. G. Chadsey (Eds.), *Beyond high school: Transition from school to work* (pp. 234–264). Belmont, CA: Wadsworth.

Harris Interactive, Inc. (2002). *Harris survey of Americans with disabilities.* New York: National Organization on Disability.

Hood, E. L., Test, D. W., Spooner, F., & Steele, R. (1996). Paid co-worker support for individuals with severe and multiple disabilities. *Education and Training in Mental Retardation and Developmental Disabilities, 31,* 251–265.

Jackson & Associates (1985). *Executive summary, National Leadership Institute on Supported Employment.* Olympia, Washington. Unpublished paper.

Katsiyannis, A., Zhang, D., Woodruff, N., & Dixon, A. (2005). Transition supports to students with mental retardation: An examination of data from the national longitudinal transition study 2. *Education and Training in Developmental Disabilities, 40*(2), 109–116.

Kraemer, B., McIntyre, L., & Blacher, J. (2003). Quality of life for young adults with mental retardation during transition. *Mental Retardation, 41,* 250–262.

Mank, D. (1996). Natural supports in employment for people with disabilities: What do we know and when did we know it? *Journal of the Association for Persons with Severe Handicaps, 21,* 174–177.

Mank, D., Cioffi, A., & Yovanoff, P. (1997). Analysis of the typicalness of supported employment jobs, natural supports, and wages and integration outcomes. *Mental Retardation, 35*(3), 185–197.

Mank, D., Cioffi, A., & Yovanoff, P. (2000). Direct support in supported employment and its relation to job typicalness, co-worker involvement, and employment outcomes. *Mental Retardation, 38,* 506–516.

McMahan, R., & Baer, R. (2001). IDEA transition policy compliance and best practice: Perceptions of transition stakeholders. *Career Development for Exceptional Individuals, 24,* 169–184.

Menchetti, B., & Garcia, L. (2003). Personal and employment outcomes of person centered planning. *Education and Training in Developmental Disabilities, 38*, 145–156.

Michaels, C. (1999). *Transition to employment*. Austin, TX: Pro-Ed.

Murphy, S. T., & Rogan, P. M. (1994). *Developing natural supports in the workplace: A practitioner's guide*. St. Augustine, FL: Training Resources Network, Inc.

Murphy, S., & Rogan, P. (1995). *Closing the shop: Conversion from sheltered to integrated work*. Baltimore: Paul Brookes.

O'Brien, J. (1987). A guide to life-style planning: Using the activities catalog to integrate services and natural support systems. In B. Wilcox & J. Knoll (Eds.), *A comprehensive guide to the activities catalog: An alternative curriculum for youth and adults with severe disabilities* (pp. 175–189). Baltimore: Paul H. Brookes.

Pancsofar, E., & Steere, D. (1997). The C.A.P.A.B.L.E. Process: Critical dimensions of community-based assessment. *Journal of Vocational Rehabilitation, 8*, 99–108.

Pendergast, M., & Storey, K. (1999). Individual Program Plan differentials in segregated and integrated work programs for adults with developmental disabilities. *Journal of Vocational Rehabilitation, 13*, 15–19.

Rabren, K., Dunn, C., & Chambers, D. (2002). Predictors of post high school employment among young adults with disabilities. *Career Development for Exceptional Individuals, 25*, 25–40.

Reid, D., Parsons, M., & Green, C. (2001). Evaluating the functional utility of congregate day treatment activities for adults with severe disabilities. *American Journal on Mental Retardation, 106*, 460–469.

Rizzo, D. C. (2002). With a little help from my friends: Supported self-employment for people with severe disabilities. *Journal of Vocational Rehabilitation, 17*, 97–105.

Roessler, R., Shearin, A., & Williams, E. (2000). Three recommendations to improve transition planning in the IEP. *The Journal for Vocational Special Needs Education, 22*(2), 31–36.

Rojewski, J. W. (2002). Career assessment for adolescents with mild disabilities: Critical concerns for transition planning. *Career Development for Exceptional Individuals, 25*, 73–95.

Rusch, F., & Braddock, D. (2004). Adult day programs versus supported employment (1988–2002): Spending and service practices of mental retardation and developmental disabilities state agencies. *Research and Practice for Persons with Severe Disabilities, 29*, 237–242.

Shafer, M. S., Revell, G. W., & Isbister, F. (1991). The national supported employment initiative: A three-year longitudinal analysis of 50 states. *Journal of Vocational Rehabilitation, 1*(1), 9–17.

Storey, K., & Garff, J. (1999). The effect of co-worker instruction on the integration of youth in transition in competitive employment. *Career Development for Exceptional Individuals, 22*, 69–84.

Strain, P. S. (1983). Generalization of autistic children's social behavior change: Effects of developmentally integrated and segregated settings. *Analysis and Intervention in Developmental Disabilities, 3*, 23–34.

Szymanski, E. (1994). Transition: Life-span and life-space considerations for empowerment. *Exceptional Children, 60*, 402–410.

Taylor, S. (1988). Caught in the continuum: A critical analysis of the principle of least restrictive environment. *Journal of The Association for Persons with Severe Handicaps, 13*, 41–53.

U.S. Department of Labor. (2004). Occupational outlook handbook, 2004–2005. Washington, DC: Author.

Wehman, P. (1981). *Competitive employment: New horizons for severely disabled individuals*. Baltimore: Paul H. Brookes.

Wehman, P. (1992). *Life beyond the classroom: Transition strategies for young people with disabilities*. Baltimore: Paul H. Brookes.

Wehman, P. (1999). Supported employment: Toward reducing the impact of disability. *Journal of Vocational Rehabilitation, 12*, 131–133.

Wehman, P., & Bricout, J. (1997). Supported employment: Critical issues and new directions. In G. Revell, K. J. Inge, D. Mank, & P. Wehman (Eds.), *The impact of supported employment for people with significant disabilities: Preliminary findings from the national supported employment consortium*. Virginia Commonwealth University Rehabilitation Research and Training Center on Supported Employment.

Wehman, P., Brooke, V., & Inge, K. (2001). Vocational placements and careers. In P. Wehman (Ed.), *Life beyond the classroom: Transition strategies for young people with disabilities* (3rd ed.) (pp. 211–246). Baltimore: Paul Brookes.

Wehman, P., & Kregel, J. (1984). A supported work approach to competitive employment of persons with moderate and severe handicaps. *Journal of the Association for Person with Severe Handicaps, 10*(1), 3–9.

Wehman, P., Revell, G., & Kregel, J. (1998). Supported employment: A decade of rapid growth and impact. *American Rehabilitation, 24,* 31–43.

Wehman, P., & Targett, P. (2002). Supported employment: The challenge of new staff recruitment, selection and retention. *Education and Training in Mental Retardation, 37*(4), 434–446.

Wehman, P., West, M., & Kregel, J. (1999). Supported employment program development and research needs: Looking ahead to the year 2000. *Education and Training in Mental Retardation and Developmental Disabilities, 34*(1), 3–19.

CHAPTER 10

CURRICULUM FOR STUDENTS IN TRANSITION

CHAPTER OBJECTIVES

Upon completion of this chapter, you will be able to

1. describe functional life skills that all students in transition need to master for successful adult living.
2. describe skills that business and industry value in employees who are entering the workforce.
3. infuse functional life skills topics into general education content lessons.
4. design community-based instructional experiences that allow students to learn important work and community skills.
5. design, adapt, and modify curricular content to assist students to achieve their desired postschool outcomes as they transition to adult life.

KEY TOPICS TO LOOK FOR IN THIS CHAPTER . . .

- Functional skills for adult living: In this chapter, we discuss ways to help young people learn functional skills needed in adult life. Look for the range of strategies that may be used to ensure that these skills are taught.
- Prioritizing curriculum content: What are the most important skills for young people who are in transition to learn? Look for the range of responses to this question throughout this chapter, and consider your role in helping young people learn these skills.
- School-based versus community-based learning: How do each of these approaches contribute to student learning?

From at least age sixteen, when transition planning begins, to students' transition out of the education system, they should continue to learn and master skills that they will need for success during the next phase of their lives. For some students, this will mean attending community college or a four-year university. For others, this will mean entering the workforce directly, with or without support from adult service agencies. For many students, this transition will entail moving out of their family's home to a dorm room or an apartment. Increased mobility in the community and responsibility for financial obligations will be required. Clearly, young people need to learn a great deal from their teens to their early twenties.

Much of what needs to be learned will be part of the school curriculum, while other important skills will be learned primarily from family and friends through activities that take place in the home or in the community. Although schools cannot possibly teach all skills that are required in adulthood, they do play a critical role in preparing young people for a successful transition to adult living. A strong partnership among students, their families, school personnel, and representatives of adult service agencies or postsecondary institutions will help to ensure that students are well prepared.

In this chapter, we will discuss the structure and design of curriculum for students in transition. We will describe the role that state standards play in prescribing required curricular content for students at different grade levels, as well as ways to infuse functional skills into these content areas. We will also discuss the development of important skills through school- and community-based instruction. Finally, we will discuss the importance of connecting curricula to desired postschool outcomes for students who are leaving the special education system.

RESEARCH RELATED TO SECONDARY-LEVEL CURRICULUM AND TRANSITION

Before describing key ingredients into effective curricula for transition-aged students, we provide a brief overview of pertinent research regarding such curricula. Specifically, we will review research related to important curriculum content for secondary-level students and to strategies for promoting better access and participation in the general education curriculum.

A key focus of the literature regarding curriculum for students in transition concerns what is considered to be the most important curriculum content. Clark, Field, Patton, Brolin, & Sitlington (1994), wrote a position statement on behalf of the Division on Career Development and Transition (DCDT) of the Council for Exceptional Children (CEC), in which they argued that the instruction in functional life skills is a necessary component of the curriculum for all students with disabilities, not just those with more severe disabilities. This focus on the need for the development of functional life skills in curriculum development is based on the demands of adult life in the domains of employment, independent living, and community participation and is a consistent theme in literature on effective transition planning. Grigal and Neubert (2004) conducted a survey of 234 parents of transition-aged students in two urban school districts to determine their perceptions of their children's school program and of postschool outcomes. Parents of low incidence disabilities (i.e., more severe disabilities) ranked community-based instruction and life skills instruction more highly, while parents of higher incidence disabilities ranked academic instruction more highly. This study highlights families' concerns about their children's future and the relationship of current curriculum content to future aspirations. Agran, Swaner, and Snow (1998) reported on a survey that they conducted with middle and secondary school personnel regarding the inclusion of work safety skills instruction in the curriculum.

Respondents indicated that, although they felt that work safety skills instruction is important, it is typically not taught in a systematic manner. The authors speculated that this was perhaps due to teachers' assumptions that other people will address this aspect of the curriculum or that students already know this content. Wehmeyer and Schwartz (1998) reviewed IEPs for 136 students with mental retardation and other developmental disabilities to determine the degree to which goals included an emphasis on instruction in self-determination skills. Of 895 transition goals that were reviewed, none targeted instruction or learning related to specific self-determination skills. The implication of this study is that direct instruction in self-determination skills must be included as part of the overall high school curriculum. This is particularly important, as increased self-determination and active student involvement in the assessment and planning processes can have significant impact on the content of transition IEPs and, consequently, on curriculum (Field, Martin, Miller, Ward, & Weymeyer, 1998). Bouck (2004) argued for direct instruction in functional life skills for students with mild mental retardation as opposed to participation in a "watered down" version of the general education curriculum. In this article, the author argued that efforts to focus too narrowly on the general education content for students with mild mental retardation may result in important functional skills being neglected. Elksnin and Elksnin (1998) described the importance of teaching occupational social skills to students with disabilities. They base their assertion, in part, on the report of the Secretary's Commission on Achieving Necessary Skills (SCANS), which reported important skills that high school students should develop in order to be successful in today's business and industry. Several of the skills identified in the SCANS report (for example, participating as a member of a team, teaching others new skills, serving clients or customers, exercising leadership, negotiating, and working with people from diverse backgrounds) involved occupational social skills. The importance of the SCANS report for curriculum development will be described in greater detail later in this chapter. Patton, Cronin, and Wood (1999) describe strategies for infusing functional life skills instruction into existing curricular content areas. These authors describe three main strategies for teaching such functional life skills: teaching these skills through direct course work, augmentation (using a portion of a general education lesson to address functional skills), or infusing these skills into general education lessons by connecting key words (content referents) in the general education lesson to life skills topics. More will be discussed about the curriculum infusion strategy later in this chapter.

Several authors have addressed instructional content and strategies that result in more positive transition outcomes for students with disabilities. Kohler (1994) evaluated the impact of on-the-job work skills training on fifty-eight students with mild disabilities, and reported improvements in both work skills and work related behaviors. Other authors have also asserted the importance of work experience while students are in school (Baer, Flexer, & McMahan, 2005; Hanley-Maxwell & Collet-Klingenberg, 2004; Inge, Wehman, Clees, & Dymond, 1996). Benz, Lindstrom, and Yovanoff (2000) reported on two studies that they conducted about transition practices in connection with Oregon's Youth Transition Program. The results of their studies indicated that student participation in two or more career-related paid work experiences while they were in school and the completion of four or more student-identified transition goals were positive predictors of graduation with a standard diploma and engagement in postschool work or schooling. Lindstrom, Benz, and Doren (2004) used a case study approach to examine barriers and facilitators of career choice among young women with learning disabilities. They interviewed six women, three of whom were in "traditional" female occupations, and three of whom were in nontraditional occupations. Based on the results of their extensive interviews, variables that appeared to influence career choice included (1) gender roles, (2) disability, (3) family and childhood experiences, (4) early work experiences, and (5) career exploration and counseling. Implications of this study are that paid work experiences and active involvement in career exploration in a wider range of professions are important for young women in transition. Sitlington, Neubert, Begun, Lombard, and Leconte (1996) recommended that assessment practices in transition be designed to address specific purposes: to clarify and determine individual student's level of career development, to help students clarify their interests, to determine placements, to facilitate the development of self-determination, and to determine supports, accommodations, and services that are needed. They also recommended that assessment strategies be closely tied to four phases of career development (career awareness, career exploration, career preparation, and career assimilation).

More recently, several studies have addressed strategies for helping students with disabilities to gain access to and progress through standards-based general education curriculum. Wehmeyer, Lattin, and Agran (2001) described a curriculum decision-making model for including students with mental retardation in the general education curriculum. Their model begins with the assumption that participation in the general education curriculum is the preferred approach unless the student cannot benefit from it without modification. If not, then assistive technology is considered, followed by adaptations to the curriculum (i.e., modifications to the presentation and representation of the curriculum and ways that students engage with it). Curriculum adaptations include different ways that the curriculum is presented and different ways for students to respond to content. If these are not sufficient, then curriculum augmentation strategies are introduced, which include teaching the students to use strategies such as self-regulation or cognitive learning strategies that allow them to increase their ability to benefit from the curriculum. Curriculum augmentation also includes teaching specific self-determination skills to students to gain greater control over their own learning. If the above interventions are insufficient, then curriculum alterations may be considered to better address functional skill needs of students. Wehmeyer, Lance, and Bashinski (2002) extended this model by including a discussion of universal design principles to allow better access to general education curricula by students with mental retardation. The concept of universal design for learning (UDL) was further described by representatives of the Center for Applied Special Technology (CAST) (Hitchcock, Meyer, Rose, & Jackson, 2002). Basic principles of UDL included (1) wording learning goals broadly enough to allow access by a wide variety of learners to the essence of the goals; (2) flexible formats for curriculum materials; (3) flexible methods for students to interface with the curriculum content; and (4) flexible methods for assessment of student mastery. The overall purpose of the UDL approach is to allow access to, participation in, and progress through the general education curriculum (Hitchcock et al., 2002).

Wehmeyer, Field, Doren, Jones, and Mason (2004) described the evolution and development of strategies for enhancing the self-determination of individuals with disabilities since 1990 and the relationship of self-determination to standards-based curriculum. These authors assert that the recent mandates for all students to be assessed on state standards-based content provides an opportunity to more fully infuse self-determination into the curriculum because (1) many state standards focus on component skills of self-determination, such as goals setting, problem solving, and decision making, and (2) teaching self-determination skills such as self-regulation, self-management, problem-solving, and goal setting will lead to better engagement in and progress through the general education curriculum.

Several studies have investigated the impact of instruction in self-management skills, which are component skills of self-determined behavior. Hughes, Copeland, Agran, Wehmeyer, Rodi, and Presley (2002) taught self-monitoring skills to four secondary-level students with mental retardation in order to help them improve their performance in general education classes. This study demonstrated that these students could be taught to increase needed skills, including holding one's head up and saying thank you, in inclusive settings through self-monitoring. Palmer, Wehmeyer, Gipson, and Agran (2004) taught problem-solving and study planning skills that were linked to standards-based curricula in the areas of language arts, science, and social studies to middle school students with intellectual disabilities. The problem-solving and study-planning skills were taught using the Self Determined Learning Model of Instruction (SDLMI; Agran, Blanchard, & Wehmeyer, 2000). This model of teaching incorporates principles of self-determination and is based on twelve questions that are organized into three phases: Set a Goal, Take Action, and Adjust the Goal or Plan. In the Palmer and colleagues (2004) study, the students in the treatment groups who received the self-management skills training made significant improvement over control groups who did not receive the training. McGlashing-Johnson, Agran, Sitlington, Cavin, and Wehmeyer (2003) used the SDLMI with four students with moderate to severe disabilities in a community job placement situation. Three of the four students learned to set goals, develop and implement action plans, and adjust their goals and action plans. The fourth student made significant gains in mastering these skills. Agran, Sinclair, Alper, Cavin, Wehmeyer, and Hughes (2005) investigated the effects of instruction in self-monitoring on the direction-following abilities of six students with moderate to severe disabilities in general education settings. Students were taught to acknowledge a direction, complete the task, and monitor their performance. The students in this study successfully learned to monitor their own direction-following ability. A major implication that the authors draw from this study is that students with disabilities need supports to succeed in inclusive settings and that self-monitoring is a powerful "self support" strategy.

In summary, the work of these authors highlights several key issues regarding curriculum development for students in transition:

- All students of transition age need to develop functional skills that are required in daily adult life.

- Work experience and the development of skills that are valued by business and industry are important for later success.
- The majority of students with disabilities can participate in the standards-based general education curriculum, with modifications and supports if necessary. These supports include self-management skills and other skills and behaviors that constitute self-determination.
- The development of the skills, knowledge, and attitudes of self-determination must be infused throughout the entire curriculum, as they are essential to students' active participation in their own transition planning.
- Career awareness should be introduced early during the secondary years in order to help students make initial choices about areas of future interest.
- The development of career awareness and functional life skills can be addressed through infusion into general education lessons.

POSTSCHOOL OUTCOMES: THE GUIDING FORCE IN CURRICULUM DEVELOPMENT

For students with disabilities who are in transition, their desired postschool outcome statements from their transition IEPs should be the major guiding force in the selection, design, and adaptation of educational curricula. As an outcome-oriented process to promote successful movement from school to postschool activities, instruction for transition-aged students should help prepare them for the next steps in their lives. Consider Sue Anne and Mike, as described below.

Sue Anne

When she was in high school, Sue Anne dreamed of going to college in order to learn how to become an early childhood educator. She knew that, in order to fulfill this dream, she would need to complete her coursework in English, the sciences, and math, and that her grades would need to be high enough for her to be admitted to the college of her choice. Besides everything that she was learning in school, Sue Anne knew that she would need to learn more about skills of everyday living: doing laundry, cooking, cleaning her house, getting around the community, and so forth. Her family was her main support system in learning these skills, and, as she got older, she assumed more responsibilities for the completion of some of these tasks around her home. She also needed to gain more experiences working with young children through babysitting and volunteer activities. She also needed to maintain her health and stay fit even when she went to college. Finally, she needed to learn how to apply to colleges, seek out scholarships and student loans, and how to contact the College Disability Support Services Office in order to arrange for her accommodations. There was so much to learn and to accomplish to get ready for college!

Mike

Mike also has a great deal to learn, although he may not be aware of this. He is, however, quite aware that something is changing in his day-to-day life. He is gaining work experience as part of his school curriculum and, although he does not know it now, this experience will be valuable to him in obtaining paid employment as an adult. The experiences that he is getting now will also help convince adult service agencies that he can indeed work, if provided with appropriate support. But work is only one aspect of Mike's future life. He needs to learn skills associated with home living, such as cooking, doing his laundry, cleaning the dishes, and cleaning his home. He needs to learn how to shop at the grocery store and in other community locations. He needs to learn how to use money, how to use a calendar, how to read a shopping list, and how to cross streets safely. He also needs to learn how to take a shower with greater independence, how to care for his teeth, and how to recognize when he is feeling sick. His family and circle of support know that he will probably always need some level of support to work, live in an apartment, and get around the community, but he is still learning. There is just so much for him to learn . . .

As illustrated through Sue Anne and Mike, students in transition have a great deal to learn within a finite period of time. This requires prioritization of what is most important to learn. As described in Chapter 4, desired postschool outcomes should drive the selection of annual goals and short-term objectives. That is, the postschool outcome provides a rationale for what is taught within a given school year, which is described through annual goals and short-term objectives. Annual goals and short-term objectives are only included in the IEP if it is clear to the educational team that the mastery of these goals and objectives will help lead to the attainment of the desired postschool outcomes. Figures 10.1, 10.2, and 10.3 provide examples of the connection between desired postschool outcomes and annual goals and short-term objectives for a student with mental retardation who requires limited support needs (Steere & Cavaiuolo, 2002). Notice in these examples that the mastery of the skills

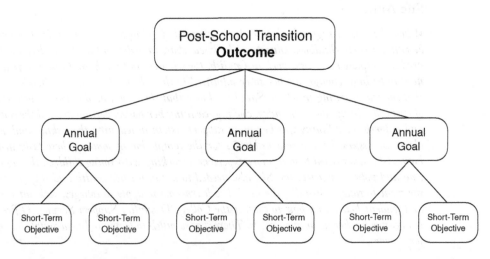

FIGURE 10.1 Relationship of Transition Outcomes to Annual Goals and Short-Term Objectives

Source: "Connecting Outcomes, Goals, and Objectives in Transition Planning" by Daniel Steere and Domenico Cavaiuolo, *Teaching Exceptional Children*, Vol. 34, 2002, pp. 54–59. Copyright 2002 Council for Exceptional Children. Reprinted with permission.

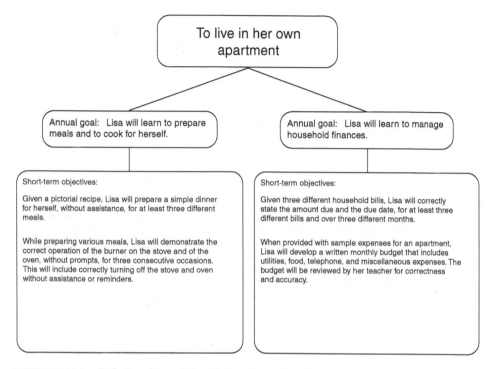

FIGURE 10.2 Relationship of Transition Outcome for Community Living to Associated Annual Goals and Short-Term Objectives

Source: "Connecting Outcomes, Goals, and Objectives in Transition Planning" by Daniel Steere and Domenico Cavaiuolo, *Teaching Exceptional Children,* Vol. 34, 2002, pp. 54–59. Copyright 2002 Council for Exceptional Children. Reprinted with permission.

contained in the annual goals and short-term objectives have a clear connection to the desired transition outcomes.

FUNCTIONAL ADULT LIVING SKILLS FOR ALL STUDENTS

All young people who are making the transition from school to adulthood, regardless of ability or disability, need to learn a wide range of functional skills that will allow them to live successfully as adult members of the community (Wehman & Targett, 2004). Even students with mild disabilities who aspire to postsecondary education must be able to take care of their apartment, wash their clothes, maintain their bank accounts, and so forth. As shown in Table 10.1, a wide range of functional skills are needed for success in the major domains of adult living. Many of these functional skills may be taught in the school and/or in the home. When they are taught in school, they may be infused into general education content areas or they may be taught directly; both strategies are discussed later in this chapter. For now, however, we simply want

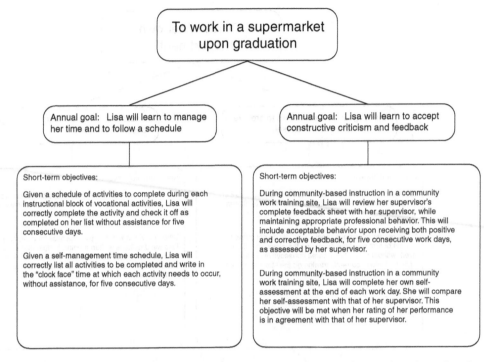

FIGURE 10.3   Relationship of Transition Outcome for Employment to Associated Annual Goals and Short-Term Objectives

Source: "Connecting Outcomes, Goals, and Objectives in Transition Planning" by Daniel Steere and Domenico Cavaiuolo, *Teaching Exceptional Children*, Vol. 34, 2002, pp. 54–59. Copyright 2002 Council for Exceptional Children. Reprinted with permission.

to emphasize that these functional skills are needed by all students in transition, not just those with more severe disabilities (Clark et al., 1994).

One of the pioneers of the development of functional curricular content for students of transition age was Donn Brolin. (See Sidebar 10.1.) Many authors have developed curricula to address the functional life skills needed by students in transition. Brolin's Life Centered Career Education model (1997, 2004) addresses twenty-two competencies and numerous sub-competencies in the adult living domains of *daily living skills, personal-social skills*, and *occupational guidance and preparation*. The LCCE contains three important features (www.cec.org, 2005). First, the competencies in the three domains focus on functional skills needed by students who are making the transition to adult living. Second, the competencies are sequenced in terms of complexity. These reflect a progression of career development from self- and career-awareness to career exploration and then to career preparation. Third, the LCCE focuses on skill development in school, through infusion in academic classes and other inclusive settings, but also through home and community-based experiences.

Other authors have developed curricula that focus on functional skills for adult living. Cronin and Patton's Domains of Adulthood (1993) covered the areas of

TABLE 10.1 Example of Functional Skills Needed by Most Students with and without Disabilities

DOMAIN OF ADULT LIVING	EXAMPLE OF FUNCTIONAL SKILLS NEEDED FOR SUCCESS
Home Living	■ Cooking meals ■ Doing laundry ■ Cleaning one's home ■ Completing self care activities ■ Making simple repairs within the home
Community Use	■ Using public transportation ■ Safely crossing streets ■ Making purchases in community stores ■ Accessing services in the community (e.g., dentists, physicians, banks, cleaners, etc.) ■ Dressing appropriately for the weather
Employment	■ Reading and understanding a paycheck ■ Following posted rules ■ Following verbal or written directions ■ Using equipment safely ■ Receiving feedback and criticism
Financial Planning	■ Using an ATM or debit card ■ Carrying money safely ■ Reading and comparing prices on items ■ Reading and paying bills ■ Spending within one's means
Recreation and Leisure	■ Cooperating with others ■ Following rules ■ Using equipment correctly ■ Following safety precautions ■ Using functional reading or math
Health and Safety	■ Reading medicine bottles/dosages ■ Using a thermometer ■ Handling and storing food safely ■ Recognizing and responding to fire hazards ■ Distinguishing illnesses that require a doctor

employment/education, home and family, leisure pursuits, community involvement, physical/emotional health, and *personal responsibility and relationships.* These six curriculum domains were then further delineated through a set of sub-domains or competency areas. For example, the domain of *home and family* addresses competencies related to *home management, financial management, family life,* and *child rearing.* The domain of *leisure pursuits* is further sub-divided into the competency areas of *indoor activities,*

■ ■ ■ ■ ■ ▬▬▬▬▬▬▬▬▬▬▬▬▬▬▬▬▬▬▬▬▬▬▬▬▬▬▬▬▬▬▬▬▬▬▬▬▬▬▬

SIDEBAR 10.1
SPOTLIGHT ON HISTORY: DONN BROLIN

The late Donn Brolin was a true pioneer in the conceptualization and design of curricular content for students with disabilities in transition to adulthood. Prior to his death in 1996, Brolin was professor emeritus of educational and counseling psychology at the University of Missouri at Columbia. Dr. Brolin received his Ph.D. in special education and rehabilitation psychology from the University Wisconsin-Madison, and he served as the first president of the Division on Career Development and Transition (DCDT) of the Council for Exceptional Children. In 1990, he received the prestigious J. E. Wallace Wallin Education of Handicapped Children award from CEC, which is awarded to one professional each year who has made outstanding contributions to the education of students with disabilities.

Brolin's major contribution to the field of special education was the development of the Life Centered Career Education (LCCE) Curriculum. The LCCE Curriculum addresses functional adult living needs in three curriculum domains: Daily Living Skills, Personal-Social Skills, and Occupational Guidance and Preparation. Each domain, in turn, is divided into competencies, for a total of twenty-two competencies across the three domains. For example, under the curriculum domain of *Daily Living Skills*, a competency is *managing personal finances*. Each competency is then further delineated into subcompetencies that increase in complexity. For example, the subcompetencies under the aforementioned competency of *managing personal finances* include (1) making change, (2) making responsible expenditures, (3) keeping basic financial records, (4) calculating and paying taxes, (5) using credit responsibly, and (6) using banking services. The entire curriculum is constructed to assist secondary students with disabilities to master these competencies and subcompetencies in order to be better prepared for adult living.

The LCCE was one of the earliest curriculum models that directly addressed the needs of adult living and attempted to teach these important skills directly. The LCCE was recently revised and is available through CEC (www.cec.org). Thanks to the pioneering work of Donn Brolin, educators of transition-aged students continue to include important skills necessary for successful adult living in the curriculum.

▬▬▬

outdoor activities, community/neighborhood activities, travel, and *entertainment*. Similarly, the remaining four domain areas are further defined and described through competency categories. Smith and Schloss's Community-referenced Curriculum (1988) addressed the areas of *work, leisure and play, consumer, education and rehabilitation*, and *transportation*. Dever's Community Living Skills Taxonomy (1988) addressed the areas of *personal maintenance and development, homemaking and community life, vocational, leisure*, and *travel*. The common feature of these various curricula is that they have all attempted to clarify functional skills that students in transition need to learn to assist them in living successful adult lives (Patton, Cronin, & Wood, 1999).

Consider This!   Think back to your own high school experience. As you look back to this time in your life, what were some of the more functional skills that you learned and that you still use on a regular basis? Where did you learn these skills (e.g., within a class at school, with your friends in the community, or from your family)? What skills did you learn during high school that you consider of limited or no use to you now?

CURRICULUM STANDARDS AND INFUSION OF FUNCTIONAL SKILLS

Weymeyer and colleagues (2004) point out that the context for curriculum development for students within the special education system has changed dramatically over the past several years. First, the 1997 amendments to IDEA (P.L. 105-17) required that all IEPs for identified students contain statements about how students' disabilities affected their participation in the general education curriculum (614[d]). The reauthorization, Individuals with Disabilities Education Improvement Act of 2004 (H.R. 1350), specifies, more broadly, participation in general education programs (614[a]). As Weymeyer and colleagues (2004) point out, the intent of the former was to ensure that students with disabilities were not excluded from participation in the general curriculum or from curricular reform efforts. IDEA 2004 could be interpreted to be more inclusive of all program curricula. The requirements that all students, including those with severe disabilities, participate in state assessments are further evidence of this intent. Second, states have established academic standards that specify skills to be mastered at different grade levels within the major academic domains. These standards provide direction for curriculum development and the basis for state academic assessments. These standards also provide the basis for the preparation and certification of teachers, in accordance with the No Child Left Behind Act.

Table 10.2 lists the academic areas for which standards have been written or are in preparation for the Commonwealth of Pennsylvania as of December 2005 (www.pde.state.pa.us). The categories of standards listed in Table 10.2 are representative of those in other states and provide an indication of the academic areas that are typically addressed. Also shown in Table 10.2 are the three options for the assessment of student mastery of the specified state academic standards. As indicated by this table, the requirement for curriculum to address state academic standards and for students to be tested to determine the impact of the standards-based curriculum affect *all* students with disabilities, including those with severe and multiple disabilities.

The impact of these curricular reform efforts is positive in that high expectations are held for students with disabilities and they are expected to be included in the general education curriculum. On the other hand, these reforms have also made it more difficult for educators to teach the functional life skills mentioned earlier, as the demands of addressing state academic standards dictate that such instruction takes precedence (Wehman, 2001).

Consider how different students may be affected by the standards-based curriculum requirements. Students who require minor accommodations to access the general education curriculum can do so with little adaptation to the method of instruction or content. For these students, functional daily living skills are typically taught by the family and are not addressed as part of the general education curriculum. These students are mostly involved with academic subjects and, in many cases,

TABLE 10.2 Sample State Academic Standards and Options for Assessment

Academic Standards
Listed below are categories for state academic standards for the Commonwealth of Pennsylvania. All areas are final except where noted.

- Arts and humanities
- Career education and work (in progress)
- Civics and government
- Economics
- Environment and ecology
- Family and consumer sciences
- Geography
- Health, safety, and physical education
- History
- Mathematics
- Reading, writing, speaking, and listening
- Science and technology
- World languages (in progress)

Options for Assessment of Mastery of the Standards

1. State assessment process with no modifications or accommodations
2. State assessment process with accommodations for documented disabilities, including quiet testing environment, extended time for completion of the test, use of calculators, etc.
3. State alternative assessment process designed for students with the most severe disabilities, typically limited to approximately 1% of the school-aged population. These assessments test functional demonstrations of skills that are linked conceptually to the essence of state academic standards.

are preparing for postsecondary education. On the other hand, students with very severe intellectual and/or multiple disabilities are typically not involved in the general education academic curriculum at the high school level. These students must be taught functional skills that will allow them to live, work, and use the community with support upon exiting high school. Often, these students are involved with community-based instruction that allows them to experience the actual cues and conditions that exist in community environments such as work places, stores, and restaurants (Rose, Rainforth, & Steere, 2003; Steere, Rose, & Fishbaugh, 1999). For these students, the community is, in essence, an extension of the school, and inclusion efforts must be pursued within that context (Steere et al., 1999). For a third group of students, those who have moderate disabilities and are continuing to be taught content that is directly related to state academic standards but who require more substantial modifications to the curriculum, the challenge is somewhat more complex. These are students who may not aspire to postsecondary education and who will require functional skills to be taught directly. They are frequently several grade levels behind in their progress, yet continue with academic subject areas.

Patton and colleagues (1999) specify three ways that life skills curricular content can be addressed within the curriculum. The first approach is to teach these skills within courses that specifically address the skills in question. For example, a course on personal finances can cover important skills for adult home and community living. The second two approaches attempt to integrate life skills topics within existing general education curricula. The *augmentation* method involves dedicating a portion of a class period to a functional life skills topic. For example, the last twenty minutes of a math class could be used to address personal finance. The *infusion* method involves connecting life skills topics to the content of general education curricula and then using these connections in a creative way to address functional life skills. In using this method, teachers analyze the content of the general education curriculum for *content referent*, which are key concepts, vocabulary, or skills that are addressed. These content referents are then linked to possible life skills topics within specified domains of adult living. Table 10.3 provides a sample of this connection process. In recommending the infusion method, Patton and colleagues (1999) note that this method is preferred when students are locked into a prescribed curriculum sequence and have limited opportunities for specific coursework in functional life skills. They also caution that the infusion method has the limitation that life skills may not be comprehensively covered.

PERSPECTIVES OF BUSINESS AND INDUSTRY

Another perspective that is important in the curriculum design process is that of the business and industry community (Evers & Elksnin, 1998; U.S. Department of Labor, 1991). The U.S. Department of Labor initiative entitled the Secretary's Commission

TABLE 10.3   Examples of Infusion of Life Skills Topics into General Education Curricula

Example #1:

Curriculum Content Area: History

Lesson Focus: History of civil rights movement, with a focus on the rights of minorities to vote

Content Referents: Voting, voter registration

Domains of Adult Living: Community participation (registering to vote, the voting process), leisure (reading a newspaper)

Example #2:

Curriculum Content Area: Math

Lesson Focus: Addition, subtraction, multiplication, and division using numbers in decimal form

Content Referents: Decimals, calculator use

Domain of Adult Living: Personal finances (checkbook balancing, reading bank statements, etc.), community participation (shopping)

TABLE 10.4   Skills and Competencies Recommended by the Secretary's Commission on Achieving Necessary Skills (SCANS)

Foundation Skills

1. Basic Skills—reading, writing, arithmetic, mathematics, listening, speaking
2. Thinking Skills—creative thinking, decision making, problem solving, seeing things in the mind's eye, knowing how to learn, reasoning
3. Personal Qualities—responsibility, self-esteem, sociability, self-management, integrity, honesty

Competencies

1. Resources—identifies, organizes, plans, and allocates: time, money, materials, facilities, human resources
2. Information—acquires and uses information: acquires and evaluates, organizes and maintains, interprets and communicates, uses computers
3. Systems—understands complex inter-relationships: understands systems, monitors and corrects performance, improves or designs systems
4. Technology—works with a variety of technologies: selects, applies, maintains, and troubleshoots equipment
5. Interpersonal—works with others: participates as a member of a team, teaches others new skills, serves clients and/or customers, exercises leadership, negotiates, works with diversity

on Achieving Necessary Skills (SCANS) resulted in recommendations for skills that students exiting high school should possess in order to be successful in a competitive labor market. These competencies or skills became the basis for educational reform legislation, including the Goals 2000 (P.L. 103-227) and the School-to-Work Opportunities Act (P.L. 103-239; Evers & Elksnin, 1998). Table 10.4 shows the SCANS components. The SCANS skills and competencies provide school personnel with valuable information about what business and industry is looking for in successful employees. Note that many of these skills are infused throughout typical general education curricular content areas and that many are developed longitudinally, beginning in the elementary grades and refined at higher grade levels.

Consider This!   Look over the SCANS list of skills and competencies, shown in Table 10.4. Now, consider how these skills are addressed at the elementary level within typical classrooms. How are these skills and competencies developed in typical youngsters? Now, consider the same question, but this time focus on typical high school students.

USING THE COMMUNITY FOR INSTRUCTION

For many transition-aged students, particularly those with more significant disabilities, community-based instruction is an essential component of their curriculum

(Johnson & Wehman, 2001; Wehman, 2001; Wehman & Targett, 2004). Several considerations for implementing community-based instruction are described below.

Develop Relationships with Community Businesses

Educators in school transition programs must first develop positive relationships with area business establishments. These relationships will tend to make the owners and staff of such businesses more receptive to having students frequent these locations for purposes of instruction. In some cases, this can also lead to potential work training or assessment sites for specific students. To develop a positive relationship, transition coordinators should make a point of visiting each business to introduce themselves and to leave written material that describes the structure and purposes of the school's transition program. In some school districts, these individuals are called job development specialists or employment specialists. A follow-up interview with a business owner may also be requested. Perhaps the best way to develop positive relationships with area businesses is to visit them on a regular basis so that school personnel and their students are recognized as "regulars" within these establishments.

Ensure Connection to the IEP

Community-based instruction should be listed as a necessary transition service in each student's IEP. (Refer back to Chapter 4 for a discussion of transition planning and the transition IEP.) It must be clarified to all members of the team that community-based instruction does not constitute merely "field trips," but instead is an integral part of each student's educational program. This also ensures accountability in terms of frequency and duration of community-based instruction.

Address Multiple Skills

Time in the community should be used wisely to address multiple skill areas identified in students' IEPs. Objectives related to money use, social interaction, mobility, positive behavior, and communication can all be addressed within a single visit to a local store to make a purchase. Teachers should record data on how students performed during community trips in relation to specific IEP goals and objectives. A key issue during such community-based instruction is to determine how students responded to cues and stimuli within community locations (Pancsofar & Steere, 1997). Because the ability to respond to social and environmental cues is an indicator of greater independence, instructors should note what salient cues were present, how students responded to these cues (if at all), and what intensity of prompting was necessary to assist the learner to respond correctly to the cues. Table 10.5 provides an example of this form of data recording.

Schedule Regular Instruction in the Community

Community-based instruction should be scheduled on a regular basis. Weekly instruction is a minimum for many students, and transition coordinators may need to increase this to more frequent instruction for specific students. Instruction that occurs

TABLE 10.5   Format for Recording Student Reactions to Cues during Community-Based Instruction

Name: Ryheed Washington

Objectives Addressed:

- During community-based instruction, Ryheed will make purchases up to $5.00 using the next dollar strategy, without prompts for three consecutive purchases.
- During community-based instruction, Ryheed will successfully cross the street without prompts, over five consecutive opportunities.
- During community-based instruction, Ryheed will interact appropriately with store clerks by saying "Hi" and "Thank you" and without screaming, for three consecutive opportunities.

Date: 10/25/05
Location: Dollar Store

CUES	REACTIONS	PROMPTING REQUIRED FOR SUCCESS
Cross walk signal	R. did not look at the signal	Verbal prompts necessary to get him to look
Cashier stating the amount due and the cash register display	R. looked at the price of one item only	Verbal prompts and gestural prompts toward the cash register display
Cashier saying "Thank you and have a good day!"	R. said "Thank you"	None needed

Notes:
This cashier recognizes us and seems to like Ryheed. Very positive response to our presence and willing to be patient as we teach him to count out the correct number of dollar bills.

less frequently than once per week is of limited utility, particularly for students with more severe disabilities who learn slowly and have poor generalization and maintenance skills.

Promote Inclusion in the Community

Finally, community-based instruction is not designed merely to teach students new skills and abilities. Rather, it is designed to promote the inclusion of students into their local communities (Storey, 2002). Such inclusion may lead to a more meaningful inclusion through employment or through more active participation in the community in adulthood. As students approach the transition to adulthood, educators must help students be included within the life of the school but also that of the larger community they will join upon graduation.

CHAPTER SUMMARY

This chapter has provided an overview of the issues that need to be taken into consideration in designing curricula for students in transition. It is essential that what students are learning is clearly leading toward the attainment of their desired postschool outcomes. Therefore, annual goals and short-term objectives on student IEPs must be clearly tied to the transition outcomes that have been established by the team, with the active participation of the student and family. All students in transition, not just those with more severe disabilities, need to master the functional life skills they will need for success in adult life. However, because curriculum reform efforts have resulted in the mandate for schools to address state academic standards, educators must be creative in either finding opportunities to teach important life skills directly or to infuse these topics into existing general education academic areas. We also discussed the perspectives of business and industry and what this segment of the adult world feels are important and necessary skills for students leaving high school to possess. Finally, we discussed the importance of community-based instruction for teaching necessary skills and for promoting community inclusion of students in transition.

APPLICATION ACTIVITIES

The application activities listed below are essential for your continued learning and skill development in transition planning. Each of the activities will require your time and energy, but will help you develop your professional skills in this area.

For Practice and Enhanced Understanding:

Find and download the state academic standards for high school students in your state. As you review these standards, note academic areas in which functional life skill areas are addressed or could be infused.

If you are currently teaching, review your own curricular content to identify where important life skills are or may be addressed. For elementary and middle school teachers, this may include skills that form the foundation for adult living skills. Do you teach these functional life skills directly or do you infuse them in more traditional educational curricula? If the latter, is enough practice provided that these skills are learned, maintained, and generalized?

For Your Portfolio:

If you are currently working with transition-aged students, determine where in their curriculum functional living skills are addressed. Are they addressed directly through course work or are they infused into academic curricula?

Conduct a survey of the community surrounding your school. What businesses are located within a reasonable distance from the school? If you have not done so, develop a transition program brochure to give to local businesses and then make introductory visits to explain the purpose of your transition program. Keep a record of whom specifically you spoke to, when you made the introductory visit, and what materials you left.

Design a form for use in assessing students during community-based instruction, using Table 10.5 as an example. Then, use this form consistently to track your students' progress on specific IEP objectives during community-based instruction. In particular, note their responses to natural cues and what level of prompting is necessary to elicit correct responses to these cues.

RESOURCES AND WEBSITES

The following resources and websites will allow you to extend your knowledge about curricula for students in transition. Consider including these resources in your professional portfolio.

Beach Center on Disabilities

Contact the Beach Center for information regarding the Self-Determined Learning Model of Instruction (SDLMI).
www.beachcenter.org

Division on Career Development and Transition (DCDT) of the Council for Exceptional Children (CEC)

Contact the DCDT for position statements and publications regarding best practices in transition.
www.dcdt.org

Council for Exceptional Children

Contact CEC for information about the Life Centered Career Education (LCCE) curriculum materials.
www.cec.sped.org

Secretary's Commission on Achieving Necessary Skills (SCANS)

Contact this website for more detailed information regarding the SCANS competencies.
wdr.doleta.gov/scans/

REFERENCES

Agran, M., Blanchard, C., & Wehmeyer, M. (2000). Promoting transition goals and self-determination through student self-directed learning: The self-determined learning model of instruction. *Education and Training in Mental Retardation and Developmental Disabilities, 35,* 351–364.

Agran, M., Sinclair, T., Alper, S., Cavin, M., Wehmeyer, M., & Hughes, C. (2005). Using self-monitoring to increase following-direction skills of students with moderate to severe disabilities in general education. *Education and Training in Developmental Disabilities, 40,* 3–13.

Agran, M., Swaner, J., & Snow, K. (1998). Work safety skills: A neglected curricular area. *Career Development for Exceptional Individuals, 21,* 33–44.

Baer, R., Flexer, R., & McMahan, R. (2005). Transition models and promising practices. In R. Flexer, T. Simmons, P. Luft, & R. Baer (Eds.), *Transition planning for secondary students with disabilities* (2nd ed.) (pp. 53–82). Upper Saddle River, NJ: Pearson Merrill Prentice Hall.

Benz, M., Lindstrom, L., & Yovanoff, P. (2000). Improving graduation and employment outcomes of students with disabilities: Predictive factors and student perspectives. *Exceptional Children, 66,* 509–529.

Brolin, D. (1997). *Life centered career education: A competency-based approach* (5th ed.). Reston, VA: Council for Exceptional Children (CEC).

Bouck, E. (2004). State of curriculum for secondary students with mild mental retardation. *Education and Training in Developmental Disabilities, 39,* 169–176.

Clark, G., Field, S., Patton, J., Brolin, D., & Sitlington, P. (1994). Life skills instruction: A necessary component for all students with disabilities: A position statement of the Division on Career Development and Transition. *Career Development for Exceptional Individuals, 17,* 125–134.

Council for Exceptional Children (CEC) Website. (2005). www.cec.sped.org.

Dever, R. (1988). *Community living: A taxonomy.* Washington, DC: American Association on Mental Retardation (AAMR).

Elksnin, N., & Elksnin, L. (1998). *Teaching occupational social skills.* Austin, TX: Pro-Ed.

Evers, R., & Elksnin, N. (1998). *Working with students with disabilities in vocational-technical settings.* Austin, TX: Pro-Ed.

Field, S., Martin, J., Miller, R., Ward, M., & Wehmeyer, M. (1998). Self-determination for persons with disabilities: A position statement of the Division on Career Development and Transition. *Career Development for Exceptional Individuals, 21,* 113–128.

Grigal, M., & Neubert, D. (2004). Parents' in-school values and post-school expectations for transition-aged youth with disabilities. *Career Development for Exceptional Individuals, 27,* 65–85.

Hanley-Maxwell, C., & Collet-Klingenberg, L. (2004). Preparing students for employment. In P. Wehman and J. Kregel (Eds.), *Functional curriculum for elementary, middle, and secondary age students with special needs* (pp. 205–243). Austin, TX: Pro-Ed.

Hitchcock, C., Meyer, A., Rose, D., & Jackson, R. (2002). Providing new access to the general curriculum: Universal design for learning. *Teaching Exceptional Children, 35,* 8–17.

Hughes, C., Copeland, S., Agran, M., Wehmeyer, M., Rodi, M., & Presley, J. (2002). Using self-monitoring to improve performance in general education high school classes. *Education and Training in Developmental Disabilities, 37,* 262–272.

Individuals with Disabilities Education Act Amendments of 1997 (P.L. 105-17), *et seq.* § 16(d).

Individuals with Disabilities Education Improvement Act of 2004 (H.R. 1350), *et seq.* § 16(a).

Inge, K., Wehman, P., Clees, T., & Dymond, S. (1996). Transition from school to adulthood. In P. McGlaughlin & P. Wehman (Eds.), *Mental retardation and developmental disabilities* (2nd ed.) (pp. 69–84). Austin, TX: Pro-Ed.

Johnson, S., & Wehman, P. (2001). Teaching for transition. In P. Wehman (Ed.), *Life beyond the classroom: Transition strategies for young people with disabilities* (3rd ed.) (pp. 145–170). Baltimore: Pro-Ed.

Kohler, P. (1994). On-the-job training: A curricular approach to employment. *Career Development for Exceptional Individuals, 17,* 29–40.

Lindstrom, L., Benz, M., & Doren, B. (2004). Expanding career options for young women with learning disabilities. *Career Development for Exceptional Individuals, 27,* 43–63.

McGlashing-Johnson, J., Agran, M., Sitlington, P., Cavin, M., & Wehmeyer, M. (2003). Enhancing the job performance of youth with moderate to severe cognitive disabilities using the Self-determined Learning Model of Instruction. *Research and Practice for Persons with Severe Disabilities, 28,* 194–204.

Palmer, S., Wehmeyer, M., Gipson, K., & Agran, M. (2004). Promoting access to the general curriculum by teaching self-determination skills. *Exceptional Children, 70,* 427–439.

Pancsofar, E., & Steere, D. (1997). The C.A.P.A.B.L.E. process: Critical dimensions of community-based assessment. *Journal of Vocational Rehabilitation, 8,* 99–108.

Patton, J., Cronin, M., & Wood, S. J. (1999). *Infusing real-life topics into existing curricula: Recommended procedures and instructional examples for the elementary, middle, and high school levels.* Austin, TX: Pro-Ed.

Pennsylvania Department of Education Website (2005). www.pde.state.pa.us.

Rose, E., Rainforth, B., & Steere, D. (2003). Guiding principles for the education of youth with severe and multiple disabilities. In F. Obiakor, C. Utley, & A. Rotatori (Eds.), *Advances in special education: Psychology of effective education for learners with exceptionalities* (pp. 155–180). Boston: JAI Press.

Sitlington, P., Neubert, D., Begun, W., Lombard, R., & Leconte, P. (1996). *Assess for success: Handbook on transition assessment.* Reston, VA: Council for Exceptional Children.

Smith, M., & Schloss, P. (1988). Teaching to transition. In P. Schloss, C. Hughes, & M. Smith (Eds.), *Community integration for persons with mental retardation* (pp. 1–16). Austin, TX: Pro-Ed.

Steere, D., & Cavaiuolo, D. (2002). Connecting outcomes, goals, and objectives in transition planning. *Teaching Exceptional Children, 34,* 54–59.

Steere, D., Rose, E., & Fishbaugh, M. S. (1999). Integration in the secondary school for students with severe disabilities. In M. Coutinho & A. Repp (Eds.), *Inclusion: The integration of children with disabilities* (pp. 333–365). Atlanta: Wadsworth Publishing Co.

Storey, K. (2002). Curriculum design and programmatic issues involving youth in transition. In K. Storey, P. Bates, & D. Hunter (Eds.), *The road ahead: Transition to adult life for persons with disabilities* (pp. 1–5). St. Augustine, FL: TRN.

U.S. Department of Labor (1991). *What work requires of schools: A SCANS report for America 2000.* Washington, DC: Author.

Wehman, P. (2001). *Life beyond the classroom: Transition strategies for young people with disabilities* (3rd ed.). Baltimore: Brookes.

Wehman, P., & Targett, P. S. (2004). Principles of curriculum design: Road to transition from school to adulthood. In P. Wehman and J. Kregel (Eds.), *Functional curriculum for elementary, middle, and secondary age students with special needs* (2nd ed.) (pp. 1–36). Austin, TX: Pro-Ed.

Wehmeyer, M., & Schwartz, M. (1998). The self-determination focus of transition goals for students with mental retardation. *Career Development for Exceptional Individuals, 21,* 75–86.

Wehmeyer, M., Field, S., Doren, B., Jones, B., & Mason, C. (2004). Self-determination and student involvement in standards-based reform. *Exceptional Children, 70,* 413–425.

Wehmeyer, M., Lance, D., & Bashinski, S. (2002). Promoting access to the general curriculum for students with mental retardation: A multi-level model. *Education and Training in Developmental Disabilities, 37,* 223–234.

Wehmeyer, M., Lattin, D., & Agran, M. (2001). Achieving access to the general curriculum for students with mental retardation: A curriculum decision-making model. *Education and Training in Mental Retardation and Developmental Disabilities, 36,* 327–342.

CHAPTER 11

RECREATION, LEISURE, AND HEALTHY LIVING FOR STUDENTS IN TRANSITION

CHAPTER OBJECTIVES

Upon completion of this chapter, you will be able to

1. describe recreation and leisure activities that exist within most communities and that may be appropriate for students of transition age.

2. describe the benefits of participation in recreation and leisure activities.

3. assist students in deciding on recreation and leisure activities that are right for them and that can contribute to their overall quality of life.

4. assist students in transition to develop patterns of behavior that are associated with a healthy lifestyle.

5. assist students in transition to develop appropriate recreation and leisure activities at home and in the community and to develop healthy adult lifestyles.

KEY TOPICS TO LOOK FOR IN THIS CHAPTER . . .

- Options for recreation and leisure: As we will discuss in this chapter, planning for recreation and leisure for a healthy adult life is often neglected during transition planning. In this chapter, look for the range of potential options for recreation and leisure for young people.

- Self-determination and healthy living: Students with disabilities often lack the knowledge and skills that they need to live healthy adult lives. Look for information about healthy living that young people in transition need to learn and ways to increase their knowledge so that they have greater control over this aspect of their adult lives.

In this book, as in many texts and articles about transition to adulthood, there is a strong focus on transition to employment in the community. This emphasis is logical: employment and a satisfying career are key to a successful and fulfilled adult life. However, the development of satisfying recreation and leisure outlets is equally important, although this is a neglected area in many transition programs (McNulty, Mascia, Rocchio, & Rothstein, 1995; Strand & Kreiner, 2005). Recreation activities and leisure time provide a balance to our working life and allow us to focus our creativity and mental and physical energy to explore new and exciting areas outside of our careers. These activities also can play a major role in helping us to develop and maintain healthy lifestyles in adulthood and to offset the stresses of the workplace. Recreation and leisure activities are also opportunities for social interaction with current friends and potential friends. As shown in Table 11.1, recreation and leisure activities have numerous benefits. (As you read this chapter, please keep in mind that it is good practice to consult the family or the family physician as to the health consequences of an individual engaging in sports or fitness activities.)

The importance of recreation and leisure and their relationship to healthy living cannot be overemphasized. Certain recreation and leisure activities contribute to overall fitness for adults in our society. The development of such recreation and leisure activities for young people in transition is particularly important in light of research that indicates poorer cardiovascular fitness levels in individuals with mental retardation (Gillespie, 2003). Kozub (2003) reviewed research that indicates that, as a group, individuals with disabilities are less fit than their non-disabled counterparts and have fewer opportunities to participate in sports programs.

In this chapter, we will discuss the development of recreation and leisure opportunities for students with disabilities who are in transition to adulthood. We will also describe ways to assist these students to develop patterns of adult living that are healthy and safe. We will discuss strategies for helping young people to choose and participate in recreation and leisure activities that are best matched to their interests and abilities and that help them be included with others without disabilities.

TABLE 11.1 Potential Benefits of Recreation and Leisure for Adults with Disabilities

---

Recreation and leisure activities can provide adults with disabilities opportunities to:

- release physical energy and stress
- learn new skills and develop new abilities
- meet new people and possibly make friends who have common interests
- contribute to a group effort or to the betterment of the local community/neighborhood
- fill time in a more productive or interesting manner
- relax and find enjoyment
- spend money for meaningful or enjoyable pursuits
- balance or offset one's working and domestic responsibilities
- achieve better physical health or conditioning
- be included in community activities and to be recognized within the community

---

RESEARCH RELATED TO RECREATION, LEISURE, AND HEALTHY LIVING FOR PEOPLE WITH DISABILITIES

A number of authors have written about the importance of healthy diet, exercise, and outlets for recreation and leisure for healthy adult living. Strand and Kreiner (2005) described the role of recreation and leisure as key ingredients to a healthy and fulfilling adult life and the need to incorporate student choices into the selection of recreation and leisure activities. They also recommend that connections with community recreation and leisure activities should begin well before students exit the special education system to increase the likelihood that they will have the chance to participate in inclusive settings with adequate supports. Yu, Spevack, Hiebert, Martin, Goodman, Martin, Harapiak, and Martin (2002) compared happiness indices during work and leisure activities for individuals with severe versus profound disabilities, and found that both groups showed greater happiness during leisure activities than they did during work activities. The importance of exercise is particularly important for students of transition age. Research suggests that students with intellectual disabilities have poorer cardiovascular fitness than their non-disabled peers and tend to have fewer opportunities to engage in activities requiring vigorous exercise. Gillespie (2003) compared the cardiovascular fitness levels of thirty children with mental retardation and thirty without disabilities and found that the students without disabilities had significantly greater levels of aerobic fitness. The author concludes that current opportunities, such as adaptive physical education and Special Olympics, are insufficient to help young adults with intellectual disabilities maintain adequate fitness levels and avoid a sedentary lifestyle. Kozub (2003) investigated the activity patterns of seven adolescents with mental retardation over a seven-day period and found that they engaged in short bouts of movement that may be insufficient to affect cardiovascular health. The lack of movement may also be influenced by the lack of intrinsic motivation to engage in more vigorous exercise, and movement may in fact decrease with age, as young adults establish a sedentary lifestyle. Braunschweig, Gomez, Sheean, Tomey, Rimmer, and Heller (2004) assessed 48 community-dwelling adults with Down syndrome and found that 89 percent were overweight or obese, 54 percent had large waist circumferences, and that none met the guidelines for fruit and vegetable intake. Yamaki (2005) measured the prevalence of obesity, overweight, or healthy weights among adults with intellectual disabilities, using data from the National Health Interview Survey from 1985–2000. Body mass index was used as the measure of weight status for this study. The percentage of adults with intellectual disabilities in the obese category was higher than the general population and increased over the time frame of the study. A smaller proportion of adults with intellectual disabilities kept their weight in the healthy range than did individuals without disabilities. The authors offer four possible explanations for these findings: (1) people with intellectual disabilities may be less conscious of health risks; (2) they may have fewer opportunities to gain such knowledge; (3) people with intellectual disabilities are often of lower income status and therefore may eat less healthy foods; and (4) less restrictive community settings present increased choices for people with intellectual disabilities, including non-healthy fast food diets. Ayvazoglu, Ratcliffe, and Kozub (2004) summarized concerns about the lack of movement opportunities for students with intellectual disabilities and their resulting sedentary lifestyles as they enter adulthood. These authors also provide helpful suggestions for using the IEP planning process to discuss ways to increase students' exposure to a wider variety of activities at an earlier age and to collaborate with the family to address this important area.

The concerns raised by these studies have resulted in research into ways to improve the cardiovascular fitness of individuals with disabilities, particularly intellectual disabilities. Rimmer, Heller, Wang, and Valerio (2004) evaluated the effects of an exercise program on fifty-two adults with Down syndrome. The program consisted of thirty minutes of cardiovascular exercise and fifteen minutes of strength training, three times a week for twelve weeks. Compared to a control group, the participants made significant improvements in cardiovascular fitness, strength, and endurance. Also, a slight but significant reduction in body weight was reported. In a related study, Heller, Hsieh, and Rimmer (2004) measured the attitudinal and psychosocial outcomes of a fitness and health program with fifty-three adults with Down syndrome. The program consisted of the same exercise as that reported in the previous study coupled with a health education component to teach participants the benefits of exercise, to increase their self-efficacy, and to help them set goals and establish action plans. The authors reported three significant differences in attitudes that they attributed to the intervention: (1) the experimental group perceived fewer barriers to exercise; (2) these participants reported higher levels of outcome expectancy; and (3) they reported increased confidence in their ability to perform exercise. The participants also reported increased levels of life satisfaction.

Several articles have described programs or strategies for increasing recreation and leisure activities for individuals with disabilities. Schleien and Ray (1997) described Minnesota's SCOLA Project (School + Community = Opportunity for Leisure Activity) and the steps that were taken to build community collaboration for increased leisure activities for young people with disabilities. They recommend that leisure education be incorporated into the transition planning process and that leisure programming be provided in typical community recreation environments. They also indicate that collaboration among schools, families, and community agencies is essential for designing recreation programs that have positive health and other benefits. Stopka, Pomeranz, Siders, Dykes, and Goodman (1999) describe a special physical education program at the University of Florida that conducts a program of health, fitness, sports, and recreation with age peers with mental retardation. Programs such as this, which use university settings to address the needs of young people with disabilities, are an effective way to facilitate interaction among people with and without disabilities while increasing recreation and leisure outlets. McNulty and colleagues (1995) described 5 guidelines for establishing recreation and leisure options for individuals with dual sensory impairments: (1) establish communication and rapport; (2) use person centered planning as an assessment approach; (3) assess community leisure and recreation opportunities; (4) provide appropriate instruction;

and (5) identify and furnish supports. Ohtake (2004) reviewed standards that any game modification should meet to ensure participation of students with severe and multiple disabilities in team sports games. These guidelines are that activities should (1) be challenging, (2) have adequate safety provisions, (3) minimize deviations to integrity to the intent and format of the game, (4) avoid undue burdens of cost and time, and (5) ensure that the participation of the student with disabilities is an essential part of the game.

Finally, several authors have described the importance of inclusive recreation and leisure activities (Moon, 1994; Schleien, Green, & Stone, 2003; Walker & Shoultz, www.open.org). Walker and Shoultz (www.open.org) described five elements that are important to the promotion of social inclusion through recreation. These elements are (1) the involvement with other children with the assistance of a facilitator, (2) modeling for others by the facilitator, (3) backing off to let things happen on their own, (4) observing interactions within the context of activities, and (5) providing opportunities for friendships to occur. Moon (1994) described nine elements that are important to the design of inclusive recreation programs:

- The enjoyable use of free time;
- Choice;
- Age appropriateness;
- Family involvement;
- Professional roles to support recreation efforts;
- Leisure education to increase recreation skills;
- Focus on physical fitness and motor skills;
- Partial participation; and
- Focus on peer relationships.

Schleien and colleagues (2003) described three levels of inclusion (physical inclusion, functional inclusion, and the highest level, social inclusion) and stated that both intrinsic and extrinsic strategies may be used to promote social inclusion through recreation. Intrinsic strategies are those designed to promote change within the individual (e.g., to teach new recreation skills) while extrinsic strategies include those designed to change the recreation environment (e.g., the creation of a Circle of Friends). These authors also describe the important role that families play in facilitating social inclusion through recreation.

Together, the studies described above highlight three important issues. First, there are numerous benefits of recreation and leisure activities in adult life. Second, individuals with disabilities are frequently lacking in either skills or in opportunities to participate in such activities. Third, direct efforts to plan for the participation of young people with disabilities in inclusive recreation and leisure activities can result in increased social inclusion and the development of potential friendships. See Sidebar 11.1 for the story of Stuart Schleien, a leader in the development of recreation and leisure activities for people with disabilities.

■ ■ ■ ■ ■

SIDEBAR 11.1
SPOTLIGHT ON HISTORY: STUART SCHLEIEN

Stuart J. Schleien, Ph.D., CTRS/CPRP, is a Professor and Department Head of Recreation, Parks, and Tourism at the University of North Carolina at Greensboro since 1997. Dr. Schleien has been a leader in the development of quality recreation and leisure activities for people with disabilities. In particular, he has been a consistent advocate for the creation of inclusive recreational activities that result in opportunities for meaningful friendships to occur between people with and without disabilities. Dr. Schleien is a Certified Therapeutic Recreation Specialist and has used his expertise in this area to advocate for change at multiple levels to allow inclusive recreation and leisure activities to occur. He has published extensively on recreation and friendship skills development and the social inclusion of individuals with disabilities in community settings. He has written seven books and over one hundred journal articles and book chapters on these topics. His most recent text, entitled *Community Recreation and People with Disabilities: Strategies for Inclusion* (2nd edition), is used extensively to educate professionals and families about the creation of inclusive recreation opportunities. Throughout his career, Dr. Schleien has presented extensively throughout the United States and abroad.

Source: From the website of the University of North Carolina at Greensboro, www.uncg.edu

RECREATION AND LEISURE FOR STUDENTS IN TRANSITION

As shown in Table 11.1, there are numerous potential benefits for engaging in recreation and leisure activities. Leisure activities may take place within the community or they may occur in the home. In this section, we will discuss recreation and leisure options that may be most beneficial for students with disabilities.

Options for Community Recreation

Recreation options within most communities are varied and numerous. A perusal of most local newspapers will reveal a wide range of possible community recreation and leisure activities that are available to local citizens, including those with disabilities. For example, Table 11.2 shows recreation and leisure activities identified by one of the authors by reviewing the local paper for the local town surrounding area. Although some of the events listed in Table 11.2 are clearly seasonal activities, it is likely that a similar range of activities is available at any given time of year. Also, additional activities were not listed in this particular issue of the local paper, but do take place during a typical week (e.g., attending school sporting events, local bingo games, etc.). Another option is to consult with the local Independent Living Center, if there is one in your community, to find out what they offer or would recommend.

TABLE 11.2   Community Recreation and Leisure Activities Listed in
The Pocono Record, **October 31, 2004**

- Holiday parade
- Golfing
- Hunting
- Fishing
- Leaf watching
- Hiking
- Plays in local theaters
- Movies
- Restaurants (going out for breakfast, lunch, or dinner)
- Musical concerts
- Shopping at local stores and the mall
- Arts and crafts festival
- Dance performance
- Skating
- Art exhibit
- Local performers (clown, singer, musical group)
- Tournament baseball league
- Book show
- Recreational soccer league
- Recreational bowling league
- Recreational basketball league
- Recreational volleyball league
- Ski club (announcement for upcoming event)
- Wrestling tryouts for school (announcement for)
- Cheerleading tryouts for school (announcement for)
- Political party reception at a local VFW
- Gymnastics school (children through adult)
- AAA seminar on how to pack and prepare for a vacation trip
- Local orchard sale on pumpkins, potatoes, squash, etc.
- Wellness and sports center
- Local museums and historical sites

Table 11.3 shows a chart of potential activities that appeared in a publication that was developed in New Hampshire for parents of students with disabilities (Hackett, 1994). This table is comprehensive and allows students and families to indicate what activities young people have tried or would like to try. This is an excellent planning tool to promote the systematic selection of community recreation and leisure activities that will best meet students' needs, interests, and preferences.

Dymond (2004) describes the importance of teaching skills for community participation within the context of a functional curriculum for students with disabilities.

TABLE 11.3 Chart of Potential Recreation and Leisure Activities

STARTER LIST OF COMMUNITY RECREATION OPPORTUNITIES

ACTIVITY	PARTICIPATES NOW	HAS PARTICIPATED	WOULD LIKE TO TRY	NOT INTERESTED
Sports/Outdoors/Exercise				
Aerobics				
Archery				
Backpacking/camping				
Badminton				
Basketball				
Bicycling				
Bowling				
Canoeing				
Field hockey				
Fishing				
Football				
Golf				
Gymnastics				
Hiking				
Horseback riding				
Horseshoes				
Hunting				
Ice hockey				
Jogging/running				
Judo/Karate/martial arts				
Lacrosse				
Mountain climbing				
Racquetball				
Sailing				
Skating				
Skiing (downhill)				
Skiing (cross country)				

TABLE 11.3   Continued

ACTIVITY	PARTICIPATES NOW	HAS PARTICIPATED	WOULD LIKE TO TRY	NOT INTERESTED
Soccer				
Softball				
Squash				
Swimming				
T-Ball				
Tennis				
Volleyball				
Walking				
Weight training				
Voga				
Other:				
Dance				
Aerobic				
Ballet				
Folk				
Jazz				
Modern				
Square				
Tap				
Other:				
Arts/Crafts/Hobbies				
Birdwatching				
Calligraphy				
Carpentry				
Ceramics				

(continued)

TABLE 11.3   Continued

ACTIVITY	PARTICIPATES NOW	HAS PARTICIPATED	WOULD LIKE TO TRY	NOT INTERESTED
Collecting (stamps, coins)				
Cooking				
Crocheting				
Drawing				
Gardening				
Knitting				
Latchhook				
Listening to music				
Painting				
Photography				
Playing instruments				
Pottery				
Reading				
Sculpting				
Singing				
Woodcarving				
Writing (stories, poems)				
Other:				
Games				
Billiards/pool				
Bingo				
Cards				
Checkers				
Chess				
Crossword puzzles				
Dominoes				
Ping pong				

TABLE 11.3 Continued

ACTIVITY	PARTICIPATES NOW	HAS PARTICIPATED	WOULD LIKE TO TRY	NOT INTERESTED
Puzzles				
Scrabble				
Video games				
Other:				
Trips/Social Events				
Barbecues/picnics				
Concerts				
Cultural				
Historic				
Movies				
Restaurants				
Shopping				
Sporting events				
Other:				

Source: From *Everybody Belongs: Tips for Including Your Child in Community Recreation* by Louise Kennedy Hackett, 1994. Copyright New Hampshire Developmental Disabilities Council. Reprinted by permission.

She lists eight categories of non-work activities in which individuals typically engage in their local communities. These are:

- Going to restaurants/eateries
- Going to grocery stores
- Shopping at retail stores, such as clothing, drug, sporting goods, music, video, pet, and toy and hobby stores
- Using services such as banks, salons (hair and nail), dry cleaners, laundromats, and physicians
- Using public facilities, such as libraries, churches, and post offices
- Using recreation facilities, such as the YMCA, fitness centers, museums, skating rinks, movie theaters, and arcades
- Volunteer work, such as Meals on Wheels, Red Cross, and United Way
- Transportation, including school buses, public buses, taxis, trains/subways, bicycle, walking, riding in or driving cars

Readers should note how many of the activities that Dymond (2004) lists are ones that may be enjoyable to most people, that is, are recreation and leisure activities. It should also be noted that the ability to travel and move about one's local community to engage in activities such as these is a major factor that contributes to the sense of self-determination for young people in transition (West, Wittig, & Dowdy, 2004).

West (2001) cautions that, too often, people with disabilities have been restricted to recreation and leisure activities that are either segregated or focused on a narrow range of activities such as bowling, swimming, or arts and crafts. These may certainly be appropriate activities, but only if people *choose* to participate in them. West goes on to point out that many people with disabilities often have limited experiences and repertoires of skills to make such choices. Because of this limited exposure, West suggests the following considerations in helping people with disabilities select and engage in leisure activities of their choice:

- People with disabilities may need to experiment and experience a range of different leisure and recreation activities before making choices about particular preferences.
- A range of both group and solitary activities should be offered.
- It is important to remember that people with disabilities do not have to be particularly good at an activity in order to participate, as long as adaptations to the activities are acceptable to other participants.
- People may certainly choose to participate in segregated recreation and leisure activities, but they should be afforded the opportunity to participate in the same or similar activities in an integrated context.

Consider This!   What community recreation and leisure activities have you participated in during the past month? Look back over your calendar and make a list of all activities during this time period, and then categorize them according to the type of recreation and leisure activity (for example, watching sporting events, hiking, outdoor sports, etc.). Now, as you look back over this list of activities in which you have participated, how many of them do you remember specifically being positive or enjoyable events? Why were these events so positive that you remember them specifically?

Sue Anne

While she was in high school, Sue Anne's recreation and leisure activities were typical of others her age: she hung out with her best friends, went shopping, and participated in extracurricular events through her school. She also did many things with her family, including going out to dinner, going to movies, shopping, and taking family day trips and vacations. She was also involved in her church. As Sue Anne made the transition to college, her recreation and leisure activities focused more on campus events. She joined a student organization for early childhood education majors, and through that organization she participated in local fundraising and service activities. She also made new friends, with whom she would go shopping, go to sporting events on campus, and meet at the college fitness center to work out together. When she went home for the weekend or during holidays, she would continue to engage in community recreation and leisure activities with her family.

Mike

For some time, Mike has been involved in community recreational activities with his family and relatives. He shops at the mall, goes to the local park, and eats out at McDonald's. He also goes to community fairs, goes to movies with his family, and participates in therapeutic horseback riding. Mike participates in a softball league for people with disabilities, and he is involved with his church and in activities that are sponsored through the church. Although Mike's family is satisfied with his involvement in these activities, they have a natural concern about who will support his involvement in the future when he moves into supported living or when they are unable to take him to community events. For now, however, they know that Mike enjoys these varied activities, because he is clearly more relaxed during these outings and because he looks forward to them.

Options for Recreation in the Home

Recreation options within the home are equally important. These activities allow recreation to occur when people are alone or with others, and they typically require less expenditure of time, money, or energy than do some community recreation activities. These activities allow people to "regenerate" themselves physically and mentally and to engage in unique and interesting pursuits. Table 11.4 lists leisure and recreation activities that may occur in the home. Many of these activities are potential recreation and leisure outlets for young people with disabilities.

Francois is in his fifties and has mental retardation requiring extensive supports. He has a complex seizure disorder and he is hemiplegic on his left side. Francois has limited verbal language, consisting of a few words in English and French, which are reflective of his French-Canadian family ties. Francois lives in a group home with three other people. He attends a rehabilitation facility (sheltered workshop) during the day. When he is home, Francois is never at a loss for what to do. His favorite activity is rug-hooking, and he has developed an effective method of holding the rug pattern down with his left arm and hand, thereby freeing up his

TABLE 11.4 Leisure and Recreation Activities That May Take Place in the Home

■ Watching television	■ Exploring the Internet
■ Listening to music	■ Drawing or painting
■ Playing an instrument or singing	■ Building models or other craft activities
■ Cooking	■ Exercising
■ Gardening	■ Playing video games
■ Reading	■ Collecting objects with a common theme
■ Playing cards or other games	■ Knitting, weaving, or crocheting
■ Conversing with a friend, either in person, by telephone, or through email	■ Sewing
	■ Decorating for holidays or other events

right hand to insert strands of yarn and to hook them. He is proud of his rugs, which he makes from kits, and his room has several on the floor. Francois is also active in his church, and non-disabled members of the parish have made it their responsibility to take turns picking him up at the group home to drive him to service on Sundays. Overall, Francois has a satisfying and fulfilling life of recreation and leisure.

Friends and Community Connections

Condeluci (1996) argued that "... relationships become the key element to interdependence and a tangible outgrowth in our ability to go beyond difference" (p. xxxv). Connections to other people within our workplaces and communities are an important element to an overall quality of life for most people (Hughes, Copeland, Fowler, and Church-Pupke, 2002). For most people, satisfying relationships with family and friends are essential ingredients to a happy and fulfilled life, or what Powell (2004) refers to as the "American Dream." Friendships cannot be taught or arranged, but can only evolve through reciprocal and longitudinal interactions and through participation in activities of mutual interest. Clearly, engagement in recreation and leisure activities is one important avenue to the development of potential friendships.

Most people who live within a particular community for an extended period of time start to develop connections to their communities. These connections need not be extensive, but they should occur with regularity. Typically, one begins to be recognized as a "regular" within certain community stores, restaurants, and other locations. When people are recognized by others in the community, a sense of belonging can occur, that is, a sense of membership and importance within the community. Feeling connected or accepted can, in turn, contribute to one's self esteem (Chandler & Pankaskie, 2004). The point here is that *regular* participation in community recreation and leisure activities can also lead to a deeper sense of community membership. The longitudinal development of community connections takes time and, for some people, more intense support. For example, Harlan-Simmons, Holtz, Todd, and Mooney (2001) described a Community Membership Project to assist older adults with developmental disabilities to develop social relationships through participation in community activities. Community activities were selected for each participant based on individual interests and preferences including participation in the YMCA, a local senior citizens center, and a community woodworking shop. Although the participants developed more social relationships with the support of staff members called "community builders," Harlan-Simmons and colleagues (2001) point out that the development of true friendships is typically more elusive and requires "... a great deal of time and concerted effort to cultivate, along with plain good luck of the right interpersonal chemistry" (p. 179).

Addressing Recreation and Leisure through the Curriculum

Perhaps the most appropriate ways to address recreation and leisure activities are through the physical education curriculum and through extracurricular clubs, sports, and other activities. Recreation and leisure activities are often incorporated into the physical education curriculum at the middle and high school levels, and these activities provide a valuable outlet for release of energy and stress for young people who are spending the majority of their day working on more sedentary academic activities. Most middle and high schools offer extracurricular sports including school-sponsored athletic events (soccer, football, field hockey, etc.) that are potential activities for young people with disabilities. It should be noted, however, that such teams become increasingly competitive at the higher grade levels. Middle and high schools also offer a wide variety of clubs and organizations, such as chess clubs, Future Business Leaders of America, computer clubs, drama club, band, and a variety of academic or scholastic contests and activities (e.g., spelling or math contests). Some of these many options may be appropriate for certain students with disabilities. Also, peer buddy programs are often an especially effective way to involve students with disabilities in such activities with the support of non-disabled age peers (Hughes & Carter, 2000). Peer buddy programs create structured ways for students with and without disabilities to interact with one another, often through for-credit courses. For example, one high school program in New Jersey created a one-credit elective course on assistive technology, and students with and without disabilities had to research and brainstorm options that would help specific members of the class (E. Thayler, personal communication, April 20, 2000).

Processes for Identifying Appropriate Recreation and Leisure Activities

McNulty and colleagues (1995) described five guidelines in selecting recreation and leisure activities for students in transition who have dual sensory impairments (deaf-blind). Although written about students with dual sensory impairments, these guidelines are appropriate for consideration for a wide variety of students in transition. The five guidelines are described below, with the example of their use with Mike.

Guideline #1: Establish Communication and Rapport. The first guideline recommended by McNulty and colleagues (1995) is for people who will be with students in transition to establish communication and rapport with them. For example, Mike's family wanted him to participate in a wider range of community activities with a volunteer "peer buddy" from the local university. Once Jarrod, a peer buddy from the university, was identified, the first step was for him to spend time with Mike to get to know him. At first, this happened in Mike's home and with Mike's family present, and Jarrod and Mike did things together that Mike already liked to do.

Guideline #2: Use Person Centered Planning as an Assessment Technique. As described in Chapters 2 and 4, person centered planning strategies are very effective in helping to develop comprehensive personal profiles of students with disabilities and in organizing family and friends to assist these people to work toward the attainment of future aspirations. Mike already had a circle of support, so it was easy for Jarrod to start participating and to get to know Mike's specific likes, dislikes, and interests. This information was essential for planning recreation activities that are well matched to Mike.

Guideline #3: Assess Community Leisure and Recreation Opportunities.   The circle of support decided to try to find new places for Mike to go in the community with Jarrod. Mike likes to walk, and he likes to eat out at McDonald's. He also likes animals. Jarrod volunteered to look for new restaurants that Mike might like near farms, petting zoos, or pet stores in the area. His idea was to take Mike out for lunch and then to a local community location to see animals. Mike also likes music and movies, so Jarrod could also take him to the mall to shop for music CDs or movies on DVD to watch at home. Because Mike's family was concerned about him maintaining his health and not gaining weight, they indicated that it would be important for Mike to do a lot of walking. Also, they wanted Jarrod to introduce him to a more varied and healthy menu at these new restaurants, including salads.

Guideline #4: Provide Appropriate Instruction.   Once in a new restaurant, Mike needed to be taught how to order food. He was used to McDonald's and what they serve, but was not familiar with other fast food restaurants (Burger King, Taco Bell, Subway, etc.) or with local deli restaurants that serve more traditional sandwiches and salads. Jarrod decided to take pictures of the menus in these various restaurants, and he introduced these to Mike in Mike's home. This way, Mike was already somewhat familiar with what his choices were when he went to new restaurants. Also, Jarrod introduced new foods to Mike while they were at Mike's home to assess his preferences. This made it easier to know what foods Mike would accept while out in the community.

Guideline #5: Identify and Furnish Supports.   The community activities with Jarrod were successful, and Mike looked forward to these new outings, which happened about twice a month. Mike's family took photographs of Jarrod to attach to the calendar so they could try to teach Mike to predict when Jarrod would come over to do things. However, Mike's parents knew that Jarrod would be student teaching soon and would then graduate, so he may not be able to continue to be Mike's peer buddy the following year. Mike's family contacted the Best Buddies coordinator at the university to start making arrangements for a new peer buddy who could spend time with both Mike and Jarrod in order to ensure some continuity of community activities for Mike once Jarrod was no longer available.

DEVELOPING PATTERNS OF HEALTHY LIVING

Dimensions of a Healthy Adult Lifestyle

A healthy adult lifestyle is one that is characterized by physical health, psychological health, and prevention of accidents and sickness. Maintenance of physical health requires understanding and appropriate use of medications, a healthy diet, exercise, and proper hygiene skills. Psychological health includes stress management, a sense of control and self-efficacy, a positive outlook on life, and an awareness and understanding of one's own strengths and positive attributes. Psychological health also includes satisfaction with career, home, and interpersonal relationships. Prevention of illness, accidents, poor eating or drinking habits, and threats to psychological wellness are also key to a healthy adult lifestyle.

Hughes and colleagues (2002) summarized potential dimensions of a quality of life. They note that quality of life must be individually defined and can vary from person to person. The dimensions of quality of life that they review include:

- social relationships
- psychological well-being
- employment
- self-determination
- recreation and leisure
- independent living skills
- residential environment
- community participation
- lifestyle patterns
- support received
- individual and family resources
- personal development
- social acceptance
- physical and material well-being
- civic rights and responsibility

In reviewing this list of possible indicators of a quality of life, it is important to note that several relate to physical and psychological health and to recreation and leisure and satisfying relationships.

Threats to Healthy Living

Young people who are of transition age face many potential risks that can jeopardize patterns of healthy living. First, poor diet and lack of exercise can lead to poor health later in life. Second, risk-taking behaviors can result in accidents and, in some cases, disability. For example, young people in their adolescence or young adulthood are at risk of experiencing traumatic brain injuries due to motor vehicle accidents, falls, and sporting accidents (Wehman, Keyser-Marcus, West, Targett, & Bricout, 2001). Third, communities often present other dangers, such as unsafe strangers, vehicle accidents involving pedestrians, falls on icy surfaces, and so forth. Fourth, young people who are living on their own for the first time may be presented with risks due to fire, burns or cuts while cooking, or accidents in the bathroom. Fifth, many workplaces present their own risks for accidents to occur. Sixth, the availability of alcohol and drugs presents its own set of risks to young people who may experience peer pressure and who may have greater freedom to make decisions on their own. Finally, young people who are sexually active face risks of sexually transmitted diseases, including HIV and AIDS (Agran, 2004). See Chapter 7, "Transition to Postsecondary Education," for a discussion of these issues related to students with disabilities on college campuses.

Agran (2004) wrote that the area of safety skills instruction is a neglected part of the curriculum, despite the risks that young people face. According to Agran (2004), this oversight may be due to several factors:

- Educators and parents may have assumed that these risks were of low probability, and consequently did not need to be directly addressed in the curriculum;
- They may also have felt that young people with disabilities could not understand the sometimes subtle cues associated with such risks, and
- It may have been assumed that young people would learn these skills without formal instruction.

Agran (2004) argues that such assumptions are poor reasons to neglect direct instruction in safety skills. His assertions are particularly important for young people who are in transition to more independent adult lives.

Addressing Healthy Living through the Curriculum

Agran (2004) recommends that safety skills be directly taught through curricular content related to the following seven areas:

- Home and community safety
- Work safety
- Fire safety
- Crime prevention
- HIV/AIDS prevention
- Substance use prevention
- Self-medication/heath care

He recommends that these areas be addressed longitudinally throughout the curriculum, starting at the elementary level in increasing complexity and sophistication of skills and judgment through the middle and secondary school curriculum. For example, at the elementary level, students might be taught to identify the function of medication that is prescribed. They could then be taught side effects of medication at the middle school level, and then, at the high school level, how to seek assistance or attention if too much or too little medication is taken (Agran, 2004). We should note that, as with many functional skills associated with successful adult living, such safety skills require young people to develop generalized skills. For example, the ability to determine proper dosages of medication would require the generalized ability to do so for any type of medication that may be encountered.

CHAPTER SUMMARY

In this chapter, we have described the importance of the development of recreation and leisure opportunities for young people in transition. There are numerous benefits to participation in recreation and leisure activities, and such participation is associated with physical and mental health and with an overall positive quality of life. Recreation and leisure activities can occur within the home, or they can take place within the community. Regular participation in recreation and leisure activities within the community help to create connections and bonds to one's local community and open the possibility for the development of friendships. A key point in this chapter is that there are many recreation and leisure opportunities that take place on a regular basis in most typical communities. Students in transition should be given the opportunity to take part in a range of these activities so that their own preferences and interests can be established. The transition planning team should also address recreation and leisure as an important outcome area to target for planning for students' adult lives.

In this chapter, we also addressed issues associated with the development of healthy adult lifestyles. A particular concern is the development of recreation and leisure activities that increase or maintain physical fitness of young people with disabilities. Students in transition also need to be taught specific skills associated with safe and healthy living, including diet and nutrition, how to deal with illness, and community safety.

APPLICATION ACTIVITIES

The application activities listed below are essential for your continued learning and skill development in transition planning. Each of the activities will require your time and energy, but will help you develop your professional skills in this area.

For Practice and Enhanced Understanding:

If you are currently teaching or are associated with a school system, review the school's curriculum to determine where issues of health and safety are addressed. At what grade levels are these issues addressed? Do students receive longitudinal instruction regarding the dangers of drugs and alcohol abuse or of sexually transmitted diseases?

If you work in a school system, find out about all of the school clubs and organizations that your school offers to students. What are the criteria for membership in the different clubs and organizations? Can anyone join? Which of these clubs and organizations seem to be good options for students with disabilities?

Using the information gained from the preceding activity, as a guide, consider starting a school club or organization that would introduce students with and without disabilities to your own personal interests. For example, one fifth-grade teacher started a bird-watching club, because that is one of his personal avocations (B. Butler, personal communication, May 5, 2001). This organization is now a potential recreation option that is appropriate for a wide range of students.

Consider researching and then starting a peer buddy program within your school. There are a number of models that have been described and that could provide you with guidance. (See Hughes and Carter, 2000, for a description of a peer buddy program.) Although the development of a peer buddy program would entail a substantial amount of work, it can result in numerous opportunities for students with and without disabilities to develop potential friendships. At the very least, they will learn more about one another.

For Your Portfolio:

Survey your local community to determine what recreation and leisure activities take place on a regular basis. Make a comprehensive list of these events, along with contact information, meeting times and locations, and so forth. Keep this information for future students to look at in order to try to determine their individual interests and preferences.

If you are currently teaching, conduct surveys or interviews with your students to determine interests and preferences for recreation and leisure activities. Then, use the information you gathered above to match students to potential adult community recreation and leisure activities.

RESOURCES AND WEBSITES

The following resources and websites will allow you to extend your knowledge about how to assist people with disabilities to access and enjoy recreation and leisure activities in their local communities. Consider including these resources in your professional portfolio.

American Therapeutic Recreation Association

National professional organization for recreation therapists.
www.atra-tr.org

National Recreation and Park Association

Mission is to advance parks, recreation, and environmental conservation efforts that enhance the quality of life for all people. Includes publications related to therapeutic recreation.
www.nrpa.org

National Center on Accessibility

Promotes access for people with disabilities in recreation.
www.ncaonline.org

REFERENCES

Agran, M. (2004). Health and safety. In P. Wehman & J. Kregel (Eds.), *Functional curriculum for elementary, middle, and secondary age students with special needs* (2nd ed.) (pp. 357–384). Austin, TX: Pro-Ed.

Ayvazoglu, N., Ratliffe, T., & Kozub, R. (2004). Encouraging lifetime physical fitness. *Teaching Exceptional Children, 37,* 16–20.

Braunschweig, C., Gomez, S., Sheean, P., Tomey, K., Rimmer, J., & Heller, T. (2004). Nutrition status and risk factors for chronic disease in urban-dwelling adults with Down syndrome. *American Journal on Mental Retardation, 109,* 186–193.

Chandler, S., & Pankaskie, S. (2004). Socialization, peer relationships, and self-esteem. In P. Wehman & J. Kregel (Eds.), *Functional curriculum for elementary, middle, and secondary age students with special needs* (2nd ed.) (pp. 165–204). Austin, TX: Pro-Ed.

Condeluci, A. (1996). *Beyond difference.* Delray Beach, FL: St. Lucie Press.

Dymond, S. (2004). Community participation. In P. Wehman & J. Kregel (Eds.), *Functional curriculum for elementary, middle, and secondary age students with special needs* (2nd ed.) (pp. 259–292). Austin, TX: Pro-Ed.

Gillespie, M. (2003). Cardiovascular fitness of young Canadian children with and without mental retardation. *Education and Training in Developmental Disabilities, 38,* 296–301.

Hackett, L. (1994). *Everybody belongs: Tips for including your child in community recreation.* Concord, NH: New Hampshire Developmental Disabilities Council.

Harlan-Simmons, J., Holtz, P., Todd, J., & Mooney, M. (2001). Building social relationships through valued roles: Three older adults and the community membership project. *Mental Retardation, 39,* 171–180.

Heller, T., Hsieh, K., & Rimmer, J. (2004). Attitudinal and psychosocial outcomes of a fitness and health education program on adults with Down syndrome. *American Journal on Mental Retardation, 109,* 175–185.

Hughes, C., & Carter, E. (2000). *The transition handbook: Strategies high school teachers use that work!* Baltimore: Paul Brookes.

Hughes, C., Copeland, S., Fowler, S., & Church-Pupke, P. (2002). Quality of life. In K. Storey, P. Bates, & D. Hunter (Eds.), *The road ahead: Transition to adult life for persons with disabilities* (pp. 157–171). St. Augustine, FL: TRN Publishers.

Kozub, F. (2003). Explaining physical activity in individuals with mental retardation: An exploratory study. *Education and Training in Developmental Disabilities, 38,* 302–313.

McNulty, K., Mascia, J., Rocchio, L., & Rothstein, R. (1995). Developing recreation and leisure opportunities. In J. Everson (Ed.), *Supporting young adults who are deaf-blind in their communities: A transition planning guide for service providers, families, and friends* (pp. 159–184). Baltimore: Paul Brookes.

Moon, M. S. (1994). The case for inclusive school and community recreation. In M. S. Moon (Ed.), *Making school and community recreation fun for everyone: Places and ways to integrate* (pp. 1–13). Baltimore: Paul Brookes.

Ohtake, Y. (2004). Meaningful inclusion of all students in team sports. *Teaching Exceptional Children, 37,* 22–27.

Powell, T. (2004, October). Helping people with disabilities realize the American Dream. Presentation at the conference on disAbility, sponsored by the University of Scranton, Scranton, PA.

Rimmer, J., Heller, T., Wang, E., & Valerio, I. (2004). Improvements in physical fitness in adults with Down syndrome. *American Journal on Mental Retardation, 109,* 165–174.

Schleien, S., Green, F., & Stone, C. (2003). Making friends within inclusive community recreation programs. *American Journal of Recreation Therapy, 2,* 7–16.

Schleien, S., & Ray, M. T. (1997). Leisure education for a quality transition to adulthood. *Journal of Vocational Rehabilitation, 8,* 155–169.

Stopka, C., Pomeranz, J., Siders, R., Dykes, M., & Goodman, A. (1999). Transitional skills for wellness. *Teaching Exceptional Children, 31,* 6–11.

Strand, J., & Kreiner, J. (2005). Recreation and leisure in the community. In R. Flexer, T. Simmons, P. Luft, & R. Baer (Eds.), *Transition planning for secondary students with disabilities* (2nd ed.) (pp. 460–482). Upper Saddle River, NJ: Merrill.

The Pocono Record, October 31, 2004.

Walker, P., & Shoultz, B. *Supporting children and youth with disabilities in integrated recreation and leisure activities.* Retrieved on 9/1/05 from The Arc's Community Integration Report on Recreation and Leisure, www.open.org.

Wehman, P., Keyser-Marcus, L., West, M., Targett, P., & Bricout, J. (2001). Applications for youth with traumatic brain injury. In P. Wehman (Ed.), *Life beyond the classroom: Transition strategies for young people with disabilities* (3rd ed.) (pp. 449–490). Baltimore: Paul Brookes.

West, M. (2001). Independent living. In P. Wehman (Ed.), *Life beyond the classroom: Transition strategies for young people with disabilities* (3rd ed.) (pp. 261–274). Baltimore: Paul Brookes.

West, M., Wittig, K., & Dowdy, V. (2004). Travel and mobility training. In P. Wehman & J. Kregel (Eds.), *Functional curriculum for elementary, middle, and secondary age students with special needs* (2nd ed.) (pp. 245–258). Austin, TX: Pro-Ed.

Yamaki, K. (2005). Body weight status among adults with intellectual disability in the community. *Mental Retardation, 43*, 1–10.

Yu, D., Spevack, S., Hiebert, R., Martin, T., Goodman, R., Martin, T., Harapiak, S., & Martin, G. (2002). Happiness indices among persons with profound and severe disabilities during leisure and work activities: A comparison. *Education and Training in Mental Retardation and Developmental Disabilities, 37*, 421–426.

CHAPTER 12

INTERNATIONAL ISSUES AND PRACTICES IN TRANSITION SERVICES AND EMPLOYMENT OF INDIVIDUALS WITH DISABILITIES

CHAPTER OBJECTIVES

Upon completion of this chapter, you will be able to

1. compare policy and legislative approaches to transition and training programs in the United States and Europe, and some selected developing countries.

2. discuss policy and practice approaches to transition and training programs in the United States and the developing world.

3. discuss a number of challenges faced by people with disabilities in developing nations with respect to culture, public policy, and impairment.

4. describe specialized programs for transition and career development in two developing countries.

5. describe three areas of internationally focused careers for individuals with disabilities.

6. have a familiarity with issues, challenges, and policies on transition and employment that exist in other developed countries and in developing countries. You will also be aware of international career opportunities for individuals with disabilities.

KEY TOPICS TO LOOK FOR IN THIS CHAPTER . . .

■ As we live in an increasingly global climate, consider the impact of economic policy development and employment opportunities for individuals with disabilities in developing countries.

- Our legislation and regulations provide a foundation for individuals with disabilities to practice self-determination. For a number of reasons this has not occurred in other countries, especially in the developing world. Consider how this exacerbates the existing hardships for persons with disabilities.

- Among the many career opportunities for individuals with disabilities, those in the international arena are rarely mentioned. However, the U.S. Department of State and other organizations specialize in just such opportunities.

Previous chapters have dealt exclusively with transition issues and practices in the United States. However, as travel, trade agreements, business outsourcing, and educational opportunities abroad continue to grow it is important that educators pay attention to these developments and their effect on the lives of individuals with disabilities in the developed and developing countries. Much of the American system for treating and educating individuals with disabilities came initially from Europe and then evolved as the country grew and public education became a primary institution in American life. In Europe, countries took vastly different approaches with the more inclusive models emerging from Scandinavia (Ingstad & Whyte, 1995). However, with the emergence of the European Union (EU), member countries are studying best practices among themselves to better prepare individuals with disabilities for productive lives as adults (see www.european-agency.org/transit/index.html#international). For example, the EU has developed a five country project to improve the employment of individuals who are blind or visually impaired. The project, VISAGE/ESPVIP (Visual Impairment and Standards in Adult Guidance and Employment/Employment Support Services for Visually Impaired People) included organizations from the United Kingdom, Italy, Ireland, France, and Denmark. There were five areas of development, which involved (1) vocational guidance practices, (2) professional training and development, (3) job creation and support, (4) labor market support schemes and job retention, and (5) rehabilitation and assessment. Within three years (1997–2000), the project had produced a handbook for vocational guidance practitioners who advised individuals with visual impairments, a work placement guide for employers, and a European website for employers interested in recruiting workers with visual impairments (see www.aaa.dk/jobvision). The widespread dissemination of project materials and training provided a benefit beyond the project countries and enabled other EU member nations to tap into successful employment practices for their visually impaired and blind populations (Roy, 2002).

An extensive study, *Transition from School to Employment: Main problems, issues and options faced by students with special educational needs in 16 European countries* (European Agency for Development in Special Education Needs, 2002), essentially recommended much of the transition language that is contained in our IDEA regulations. That is, students and their parents should be highly integrated into the planning process and students should have a strong voice in making the choice for themselves as it relates to career choices and location of preparation; for example, vocational school, business location, or a less integrated program facility. In addition, there should be individualized program plans to evaluate whether or not progress is being made and that all parties are carrying out their agreed-upon responsibilities. Although comprehensive in nature, the study looked primarily at individuals with mild disabilities, especially those with learning disabilities (European Agency for Development in Special Needs Education, 2002).

Consider This!   Suppose you had the opportunity to study abroad in Europe during a semester.

- Which country would you choose and why?
- How would you prepare to become knowledgeable in the special education, vocational education, and rehabilitation service policies and practices of that country?
- If you had the opportunity to do an internship in the country, would you choose to be placed in a compulsory education school, a vocational school, a special learning center, a company that employed persons with disabilities, or another placement?
- What would you hope to learn from your experience?

EMPLOYMENT AND REHABILITATION PRACTICES IN EUROPEAN COUNTRIES

United Kingdom (UK)

Transition is planned for all students, including those with disabilities and special learning needs. Students are enrolled in a program of career education within the secondary school curriculum. This often takes place over an extended period of time, not just in the final year of statutory school, which ends when an individual reaches the age of sixteen. Students receive career guidance from a specialist attached to Career Services who interviews them to obtain information on career choices. Students develop a Career Action Plan, which includes their goals for education, training, and employment. Strategies for implementation are included. Careers Services are units independent of the schools, but have a specific responsibility to serve the needs of young people with disabilities and other special needs. Specialist career advisors for students with disabilities are familiar with what can be very complicated routes to getting the additional supports and funding from one or any combination of departments such as the Health Authority, Social Services, and the Local Education Authority (Transition Information Database, 2004).

Transition to employment includes students completing a period of work experience during the last two years of their statutory schooling and pre-vocational and vocational courses after age sixteen. Under the regulations of the Special Educational Needs Code of Practice, individuals with a designation of special educational needs, especially those with the most severe disabilities, have a transition review at age fourteen to plan for a complete transition process over their last two years of schooling. The review is multi-agency and involves a range of service providers depending on the student's disability and need for supports. These professionals may include representatives of the school, postsecondary education, learning support services, educational psychology services, and from agencies such as the Careers Service, Social Services, and the Health Authority. Parents and primary caregivers are integrally involved. The outcome of this review is a transition plan that states the student's preferences and the action to be taken by the different agencies in order to achieve the student's goals.

As part of the transition process, many special schools and mainstream schools that include students with disabilities offer "link" or "taster" courses in collaboration with postsecondary education institutions in the final two years of statutory schooling (i.e., ages fourteen to sixteen). These courses are pre-vocational and usually focus on independence or generic skills. Such courses are held at a regular time each week in a college (link courses) or for a few days (taster courses) during which time students can become accustomed to a different learning environment, instructors, and activities to help them finalize plans for their post-statutory school education and to facilitate the move to a particular college, if they have already chosen that option. It is a sign of good transition practice when there is a close collaboration between statutory schools and colleges over the content and delivery of link courses.

The term Further Education (FE) is applied to any education beyond statutory school where the qualifications of the students are considered to be at a sub-degree level or unprepared for baccalaureate level coursework. The vast majority of courses in FE are vocationally oriented, but students can enroll in academic courses that lead to qualifications for entry into higher education or baccalaureate colleges. The FE vocational courses typically lead to a work related qualification within the National Vocational Qualifications (NVQ) framework.

The Further Education Funding Council (FEFC) (in Scotland, the Scottish Further Education Funding Council) publicly funds local further education colleges in England, Wales, and Scotland. FEs are independently administered and are not under the direction of the local education authorities. All colleges that receive government funding cannot discriminate against individuals with disabilities. There are independent colleges that provide further education specifically for students with disabilities and they are mostly run by voluntary agencies. These FEs are called specialist colleges and they serve students from a wide area and are usually residential.

In addition to the normal introductory materials and course information, all UK colleges are required to have a Disability Statement, articulating their policies and services for students with disabilities. Each college must have a staff member who coordinates the services for students much like a director of Services for Students with Disabilities on campuses the United States Colleges receive a budget for supporting students with disabilities. In theory, therefore, the students should be able to receive support and specialized equipment as necessary, but there is apparently a lot of variation in practice among colleges.

In England, Wales, and Northern Ireland, students do not have to pay tuition fees up to the age of nineteen; or in Scotland, age eighteen. Colleges have the discretion to reduce or waive fees for students over the age of nineteen (eighteen in Scotland). This can reduce the financial burden on students with disabilities and their families.

Local education authorities are mandated to provide transportation for students with disabilities who attend LEA schools after age sixteen and they are obligated to do the same for students studying in further education colleges. However, in some cases, transportation to and from college is paid through the Social Services Department of the country. Additionally, local authorities can assist students beyond age sixteen with living costs and award discretionary grants. Here too, there is considerable variability in this practice across the UK.

Sweden

Swedish employment policy has focused on the theme, "Work for all," but the rising unemployment of recent years has lessened the opportunity of obtaining employment for individuals with disabilities. Sweden has two legislative acts aimed at supporting the preparation and workplace environment for persons with disabilities. *The Building and Planning Act*, states regulations for workplaces, and the *Work Environment Act* prescribes that employers must adapt the physical environment, work organizations, and the like to accommodate persons with disabilities. There are a number of employment policy measures aimed at making it easier for people with disabilities to find work on the open market. If this is not possible, there are incentives to create alternative employment opportunities such as workshops, enclaves, and job teams (Transition Information Database, 2004).

Assessment of working capacity, occupational rehabilitation, and vocational guidance is provided at Employability Institutes, administered under the national Labor Market Administration. The Institutes were recently reorganized into more decentralized units with explicit requirements concerning economic performance.

Financial contributions are made to employers who recruit employees with disabilities at pay rates and terms that apply under traditional collective bargaining agreements between trade unions and employers. Grants are available for employers who adapt their workplaces to the needs of people with disabilities, install technical aids or employ attendants and job coaches. Training for individuals with disabilities may be combined with probationary employment in the hiring company. Rehabilitation, social, and vocational training must take place over a relatively short and intensive period of time to encourage the trainees to enter the job market as quickly as possible.

Germany

Germany has a dual system of vocational education. In this system, vocational schools provide the theoretical training and companies provide the practical training. Student trainees either attend the two places of training alternately or simultaneously. Only a small percentage of students with learning disabilities are able to cope with the requirements of the dual system training. Because of the lack of success, alternative programs have been developed or "borrowed" from other European nations.

The primary goal is vocational integration through enabling individuals with disabilities to gain as many skills as possible to qualify for an occupation in the general employment market. Germany uses a variety of assessment models to determine how a disability affects learning vocational skills and job performance. They also measure the interaction between the individual and the work environment, including work behaviors and social interaction. This approach results in a recommended training program implemented in a location that will support the individual. In some areas of the country, this process is carried out through cooperative networks that include a Career Office, Rehabilitation Center, social workers, teachers, medical doctors, and others with appropriate expertise. This has given rise to a growing collaboration between mainstream (compulsory) schools and vocational schools in planning joint programs during the last year of the compulsory school. A Careers Advice Service funded through the national Office of Employment aids them in their efforts. The Careers Advice Service is responsible for supporting vocational assessment, enrollment in pre-vocational training programs, and supporting rehabilitation services.

Pre-vocational training programs are considered a successful way of selecting an appropriate career and preparing for vocational schools where the skills for that career are taught. Pre-vocational training stresses studies of successful work habits, visits to companies and work internships, and planning through a Department of Career Guidance in the Office of Public Employment. In the past, Germany has relied heavily on training and employment in sheltered workshops, but there is now a growing movement to prepare and place individuals with disabilities in community-based work environments with non-disabled employees.

The Vocational Training Act ensures that all German citizens have access to initial vocational training, further training, and re-training when needed. These training phases are to take place at regular worksites whenever possible and guarantee additional supports for individuals with disabilities, including a vocational training allowance.

Although there is no guarantee of employment when the phases of training have been completed, there are supporting services for seeking job placement and other supports throughout the working life of individuals with disabilities as specified in the Disabled Person Act (Transition Information Database, 2004).

As you can see from these policy and program descriptions, many European countries are early on in the development of legislation, programs, and agencies to include individuals with disabilities in the regular workforce. Historically, formal schooling in Europe was a gate-keeping process that controlled access to higher education and the most prestigious occupations. Those persons who did not perform well in compulsory school or were excluded from school altogether had only low status/low paying jobs available to them (Barton & Armstrong, 2001). The European nations are now making their educational systems more open to students with disabilities and the job market is likewise becoming more inclusive.

EMPLOYMENT AND REHABILITATION ISSUES IN THE DEVELOPING WORLD

Prior to 1981, the International Year of Disabled Persons (IYDP), very little was known about persons with disabilities in the developing world. The developing world is considered to be most countries outside of Europe and North America (Ingstad, 2001). However, parts of Asia (e.g., Japan and South Korea) and Australia are included in the developed world. Even today, it is difficult to obtain disability statistics from developing countries where remote areas and lack of infrastructure make it difficult to know the numbers of persons with disabilities, the types of disabilities, and the welfare of those individuals. This is complicated further by epidemics, wars, and famine that ravage whole populations, killing thousands and leaving many of the survivors with disabilities. These survivors may very well be displaced in refugee camps where there is almost no opportunity for education, vocational training, and employment.

In 1983, the United Nations General Assembly created the *World Programme of Action Concerning Disabled Persons*, which was the sendoff for the Decade for Disabled Persons (1983 to 1992). The goals of the *World Programme of Action* were to

> Promote effective measures for prevention of disability, rehabilitation and the realization of the goals of "full participation" of disabled persons in social life and development, and of "equality." (United Nations, 1983, p. 1)

During this time, many countries in the developing world created policies, laws, and planning documents to protect the rights of persons with disabilities and other special needs. Although many of these enactments were not followed by legislation, they did serve to raise awareness of people with disabilities and their connection to community and country.

Nevertheless, developing countries experience many problems in implementing rehabilitation programs, which are often based upon models developed by United Nations agencies and/or nongovernmental organizations headquartered in Europe or the United States. Rarely do these programs fit local conditions and thus, do little to improve conditions (Ingstad, 2001).

It is important to keep in mind that disabilities interact in context with the built environment and social-economic status. A severe disability will have a different effect on an individual who is poor and lives in a rural village in South America compared to an individual from a middle-income family in a suburban community in North America. For the latter, there is education and training, support services, financial services, and real opportunity for employment. For the former, none of that is likely except for family support and even that may not happen depending upon certain cultural beliefs (Schriner, 2001). Nevertheless, we know that no matter where they live, persons with disabilities are among the most economically disadvantaged populations in society, being either unemployed or underemployed.

In many developing countries, conditions for women and children with disabilities are more challenging than for men. Their prospects for economic self-sufficiency are compounded by a lack of access to health care and education, and religious and cultural norms, which limit their right to work. When allowed to work, the job conditions may be too difficult to accomplish and may often be in environments that are unhealthy, physically unsafe, or both.

Certainly, a complicating factor in the employment of people with disabilities in developing countries is the nature of work compared to that of the developed countries. Many people in developing countries work in subsistence occupations like farming, fishing, or as self-employed merchants or artisans. The developed world has oriented its economic development to the information age and its necessary technologies. The resulting jobs are not suited for most people with disabilities from developing nations because they have no opportunity to prepare for such employment nor do their countries have the infrastructures to support these jobs (Schriner, 2001). The best opportunities might lie in manufacturing hardware components if they can meet the standards of assembly at an acceptable rate, but jobs are rare enough in most developing countries such that individuals with disabilities have a competitive disadvantage.

Unemployment among adults and youth with disabilities in the developing world is due to three strong factors: culture, public policy, and impairments (Schriner, 2001).

Culture

According to Groce (1993), understanding cultural influences is critical to understanding social definitions of disability and the conditions under which people with disabilities live. Cultural understandings are important for determining perceptions of people with disabilities and their life circumstances. For example, cultures that believe in reincarnation may see a disability as punishment for transgressions in a previous life of either the parents or the child. Yet, in other cultures, individuals with a mental health condition or mental retardation may be considered "touched by God" and treated with care and respect.

Public Policy

Unlike the developed world with its history of layered policies that can both support and confuse people with disabilities, developing nations have scarce resources to fund policy programs established to specifically serve their disabled populations. Their focus is primarily on the basic issues of economic development, education, and health care with no special focus on the needs of people with disabilities (Metts & Metts, 1998). Most funding and human support comes from non-governmental organizations (NGOs) such as international aid groups, missionary groups, and governmental programs sponsored by a developed nation (Schriner, 2001). Because the funding and program requirements come from external organizations, the developing country has little to do with shaping public policy around their own ideas for service eligibility and delivery.

Impairment

The concept of impairment has played a key role in setting policies and programs of services for individuals with disabilities in the developed world. Impairment, as a construct, has been used to sort individuals out of the workforce because of their inability to perform the tasks of a job with the sufficient speed and quality required by an employer or industry standard or both. This then, entitles them to participate in the social welfare/rehabilitation system for income and health care assistance and preparation for employment in a field where their disability may not be an impairment (Gooding, 1994). In the developing world, impairment is viewed differently in economic sectors outside of manufacturing and technology. Countries with populations residing in rural villages that rely primarily on an agrarian economy have less need for an impairment designation system because slower paced, simpler jobs enable many disabled persons to participate in the economic life of their villages (Schriner, 2001).

Stephen lives with his mother, his aunt, and two cousins in the Western Cape Province of South Africa. He was born with mild mental retardation and mild cerebral palsy. Until 1995, Stephen had no school to attend. Because he is black, the previous practice of apartheid did not allow him to attend specialized schools for white children with disabilities and the local school for black children had no special education services. So, Stephen stayed in his home and was cared for by one of his cousins who would occasionally take him out to the market place. Stephen enjoyed these times and especially liked visiting the booths of men who repaired small appliances and bicycles. He would watch them intently and over time came to know how some of the repairs were made. One of the repairmen took a liking to Stephen and taught him how to work on bicycles. Stephen wanted to repair bicycles for the people in his township, but he had no tools or benches for the repairs. For a few years, Stephen's skills and desire to work were wasted.

When apartheid finally ended in South Africa and a new constitution was written that guaranteed an inclusive education system for all the people, Stephen had the opportunity to attend the Village Work Centre near Cape Town. There, to his delight, was a fully equipped workshop for repairing bicycles and wheelchairs and teachers to help him learn new skills. Stephen has been at the center for ten years now and is the lead repairman in refurbishing wheelchairs. The center is known throughout the Western Cape as the best place for repairing wheelchairs, manual or motorized. Stephen earns a salary for his work and makes a sizeable contribution to his family's budget. Recently, Stephen and his mother and aunt and cousins moved to a larger house because Stephen's salary made it possible. Once considered a difficult challenge for his family, Stephen is now a productive and valued member because of his specialized employment skills.

EMPLOYMENT AND REHABILITATION PRACTICES IN THE DEVELOPING WORLD

As cited earlier, developing nations have increased their awareness of disability, its implications for education and work, health care, and community integration. However, this awareness has been generated from outside most of these countries and few, with the exception of South Africa which has some highly developed areas, have enacted legislation or constitutional regulations that include individuals with disabilities in compulsory education, vocational education, or specialized training. Thus, the following descriptions focus more on special programs in developing countries rather than nation-wide laws and policies that create equal opportunities for persons with disabilities. The exception is Taiwan, which passed legislation related to special education, transition, and employment preparation in 1997 (Lin, 2002).

Philippines

The Special Care Development Center (SCDC) in Las Pinas City, Philippines, was established in 1990 to educate children with special learning needs. The goal is to provide them with functional independent living skills through special education, and to promote human rights and dignity for children with challenging needs through the *Life Centered Career Education* program (Brolin, 1992). Through this program, children and young adults learn regular functional activities geared toward full participation in integrative community living.

The Center's students have all types of disabilities, including mild to moderate mental retardation; behavioral and emotional disorders; learning disabilities; speech/communication problems; physical or orthopedic disabilities; autism; hearing impairments; and multiple disabilities. Students learn in natural environments that stimulate development and enable them to work at their own rate and level.

The *Life Centered Career Education* program offers activities that promote the holistic development of students with disabilities toward fuller community integration, such as transportation mobility, using community resources, and consumer education. Students also work on enhancing their social skills, speech and communication development, cognitive and self-help skills, and fine/gross motor skills.

In addition to special education and transition services, SCDC provides psychoeducational assessment, occupational therapy, physical therapy, speech/language communication therapy, counseling, behavioral therapy, therapeutic horseback riding, and tutorials. Field training internships make it possible for trainees and caregivers in these and other disciplines to learn by working in an inclusive, community-based education program (www.cec.sped.org/intl/progpract.html#spcare).

Peru

Centro Ann Sullivan del Peru (CASP) was established in Lima, by Dr. Liliana Mayo-Ortega in 1979, with the support of her parents and colleagues. Dr. Mayo-Ortega started the center because there were no schools or training centers for people with severe and profound mental retardation and autism in Peru.

CASP is a non-governmental organization (NGO) known for its contributions as a model center for research, demonstration, and training for persons with severe mental retardation, autism, and behavioral challenges. It is named for Ann Sullivan, who was Helen Keller's innovative teacher.

Professionals come from many different countries to teach and consult with the CASP staff and to observe the program. The professional development programs for the Center's staff is based in the work of these professionals, many of whom come to Peru every one or two years. CASP has a formal agreement with the Schiefelbusch Institute for Research in Life Span Studies at the University of Kansas and receives professional development training through the University of Kansas faculty in the department of special education and the department of human development and family life. Judith LeBlanc from the University of Kansas has been instrumental in working with CASP staff to develop their specialized curricula. The staff at CASP shares their training with teachers and disability specialists and parents from all over Peru and throughout South America. Trainings take place at CASP and in other countries. In addition, CASP has developed a long distance education program in cities and villages in the provinces of Peru. The number of these sites has increased annually as communication networks have grown. Educational videos and manuals are produced by CASP to demonstrate their work at the center in Lima. The Telefonica Foundation and Telefonica Peru are providing funding to expand the distance-learning program in Peru and to other countries. Plans have been developed to set up online courses in Spanish to better serve Peru and other countries in Latin America (www.cec.sped.org/intl/progpract.html#peru).

Taiwan

The transition from school to work for students with disabilities has become an important issue in Taiwan. In 1997, two significant laws were passed: The Special Education Act of 1997 and the Protection Act for Individuals with Disabilities of 1997. This legislation is meant to ensure the right to education, the right to vocational rehabilitation, the right to appropriate medical services, and the right to work for persons with disabilities (Lin, 2002). The Special Education Act acknowledges transition at four important stages, at kindergarten, at grade six in primary school, at grade nine in secondary school, and at grade twelve in high school. Like our own IDEA, the Special Education Act requires that transition planning take place during the development of an Individual Education Plan. Transition services are to include planning for education, living, employment, psychological guidance, social welfare, and other related professional services (Lin, 2002). Based upon the laws passed in 1997, transition services are seen as a coordinated set of activities, which includes early intervention, special education, postsecondary education, vocational training, integrated employment, continuing and adult education, adult services, independent living/community participation, and aging care. In spite of this, Lin (2002) reports that 78.9 percent of people with disabilities in Taiwan are unemployed. Further, Lin conducted a study of young Taiwanese adults with hearing impairments and found that 53.8 percent of the sample ($N = 26$) had never been employed; 92.3 percent had not attended a transition planning meeting at their school; and only 7.7 percent had even been invited to a transition planning meeting.

Likewise, a study conducted by Chen and Zhang (2003) of 202 Taiwanese high school students with disabilities found there is a high need for transition services, but a low correlation of those services are actually delivered. The highest need transition services were (1) professional guidance, (2) working/living environment adaptation, (3) psychological guidance, (4) personal affairs, (5) community living, and (6) adult living. The correlations between these needed services and those actually received in each of the categories were quite low and underscore the situation that the most important transition needs for disabled youth in Taiwan are not being met. Given the Taiwanese laws that tend to mirror the protections of our IDEA, these results were disappointing and suggest that stronger efforts at implementation must take place.

It is important to note that many countries in Africa, Asia, and South America were colonies of European nations, some well into the twentieth century, and the school systems established, if at all, followed the exclusionary practices of the European system. In some cases there were no institutions of higher education established during colonial times and those individuals native to a country who qualified for a college education had to have the funds to be educated abroad. Even today, many college students from developing countries attend American, European, and Australian universities. Because of this, teacher education colleges have been slow to develop preparation programs for special educators at every level, especially for adolescents and young adults with disabilities who need teachers to prepare them for employment and community life. See Sidebar 12.1 for the story of Judith Heumann's contributions to the independence of individuals with disabilities.

■ ■ ■ ■ ■

SIDEBAR 12.1
SPOTLIGHT ON HISTORY: JUDITH HEUMANN

Judith (Judy) Heumann was born in 1947. At eighteen months of age she contracted polio and subsequently became a wheelchair user. During the 1950s, very few services existed for people with disabilities and there were no federal regulations guaranteeing a free appropriate education. Her local school refused to allow Heumann to attend and referred to her as a fire hazard. After a difficult struggle waged by her mother, Judy was allowed to enroll in fourth grade.

Heumann attended college at Long Island University in Brooklyn. She wanted to become a teacher and successfully completed all the course work, but the New York City Board of Education refused to grant her a teaching certificate on the basis that she was disabled. She sued the Board and eventually won the case. Heumann taught elementary school for three years and then worked at organizing civil rights actions for people with disabilities. She and several friends founded the organization, Disabled in Action in New York City.

Disabled in Action was the first among many organizations in which Heumann had significant involvement. In 1974, she became a legislative assistant to the chairperson of the U.S. Senate Committee on Labor and Public Welfare. During this time, Judy helped draft the legislation that became the Education for All Handicapped Children Act (now named the Individuals with Disabilities Education Act).

Ed Roberts (see Chapter 7) recruited Heumann to come to California and from 1975 through 1982, she served as the deputy director of the Center for Independent Living in Berkeley, California. She later worked as special assistant to the executive director of California's State Department of Rehabilitation. In 1983, Roberts, Heumann, and Joan Leon co-founded the World Institute on Disabilities (WID). For more than ten years she was the vice president of WID and director of its Research and Training Center on Public Policy in the Independent Living division. Among her policy triumphs was helping to develop the legislation that created the Americans with Disabilities Act. In 1993, President Bill Clinton appointed her as Assistant Secretary of Education directing the Office of Special Education and Rehabilitation, a position she held until 2001. The following year, she was hired as Adviser, Disability and Development in the Human Development Network of the World Bank. In this position, Heumann leads the World Bank's work on disability and its integration into policy discussions with its client countries on projects that fully consider people with disabilities in developing countries. By initiating strategies to address the needs of the marginalized population of disabled people in poor countries around the world, Heumann's work will contribute to achieving the World Bank's goal on poverty reduction and development. Judy Heumann has contributed much to the independence of individuals with disabilities in America and now she's taking on the world.

INTERNATIONAL CAREER OPTIONS FOR STUDENTS WITH DISABILITIES

While perhaps not an obvious choice, there are significant opportunities for individuals with disabilities to work in international employment positions abroad and stateside. Mobility International USA/National Clearinghouse on Disability and Exchange (MIUSA/NCDE) has published a helpful guide entitled, "Preparing for an International Career: Pathways for People with Disabilities" (2005). The National Clearinghouse on Disability and Exchange is sponsored by the Bureau of Educational and Cultural Affairs of the U.S. Department of State. The book, which can be downloaded free at www.miusa.org/publications/books/pic, covers topics on career options, job prospects, employment qualifications, international activities in high school, international degree programs and fellowship programs in college, and tips for entering international employment. Much of the text is in the form of personal stories of individuals with disabilities who work in a variety of international positions either in the United States or in foreign countries. Like all good guides, this one follows the structure of presenting some planning questions. Considerations are whether or not an individual has a desire to live overseas and work directly with people in another country or be an administrator of international programs in the United States. Some options include working for the federal government, a not-for-profit non-governmental organization, an educational institution, or working in the private sector in business or consulting. Depending on the answers to these questions, the following options may apply.

International Exchange

Professionals in this field provide the support for study abroad programs in high schools and colleges. They might also be involved in international education programs that recruit and support international students in this country. Another area is the exchange of teachers, business professionals, researchers, and interns between the United States and other countries.

International Affairs

This is an exciting professional career focused on developing international relations through diplomacy, trade agreements, cooperative ventures, economic development, and other areas of foreign affairs. Such work usually involves issues that effect widespread global interests like treaties, military alliances, environmental issues, human rights, and immigration.

International Development

Careers in international development help create better conditions for people through improvements in fields like agriculture, health services, education, technology, human rights, employment and economic advancement, and transportation. They also work on disaster relief after wars, weather-related catastrophes, famine, and epidemics.

Employment Prospects

According to the MIUSA/NCDE guide on international careers for individuals with disabilities (2005), the prospects of being employed in one of the three areas above is good and getting better. Eighty-eight percent of students graduating in 2002 with a degree in international affairs were employed within six months. Forty-two percent of those employed found positions in the public sector. The U.S. Department of State offers a Workforce Recruitment Program (WRP) especially for high achieving students with disabilities. According to their website (www.careers.state.gov/student /programs/student_disability.html), a student is eligible for the program if he or she is a U.S. citizen, has a substantial disability, is at least sixteen years of age, and enrolled or accepted for enrollment in any high school, vocational school, or undergraduate degree program. The school must be registered with the WRP for its students to be accepted into the program.

In the next few years, the support from the federal government for international development programs is expected to grow by $5 billion and by several more billion from the private sector. International exchange programs have doubled in the past decade and are expected to continue at that pace making the need for more staff in this area critical. Entry level salaries for individuals with a bachelor's degree range from $28,000 to $36,000 with full benefit packages (MIUSA/NCDE, 2005). Individuals who want to explore international career options should take advantage of the opportunities for paid and unpaid internships, and volunteer programs. In addition to the U.S. Department of State programs cited above, there are many organizations that run programs during the summer and throughout the year. The most prominent of these organizations and their contact information are provided in the MIUSA/NCDE publication. Among those listed are the ASSE International Student Exchange Programs, Pacific Intercultural Exchange-USA, Inc., Program of International Exchange, Rotary International Youth Exchange, YMCA International Program Services, and Youth for Understanding USA. These organizations and more are described by MIUSA/NCDE (2005) along with contact information for each.

Consider This!   Suppose you had the opportunity to serve in the Peace Corps after finishing your teacher preparation program.

- Which continent or country would you choose in the developing world?
- How would you mentally prepare yourself for the cultural, economic, educational, and health care differences in comparison with the United States?
- What do you believe would be your greatest asset in working with people with disabilities in another country and culture?
- What do you think would be your greatest sacrifice in serving in the Peace Corps rather than pursuing or continuing a teaching career in the United States?

CHAPTER SUMMARY

Like the United States, European nations have developed policies and enacted legislation to protect the rights of people with disabilities in employment training and placement. They have also created national and local agencies to fund and support programs on transition from school to work. These agencies, like those in the United States, are helpful, but can vary in the quality of their support and also create confusion for individuals with disabilities and their families. It appears that member nations of the European Union will work together to share practices on how best to prepare people with disabilities for the workforce and implement fair employment practices to aid in their success.

The developing world and its challenges for all its people compounds the difficulties faced by individuals with disabilities. A general lack of educational opportunity and irregular access to health care creates enormous problems in terms of quality of life. Most of the programs available to youth and young adults with disabilities come from NGOs, developed nations, or the United Nations. In only a few cases are there national policies and programs to serve this population. Although awareness of disabilities has increased in the past two decades, little has been accomplished to substantially improve conditions for education and employment. As multinational corporations continue to base their operations in developing countries, international advocacy groups should demand that people with disabilities have an equal access to training and jobs as the general population.

In the United States, there are growing opportunities for individuals with disabilities to choose a career in the international sector. Because of the growing popularity of study abroad programs, there are more positions available in international exchange. Because there is greater globalization effecting trade and diplomacy, there are more positions available in international affairs. And, because there are more organizations involved in human rights issues and projects to educate and provide needed services for developing countries, there are more positions available in international development. Students with disabilities should take advantage of programs offered by the U.S. Department of State and a variety of other organizations to explore their interest in an international career position.

APPLICATION ACTIVITIES

The application activities listed below are essential for your continued learning in transition policies and practices. Each of the activities will require your time and energy, but will help you develop your professional skills in this area.

For Practice and Enhanced Understanding:

Make an appointment with an advisor in your international programs office and ask about study abroad programs for special education majors in developed and developing countries.

While you are there ask for the names, phone numbers, and email addresses of international students who are willing to speak to people about their country.

- Interview an international student about her or his perception of vocational training and employment opportunities for people with disabilities.
- If you can find an international student who is studying for a degree in special education or education on your campus (probably a graduate student), ask your professor if the student can be invited to class to make a presentation on transition services, vocational preparation, and employment of persons with disabilities in his or her country.

Ask a reference librarian on your campus what journals are available on international special education or disability studies (you may have to use interlibrary loan). Also, find out if you can get access to United Nations documents on their programs for training and employing people with disabilities.

For Your Portfolio:

Use your college library and Internet search engines to survey and list articles and books from economics, international affairs, political science, sociology, and disability studies to learn more about legislation and regulations that affect people with disabilities in other countries.

Study our U.S. Department of State and USAID websites for information on programs our country is initiating in the developing world on special education, vocational training programs, and economic development that includes individuals with disabilities.

REFERENCES

Barton, L., & Armstrong, F. (2001). Disability, education, and inclusion: Cross-cultural issues and dilemmas. In G. L. Albrecht, K. D. Seelman, & M. Bury (Eds.), *Handbook of disability studies* (pp. 693–710). Thousand Oaks, CA: Sage Publications.

Brolin, D. (1992). *Life centered career education.* Alexandria, VA: Council for Exceptional Children.

Chen, L.-J., & Zhang, D. (2003). Transition services in Taiwan: A comparison between service need and services received. *Education and Training in Developmental Disabilities, 38*(3), 334–340.

Council for Exceptional Children. (2004). Retrieved from www.cec.sped.org/intl/progpract.html#spcare, December 22, 2004.

European Agency for Development in Special Needs Education. (2002). *Transition from School to Employment: Main problems, issues and options faced by students with special educational needs in 16 European countries.* Retrieved from www.european-agency.org, December 19, 2004.

Gooding, C. (1994). Disabling laws, enabling acts: Disability rights in Britain and America. London: Pluto.

Groce, N. (1993). Cultural and chronic illness: Raising children with disabling conditions in the culturally diverse world. *Pediatrics, 9*(5), 1049.

Ingstad, B. (2001). Disability in the developing world. In G. L. Albrecht, K. D. Seelman, & M. Bury (Eds.), *Handbook of Disability Studies* (pp. 772–792). Thousand Oaks, CA: Sage Publications Inc.

Ingstad, B., & Whyte, S. (1995). *Disability and culture.* Berkeley: University of California Press.

Lin, H-C. (2002). *Transition from school to work for youth with hearing impairments in Taiwan.* Paper presented at the eighth Asia-Pacific Congress on Deafness: For All the World to Hear, August 3–6, 2002, Taipei, Taiwan.

Metts, R., & Metts, N. (1998). USAID, disability, and development in Ghana. *Journal of Disability Policy Studies, 9*, 31–57.

Mobility International USA/National Clearinghouse on Disability and Exchange (2005). *Preparing for an international career: Pathways for people with disabilities.* Eugene, OR: Author.

Roy, A. (2002). Supporting the transition of visually impaired adults to employment: European Union innovations. *Journal of Visual Impairment and Blindness, 96*(9), 645–654.

Schriner, K. (2001). A disability studies perspective on employment issues and policies for disabled people. In G. L. Albrecht, K. D. Seelman, & M. Bury (Eds.), *Handbook of disability studies* (pp. 642–662). Thousand Oaks, CA: Sage Publications.

Transition Information Database (2004). Retrieved from www.european-agency.org/transit/index.html, December 18, 2004.

United Nations. (1983). *World programme of action concerning disabled persons.* New York: Author.

EPILOGUE

You have arrived at the end of this book and the end of your introduction to the study of effective transition services for students with disabilities. We emphasize that this is merely an introduction, because the development and implementation of best practices to help young people with disabilities achieve successful outcomes in adulthood will take the unified efforts of researchers, practitioners, and students and their families for many years to come.

QUALITY TRANSITION SERVICES: WHAT ARE THEY WORTH?

The many strategies we have discussed throughout this text take substantial time and effort, and never are they easy to put into practice. Let's look briefly at the impact of such quality services on the lives of young people in transition and on society in general. To do so, let's take a look at the future for Sue Anne and Mike, ten years after their transition to adult life.

Sue Anne

Sue Anne is now a veteran teacher. She is twenty-eight years old, and she has been out of college for six years. From that first day as a teacher, waiting expectantly for her first fifteen students, she has continued to refine and hone her teaching skills. The other teachers in her school know her as a highly competent and caring professional who is a trusted ally to students and their families. She is now a mentor to a first-year teacher, and it amazes Sue Anne how quickly the last six years have passed. It seems like yesterday that she was just starting out.

Sue Anne is now married and has a home of her own. She and her husband are thinking seriously of having children; if this happens, it will bring another time of transition into Sue Anne's life. Between her husband's salary and her own, Sue Anne is feeling much more secure financially, and she and her husband can afford to take a vacation each summer and buy the things that they want for their new home. Sue Anne feels like she and her husband are really a part of the community now, not just because she is a recognized professional, but because they are visible in and integrated into many places within the local community.

Sue Anne has come a long way and her life has changed in many ways since she was a freshman in college. Many more changes and transitions will take place throughout the rest of her life: parenthood, the aging of her own parents, her own children's transition from childhood to adulthood and, at some point, retirement. For now, she is content to look back on her achievements and joys thus far and her success in making the transition to adult living.

Mike

Mike was entitled to special education services until age twenty-one, when his transition to the adult service system took place. It is now ten years later, and Mike is thirty-one. He lives in an apartment with one other individual who also has developmental disabilities, and they both receive support from a team of supported living professionals who alternate the responsibility of living with and supporting Mike and his roommate. The transition from Mike's home to a group home was difficult, and his confusion and distress were evident in his moody and sometimes aggressive behavior. He lived in the first group home for two years, moved to another group home for six years, and has been in the apartment now for two years. It seems to the staff of the residential service provider agency that Mike is finally settling into a comfortable living arrangement. The staff are not sure why this is: perhaps Mike is just older and is less subject to the stresses of adolescence, or maybe the quieter setting of the apartment just works better for him. In any case, he seems happier. Mike's parents, who have been actively involved in supporting Mike since his move out of their home, feel the same way, and they are cautiously optimistic that Mike has turned a positive corner, at least for now.

Mike is supported by a different service provider agency for his "day" services. He works three days a week in a supported employment site with the support of an employment specialist. He works in the local mall with one other worker with disabilities, doing janitorial work. He really enjoys the pet store and watching the fish and colorful parakeets in the window, and his employment specialist has to remind him to keep working. Mike has been working in the mall for two years now, and store and shop owners now recognize him. One woman at the hot pretzel store knows just what kind of pretzel to have ready when it is time for Mike's break, and she is patient as he counts out his money. Likewise, the bank tellers know Mike and his co-worker, and they look forward to helping them cash their paychecks. When Mike is not working, he returns to the agency's facility, where he works in their sheltered workshop. He does not like this, and it shows in his behavior. Mike's parents have had an ongoing disagreement with the agency, because they feel it would be better for Mike to be out in the community, even on the days when he is not working. Unfortunately, funding is always a problem, so the agency does not feel that they can afford to assign a person to work one on one with Mike on his non-work days. Mike's family is considering hiring someone privately to spend time with Mike in the community. The agency is looking for additional work for Mike so that he can increase his number of hours of working in the community.

When he is not working, Mike has an active schedule of community recreation activities. His supported living staff takes him out frequently to shop, go out to eat, or spend time in the local park. Mike goes home to his family's house about once a month. Mike even went on an extended vacation to Orlando and Disney World with his roommate and two members of his supported living staff. Mike's parents were worried the entire time he was gone, but the pictures they brought back showed Mike smiling and happy.

Like Sue Anne, Mike will face additional challenges throughout his lifetime and, because of the severity of his intellectual disabilities, he will likely not understand all of these events. His parents will always watch out for him as long as they are alive, and they worry about how to protect him when they are gone. They are saving money to put into a trust fund for Mike, and they are consulting with an attorney to set up the best arrangement they can for him. In the meantime, they know he seems happy, that he has a job and a decent place to live, and that he has people throughout the community who genuinely care about him. Perhaps that is the greatest protection of all.

It seems that Mike and Sue Anne have benefited from a well-planned transition to adulthood, but how has society in general benefited? Consider these ways:

- Sue Anne and Mike are now both taxpayers. Certainly, Sue Anne's salary and resultant taxes are far greater than Mike's, but both are making a monetary contribution to society. Although Mike receives funds to support him through Social Security and the state Mental Retardation and Vocational Rehabilitation systems, he is becoming more independent with each additional hour that he works per week. He receives support from society, but he returns the support through his taxes.
- Both Sue Anne and Mike are making a contribution through the work they do, work that is needed and that contributes to the greater good of the community. Their work is valued and recognized by those around them.
- Both Sue Anne and Mike are recognized members of their communities. Both are neighbors, shoppers, and regulars at a variety of community locations. Their presence and their unique personalities enrich the lives of those who know them.

A REVIEW OF EFFECTIVE PRACTICES

Throughout this book, we have described effective practices that can contribute to the successful transition to adulthood for young people with disabilities. We review these practices briefly in this section to reinforce the key points introduced throughout the text. This review is presented within the context of the following topics in order emphasize the scope of effective transition planning:

- Active Student Involvement
- Active Family Involvement
- Proactive and Dynamic Planning
- Coordination with Adult Service Agencies
- Connections to Natural Support Systems
- Employment Experiences with a Career Focus

- Achieving Success through Continued Postsecondary Education
- A Relevant and Challenging Curriculum
- A Focus on Community Living
- A Focus on Recreation and Leisure for Healthy Living
- Recognition of an Increasingly Global Society

Active Student Involvement

Active and ongoing student involvement is a cornerstone of effective transition planning. In Chapter 2, we introduced the importance of self-determination, which we described as a combination of skills, knowledge, and attitudes or beliefs about oneself and the ability to positively affect one's own future. For many young people who are in transition, active involvement in planning may be difficult, but we also know that with the assistance of family, friends, teachers, adult service professionals, and community members, students can learn to take a more active role in the planning process and thereby develop a sense of ownership to their future plans.

Active Family Involvement

Families must also be actively involved. A key point we introduced is that many families lack the information that is necessary to negotiate the transition from special education system to adult service system. Transition of their children is often a stressful and confusing time for families, and it is incumbent upon educators and other professionals to assist families by ensuring that they have the needed information. Families should be encouraged to participate actively in the planning process. As with the facilitation of student involvement, there are many proactive and creative strategies that result in more active family involvement and a closer partnership with the school and adult agencies.

Proactive and Dynamic Planning

The attainment of successful adult outcomes only occurs when all key team members plan longitudinally in a proactive manner. We need to start the planning process as early as possible to allow students to gain experiences and make decisions. The plans that are developed must be dynamic and should reflect the changes in decision making that occur in young people as they gain experiences. The written plans should be clear, logical, and reflect the active involvement of all of the people who have an investment in it. Most of all, they should reflect students' choices and personal visions for the future.

Coordination with Adult Service Agencies

All parties in the planning process must work together toward the common goal of a successful and fulfilling adult life for young people with disabilities. Before people from different agencies can work together, they need to gain a greater understanding of their counterparts in other disciplines. Educators must strive to better understand the adult service systems, and professionals in these systems need to understand the special education system. All professionals must work together to create strategies that work to help students make a smooth transition out of special education and into the adult service world. They also need to take the necessary steps to ensure that students and their families have the information they need to work with both systems.

Connections to Natural Support Systems

Although adult services are critical for the success of many young people, equally important are natural support systems. Co-workers, friends, families, neighbors, and even familiar community members are all potential sources of assistance and support during adulthood. Almost all successful adults rely on natural support networks, and young adults with disabilities are no different. A critical point to reiterate is that the creation of strong networks of natural supports does not come easily or automatically, and instead requires sustained and longitudinal planning.

Employment Experiences with a Career Focus

A fulfilling career is a key element in a successful adult life. As we have described, people with disabilities continue to experience unemployment and underemployment, thus being denied the opportunity to experience this essential aspect of adult life. All people should have the opportunity to work in the community for pay. Some will achieve this through continued postsecondary education and training, while others will require longitudinal support through supported employment services. The key point is that those involved with transition planning must make *integrated, paid community employment* a clear goal of the planning process and then provide young people with the experiences, instruction, and support systems to achieve this outcome.

Achieving Success through Continued Postsecondary Education

Continued postsecondary education opens other possibilities for a successful adult life, and many young people with disabilities can meet the challenges of such an education. As with other aspects of transition planning, the entry into postsecondary education takes advanced preparation, training in self-determination, and a well-coordinated support system to ensure academic and social success. Coordination among student, family, school, and college or university staff is crucial.

A Relevant and Challenging Curriculum

While they are in high school, students with disabilities need to learn skills that will serve them well in adulthood. Many of these skills will be taught primarily by families, while others will fall to the schools. The *IDEA 2004* and *No Child Left Behind* have mandated that all students be challenged academically. However, a relevant curriculum goes beyond state mandated academic standards and includes functional skills for everyday living, including those skills and behaviors that are valued by employers. The process of designing relevant and challenging curriculum that will meet the needs of diverse students will continue to be a challenge for the special education system.

A Focus on Community Living

Transition planning focuses on more than just employment. Our coordinated efforts with students and their families must also prepare young people to make the transition to their first homes away from the family. This involves teaching them a wide range of skills that are required for living on one's own. For some individuals with more extensive support needs, the transition to supported living will require extremely proactive planning. As with all other aspects of transition planning, the earlier the better. We must also be concerned with helping young people become connected to their larger communities so they can have the opportunity to develop relationships and be recognized as contributing and valuable citizens.

A Focus on Recreation and Leisure for Healthy Living

This is perhaps the most neglected area of transition planning, yet it is as important as transition to employment or independent living. Young people need to learn how to maintain their physical and psychological health. They need to learn how to participate in local communities in ways that lead to a more fulfilled, well-rounded, and happy lifestyle.

Recognition of an Increasingly Global Society

Finally, we emphasized that students today are transitioning to an adult world that is based increasingly on global communication and commerce. Our U.S. society continues to become more diverse, and the likelihood that students will work for businesses with international ties is increasing. Additionally, our educational and adult service systems must continue to serve as examples for the development of quality services to citizens with disabilities in other countries.

A REMINDER: YOUR ROLE IN HELPING STUDENTS IN TRANSITION

The content of this book is worthwhile only to the degree that it helps motivate and prepare you to play a part in helping young people with disabilities make a smooth transition to productive and fulfilling adult lives. It is therefore important to remind you of your potential role in contributing to the success of students with disabilities as they leave the special education system and enter the adult world.

Educators and School Personnel

Teachers at the Elementary Level. When you began this book, you may have seen little relevance of the topic to your job responsibilities. We hope you now see that the educational experiences that you provide constitute an essential foundation for your students' later success in adulthood. Specifically, in addition to basic communication, social, motor, and academic skill development, you can develop self-determination abilities in your students. Helping students to know their own strengths and needs, to learn to make choices and decisions, and to express themselves all directly contribute to the development of greater self-determination. In addition, initial career awareness can begin at the elementary level, and the foundations of work skills can start with the completion of responsibilities in the classroom or at home, both individually, or as part of a cooperative group. Finally, you can encourage your students to have aspirations and dreams for the future.

Teachers at the Middle School Level. Like that of elementary teachers, your role is to provide a strong foundation for transition to adult life. The knowledge and skills that you impart are more sophisticated and begin to relate directly to the demands of adult life. Students' knowledge of their needs, strengths, and aspirations should become more refined at the middle school level. Career awareness is more of a focus as some students begin to develop tentative aspirations for the future. All of the skills begun at the elementary level must continue and must be developed incrementally. Your job typically ends just as students reach the age (fourteen) when transition planning needs to begin in earnest.

Secondary Level Teachers. Your role is central to successful transition planning. Whether you are a special educator or a general education teacher, you will have direct influence on the outcomes that young people achieve in adulthood. Many of you will be actively involved in the transition planning process, and almost everything we have discussed in this book will apply to your work with young people with disabilities.

Administrators. Your role is critical in supporting effective transition practices. Some administrators support these efforts by helping teachers arrange community-based instruction or by creating a transition coordinator position to guide and coordinate transition programming. You also have a critical role working with families and helping them to understand the differences between entitled special education services and the adult service system, which is basely primarily on differential eligibility criteria.

Transition Coordinators. Along with special education teachers, your role is central, and you will have overall responsibility for coordinating the transition planning process. Everything we have discussed here applies to you.

Adult Service Professionals

This is a broad category which includes vocational rehabilitation counselors, case managers/support coordinators from the MR/DD or Mental Health departments, private provider agency staff, including employment specialists and job developers, residential program staff, and representatives from the Social Security Administration. Each of you, depending on your job title and responsibilities, has a unique and important role in facilitating a smooth transition. First, you need to work closely with the schools, with families, and with young people with disabilities to ensure that they understand what your agency does and what your role is in the transition process. The closer this working relationship is, the more successful the outcomes are likely to be. One of your most important responsibilities is to educate families, students, school representatives, and representatives from other adult service agencies about your agency's services and *how and when* to best access those services.

Family Members

Along with your children, you experience the challenges and successes of transition planning most directly. As we have described throughout this book, you should be active partners with schools and adult service agencies in planning for your children's transition to the adult service system, to work, to a new home, or to postsecondary education. You likely coordinate most services and planning and you are likely to continue to do so long after your sons and daughters have left the special education system. One additional role that some of you may take on is that of mentor and educator to other family members who are just learning about transition planning or who are struggling with the process.

Students

Simply put, this book has been about helping you clarify and then reach your aspirations for a happy and successful adult life. We have tried to emphasize throughout the book that the more actively involved you are with the planning process, the more likely you are to reach your future goals. Regardless of the nature and degree of your disability, there are numerous ways for you to take an active and central role in the planning process. Your job is to develop the knowledge, skills, and attitudes/beliefs that you will need to take charge of your own life.

Community Members

This is another broad category, and it includes neighbors, friends, people in community stores, people at places of worship, and so forth. Your role may be peripheral to the planning process, and you may simply know young people with disabilities through their involvement in the community. However, some of you may be invited to take a more active role in planning by specific students with disabilities who value your input, wisdom, and guidance. If that occurs, respond and get involved! Your involvement may be an essential ingredient for success in a young person's life.

Employers

You have a unique role: you have the power to give young people a chance to become productive and contributing members of our labor force. This may require making some adjustments and accommodations, but the investment pays off in gaining reliable and motivated employees. People with disabilities may be the most untapped pool of labor in our country, and they can contribute as much to your businesses as you can contribute to their career growth and development.

Each of the aforementioned participants has a role and a vested interest in the outcome of effective transition planning for students with disabilities. It takes all of our efforts, and we as a society all benefit from the investment of time, energy, and commitment.

PLEASE REMEMBER

The impact of effective transition services extends beyond the date of exit from special education services and into adulthood. Effective transition services have a positive impact on the lives of students with disabilities, their families, and on the communities in which they live. Many people, including school personnel, adult service professionals, families, community members, employers, and students, play a critical role in the success of transition efforts. All citizens should have a vested interest in the achievement of successful outcomes from all students leaving our school systems. The strategies discussed throughout this book can result in better transition outcomes for students with diverse disabilities, such as Sue Anne and Mike.

Our very best wishes,
Dan, Ernie, and Domenico

INDEX